PLURALIST CONSTITUTIONS IN SOUTHEAST ASIA

This book examines the presence of ethnic, religious, political, and ideational pluralities in Southeast Asian societies and how their respective constitutions respond to these pluralities. Countries covered in this book are Brunei, Cambodia, Indonesia, Laos, Malaysia, Myanmar, the Philippines, Singapore, Thailand, and Vietnam. The chapters examine: first, the range of pluralist constitutional values and ideas embodied in the constitutions; secondly, the pluralist sources of constitutional norms; thirdly, the design of constitutional structures responding to various pluralities; and fourthly, the construction and interpretation of bills of rights in response to existing pluralities. The 'pluralist constitution' is thus one that recognises internal pluralities within society and makes arrangements to accommodate, rather than eliminate, these pluralities.

Constitutionalism in Asia series

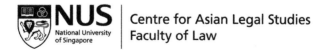

Pluralist Constitutions in Southeast Asia

Edited by
Jaclyn L Neo
and
Bui Ngoc Son

·HART·
OXFORD · LONDON · NEW YORK · NEW DELHI · SYDNEY

HART PUBLISHING

Bloomsbury Publishing Plc

Kemp House, Chawley Park, Cumnor Hill, Oxford, OX2 9PH, UK

HART PUBLISHING, the Hart/Stag logo, BLOOMSBURY and the Diana logo are trademarks of Bloomsbury Publishing Plc

First published in Great Britain 2019

Reprinted 2019

Copyright © The editors and contributors severally 2019

The editors and contributors have asserted their right under the Copyright, Designs and Patents Act 1988 to be identified as Authors of this work.

All rights reserved. No part of this publication may be reproduced or transmitted in any form or by any means, electronic or mechanical, including photocopying, recording, or any information storage or retrieval system, without prior permission in writing from the publishers.

While every care has been taken to ensure the accuracy of this work, no responsibility for loss or damage occasioned to any person acting or refraining from action as a result of any statement in it can be accepted by the authors, editors or publishers.

All UK Government legislation and other public sector information used in the work is Crown Copyright ©. All House of Lords and House of Commons information used in the work is Parliamentary Copyright ©. This information is reused under the terms of the Open Government Licence v3.0 (http://www.nationalarchives.gov.uk/doc/open-government-licence/version/3) except where otherwise stated.

All Eur-lex material used in the work is © European Union, http://eur-lex.europa.eu/, 1998–2019.

A catalogue record for this book is available from the British Library.

Library of Congress Cataloging-in-Publication data

Names: Neo, Jaclyn L., editor. | Bui, Ngoc Son, editor. | National University of Singapore. Centre for Asian Legal Studies, sponsoring body.

Title: Pluralist constitutions in Southeast Asia / edited by Jaclyn L Neo, Bui Ngoc Son.

Description: Oxford, UK ; Portland, Oregon : Hart Publishing, 2019. | Series: Constitutionalism in Asia | Includes bibliographical references and index.

Identifiers: LCCN 2018052894 (print) | LCCN 2018055178 (ebook) | ISBN 9781509920464 (EPub) | ISBN 9781509920457 (hardback)

Subjects: LCSH: Constitutional law—Southeast Asia | BISAC: LAW / Comparative.

Classification: LCC KNC524 (ebook) | LCC KNC524 .P58 2019 (print) | DDC 342.59—dc23

LC record available at https://lccn.loc.gov/2018052894

ISBN: HB: 978-1-50992-045-7
ePDF: 978-1-50992-047-1
ePub: 978-1-50992-046-4

Typeset by Compuscript Ltd, Shannon
Printed and bound in Great Britain by TJ International Ltd, Padstow, Cornwall

To find out more about our authors and books visit www.hartpublishing.co.uk. Here you will find extracts, author information, details of forthcoming events and the option to sign up for our newsletters.

ACKNOWLEDGEMENT

This book is a part of a research project funded by the Centre for Asian Legal Studies (CALS) at the National University of Singapore, Faculty of Law. We are grateful to Dan W. Puchniak and CALS for supporting this project; Hart Publishing, Kevin YL Tan and Li-ann Thio, editors of Hart's series in *Constitutionalism in Asia* for supporting the publication of this book; and the contributors for their excellent work. We would also like to thank our student research assistants – Louis Lai Wei Kang, Alfie Lim Si-En, Sheiffa Safi Shirbeeni, Andrea Ong Hui Xian, Damian Wong, and Daryl Yang. Finally, we are thankful to our respective institutions for their continued support.

Jaclyn Neo & Bui Ngoc Son

CONTENTS

Acknowledgement v
List of Contributors ix
Table of Cases xiii
Table of Legislation xv

1. *Pluralist Constitutions and the Southeast Asian Context 1*
   Jaclyn L. Neo and Bui Ngoc Son

2. *Constitutionalising Multiple Pluralities in Malaysia 25*
   Dian A. H. Shah

3. *The Imperative of Integrative Pluralist Constitutionalism: Going Beyond Formal Equality, Eschewing Rights, and Accommodation of Differences in Singapore 51*
   Eugene K B Tan

4. *Pluralism in Brunei's Constitution? Ethnicity, Religion and the Absolute Monarchy 83*
   Kerstin Steiner and Dominik M Müller

5. *Indonesia's Constitutional Responses to Plurality 115*
   Herlambang P. Wiratraman and Dian A. H. Shah

6. *Myanmar's Pluralist Constitution: Nation-Building versus State-Building 143*
   Nyi Nyi Kyaw

7. *Pluralist Constitution in Cambodia 169*
   Taing Ratana

8. *Constitutions in Ethnically Plural Societies: Laos and Vietnam 203*
   Bui Ngoc Son

9. *Volcanic Constitution: How is Plurality Turning Against Constitutionalism in Thailand? 225*
   Apinop Atipiboonsin

10. *The Philippine People Power Constitution: Social Cohesion through Integrated Diversity 251*
    Bryan Dennis Gabito Tiojanco

Index 283

LIST OF CONTRIBUTORS

Apinop ATIPIBOONSIN is a young scholar in the fields of comparative constitutional law and administrative law from Thailand. After receiving his LL.B., with honors, from the Faculty of Law, Thammasat University in 2012, he began his academic career at his alma mater as a lecturer, where he was appointed as an editorial committee of the prestigious *Thammasat Law Journal*. He later graduated from LL.M. program at Columbia Law School in New York as Harlan Fiske Stone Scholar in 2016. After his return to Thammasat University, he works under the Department of Public Law, teaching courses such as constitutional law, administrative law, and fundamental rights. Currently, his research concentrates extensively on constitutional law in Southeast Asia with a focus on the role of constitutional courts in coping with political conflicts. He also frequently gives advice to Law Reform Commission of Thailand as a legal expert.

BUI Ngoc Son is an Assistant Professor at the Chinese University of Hong Kong Faculty of Law. His areas of interest include comparative constitutional law and comparative law. He holds law degrees from The University of Hong Kong (Ph.D) and Vietnam National University-Hanoi (LL.M; LL.B). He is the author of *Confucian Constitutionalism in East Asia* (Routledge 2016) and articles published or forthcoming in the *American Journal of Comparative Law*, the *Law & Social Inquiry*, the *International Journal of Constitutional Law*, the *University of Illinois Law Review*, the *Fordham International Law Journal*, the *Washington University Global Studies Law Review*, and the *Washington International Law Journal*, among others. He was previously a research fellow at the Centre for Asian Legal Studies in the National University of Singapore Faculty of Law.

Nyi Nyi KYAW is a postdoctoral research fellow at the Centre for Asian Legal Studies at the National University of Singapore. A political scientist by training, he is interested in socio-legal and political aspects of topics such as law, religion, social movements, citizenship, nationalism, and constitutionalism all of which are deeply interrelated in Myanmar in transition. His work so far focuses on Myanmar but he closely follows what is happening in Sri Lanka for his keen interest in Buddhist nationalism and Muslim identity. His research has been published or accepted for publication in the *Review of Faith & International Affairs*, *Journal of Immigrant & Refugee Studies*, and *Social identities*. He has also contributed or is going to contribute chapters in several edited volumes on Muslim identity, citizenship, Buddhist-Muslim relations, and constitutionalism.

Dominik M MÜLLER is Head of the Emmy Noether Research Group 'The Bureaucratization of Islam and its Socio-Legal Dimensions in Southeast Asia' at the Max Planck Institute for Social Anthropology, Law & Anthropology Department. He has been an 'Islamic Legal Studies Program: Law and Social Change' (ILSP: LSC) Visiting Fellow at Harvard University in 2018, while working on the contribution to this volume. He also holds a non-resident fellowship appointment at the National University of Singapore's Centre for Asian Legal Studies (CALS) as part of an Emmy Noether project cooperation. He is a political anthropologist, presently particularly focusing on the anthropology of bureaucracy and its potentials to generate new perspectives on state-Islam relations in Southeast Asia.

Jaclyn L NEO is an Associate Professor of Law at the National University of Singapore (NUS). She specializes in comparative constitutional law, with a focus on Southeast Asia and comparative constitutional law and religion. She is the sole editor of *Constitutional Interpretation in Singapore: Theory and Practice* (Routledge, 2017) and has served as a guest editor for the *Singapore Academy of Law Journal*, *Journal of Law, Religion, and State*, as well as the *Journal of International and Comparative Law*. Her articles have appeared in the *International Journal of Constitutional Law* (I-CON), *Oxford Journal of Law and Religion*, *Human Rights Quarterly*, and the *Singapore Journal of Legal Studies*.

Dian A H SHAH is an Assistant Professor at the Faculty of Law, National University of Singapore. She was previously a Research Fellow of the Centre for Asian Legal Studies, and a Senior Lecturer at the Faculty of Law, University of Malaya, where she taught constitutional law. Dian completed her LL.M and S.J.D degrees at Duke University Law School, and prior to that she graduated with an LL.B from Warwick University. Her research interests span the fields of constitutional history, comparative constitutional law, and human rights, and her work focuses on the interaction of law, religion, and politics in plural and divided societies. Dian is the author of *Constitutions, Religion and Politics in Asia: Indonesia, Malaysia and Sri Lanka* (CUP 2017) and the co-editor of a volume on *Law and Society in Malaysia: Pluralism, Religion and Ethnicity* (Routledge 2018). She has also published in the *International Journal of Constitutional Law* (I-CON), *Oxford Journal of Law and Religion*, and the *Indonesian Journal of International and Comparative Law*. She serves as the Deputy Editor of the *Asian Journal of Comparative Law* (AsJCL) and the Editor of the AsJCL's Special Issue on 'Religion and Constitutional Practices in Asia' (December 2018).

Kerstin STEINER is Associate Professor at the Law School, La Trobe University. She is also a Senior Associate at the Centre for Indonesian Law, Islam and Society (CILIS) and Associate at the Asian Law Centre (ALC) both at the University of Melbourne. She is researching on the intersection of law, politics, society, and religion in Southeast Asia. With Professor Tim Lindsey she is co-author of the two volumes on Islam, Law and the State in Southeast Asia in Singapore, and Malaysia and Brunei respectively. Together with Professor MB Hooker they are currently holding an Australian Research Council funded Discovery Project on 'Islam, Law, and the State in the Philippines'. Other noteworthy publications on Brunei include 'Rule of Law in Brunei' in *Rule of Law in ASEAN Region: Update on the Baseline Study* commissioned by the Human Rights Resource Centre (2016); 'Comparative Law in Syariah Courts: A Case Study of Singapore, Malaysia and Brunei' in Mads Adenas and Duncan Fairgrieve (eds) *Comparative Law before the Courts* (2015); and with Tim Lindsey 'Islam, the Monarchy and Criminal Law in Brunei: The Syariah Penal Code Order, 2013' 2016 25(4) *Griffith Law Review*.

Ratana TAING is currently the Secretary General of the Constitutional Council of Cambodia (with rank Secretary of State). He has worked for the Constitutional Council for nearly 13 years. Since 2005 he was promoted to various positions: Director of Cabinet of the President of the Constitutional Council (July 2017), Advisor to the President (with rank under secretary of state) in 2017, Legal officer of Bureau of Litigation (2005–2009), Deputy Chief of Bureau of Legal Affairs (2009), and Chief of Bureau III (2009–2014). In 2014, he was appointed to be Under Secretary General (Under Secretary of State) of the National Committee for Organizing National and International Festival (NCONIF); Legal advisor to the Theravada Buddhist Order of the Kingdom of Cambodia (given Buddhist title *Maha Buddha Jinarasa*); Professor of Law, Paññāsāstra University of Cambodia (PUC). He is a holder of various degrees: Executive Master of Advanced Studies (MAS) in Development Studies from the Graduate Institute of International and Development Studies (IHEID), Geneva, Switzerland; LL.B and LL.M from Royal University of Law and Economics (RULE), Phnom Penh; Bachelor of English Literature from Build Bright University (BBU); and DDS from University of Health Sciences (UHS), Phnom Penh. Ratana is also a member of KAS research group on Constitutionalism in Asia, an alumnus of International Visitor Leadership Program (IVLP), the US State Department; and an alumnus of Intellectual Property Rights for Least Developed Countries (LDCs), WIPO-Sida.

Eugene KB TAN is an Associate Professor of Law at the Singapore Management University (SMU). He is also an adjunct faculty at the Singapore University of Technology and Design, and has taught, as a visiting professor, at the Yonsei University Law School in Seoul, South Korea. An advocate and solicitor of the Supreme Court of Singapore, Eugene was educated at the National University of Singapore, London School of Economics and Political Science, and Stanford University where he was a Fulbright Fellow. He has published in various edited volumes and peer-reviewed journals, including *Journal of Church and State, Israel Law Review, The China Quarterly, Ethnic and Racial Studies, Ethnopolitics, Law and Policy, Singapore Year Book of International Law, Hong Kong Law Journal, Citizenship Studies, Terrorism and Political Violence, Intersections: Gender and Sexuality in Asia and the Pacific, Yonsei Law Journal, Singapore Law Review, Asian Journal of Business Ethics, Australian Journal of Asian Law*, and *Journal of Asian Business*. Between February 2012 and August 2014, Eugene served as a Nominated Member of Parliament in Singapore's 12th Parliament.

xii *List of Contributors*

Eugene's inter-disciplinary research interests include constitutional and administrative law, law and public policy, the regulation of ethnic conflict, and the government and politics of Singapore.

Bryan Dennis Gabito TIOJANCO is a postdoctoral fellow at the National University of Singapore Faculty of Law's Centre for Asian Legal Studies. He obtained his Doctor of the Science of Law (J.S.D.) and Master of Laws (LL.M.) degrees from Yale Law School. He obtained his Juris Doctor (J.D.) degree (cum laude) from the University of the Philippines College of Law. He is a member of the Integrated Bar of the Philippines. He was an editor of the *Yale Journal of Law & the Humanities* and the *Philippine Law Journal*. His works have been published in the *Philippine Law Journal*, the *Philippine Daily Inquirer*, the *New Mandala*, the *Manila Times*, the *Philippine Law Register*, the *UP Law Center Press*, *Vibal Publishing*, and the *Max Planck Encyclopaedia of Comparative Constitutional Law*.

Herlambang Perdana WIRATRAMAN is a lecturer in the Constitutional Law Department and the Executive Director of the Centre of Human Rights Law Studies (HRLS), Faculty of Law, Universitas Airlangga (Surabaya, Indonesia). He completed his Master of Arts on Human Rights and Social Development at Mahidol University, Thailand and PhD at the Van Vollenhoven Institute, Leiden Law School, the Netherlands in 2014. He has written numerous books, including *Good Governance and Legal Reform in Indonesia* (Bangkok, 2007) and *Press Freedom, Law and Politics: A Socio-Legal Study* (Zutphen, 2014), and several book chapters and journal articles. He was previously a Visiting Professor in Graduate Studies of International Development department at Nagoya University (2015) and a Visiting Lecturer at the Vietnam National University (VNU) Law School (2017). He previously served as a Chairperson of the Indonesian Association of Legal Philosophy (AFHI, 2013–2014) and the Indonesian Lecturers Association for Human Rights (SEPAHAM Indonesia, 2014–2017). His research interests include human rights, constitutional law, law and society, freedom of expression, freedom of the press, and academic freedom.

TABLE OF CASES

Azmi Mohamad Azam v Director of Jabatan Agama Islam Sarawak and Others
[2016] 6 CLJ 562...44
Banda v Ermita (2010) G.R. No. 166620 268
Belgica v Executive Secretary [2013] 721 Phil 416 .... 270, 277
Biraogo v The Philippine Truth Commission of 2010 (2010)
GR. Nos. 192935-36 268–69
Buklod ng Kawaning EIIB v Executive Secretary (2001) G.R. No. 142801-802 268
Cruz v National Commission on Indigenous Peoples (2000) G.R. No. 135385 259,
261, 275
Dalip Kaur v Pegawai Polis Daerah, Balai Polis Daerah, Bukit Mertajam &
Another [1992] 1 MLJ 1. 40
Dato' Seri Dr Zambry Abdul Kadir v Dato' Seri Ir Hj Mohammad
Nizar Jamaluddin; Attorney General (Intervener) [2009] 5 CLJ 265
(Court of Appeal) 46
Dato' Seri Ir Hj Mohammad Nizar Jamaluddin v Dato' Seri Dr Zambry
Abdul Kadir [2009] 5 MLJ 108 (High Court). 46
Dato' Seri Ir Hj Mohammad Nizar Jamaluddin v Dato' Seri Dr Zambry
Abdul Kadir; Attorney General (Intervener) [2010] 2 Current Law
Journal 925 (Federal Court)..46
Defensor Santiago v. Commission on Elections (1997) 336 Phil. 848.....................266
Disomangcop v Secretary of the Department of Public Works and Highways
(2004) G.R. No. 149848 .... 270, 272
Estrada v Desierto (2001) G.R. Nos. 146710-15 .... 260, 276
Estrada v. Escritor, A.M. No. P-02-1651 (4 August 2003) <http://sc.judiciary.gov.
ph/jurisprudence/2003/aug2003/am_p_02_1651.htm> accessed
18 September 2018. 262
Estrada v. Escritor, A.M. No. P-02-1651 (22 June 2006) <http://sc.judiciary.gov.
ph/jurisprudence/2006/june2006/A.M.%20No.%20P-02-1651.htm>
accessed 18 September 2018. 262
Funa v Chairman of the Civil Service Commission (25 November 2014)
G.R. No. 191672.. 171, 270
Ganzon v. Court of Appeals (1991) G.R. No. 93252 271
Garcia v. Commission on Elections (1993) G.R. No. 111511 259
J.P. Berthelsen v Director General of Immigration [1987] 1 MLJ 134......................38
Larin v Executive Secretary (1997) G.R. No. 112745..268
Latifah bte Mat Zin v Rosmawati bte Sharibun & Another [2007] 5 MLJ 101. 40

Lawyers against Monopoly and Poverty v Secretary of Budget and Management
(2012) G.R. No. 164987 276
Lawyers League for a Better Philippines v. Corazon C. Aquino (1986)
G.R. No. 76180..276
Lina Joy v Majlis Agama Islam Wilayah & Another [2007] 4 MLJ 585,
630 (dissenting opinion of Justice Richard Malanjum). 40, 43
Md Hakim Lee v Majlis Agama Islam Wilayah Persekutuan, Kuala Lumpur
[1998] 1 MLJ 681..40
*Menteri Dalam Negeri & Others v Titular Roman Catholic Archbishop
of Kuala Lumpur,* [2013] 6 MLJ 468. 47
Myers v United States (October 25, 1926) 272 U.S. 52. 268
*Neri v Senate Committee on Accountability of Public Officers
and Investigations, G.R. No. 180643 (Sep. 4, 2008)*...267
Pathmanathan Krishnan v Indira Gandhi Mutho & Other Appeals [2016]
1 CLJ 911. 42
Persatuan Aliran v Minister for Home Affairs [1988] 1 MLJ 440. 38
*Petition for Prohibition with the Supreme Court of the Philippines,
Social Justice Society v. Hon. Franklin Drilon (28 August 2013)*
G.R. No. 208493 277
Philippine Constitution Association v Enriquez (1994) G.R. No. 113105.............276
Philippine Gamefowl Commission v Intermediate Appellate Court (1986)
G.R. No. 72969-70...270
*Province of North Cotabato v. Government of the Republic of the Philippines
Peace Panel on Ancestral Domain (2008) G.R. No. 183591* 272
Shamala Sathiyaseelan v Dr Jeyaganesh C Mogarajah & Another
[2004] 2 MLJ 648..44
*Siti Hasnah Vangarama Abdullah v Tun Dr Mahathir Mohamad
(as President of PERKIM)* [2012] 7 CLJ 845...44
Soon Singh v Pertubuhan Kebajikan Islam Malaysia (PERKIM) Kedah
[1999] 1 MLJ 489...40
Subashini a/p Rajasingam v Saravanan a/l Thangathoray and other appeals
[2008] 2 MLJ 147... 42, 44
Subic Bay Metropolitan Authority v. Commission on Elections (1996)
330 Phil. 1082... 259, 266
Viran Nagapan v. Deepa Subramaniam & Other Appeals [2016] 3 CLJ 505..........47

TABLE OF LEGISLATION

Constitutional material

Constitution of the Kingdom of Cambodia, 21 September 1993
    www.refworld.org/docid/3ae6b5428.html accessed 18 September 2018.........17
Constitution of Brunei Darussalam 1959 (2011 Rev Ed)................................. 18, 84
Ferdinand E Marcos, Code of Muslim Personal Laws of the Philippines
    Presidential Decree No. 1083 (1977)..265
The 1987 Constitution of the Republic of the Philippines............. 256, 259–71, 273

Statutory material

Administrative Code of 1987, Executive Order No. 292 (1987) 268
Amending Further Executive Order No. 120 (s.2012), as Amended
    by Executive Order No. 187 (s 2015), on the Bangsamoro Transition
    Commission and for Other Purposes, Executive Order No. 08
    (s 2016) (2016)..259
An Act Appropriating Funds for the Operation of the Government of the
    Republic of the Philippines from January One to December Thirty-One,
    Two Thousand and Seventeen and for Other Purposes (2016) 269
An Act Expanding the Jurisdiction of the Court of Tax Appeals (CTA),
    Elevating its Rank to the Level of a Collegiate Court with Special
    Jurisdiction and enlarging its Membership, amending for the purpose
    certain sections of Republic Act No. 1125, as amended, otherwise
    known as the Law Creating the Court of Tax Appeals, and for other
    purposes, Republic Act No. 9282 (2004)..267
An Act Providing for an Organic Act for the Cordillera Autonomous
    Region, Republic Act No. 6766 (1989) 259, 266
An Act Providing for an Organic Act for the Autonomous Region
    in Muslim Mindanao, Republic Act No. 6734 (1989) 259, 272
An Act Reorganizing the Judiciary, Appropriating Funds therefor,
    and for other Purposes, Batas Pambansa Blg. 129 (1981) 267
An Act to Establish the Cordillera Autonomous Region,
    Republic Act No. 8438 (1997)... 259, 266
An Act to Strengthen and Expand the Organic Act for the Autonomous
    Region in Muslim Mindanao, Amending for the Purpose Republic
    Act No. 6734, entitled 'An Act Providing for the Autonomous Region
    in Muslim Mindanao' as amended, Republic Act No. 9054 (2001)....... 259, 272

xvi *Table of Legislation*

Constituting the Transition Commission and for Other Purposes, Executive
    Order 120 (s 2012) (2012) 259
General Appropriations Act, FY2017 269
Local Government Code of 1991, Republic Act No. 7160 (1991) 259, 266,
    270, 274
National Commission on Muslim Filipinos Act of 2009, Rep. Act No. 9997
    (2009) 265
Organic Law for the Bangsamoro Autonomous Region in Muslim
    Mindanao, Republic Act No. 11054 (2018) 259, 265, 272–73
Republic Act No. 11054 (2018) 259, 265, 273
The Indigenous Peoples' Rights Act of 1997, Republic Act No. 8371
    (1997) 259, 261
The Initiative and Referendum Act, Republic Act No. 6735 (1989) 259, 266
The Responsible Parenthood and Reproductive Act of 2012 (2012),
    <www.officialgazette.gov.ph/2012/12/21/republic-act-no-10354/>
    accessed 18 September 2018. 275

1

Pluralist Constitutions and the Southeast Asian Context

JACLYN L. NEO AND BUI NGOC SON

I. Introduction: Constitutions and Pluralities in Southeast Asia

Southeast Asia is a region of vast pluralities. An introductory text on Southeast Asia describes the region in these terms: 'No comparative area of the world has such a range of demographic, ethnic, linguistic, religious diversity as does Southeast Asia.'[1] This diversity has sometimes complicated attempts to properly define Southeast Asia, and indeed Asia in general, beyond a geographical concept. Indeed, the geographical boundaries where Southeast Asia begins and ends have been a fluid one. Nonetheless, regional groupings depend heavily on self-conscious definition. As Asia becomes 'Asianized' through a process of self-conscious coming together,[2] Southeast Asia has become increasingly defined through a voluntary regional grouping under the Association of Southeast Asian Nations (ASEAN). This book therefore adopts the ASEAN grouping as its starting point for defining Southeast Asia. In this regard, its focus is on the exploration of *how the constitutions respond to pluralities in this self-conscious grouping of ASEAN.*[3]

ASEAN consists of ten Member States, namely Brunei, Cambodia, Indonesia, Laos, Malaysia, Myanmar, Philippines, Singapore, Thailand, and Vietnam.[4] It is one of the most religiously diverse regions in the world, being home to the largest population of Muslims globally (Indonesia), the largest population of Roman Catholics outside of Latin America (the Philippines), a population with the largest percentage of Buddhists anywhere in the world (Thailand), and the most

---

[1] Clark D Neher, *Southeast Asia: Crossroads of The World* (Northern Illinois University Press 2010).
[2] Yoichi Funabashi, 'The Asianization of Asia' (1993) 72(5) Foreign Affairs 75.
[3] We are aware that such a position may be problematic as the region could extend beyond ASEAN. To be clear, we do not assert or adopt any political position concerning regionalism in Southeast Asia by adopting the ASEAN grouping.
[4] See the website of the ASEAN: 'Association of Southeast Asian Nations' <https://asean.org/> last accessed 18 September 2018.

religiously diverse country in the world (Singapore).[5] The spread of religions further follows an intra-regional pattern, where an overwhelming majority of Southeast Asian Muslims live in Indonesia, Malaysia, and Brunei, while Buddhism and Catholicism dominate the Myanmar-Indochina region and the Philippines respectively.

On top of its religious diversity, Southeast Asia is also ethnically diverse. Two types of ethnic diversity have been emphasised in the region: first, indigenous ethnic diversity arising from regional variations of cultural and linguistic groups; and second, diversity arising from immigration – primarily of people from the Chinese and the Indian races.[6]

Furthermore, another distinctive feature within Southeast Asia is that all Southeast Asian countries had been colonised by western countries with the sole exception of Thailand. Colonial history, while a seemingly common trait, actually reveals shades of difference among ASEAN countries as the colonial experience in the region is varied. The British empire ruled over Brunei, Malaysia (Malaya, Sabah, and Sarawak), Myanmar (or Burma), and Singapore; while the US controlled the Philippines. Indochina, comprising Cambodia, Laos, and Vietnam, was colonised primarily by France and Indonesia was colonised by the Dutch.[7] The legacies of colonialism varied across these countries, not just in reception of colonial legal, political, social and economic systems, but also in terms of their rejection. As Tan highlights, communism and nationalism fuelled opposition to colonial rule in Southeast Asia and revolution featured prominently as a theme among some post-colonial societies.[8] Thus in apparent attempts to 'restore' the mythical glorious pre-colonial past, several Southeast Asian states eventually jettisoned or at least modified colonially-imposed or influenced constitutional orders.

The impact of colonialism on the legal systems in Southeast Asia is obvious. English common law is adopted by Brunei, Malaysia, Myanmar, and Singapore; whereas civil law is practised in the rest of Southeast Asia. The Philippines, having both Spanish and US influence, practice a mixed legal system instead.[9] Even within each country, there is significant legal pluralism. Thus, systems such as those of Confucian, Islamic, Hindu, Buddhist, and various chthonic or indigenous laws continue to be practised in various Southeast Asian countries. In fact, there is increasing recognition that these underlying traditional legal systems continue to influence law and society.

---

[5] Pew Research Centre, 'Global Religious Diversity: Half of the Most Religiously Diverse Countries Are in Asia-Pacific Region' (*Pew Forum*, 4 April 2014) www.pewforum.org/2014/04/04/global-religious-diversity/ accessed 18 September 2018.

[6] Charles Hirschman, 'Ethnic Diversity and Change in Southeast Asia' in Calvin Goldscheider (ed), *Population, Ethnicity, and Nation Building* (Westview Press 1995) 22.

[7] See generally, Paul H Kratoska (ed), *South East Asia: Colonial History* (Routledge 2001).

[8] Kevin YL Tan, 'The Making and Remaking of Constitutions in Southeast Asia: An Overview' (2002) 6 Singapore Journal of International & Comparative Law 1, 3.

[9] For comprehensive survey of law in Southeast Asia, see M B Hooker, *Laws of South-East Asia, Volume I, The Pre-Modern Texts* (Butterworth 1986); M B Hooker, *Laws of South-East Asia, Volume II, European Laws in South-East Asia* (Butterworth 1988).

Consonant with its religious, ethnic and legal plurality and varied colonial histories, Southeast Asia is a kaleidoscopic collection of constitutional experiments. Constitutional dynamism and resistance to it is also driven significantly by state-building, economic development, and globalisation.[10] Thailand enacted 20 constitutions as of 2017 but retains fundamentally the same political structure: a constitutional monarch, a Westminster-style government, and a German-style constitutional court.[11] Indonesia's constitution was adopted in 1945 when it declared independence but substantively revised it in the 2000s to firmly establish a presidential system and introduce a constitutional court, among other things.[12] In the Philippines, the current Constitution, which provides the framework for a presidential system modelled after the American system, was enacted in 1987 without any subsequent amendment despite several attempts of constitutional reform.[13]

The constitutional epochs of the British colonists are varied. Brunei practises an absolute monarchy defined by the Constitution of 1959, which was retained even after the constitution was amended in 1984.[14] In Malaysia, the current constitution, enacted in 1957 and frequently amended afterward, establishes a constitutional monarch alongside its Westminster-style government.[15] Singapore is a constitutional republic with a Westminster-style government within the framework established by the Constitution of 1965 and subsequent amendments.[16] Myanmar enacted three constitutions in 1947, 1974, and 2008 – each of which created different types of government.[17]

The former countries of Indochina do not have a single constitutional path either. While Cambodia aspires to implement a liberal constitutional democracy within the 1993 Constitution drafted under the auspices of the United Nations and repeatedly amended afterward,[18] Laos and Vietnam follow a socialist constitutional model which remains in their newly-enacted constitutions of 2015 and 2013 respectively.[19]

---

[10] See generally, Kevin Tan, 'Making and Remaking of Constitutions' (n 8); Wen-chen Chang, Li-ann Thio, Kevin YL Tan and Jiunn-rong Yeh, *Constitutionalism in Asia: Cases and Materials* (Hart 2015).

[11] See generally, Andrew Harding and Peter Leyland, *The Constitutional System of Thailand: A Contextual Analysis* (Hart 2011).

[12] See generally, Timothy Lindsey, *The Constitution of Indonesia: A Contextual Analysis* (Hart 2011).

[13] See generally, Rufus B Rodriguez, *Constitutionalism in the Philippines* (Rex Book Store 1997).

[14] See generally, Hussainmiya, *The Brunei Constitution of 1959: An inside History* (Brunei Press 2000).

[15] See generally, Andrew Harding, *The Constitution of Malaysia: A Contextual Analysis* (Hart 2012).

[16] See generally, Kevin YL Tan, *The Constitution of Singapore: A Contextual Analysis* (Hart 2014).

[17] See generally, Andrew Harding, *Constitutionalism and Legal Change in Myanmar* (Hart 2017).

[18] See generally, Hor Peng, Kong Phallack and Jörg Menzel (eds), *Cambodian Constitutional Law* (Konrad-Adenauer-Stiftung 2017).

[19] See generally, Gerald Leather, 'Laos: A Constitution in Search of Constitutionalism,' in Clauspeter Hill and Jörg Menzel (eds), *Constitutionalism in Southeast Asia, Vol 2* (Konrad-Adenauer-Stiftung 2008) 125; Mark Sidel, *The Constitution of Vietnam: A Contextual Analysis* (Hart 2009); Bui Ngoc Son, 'Vietnamese Constitutional Debate in Comparative Perspective' (2017) 11(2) Asian Journal of Comparative Law 189, and the rest of the articles in the special issue on Vietnamese and Comparative Constitutional Law.

These varied constitutional histories and developments make Southeast Asia a particularly rich region for empirical and theoretical examination. Much can be said about the common themes and divergences within the region, the international, regional, and local influences on constitution-making, and how constitutional histories and developments in different countries affect others in the region.[20] As mentioned, the focus for this book is the presence of pluralities and how the various constitutions respond to the extant range of these within each constitution's respective jurisdictions. We propose to conceptualise this phenomenon as one of 'pluralist constitutions' – *a constitution that recognises internal pluralities within society and makes arrangements to accommodate rather than eliminate these pluralities.*

This chapter critically reviews relevant scholarship in Part II, and discusses institutional design in these pluralist constitutions in Part III. Part IV contains our proposed conceptual framework of pluralist constitutions, which we then apply to analysing Southeast Asian constitutions in Part V. We conclude with further reflections in Part VI.

II. Constitutions in Pluralist Societies in Southeast Asia: A Gap in Comparative Constitutional Law Scholarship

While comparative and country-based studies on constitutional law in Southeast Asia abound, this is the first study to approach the issue from a pluralist perspective. This study contributes to existing scholarship on the matter in three ways. First, it offers a constitutional framework to analyse constitutional practices in Southeast Asia where societies are marked by significant pluralities. Secondly, it pluralises the field of comparative constitutional law by identifying internal pluralities as a significant site of constitutional practice and meaning. Thirdly and critically, the study bridges the gap between constitutional theory and scholarship on legal pluralism.

A. Constitutional Law in Pluralistic Southeast Asia

Constitutions in Southeast Asia, in general, and their relationship with internal pluralities, in particular, are understudied in existing constitutional law scholarship.[21] Existing scholarship of Southeast Asian constitutions can be broadly divided into two forms: textualist and contextualist. Textualist approaches focus

---

[20] See further, Kevin YL Tan and Bui Ngoc Son (eds), *Constitutional Foundings in Southeast Asia* (Hart Publishing forthcoming).

[21] For example, there are no substantive accounts on the relations of constitutions to pluralities in two recent leading books on Asian constitutional law. See Chang (n 10); Rosalind Dixon and Tom Ginsburg, *Comparative Constitutional Law in Asia* (Edward Elgar 2015).

on the texts of the Southeast Asian constitutions, usually providing doctrinal analysis or cross-text comparisons.[22] Textualist accounts do not usually substantively address the questions of how the constitutional texts in Southeast Asia are informed by the realities of plurality.

Contextualist accounts on the other hand do better in accounting for the realities of plurality do not always draw a sufficient connection between these pluralities to constitution-making or design. Furthermore, there is a tendency for some contextualist accounts to focus on single-country study or on a small handful of countries for comparative study. All of these approaches underestimate the relations of the constitution to internal pluralities.

Contextualist accounts can be further divided into macro-historical, political, and social approaches. On the first, macro-historical contextualism situates the Southeast Asian constitutions within their historical surroundings and identify a variety of constitutional models in the regions. Chen, for example, identifies:

1. Marxist-Leninist constitutional systems in Vietnam and Laos;
2. stable hybrid constitutional systems in Singapore and Malaysia which combine both liberal and authoritarian elements;
3. unstable liberal constitutional systems in Philippines, Thailand, and Indonesia;
4. liberal constitutional systems with international intervention in Cambodia and East Timor; and
5. authoritarian constitutional systems in Myanmar and Brunei.[23]

Similarly, Neo presents a typology of three models of state-religion relationships in Southeast Asia. These are, namely:

1. formal prioritisation of religion (Brunei, Cambodia, Indonesia, Malaysia, Myanmar, Thailand);
2. statist or communitarian states that tend to regard religion as an aspect of state control (Laos, Vietnam, Singapore); and
3. formalised separation of state and religion (the Philippines).[24]

These typologies focus the plurality of constitutional experiences *among* Southeast Asian nations. Our study, however, is instead concerned with pluralist constitutional experiences *within* individual Southeast Asian nations.

---

[22] See the three volumes by Clauspeter Hill and Jörg Menzel (eds), *Constitutionalism in Southeast Asia* (Konrad-Adenauer-Stiftung 2008).

[23] Albert H Y Chen, 'Western Constitutionalism in Southeast Asia: Historical and Comparative Observations' in Dirk Ehlers, Henning Glaser and Kittisak Prokati (eds), *Constitutionalism and Good Governance: Eastern and Western Perspectives* (Nomos Publishers 2014) 6.

[24] Jaclyn L Neo, 'Realizing the Right to Freedom of Thought, Conscience, and Religion: The Limited Normative Force of the ASEAN Human Rights Declaration' (2017) 17(4) Human Rights Law Review 729.

Secondly, political contextualism locates the constitutions and constitutional practice in Southeast Asia within political contestation.[25] Domestic pluralities however tend to be viewed as a source of constitutional contestations rather than as a source of constitutional dynamism.

Finally, social contextualism locates the constitutions in South East Asia (and other Asian parts) based on various types of social difference, including religion, ethnicity/race, urban/rural divisions, language, gender, and sexual orientation.[26] Social contextualists tend to focus on the functional question of how the constitutions deal with difference but do not substantively address this ontological question: what is the nature (not only function) of a constitution when it engages with plurality?

Pluralist constitutionalism recognises – indeed even celebrates – contextualism. However, it is also methodologically pluralistic on two levels. First, it adopts contextualism broadly, including macro-historical, political, and social contextualism. Secondly, it is methodologically pluralistic in that the embrace of contextualism does not exclude the formal text and law. Since constitutional texts are embodiments of domestic pluralities, textualist accounts are still important. Pluralist constitutionalism emphasises that there is connection between text and context, as formal texts must be located within the historical, political and social contexts. Consequently, pluralist constitutionalism adopts an integrated approach towards text and context whereby contextualism must be integrated with textualist considerations. Such methodological pluralism is also directed to a range of ontological, functional, and consequential questions related to constitutional engagement with plurality. These include inquiries into the nature of the constitution, its functions, as well as the results of any constitutional engagement with plurality.

B. Comparative Constitutional Law

Following from constitutional theory's limited engagement with pluralities within constitutional systems in Asia, studies in comparative constitutional law have also tended to overlook the significance of internal plurality within Southeast Asian constitutions. This partly stems from the epistemological foundations of comparative constitutional inquiry. First, comparative constitutional inquiry is dominated by institutionalism, especially juricentrism. While it is important to explore judicial review, constitutional cases, and more recently the making and amendment of constitutions, this does not sufficiently account for the plural social contexts of constitutional design and practice.[27] Second, the prevalent use

---

[25] Marco Bünte and Björn Dressel, *Politics and Constitutions in Southeast Asia* (Routledge 2017). See also, Victor V Ramraj, 'Constitutional Tipping Points: Sustainable Constitutionalism in Theory and Practice' (2010) 1(2) Transnational Legal Theory 191.

[26] Susan H Williams (ed), *Social Difference and Constitutionalism in Pan-Asia* (CUP 2014).

[27] For some recent works in these lines, Conrado Hübner Mendes, *Constitutional Courts And Deliberative Democracy* (OUP 2014); Samuel Issacharoff, *Fragile Democracies: Contested Power in the Era of*

of functionalism and universalism[28] in comparative constitutional inquiry tends to focus on global constitutional convergence.[29] This results in these inquiries underestimating factors that induce internal constitutional divergence.[30] Third, eurocentrism dominates comparative constitutional inquiry, which makes the field focus mainly on a limited set of constitutional systems sharing similar features such as the separation of power, the bill of rights, and judicial review. This unfortunately marginalises constitutional experience of the global south.[31] While there is a growing body of Asian comparative constitutional scholarship,[32] this literature has also been dominated by the institutional approach and has yet to fully accounted for the pluralist foundations of constitutional institutions save for a few exceptional studies.[33]

C. Legal Pluralism and Constitutional Theory

Thirdly, this book hopes to bridge the gap between two scholarships on constitutional theory and legal pluralism. There are extensive studies of legal pluralism in Southeast Asia,[34] but this body of scholarship focuses on the existence of two or more legal systems within a Southeast Asian country – particularly the coexistence of colonial law with traditional or indigenous law. Literature on legal pluralism does not always address the influence of, and its impact on, constitutional arrangements and practices across different countries. Theories of legal pluralism

---

Constitutional Courts (OUP 2014); Sujit Choudhry and Tom Ginsburg, *Constitution Making* (Edward Elgar Publishing 2016); Richard Albert, Xenophon Contiades and Alkmene Fotiadou, *The Foundations and Traditions of Constitutional Amendment* (Hart 2017).

[28] On these two constitutional epistemologies, see Vicki Jackson, 'Comparative Constitutional Law: Methodologies' in Michel Rosenfeld and András Sajó (eds), *The Oxford Handbook of Comparative Constitutional Law* (OUP 2012) 54.

[29] For reviews and discussions of several theories of constitutional convergence, see Rosalind Dixon & Eric Posner, 'The Limits of Constitutional Convergence' (2011) 11 Chicago Journal of International Law 399.

[30] Jaakko Husa, 'Global Constitutionalism – Some Critical Remarks,' (2017) 47 Hong Kong Law Journal 13; David Law, 'Alternatives to Liberal Constitutional Democracy' (2017) 77 Maryland Law Review 223.

[31] Ran Hirschl, *Comparative Matters: The Renaissance of Comparative Constitutional Law* (OUP 2014).

[32] For a review of this scholarship, see Andrew Harding and Bui Ngoc Son, 'Recent Work in Asian Constitutional Studies: A Review Essay' (2016) 11(1) Asian Journal of Comparative Law 163–183.

[33] Such exceptions include: Benjamin Schonthal, 'Formations of Buddhist constitutionalism in South and Southeast Asia' (2017) 15(3) International Journal of Constitutional Law 705–733; Pranoto Iskandar, 'Indigenizing Constitutionalism: A Critical Reading of Asian Constitutionalism' (2017) Oxford Unversity Comparative L Forum 2 https://ouclf.iuscomp.org/indigenizing-constitutionalism-a-critical-reading-of-asian-constitutionalism/ accessed 18 September 2018.

[34] Hooker M B, *Legal Pluralism: An Introduction to Colonial and Neo-colonial Laws* (Oxford: Clarendon Press 1975); Gary Bell (ed), *Pluralism, Transnationalism and Culture in Asian Law: A Book in Honour of M.B. Hooker* (ISEAS Yusof Ishak Institute 2017); Poh-Ling Tan (ed), *Asian Legal Systems: Law, Society, and Pluralism in East Asia* (Butterworths 1997). See also, Adam Possamai, James T Richardson and Bryan S Turner (eds), *Legal Pluralism and Shari'a Law* (Routledge 2016), with particular regard to ch 5.

problematised the idea of law as a closed system, and saw 'societies, states and "tribes" as self-contained, decontextualized units'.[35] Legal pluralists propose a conception of law that recognises and emphasises its plurality (beyond state-made law), fluidity (between different legal systems and sub-systems), the importance of private law-making (presence of social norms and conventions), and the presence and influence of unwritten norms (whether in the form of natural law, social norms or religious norms).[36] Legally, pluralist arrangements involving the state also tend to be given less focus, as unfortunately reflected by the term 'weak' legal pluralism.[37] Our account seeks to provide a link between legal pluralism and constitutionalism.

III. Institutional Design and Pluralist Constitutions

In comparison, the political scientists do a better job in addressing the impact of pluralities on constitutions. Specifically, scholars working on ethnic plurality have long advocated various forms of constitutional engineering to promote stable democracy in deeply divided societies.[38]

Arend Lijphart's consociationalism proposes grand coalitions among political elites to ensure inter-ethnic power sharing,[39] whereas Donald Horowitz's work examines, inter alia, electoral systems and the role of race-based parties in exacerbating existing ethnic division.[40] Lijphart's consociational approach relies on elite cooperation between leaders of different communities.[41] This entails grand coalition cabinets, elections with proportional representation, minority veto powers, and communal autonomy – all of which are meant to maximise the independence and influence of each main ethnic community.[42]

---

[35] William Twining, *Globalisation and Legal Theory* (Butterworths 2000) 7. See also, Gad Barzilai, 'Beyond Relativism: Where is Political Power in Legal Pluralism?' (2008) 9 Theoretical Inquiries in Law 395, 396.

[36] Werner Menski, *Comparative Law in a Global Context: The Legal Systems of Asia and Africa*, (CUP 2006) 34.

[37] For a description of the types of legally pluralistic orders (and more), see William Twining, 'Normative and Legal Pluralism: A Global Perspective' (2010) 20 Duke Journal of Comparative & International Law 473.

[38] Donald L Horowitz, Ethnic Groups in Conflict (University of California Press 1991).

[39] For Arend Lijphart's work, see *Democracy in Plural Societies: A Comparative Exploration* (Yale University Press 1977).

[40] For Donald Horowitz's work, see *A Democratic South Africa? Constitutional Engineering in a Divided Society* (University of California Press 1991); 'Constitutional Design: An Oxymoron?' in Stephen Macedo and Ian Shapiro (eds), *Designing Democratic Institutions* (Nomos XLII 2000) 253–284 and (2000) 3 Democratic Culture 117–147; 'Constitutional Design: Proposals Versus Processes' in Andrew Reynolds (ed), *The Architecture of Democracy: Constitutional Design, Conflict Management, and Democracy* (OUP 2002) 1, 15–36; 'Conciliatory Institutions and Constitutional Process in Post-Conflict States' (2008) 49 William and Mary Law Review 1213–1248; 'Encouraging Electoral Accommodation in Divided Societies' in Brij Lal & Peter Larmour (eds), *Electoral Systems in Divided Societies: The Fiji Constitution* (ANU Press 2012).

[41] Lijphart (n 39).

[42] ibid.

In contrast to consociational approaches, centripetalism denotes institutional designs that encourage inter-communal moderation and cooperation. This is achieved by promoting multi-ethnic political parties, cross-cutting electoral incentives and inter-group accommodation.[43] Benjamin Reilly's exposition of centripetalism focuses on putting in place institutional incentives for cross-ethnic behaviour in order to encourage cooperation between rival groups.[44] A third approach identified, communalism, is explained by Reilly as encompassing the use of explicit ethnic criteria of representation.[45] Quotas, for instance, would be a form of communal approach.

Theorists of constitutional designs for pluralist societies have further identified two competing models: accommodation and integration.[46] While integrationists promote a single public identity, accommodationists advocate for dual or multiple public identities.[47]

Inspired by these developments in political science, several scholars of comparative constitutional and other fields of law have turned to questions of constitutional design in pluralist or divided societies in recent times.[48] This literature in both political science and comparative constitutional studies has provided important normative theories and detailed institutional recommendations.

That said, the term 'design' suggests a technocratic and systematic approach to constitution-making.[49] However, scholars have identified difficulties with a design-oriented approach to constitutions, including the fact that institutional designs are often based on speculative predictions of how institutions will actually function, and thus be distorted by bias and self-interest.[50] We will identify and address some limitations among the wider range of criticisms below.

First, the existing scholarship is concerned with ameliorating pluralities since its focus is on divided societies. This results in an over-emphasis on internal plurality as a source of social division, and fails to see plurality as engendering a host of

---

[43] Benjamin Reilly, 'Institutional Designs for Diverse Democracies: Consociationalism, centripetalism and Communalism Compared' (2012) 11 European Political Science 259.

[44] ibid. See also, Benjamin Reilly, 'Centripetalism: Cooperation, Accommodation, and Integration', in Stefan Wolff & Christalla Yakinthou (eds), *Conflict Management in Divided Societies: Theories and Practice* (Routledge 2012).

[45] ibid 260.

[46] See John McGarry, Brendan O'Leary and Richard Simeon, 'Integration or Accommodation? The Enduring Debate in Conflict Regulation,' in Sujit Choudhry (ed) *Constitutional Design for Divided Societies: Integration or Accommodation?* (OUP 2008) 42.

[47] ibid.

[48] See generally, Sujit Choudhry (ed), *Constitutional Design for Divided Societies: Integration or Accommodation?* (OUP 2008); Hanna Lerner, *Making Constitutions in Deeply Divided Societies* (Cambridge University Press, 2011); Jaime Lluch, *Constitutionalism and The Politics of Accommodation In Multinational Democracies* (Palgrave Macmillan 2014); Michel Rosenfeld, *Constitutionalism, Identity, Difference, and Legitimacy: Theoretical Perspectives* (Duke University Press 1994); Aslı Ü Bâli and Hanna Lerner, *Constitution Writing, Religion and Democracy* (CUP 2017).

[49] Tom Ginsburg (ed), *Constitutional Design* (CUP 2012).

[50] See Horowitz, 'Constitutional Design: Proposals Versus Processes' (n 40). See also Horowitz's article in 'How to Study Constitution-Making: Hirschl, Elster and the Seventh Inning Problem' (2016) 96 Boston University Law Review 1347.

social and political relationships of differing intensities. Furthermore, by focusing on divided societies, societies that are less divided are given less attention although they are no less pluralistic. This is especially problematic as these less divided societies may provide more insight into constitutional arrangements that have been successful in managing plurality. Thus, a primary concern with divided societies may result in an under-appreciation of crucial functions that constitutions play in such pluralistic societies, such as an instrument to mitigate social polarisation while permitting expressions of plural public identities.

Secondly, the design options are created for *deeply* divided societies. Their applicability therefore depends on there being deep division within societies. Many societies, including those within Asia, may not themselves be deeply divided or have started out as such. It would be difficult to determine if applying institutions designed to address deep division in turn reinforces and deepens those divisions, since it requires an exercise in the counterfactual. Nonetheless, it would be an important question to ask if these institutional options are suited for societies that are less deeply divided.

Thirdly, where existing scholarship focuses mainly on ethnic pluralities, it may to overlook other forms of pluralities, such as those of religion, values, ideas, and even systems. Ethnic identity may be distinguished from religious identity since religion may often be considered as more fluid – particularly where the state does not restrict religious choice or conversion. In most instances where the state does impose such restrictions, religious identity is arguably seen as a form of ethnic identity and/or as intertwined with ethnic identity, which often results in greater politicisation of racial/religious identity.[51] Ideational differences are also distinct from ethnic differences since they are based on ideological commitments, which are not necessarily intertwined with identity. While there is little difference in the level of difficulty in overcoming ideological commitments, religious identity politics or ethnic identity politics, we suggest that constitutional designs specifically for ethnic identity politics may not always be suitable where different forms of plurality are involved.

Consequently, we have not adopted the lens of deeply divided societies nor their common framework of choices. Instead, this book investigates options that may not neatly fall within these options and considers ways in which various forms of plurality have been addressed within the region.

IV. Pluralism-in-fact and the Pluralist Constitution

The question of plurality and pluralism has increasingly become a crucial focus of constitutional scholarship in recent times. Michel Rosenfeld's work in this area

---

[51] See Jaclyn Neo, 'What's in a name? Malaysia's "Allah" controversy and the judicial intertwining of Islam with ethnic identity' (2014) 12(3) International Journal of Constitutional Law 751–768.

is of particular importance. He distinguishes 'pluralism-in-fact' from 'pluralism-as-a-norm', where the former denotes 'societies marked by the coexistence of a number of competing and often antagonistic conceptions of the good.'[52] This may be the result of diversities between and within groups and individuals.[53] However, as Rosenfeld rightly points out, 'the fact of pluralism ... does not tell us anything about how we ought to deal with conflicts arising within pluralistic societies.'[54] There are many possible approaches to addressing plurality within society. One such approach is liberal constitutionalism which emphasises the neutral State and equality; but it is not necessarily the only one.

'Pluralism-as-a-norm', or normative pluralism, posits that pluralism in fact is good.[55] Conflicts in a pluralistic society thus 'ought to be handled in a way that is designed to preserve and enhance pluralism.'[56] In other words, pluralism-as-a-norm entails 'the pursuit of pluralism on normative grounds.'[57] It is a conception of the good, and does not assume a position of genuine neutrality as regards to other competing conceptions.[58] Nonetheless, normative or comprehensive pluralism does seek to be inclusive of these other conceptions of the good. It is thus distinguishable from monism where it does not take the view that there is a single conception of the good that is preferable.[59] Even more boldly, Rosenfeld distinguishes normative pluralism from relativism, thus rejecting the view that all value preferences are ultimately purely subjective and contingent.[60] His pluralism-as-a-norm is therefore propounded as 'a critical counterfactual ideal [that] yields the best possible normative criterion for the reconciliation of self and other within a pluralistic in fact society, in a way that maximizes the potential for justice while minimizing that for violence.'[61] It is premised upon a dual emphasis on equalising all conceptions of the good and including them, rather than relying on hierarchy and exclusion.[62] Pluralist constitutional ordering as such involves 'multiple sets of norms that intersect, overlap, divide the field, or relate to one another horizontally rather than vertically.'[63]

While it remains to be seen if Rosenfeld's proposal for normative pluralism is the preferred way of addressing 'pluralism-in-fact', we agree that it is necessary

---

[52] Michel Rosenfeld, *Just Interpretations: Law between Ethics and Politics* (University California Press 1998) 200–201.
[53] ibid 201–3.
[54] ibid 200.
[55] ibid 206.
[56] ibid 201.
[57] ibid.
[58] ibid.
[59] ibid 206.
[60] ibid.
[61] ibid 207.
[62] ibid 208. There are of course important criticisms to Rosenfeld's attempt to straddle the middle ground between monism and relativism, though it is not necessary to go into these criticisms for this book.
[63] Michel Rosenfeld, 'Rethinking constitutional ordering in an era of legal and ideological pluralism' (2008) 6(3–4) International Journal of Constitutional Law 415, 417.

to distinguish between factual and normative pluralisms to resist constitutional monism. Our proposal of a pluralist constitution is more modest. Ontologically, we see the pluralist constitution as *a constitution that recognises and accommodates (and not eliminate) internal pluralities within a given society*. It does not go as far as Rosenfeld's normative pluralism to prescribe a comprehensive doctrine to equalise and include a plurality of conceptions of the good. Pluralist constitutions are therefore minimalist: they abjure attempts to eradicate pluralities, but may at times provide incentives for individuals and groups to abandon pluralities. Thus, for instance, a proposal for ideas of national citizenship transcending inter-group differences may persuade groups to shift their loyalties to the nation.

What the pluralist constitution clearly rejects is any attempt to ignore or *coercively* eliminate individual and group identity that is not in line with the predominant identity. This conception of pluralist constitutions can accommodate a more flexible range of constitutional choices between inclusion and exclusion, and between equality and non-equality. It is minimalist in terms of the degree of inclusion and equality. Within the pluralist constitution is a combination of hierarchical and heterarchical legal relationships. Multiple sets of norms in such constitutions may interact sometimes vertically, and other times horizontally. The consequence of this interaction may be what we call 'state constitutional pluralism': a concept that denotes competing claims to constitutional meanings by different institutional and social actors within a state.[64] Thus, what is distinctive about the pluralist constitution is the dynamism with which it develops in response to a society's range of pluralities.

A pluralist constitution is likely to reflect a political compromise among constituents with divergent interests and ideologies. It signifies that proponents of divergent interests 'have agreed to set aside their political differences concerning the subject matter of the law and to converge, for the time being, around legislation.'[65] Thus, it is possible that constitutional settlements within the pluralist constitution are much less permanent since the dynamics of convergence and divergence remain in play within the constitutional order. Interpretation of the constitutional 'settlement' becomes a focal point in promoting and defending key constitutional values even after the constitution has been agreed upon. While courts may be an important forum for this contestation, constitutional interpretation outside courts, such as in the social and political arena, also reflects the dynamism of the pluralist constitution.

Another dynamic aspect of this pluralist constitution is that the class of legitimate participants of constitution-making and re-making is not closed. While certain forms of pluralities may be accounted for when the constitution was initially made, the 'people' is not a closed category. Therefore, a pluralist

---

[64] We explore this concept in a separate study in engagement with the European concepts of supranational constitutional pluralism.

[65] Rosenfeld (n 63), 421–2.

constitution should be able to reconsider new constitutional claims and modify its existing settlement to address them. While possibly disruptive, this dynamism would better reflect the practice of constitutional law in many pluralist countries.

One further advantage of conceptualising constitutions as pluralist is also to highlight that constitutional 'settlements' should not be taken for granted. Indeed, constitutional values need to be constantly defended and negotiated in order to preserve them. Where dominant groups assume the permanent superiority of their constitutional values, they may be less prepared to defend these values against objectors both old and new. This is analogous to Mill's argument for free speech as being important to the discovery of truth. The value of freedom of speech lies in its remit to challenge opinions, which enshrines them as 'living truth' rather than dead dogma.[66] Constitutions too need to be constantly negotiated and defended in order for them to remain relevant.

Consequently, pluralist constitutionalism, as a category of constitutionalism, does not merely draw our attention to pluralist sources and contentions within a constitutional system. A crucial dynamic that pluralist accounts can surface is the tussle between the appeal of unity and the reality of plurality. Constitutions, as a tool of state and nation-building, often aspire towards political and social unity. In other words, there is often a strong monist logic inherent to the idea of a constitution. Even where Robert Dahl speaks of pluralism, he speaks of 'the existence of plurality of relatively autonomous (independent) organizations (subsystems) within the domain of a state'.[67] In this regard, the State remains the dominant forum; relative autonomy remains mediated and controlled by the state. Dahl's attention to pluralism within democracies adopts the lens of organisations, which could be organised along ideology, religion, language, ethnicity and region. However, pluralist constitutionalism, as we propose here, is concerned with not just organisational autonomy and engagement with the state within a democratic entity. In fact, we take as a given that pluralist constitutions can take non-democratic forms; indeed, some of the constitutions examined in this book are socialist constitutions while one, Brunei, is an absolute monarchy.

This tussle between unity and plurality is also played out in contests along the lines of monism and pluralism or hierarchy and hetarchy. Indeed, pluralist constitutions emphasise that plurality can result in a relationship beyond just relative autonomy mediated through a hierarchical structure. It is one that could also give rise to a dynamic that could more or less be balanced and thereby less hierarchical but more hetarархical.[68] To be clear, hetarархical relations are not

---

[66] John S Mill, *On Liberty* (1st ed, John W. Parker and Son, London 1859).
[67] Robert A Dahl, *Dilemmas of Pluralist Democracy: Autonomy vs Control* (1st ed, YUP 1983) 5.
[68] Constitutional pluralism, which has been developed in the context of the national and supranational relations within the EU, is one such hetarархical arrangement. We have also identified a form

necessary features of the pluralist constitution. Our position is simply that relative autonomy can be conceptualised in more expansive manners.

V. Pluralist Constitutionalism in Southeast Asia

It bears mentioning here that this book is the culmination of a collaborative project. We gathered a group of scholars to examine constitutions and plurality in their respective countries in Southeast Asia at a workshop held in Singapore by the Centre for Asian Legal Studies at the Faculty of Law, National University of Singapore on 27 and 28 July 2017. For each country's paper, we asked scholars to: (1) provide a brief historical account of the nation's constitutional history and the context of domestic plurality; (2) address a range of questions related to the forms, substances, functions, and consequences of constitutional engagement with plurality; and (3) offer key observations on how the pluralistic sources shape/affect constitutional law and politics. The range of questions includes the following:

Constitutional ideas and values: What are the shared common goods the nation adopts? What are the fundamental ideas and values that inform the constitutional practices of the nation? What are the similarities and differences and the interactions of these constitutional ideas and values?

Constitutional rights: What are the principles of constitutional rights? Are rights considered universal or relative or both? Is there the principle of proportionality? What are specific rights included in the Constitution to address plurality?

Sources of constitutional norms: What are the sources of constitutional law in your country? What are some of the distinctive norms of these different sources of laws? Do the norms of these different systems conflict? What are the main points of conflict? How are conflicts to be resolved?

Constitutional structure: How is the overall constitutional structure arranged? How are constitutional ideas or values related to constitutional structure? How is the legislative election system designed to respond to plurality? Does plurality affect the choice of system of government (parliamentarism, presidentialism, or mixed)? What is distinctive about the organisation, operation, and relations of the three branches of the state (legislature, executive, and judiciary) in your country? How does this institutional arrangement respond to plurality? How is the head of state selected? Does plurality affect this selection? How do the branches of government claim their legitimacy? How do they understand constitutional meaning? Are there distinctive constitutional institutions beyond the usual branches of legislature, executive, and judiciary? If yes, how are they arranged and how are they

---

of pluralism, which we denote as state constitutional pluralism, which examines hetarchical arrangements within national boundaries. See Jaclyn L. Neo and Bui Ngoc Son, 'State Constitutional Pluralism' (forthcoming).

related to plurality? Is there judicial review or other adjudicatory or administrative mechanisms to adjudicate upon the constitutionality of State action? Which institutions have the primary function of interpreting the constitution? If your country has a specialist judicial review system, how do the constitutional review bodies and the ordinary courts and other political institutions interact? How is the vertical separation of power (federalism and decentralisation) designed to respond to plurality?

These questions are intended to be fairly comprehensive in order to ensure broad comparative consistency and a productive conversation. However, scholars are not asked to address all these questions, and could focus on particular questions that are most relevant to the prominent pluralist features of their respective constitutions. We focus below on the most prominent pluralist features of the constitutions from each country's chapter, and elucidate some insights from our overall study.

First, we found that there is no single model of pluralist constitutions in Southeast Asia. As a consequence of how the region is a plurality of pluralities, there is likewise a plurality of pluralist constitutions here. Although we found that all constitutions in the region have responded to the reality of pluralities, the presence, level, and consequence of pluralist constitutions are varied. Solutions proposed to address plurality range from formal equality, minority protections, affirmative action, and federalism, with many other approaches in between and beyond.

Secondly, while ethnicity is the major source of plurality influencing constitution-making and change in Brunei, Malaysia, Myanmar and Singapore, they feature much less in other Southeast Asian countries. In Malaysia, for instance, Dian Shah points out how inter-ethnic contestation and cooperation critically affected the constitutional negotiation over fundamental rights.[69] Specifically, the pull between fundamental liberties, equal rights for *all*, and special privileges for the disadvantaged Malay majority was a crucial flashpoint for Malaysia's constitution-drafting process.

Constitutional approaches towards ethnic plurality can also change over time, as shown in Eugene Tan's account of Singapore (Chapter 3). While ethnic plurality has always been a concern for Singapore's constitution-makers, this plurality has been addressed through a combination of commitments to formal equality and substantive equality. In particular, there has been a shift in policies and constitutional solutions adopted by the Singapore government towards a preference for specific mechanisms that address ethnic plurality, rather than to rely strictly on an ethnic-blind approach guaranteed under formal equality.

In contrast to such countries which directly grappled with the different interests and demands of ethnic groups, other countries in Southeast Asia did not address the question of ethnic plurality in their constitutions. This is especially

[69] See ch 2.

curious since ethnic pluralities do exist in these other countries as a matter of fact. For instance, as Bui Ngoc Son points out in Chapter 8, both Vietnamese and Lao societies are ethnically plural. He however observes that these societies are 'not divided' along ethnic lines and that there have not been serious ethnic conflicts translating to severe political crises. This leads into an interesting argument by Bui: that while both the Vietnamese and Lao PDR constitutions are not designed to regulate ethnic plurality, their constitutions are not necessarily silent about it. In this regard, ethnic plurality could be said to function in the background of a constitution that aspires towards ethnic unity.

Thirdly, religion is another common source of plural contests within countries in Southeast Asia – though again not in all of them. Perhaps unsurprisingly, religion is a flashpoint in constitution-making and change in religiously plural countries like Brunei, Indonesia, Malaysia, Myanmar, and Singapore. For instance, in Indonesia, as Dian Shah and Herlambang Wiratraman observe, the most contentious issue debated in 1945 while the constitution was being made was whether Islam should be the religious basis of the state in Indonesia. A proposal was initially made to include the *Jakarta Charter*'s statement that obliges the state to carry out Islamic *shari'a* for its adherents[70] in the 1945 Constitution. However, this was removed after Christian nationalists in eastern islands of Indonesia threatened to secede from the newly independent state. Thus, while Indonesia has a dominant religious majority with almost 90% being Muslim, religious plurality is still a major factor in constitution-making and change.

Fourthly, ideational plurality, while often overlooked, is also a source of significant value within the constitution. This is interestingly observed in the three constitutions in the Indo-China region of Southeast Asia. In Lao PDR, Vietnam, and Cambodia, as Bui Ngoc Son highlights, there is a strong tendency towards constitutional monism and the unitary orientation of the state. This is particularly the case in Vietnam and Lao PDR which have socialist constitutions. Political monism is implemented in these two countries with their national constitutions mandating the dominance of a communist party. At face value, Laos and Vietnam may thus be easily considered as constitutionally monist as well. The stories are, however, much more complex as these two societies are ethnically plural though not divided. Their constitutions are neither exclusively informed by communist values nor silent about ethnic plurality; instead, these constitutions are relatively pluralist as the consequence of their expression of ethnic values:

> From the preamble to constitutional provisions on fundamental principles of the regime, to the bill of rights, to the structural institutions, the constitutions seek to express the reality of ethnic plurality, the aspiration to continuing ethnic unity, the sovereignty of a unified people, and the state's commitments to promotion of socio-economic development of ethnic groups and protection of their rights.[71]

---

[70] Specifically, '... *dengan kewajiban menjalankan syariat Islam bagi pemeluknya*' (in Bahasa Indonesia).
[71] See ch 8.

Pluralist Constitutions and the Southeast Asian Context 17

In contrast, Cambodia was a former member of French colonial Indochina like Vietnam and Laos, but constitution-making in the country departed from a communist path due to the influence and involvement of the international community. Ratana Taing's account in Chapter 7 highlights that the 1993 Constitution of the Kingdom of Cambodia, is nonetheless, a pluralist constitution underpinned by variety of constitutional values.[72] The Cambodian constitution therefore engages with values from transnational, local, and religious origins. The Cambodian constitution is committed to recognising and respecting 'human rights as enshrined in the United Nations Charter, the Universal Declaration of Human rights and all the treaties and conventions related to human rights, women's rights and children's rights.'[73] It also adopts western liberal values, particularly Locke's idea of a social contract, Montesquieu's model of separation of powers, as well as liberal multi-party democracy. At the same time, the constitution is also informed by local traditional values, including monarchism as an unamenable feature, and the confirmation of Buddhism as the state religion.

This ideational plurality is present in Thailand in a different but no less fascinating manner. Like its neighbour Cambodia, Thailand's constitution is informed by monarchical and Buddhist values. It is pluralist where western ideas of constitutional law struggle against the idea of *Thainess* rooted in the monarchy and Buddhism. Apinop Atipiboonsin labels Thailand's constitution as a 'volcanic constitution' in the sense that it struggles between two competing sets of constitutional ideas:

> while constitutional democracy focuses on the will of the people and give rise to opportunities for plurality to express in the regime through empowering its citizen, the idea of *Thainess* and traditional ideas limit the range of plurality allowed under the regime.[74]

Fifthly, pluralist constitutionalism can be formalised as an ideological ideal. Where this is the case, contests between unity and plurality become constitutionalised as a site of constant negotiation. The key example here is Indonesia which constitutionalises the nation's philosophy, *Pancasila*. The Indonesian Constitution's preamble defines this philosophy as the 'source of all legal sources'. Pancasila, however, has been interpreted differently over time as a response to different constitutional ideas and values in each period. This is also because Pancasila is not a single monist set of values. Further, the institutional arrangement is responsive to religious plurality and legal pluralism, which is observed in the creation of the Sharia Court and numerous Customary courts (or *Adat* courts). The latter have even influenced the decisions of the Constitutional Court.[75]

Sixthly, plurality can be overlapping and mutually reinforcing. One example is in the coincidence of the Malay race and Islamic faith in Brunei, Malaysia,

---

[72] See ch 7.
[73] Art 31 of the Constitution of the Kingdom of Cambodia, 21 September 1993 www.refworld.org/docid/3ae6b5428.html accessed 18 September 2018.
[74] See ch 9.
[75] See ch 5.

and Singapore. Another form of mutually reinforcing plurality within Southeast Asia is between ethnicity and territory, and this specifically implicates territorial division as a way to accommodate differences. This is because where ethnicity and territory coincide, there tends to be scope for identifiable political mobilisation for regional autonomy. Such regional claims are present in Myanmar where ethnic plurality coincides with regional distribution. While the state has historically insisted on a unitary state and tried to accommodate ethnic pluralities, its attempts to do so by classifying certain groups as 'citizens' has not been entirely successful. As Nyi Nyi Kyaw explains, ethnic and territorial federalism are among demands that have been repeatedly asserted to ensure some power sharing among Myanmar's ethnic groups.[76]

Another example of regional autonomy as a means to accommodate plurality can be seen in the Philippines. As Bryan Dennis Tiojanco points out, the Philippines Constitution endorses the creation of autonomous regions in Muslim Mindanao and the Cordilleras.[77] This is done with the aim of accommodating the aspirations of groups who have been historically marginalised. Tiojanco also argues that the Philippine constitution promotes civic virtue and constitutional loyalty through a 'pluralist framework of integrated diversity'. The creation of autonomous regions can be seen as a strategic embrace of pluralism in an attempt to inoculate secessionist demands and keep these regions within the 'integrated' State of the Philippines.

Lastly, it cannot be gainsaid that all constitutions are ultimately pluralist and should be conceptualised and analysed as such. Plurality of all forms influence constitution-making and change in different ways and to different extents, but it is always present regardless. Tiojanco's chapter points to networks of kin as yet another source of plurality in the Philippines, and highlights the role of civil society in pluralising politics and unifying the country on various issues.[78] He contextualises this within the Philippine constitution's 'People Power Principle', which institutionalises the revolutionary spirit of people power by promoting the right of citizens to political participation.

Furthermore, even in countries that, on first blush, appear to be constitutionally monist *de jure*, constitutional practice in these countries may in fact be more pluralist than first expected. Brunei Darussalam is an excellent example of a country that strongly exhibits constitutional monism, albeit without a robust constitutionalism that limits absolute power. While it has a written constitution, Brunei is also an absolute monarchy. There is no separation of powers as the Sultan of Brunei wields executive, legislative, as well as religious powers without any alternative locus.[79] As Kerstin Steiner and Dominik Mueller observe in their chapter, the Sultan forms a 'Personaleinheit' – an amalgamation of roles and powers in one person.[80] The Sultan's authority is formally encompassed within the state

[76] See ch 6.
[77] See ch 10.
[78] ibid.
[79] Constitution of Brunei Darussalam 1959 (2011 Rev Ed).
[80] See ch 4.

ideology of 'Melayu Islam Beraja' (Malay Islamic Monarchy). The centrality of the Sultan and his monopoly on power indicates a highly singular constitutional order. Certain pluralist values however remain present, albeit suppressed by virtue of the state's strong control. For instance, value pluralism can be found in the state ideology of Melayu Islam Beraja. While it purports to draw three ideas of legitimacy together and locate them within the single person of the Sultan, these are in fact three distinctive and potentially competing claims of authority. For instance, the idea of Beraja or monarchy rests upon hereditary authority, but one that is premised upon familial heritage and not religious heritage. The relationship between Malay and Islam are also distinctive and potentially contrasting. Even in Brunei, being Malay is an ethnic association that does not necessarily coincide with Islam-ness. Islam itself can also transcend Malay-ness. Nonetheless, as long as the Sultan wields absolute power within Brunei, pluralism remains generally suppressed.

VI. Conclusion

While this study focuses mainly on the national context of Southeast-Asian countries, it may have implications for broader global and comparative constitutional discourse. We focus here on three potential themes, namely: constitutional pluralism, pluralist constitutionalism, and pluralist global constitutionalism.

To begin with, pluralist constitutions can potentially result in constitutional pluralism within a single state. The constitution as such would not provide an exhaustive framework for its legal order, and institutional authorities may also attach different values to claims of constitutional meaning. Several scholars in this book have discussed constitutional pluralism, but this remains an important question for future research and empirical verification.

The second theme is the relationship between the pluralist constitution and pluralist constitutionalism. A pluralist constitution is not necessarily implemented in the way that makes the regime accountable to general values. It can even be implemented under authoritarianism. However, authoritarian regimes may have to adopt some constitutionalist practices in response to plurality. A pluralist constitution may thus blur the distinction between authoritarianism and constitutionalism, and its implementation may result in pluralist constitutionalism: a type of constitutionalism in which the use of political power is constrained by and accountable to domestic pluralities.

Finally, a more nuanced approach to constitutionalism around the world requires attention to plurality in a global context. Pluralist global constitutionalism has two important dimensions. First, global constitutional ideas and institutions may be localised as the consequence of their interactions with local pluralist values. Second, pluralist global constitutionalism would acknowledge and explore the diversity of constitutional experiences in different corners of the globe. In response to domestic plurality, people around the world may have a large variety of constitutional experiences and innovations.

These themes represent just some rich sites for future enquiry, and it is the aim of this collection to spark off further conversation about the impact of pluralities on constitution-making, constitutional change, and constitutional re-making.

Bibliography

—— Association of Southeast Asian Nations http://asean.org/ accessed 18 September 2018.
Albert R, Contiades X and Fotiadou A, *The Foundations and Traditions of Constitutional Amendment* (Oxford: Hart 2017).
Bâli A U and Lerner H, *Constitution Writing, Religion and Democracy* (CUP 2017).
Barzilai G, 'Beyond Relativism: Where is Political Power in Legal Pluralism?' (2008) 9 Theoretical Inquiries in Law 395, 396.
Bell G (ed), Pluralism, Transnationalism and Culture in Asian Law: A Book in Honour of M.B. Hooker (Singapore: ISEAS Yusof Ishak Institute 2017).
Bui N S (ed), 'Vietnamese Constitutional Debate in Comparative Perspective' (2017) 11(2) Asian Journal of Comparative Law 189.
Bünte M and Dressel B, *Politics and Constitutions in Southeast Asia* (Abingdon, Oxon; New York: Routledge 2017).
Chang WC, Thio LA, Tan YL K and Yeh JR, *Constitutionalism in Asia: Cases and Materials* (Oxford: Hart 2015).
Chen H Y A, 'Western Constitutionalism in Southeast Asia: Historical and Comparative Observations' in Ehlers D, Glaser H and Prokati K (eds), Constitutionalism and Good Governance: Eastern and Western Perspectives (Nomos Publishers 2014) 6.
Choudhry S (ed), Constitutional Design for Divided Societies: Integration or Accommodation? (OUP 2008).
—— and Ginsburg T, *Constitution Making* (Glouchestershire, Cheltenham; Massachusetts, Northampton: Edward Elgar Publishing 2016).
Dahl R A, Dilemmas of Pluralist Democracy: Autonomy vs Control (1st ed, YUP 1983) 5.
Dixon R & Posner E, 'The Limits of Constitutional Convergence' (2011) 11 Chicago Journal of International Law 399.
—— and Ginsburg T, *Comparative Constitutional Law in Asia* (Edward Elgar 2015).
Funabashi Y, 'The Asianization of Asia' (1993) 72(5) Foreign Affairs 75.
Ginsburg T (ed), *Constitutional Design* (CUP 2012).
Harding A, *The Constitution of Malaysia: A Contextual Analysis* (Oxford: Hart 2012).
—— *Constitutionalism and Legal Change in Myanmar* (Oxford: Hart 2017).

—— and Leyland P, *The Constitutional System of Thailand: A Contextual Analysis* (Oxford: Hart 2011).

—— & Bui N S, 'Recent Work in Asian Constitutional Studies: A Review Essay' 11 (1) Asian Journal of Comparative Law (2016) 163–183.

Hirschl R, *Comparative Matters: The Renaissance of Comparative Constitutional Law* (OUP 2014).

Hirschman C, 'Ethnic Diversity and Change in Southeast Asia', in Goldscheider C (ed), *Population, Ethnicity, and Nation Building* (Boulder: Westview Press 1995) 22.

Hill C and Menzel J (eds), *Constitutionalism in Southeast Asia* (Singapore: Konrad-Adenauer-Stiftung 2008).

Hooker M B, *Legal Pluralism: An Introduction to Colonial and Neo-colonial Laws* (Oxford: Clarendon Press 1975).

—— *Laws of South-east Asia, Volume I, The Pre-Modern Texts* (Singapore: Butterworth 1986).

—— *Laws of South-east Asia, Volume II, European Laws in South-East Asia* (Singapore: Butterworth 1988).

Horowitz D L, *A Democratic South Africa? Constitutional Engineering in a Divided Society* (Berkeley: University of California Press 1991).

—— 'Constitutional Design: An Oxymoron?' in Macedo S and Shapiro I (eds), *Designing Democratic Institutions* (Nomos XLII 2000) 253–284.

—— 'Constitutional Design: An Oxymoron?' (2000) 3 Democratic Culture 117–147.

—— 'Constitutional Design: Proposals Versus Processes' in Andrew Reynolds (ed), *The Architecture of Democracy: Constitutional Design, Conflict Management, and Democracy* (Oxford: Oxford University Press, 2002) 1, 15–36.

—— 'Conciliatory Institutions and Constitutional Process in Post-Conflict States' (2008) 49 *William and Mary Law Review* 1213–1248.

—— 'Encouraging Electoral Accommodation in Divided Societies' in Lal B & Larmour P (eds), *Electoral Systems in Divided Societies: The Fiji Constitution* (ANU Press, 2012).

—— 'How to study Constitution-Making: Hirschl, Elster and the Seventh Inning Problem' (2016) 96 Boston University Law Review 1347.

Husa J, 'Global Constitutionalism – Some Critical Remarks' (2017) 47 Hong Kong Law Journal 13.

Hussainmiya, *The Brunei Constitution of 1959: An Inside History* (Bandar Seri Bagawan: Brunei Press 2000).

Iskandar P, 'Indigenizing Constitutionalism: A Critical Reading of 'Asian Constitutionalism' (2017) Oxford Unversity Comparative Law Forum 2 https://ouclf.iuscomp.org/indigenizing-constitutionalism-a-critical-reading-of-asian-constitutionalism/ accessed 18 September 2018.

Issacharoff S, *Fragile Democracies: Contested Power in the Era of Constitutional Courts* (OUP 2014).

Jackson V, 'Comparative Constitutional Law: Methodologies' in Rosenfeld M and Sajó A (eds), The Oxford Handbook of Comparative Constitutional Law (OUP 2012) 54.

Kratoska H P (ed), *South East Asia: Colonial History* (New York: Routledge 2001).

Law D, 'Alternatives to Liberal Constitutional Democracy' (2017) 77 Maryland Law Review 223.

Leather G, 'Laos: A Constitution in Search of Constitutionalism,' in Hill C and Menzel J (eds), Constitutionalism in Southeast Asia, Volume 2 (Singapore: Konrad-Adenauer-Stiftung 2008) 125.

Lerner H, *Making Constitutions in Deeply Divided Societies* (CUP 2011).

Lijphart A, *Democracy in Plural Societies: A Comparative Exploration* (YUP 1977).

Lindsey T, *The Constitution of Indonesia: A Contextual Analysis* (Oxford: Hart 2011).

Lluch J, *Constitutionalism and The Politics of Accommodation In Multinational Democracies* (Houndmills, Basingstoke, Hampshire; New York: Palgrave Macmillan 2014).

McGarry J, O'Leary B and Simeon R, 'Integration or accommodation? The enduring debate in conflict regulation,' in Choudhry S (ed) Constitutional Design for Divided Societies: Integration or Accommodation? (OUP 2008) 42.

Mendes C H, *Constitutional Courts And Deliberative Democracy* (OUP 2014).

Menski W, *Comparative Law in a Global Context: The Legal Systems of Asia and Africa* (CUP 2006) 34.

Mill J S, *On Liberty* (1st ed, John W. Parker and Son, London 1859).

Neher, C D, *Southeast Asia: Crossroads of The World* (DeKalb: Northern Illinois University Press 2010).

Neo L J, 'What's in a name? Malaysia's "Allah" controversy and the judicial intertwining of Islam with ethnic identity' (2014) 12(3) International Journal of Constitutional Law 751–768.

—— 'Realizing the Right to Freedom of Thought, Conscience, and Religion: The Limited Normative Force of the ASEAN Human Rights Declaration' (2017) 17(4) Human Rights Law Review 729.

—— and Bui N S, State Constitutional Pluralism (forthcoming).

Peng H, Phallack K and Menzel J (eds), *Cambodian Constitutional Law* (Phnom Penh: Konrad-Adenauer-Stiftung 2017).

Pew Research Center, 'Global Religious Diversity: Half of the Most Religiously Diverse Countries Are in Asia-Pacific Region', (*Pew Forum*, 4 April 2014) www.pewforum.org/2014/04/04/global-religious-diversity/ accessed 18 September 2018.

Possamai A, Richardson J T and Turner B S (eds), Legal Pluralism and Shari'a Law (London and New York: Routledge 2016).

Ramraj V V, 'Constitutional Tipping Points: Sustainable Constitutionalism in Theory and Practice' (2010) 1(2) Transnational Legal Theory 191.

Reilly B, 'Institutional Designs for Diverse Democracies: Consociationalism, centripetalism and Communalism compared' (2012) 11 European Political Science 259.

—— 'Centripetalism: Cooperation, Accommodation, and Integration', in Volff S & Yakinthou C (eds), *Conflict Management in Divided Societies: Theories and Practice* (New York, Routledge 2012).

Rodriguez R B, *Constitutionalism in the Philippines* (Manila: Rex Book Store, 1997).

Rosenfeld M, *Constitutionalism, Identity, Difference, And Legitimacy: Theoretical Perspectives* (Durham: Duke University Press 1994).

—— *Just Interpretations: Law between Ethics and Politics* (University California Press 1998) 200–201.

—— 'Rethinking Constitutional Ordering in an Era of Legal and Ideological Pluralism' (2008) 6(3–4) International Journal of Constitutional Law 415, 417.

Schonthal B, 'Formations of Buddhist constitutionalism in South and Southeast Asia' (2017) 15(3) International Journal of Constitutional Law 705–733.

Sidel M, *The Constitution of Vietnam: A Contextual Analysis* (Oxford: Hart 2009).

Tan P L (ed), *Asian Legal Systems: Law, Society, and Pluralism in East Asia* (Sydney: Butterworths 1997).

Tan Y L K, 'The Making and Remaking of Constitutions in Southeast Asia: An Overview' (2002) 6 Singapore Journal of International & Comparative Law 1, 3.

—— The Constitution of Singapore: A Contextual Analysis (Oxford: Hart, 2014).

—— and Bui N S (eds), *Constitutional Foundings in Southeast Asia* (Hart Publishing forthcoming).

Twining W, *Globalisation and Legal Theory* (London, Butterworths 2000) 7.

—— 'Normative and Legal Pluralism: A Global Perspective' (2010) 20 Duke Journal of Comparative & Internationall Law 473.

Williams S H (ed), *Social Difference and Constitutionalism in Pan-Asia* (CUP 2014).

2
Constitutionalising Multiple Pluralities in Malaysia

DIAN A. H. SHAH

I. Introduction

The Malaysian social fabric is incredibly diverse. The latest official data estimates a population of 28.4 million, of which 63.6% are Bumiputra, 23.4% are Chinese, and 7% are Indians. The term Bumiputra means 'the sons of the soil' and typically this encompasses those from the Malay ethnic group (about 60%), the *Orang Asal* (original inhabitants), and the native tribes from Sabah and Sarawak. Ethnic cleavages, though most prominent, are only one of the many divisions that define Malaysian society. Religion is also a highly salient social marker – Islam is the dominant religion (about 61% of the population) – and there are overlapping cleavages across territorial, linguistic, and cultural lines.

This diversity has shaped and is reflected in the country's legal institutions and structures. In the lead-up to independence in 1957, the constitution-making process became mired – as we shall see in the next section – by competing demands from different sections of society on a variety of issues, especially those implicating religion (and religious laws) and ethnic interests. There were also important political interests at stake, and these played out – among others – in respect of the position of the state-level *sultans* in relation to their prerogatives and powers in matters on Islam and Malay customs. In the end, the Constitution that emerged is an amalgam of multiple legal orders and influences. Drafted by a group of Commonwealth jurists led by Lord Reid (a Judge of the Court of Appeal of England), the Constitution embodies Westminster-style constitutional traditions, but it also incorporates the concept of constitutional supremacy and a bill of rights (inspired by the Indian Constitution) and retains some traditional elements that were practised even before the colonial powers set foot in (what was then) Malaya. These elements include: (1) the Malay Sultanate; (2) Islam as the state religion; (3) the Malay language as the *lingua franca*; and (4) special privileges for the Malays.[1] Aside from

---

[1] See Tun Haji Mohd Salleh bin Abas, 'Traditional Elements of the Malaysian Constitution' in F A Trindade & H P Lee (eds), *The Constitution of Malaysia: Further Perspectives and Developments: Essays in Honour of Tun Mohamed Suffian* (OUP 1986) 1–2.

that, the Constitution also recognises the operation of native law and custom in Sabah and Sarawak, as well as customary law on land ownership in the states of Negeri Sembilan and Melaka.[2]

Against this background, this chapter examines how the plurality of constitutional sources, values, and norms in Malaysia is expressed in the Constitution and how they interact with each other. By focusing on selected issues and controversies that have emerged in the past decade, it attempts to demonstrate – empirically – that while constitutional institutions and structures were designed to accommodate and reflect the various sources of plurality in the country, and while the Constitution itself reflects a variety of constitutional ideas and values, there has also been significant friction and competing claims of authority between different constitutional institutions and sources.[3] The results of these struggles for prominence have not always been positive as far as the development of Malaysian constitutional law is concerned. For instance, as I will illustrate throughout the chapter, the space for religious freedom is increasingly constricted; in some cases implicating religion, there are repercussions on children and the family unit (such as uncertainties about custody arrangements for children who have already had to endure a broken home);[4] and the growing assertion of royal powers in politics and governance have triggered several constitutional crises in states within the Federation.[5]

II. Negotiating Pluralism: History, Constitution-Making Debates and Outcomes

Malaysia was a British colony for over eight decades before negotiations for independence began in the 1950s. The promulgation of a Constitution that was acceptable to the locals (through their representatives) was one of the preconditions for independence and a smooth transfer of power from the British colonial government. At the beginning of the constitution-making process, the British government had set specific terms of reference that would guide the constitution-making exercise. They included: (1) parliamentary democracy with a bicameral legislature; (2) a strong central government with a measure of autonomy for the states; (3) the provision of a machinery for central-state consultation on

---

[2] See art 90, Federal Constitution of Malaysia.
[3] See generally Miguel P Maduro, 'Three Claims of Constitutional Pluralism' in Matej Avbelj & Jan Komarek (eds), *Constitutional Pluralism in Europe and Beyond* (Hart Publishing 2012). For Maduro, constitutional pluralism embodies the 'legal reality of competing constitutional claims of final authority among different legal orders' within the same legal system. ibid 70–71.
[4] See eg, Maznah Mohamed, 'Making Majority, Undoing Family: Law, Religion and The Islamization of the State In Malaysia' (2010) 39(3) Economy and Society 360.
[5] See Andrew Harding, 'Nazrinian' Monarchy in Malaysia: The Resilience and Revival of a Traditional Institution' in Andrew Harding and Dian A H Shah (eds), *Law and Society in Malaysia: Pluralism, Ethnicity and Religion*, (Routledge 2018) 72–95.

certain financial matters specified in the Constitution; and (4) safeguarding the special position of the Malays and the legitimate interests of other communities.[6]

However, drafting a Constitution that is acceptable not just to the political elites (ie, the Alliance party, who represented different ethnic interests, namely, the Malays, the Chinese, and the Indians),[7] but also the Malay Rulers (the *sultans*) from the nine Malay states, proved to be a monumental task. The different actors involved in the constitution-making process were keen to ensure that their interests as well of those of the constituencies they represented were secured by the Constitution. There were thus a range of controversies that occupied the constitution-making debates. Chief among them were: citizenship arrangements for the non-Malays; national language; the special position of the Malays; the position of Islam – the religion of the majority – in the constitutional order; and fundamental liberties. The first three issues were, perhaps, the most contentious and vexing questions in the Malayan political scene since the late 1940s.[8] Intra-party bargains and negotiations, therefore, became a central feature of the constitution-making process and the outcomes of the negotiations were expressed in the Alliance memorandum to the Reid Commission.

For the purposes of this chapter, I shall focus on three issues that have had a significant influence shaping the plurality of legal orders and sources in Malaysia. The first is the position of Islam – a religion which has had a long presence in Malaya, dating back to the fourteenth-century establishment of the Melaka sultanate. The Malay State Constitutions of the nineteenth and early twentieth centuries stipulated that the Ruler of the State (the *sultan*) must be a Muslim and serve as the head of Islam in his state. During the British colonial period, some aspects of the traditional political and governance arrangements were retained: the British Residential System provided a British resident whose advice 'must be asked and acted upon' by the sultan on all questions, but the sultan retained control over matters pertaining to Islam and Malay customs.[9] The sultanate or monarchy and elements of Islamic governance in the Malay states are thus important as far as the traditional identity of the polity is concerned. I will return to the Malay sultanate question below, but here I want to focus on the constitutional arrangement that establishes Islam as the religion of the Federation and guarantees the right of other religions to be practised in 'peace and harmony'.[10] This provision is important because over time, it has opened the door for elements of Islamic law to be instituted and enforced in ever expansive ways in the country.

---

[6] See Report of the Federation of Malaya Constitutional Commission (21 February 1957), DO35/6282 (Reid Commission Report).
[7] The Alliance comprised three parties – UMNO, MCA, and MIC – representing the Malays, the Chinese, and the Indians, respectively.
[8] Joseph M Fernando, *The Making of the Malayan Constitution* (MBRAS 2002) 73.
[9] Kevin Y L Tan, 'The Creation of Greater Malaysia: Law, Politics, Ethnicity, and Religion' in Andrew Harding and Dian A H Shah (eds), *Law and Society in Malaysia: Pluralism, Ethnicity and Religion* (Routledge 2018) 3. See also Andrew Harding, *Law, Government and the Constitution in Malaysia* (Kluwer Law International 1996) 13.
[10] Federal Constitution of Malaysia, art 3.

The debates that surrounded the adoption of this provision were controversial, not least because the constitutional drafters and elected local representatives (led by The Alliance) disagreed about whether Islam should be constitutionalised as the state religion. The Alliance had pushed for a special constitutional position for Islam, owing, in part, to demands from the Malay grassroots. Interestingly, the Malay sultans initially rejected the proposal as they were concerned that it would allow the federal government to control matters on Islam and encroach on their traditional positions as the Heads of Islam in their respective states.[11] The Reid Commission was also apprehensive about any special provision for Islam; most of the Commission members thought that Malaya should be a secular state like India.[12] For Sir Ivor Jennings, in particular, Islam did not need state protection.[13] However, in anticipation of strong objections from UMNO and the Malay community, the Report of the Federation of Malaya Constitutional Commission in February 1957 ('the Reid Report') nonetheless stressed that *if* any such provision were included, the civil rights of non-Muslims would be unaffected.[14] A member of the Commission (Justice Abdul Hamid of Pakistan) who was initially supportive of the omission of a clause on Islam, also later supported the establishment of a state religion – an arrangement which he considered to be 'innocuous'. In the end, the Constitution reflected what the Alliance and Justice Abdul Hamid sought: an explicit declaration of Islam as the state religion, along with the assurance that it will not affect the religious freedom of non-Muslims. It was also emphasised that the provision does not create a theocratic state, that Malaya would retain its secular character, and that the arrangement was to model the British constitutional set-up where despite the establishment of the Anglican Church, religious freedom is nevertheless guaranteed. In addition, article 3(4) provides that the provision on Islam 'shall not derogate from other provisions in the Constitution'. In the context of fundamental rights, this means that the position of Islam as the religion of the Federation cannot be the basis for abolishing or restricting rights enshrined in the Constitution. The arrangement on Islam, as I have explained earlier, is intimately linked to the traditional role and constitutional function of the sultans as the heads of Islam in their states. But this also implicates the federal arrangement in an independent Malaya and, subsequently, in the creation of the Federation of Malaysia in 1963. Federalism thus paved the way for retaining the sultan's prerogatives in matters relating to

---

[11] Sir William Ivor Jennings, 'Hearing of Counsel on Behalf of Their Highnesses the Rulers' (14–15 September 1956) in *Papers of Sir Ivor Jennings* B/X/2/iv 20.

[12] Note on Pakistan and the Reid Commission Report, Constitutional Talks in London, May 1957 on the Future of Malaya (10 May 1957) DO35/6278.

[13] Sir William Ivor Jennings, 'Comments on the Reid Report' in *Papers of Sir Ivor Jennings* B/X/2/iv 20 ('[I] do not think that the religion of a minority or even of a majority, ought to be formally established … I have great many Muslim friends including Justice Abdul Hamid himself and I do not think that Islam needs the power of the state to support it.').

[14] See Reid Commission Report (n 6) para 169. The Commission members anticipated objections from the Malay community with respect to their position on state religion, but justified this 'in deference to views of the Malay Rulers.'

Islam in his state, and while the traditional monarchies and the existing state constitutions are retained in the nine Malay states,[15] the imposition of the constitutional monarchy and Westminster model of government on the states meant that state constitutions had to conform to the Federal Constitution and Westminster principles.[16] As Harding also notes, federalism is not unknown to the Malaysian constitutional thought and practice – in fact, the creation of the Federated Malay States (FMS) in 1895 became a forerunner to the existing federal system.[17] By accepting – through a treaty – the creation of the FMS, the sultans accepted the centralisation of executive power (with a British Resident-General based in Kuala Lumpur).[18] Legislative powers of the Member States were also affected, as state budgets and draft legislation needed to be approved by the Resident-General and, later – through a Treaty in 1909 – by a Federal Council, before they could be passed by State Councils.[19] Although there was greater devolution of legislative powers to the states from 1927 onwards, one aspect that has remained consistent is the jurisdiction of the states over customary and religious matters.

The third important issue concerns fundamental liberties and human rights provisions in the Constitution, and this inevitably relates to constitutional arrangements on special privileges for the Malays and the natives of Sabah and Sarawak, as well as the question of indigenous rights (particularly through the constitutional recognition of native law and custom in Sabah and Sarawak). The incorporation of a bill of rights into the 1957 Constitution was primarily an initiative of the Reid Commission members who drew heavily on the Indian Constitution;[20] it was thought that fundamental rights guarantees were essential features of a democratic state. However, the local leaders involved in the constitution-making process – especially those from UMNO and MCA – resisted. Tunku Abdul Rahman (the leader of the Alliance who later became the country's first Prime Minister) was concerned that extensive fundamental rights guarantees could disrupt the effectiveness of government decision-making.

There were also concerns about how a bill of rights would affect the positions and interests of the different communities in the polity. The Malays, for example, were anxious to protect their special privileges and interests, which would contradict the right to equality sought by the non-Malays. At that time, the Malays enjoyed many special rights in the states, such as preferential promotion in the civil service, free education, and an inalienable right to the most fertile land in the state.[21] To be sure, the demands for these special interests to be explicitly safeguarded in

---

[15] There were only nine Malay states that had traditional monarchies – Selangor, Pahang, Perak, Negeri Sembilan, Johor, Kedah, Kelantan, Terengganu, and Perlis. The first four states formed the Federated Malay States, and the remaining five were known as the Unfederated Malay States.
[16] Andrew Harding, *The Constitution of Malaysia: A Contextual Analysis* (Hart Publishing 2012) 54.
[17] ibid 20.
[18] ibid.
[19] ibid 21–22.
[20] Charles O H Parkinson, *Bills of Rights and Decolonization: The Emergence of Domestic Human Rights Instruments in Britain's Overseas Territories* (OUP 2007) 73.
[21] ibid 74.

the Constitution were not new: they were part of the Reid Commission's terms of reference; the original treaties between the British colonial government and the Malays states reaffirmed the special position; and the Federation Agreement of 1948 provided a clause vesting the High Commissioner with responsibility of safeguarding the special position of the Malays and legitimate interests of other communities.[22] The non-Malays, however, thought that the idea of granting special (and seemingly permanent) privileges or advantage to a certain community was irreconcilable with the promise of equal rights irrespective of race and creed. Yet, the MCA – who represented the Chinese communities – did not think that a bill of rights would be imperative. Instead, it was argued that the best means to protect the rights and interests of the Chinese community would be through citizenship and maintaining a political alliance with the UMNO.[23]

In the end, a bill of rights was eventually agreed upon among the Alliance leaders, in part due to pressures from the Indian community represented by the MIC.[24] However, compared to the guarantees expressed in the Universal Declaration of Human Rights (UDHR), the fundamental liberties chapter in the 1957 Constitution is thin and contains important limitation clauses that accord parliament with significant powers to restrict fundamental rights. Despite concerns about contradictions between a bill of rights and a provision protecting the special position of the Malays, both elements were incorporated into the Constitution, as it was thought that removing the special privileges and preferences completely would result in a serious and unfair disadvantage to the Malays. Nonetheless, it was envisioned that any need for preferential treatment and quotas would gradually cease so that 'there should be no discrimination between races and communities'.[25] When Sabah and Sarawak joined the Federation of Malaysia in July 1963, the provision on preferential treatment was amended to include the natives of Sabah and Sarawak, so that the natives would also enjoy reservations of position in public service.[26]

III. Constitutional Rights

Compared to the fundamental rights guarantees in the Indonesian Constitution, the International Covenant on Civil and Political Rights (ICCPR), and the UDHR,

---

[22] The issue of quota in public service employment is also not new, and it was inherited feature from the colonial government. Until 1953, admission to the Malayan Civil Service was only open to British subjects of European descent and to Malays, but later on one-fifth of the entrants were open to other communities.

[23] Parkinson (n 20) 90. Parkinson argues that the MCA was 'uninterested in a bill of rights' and was 'willing to endorse proposals that were not advantageous to the Chinese community in order to keep its close relationship with the United Malays National Organisation.'

[24] According to Tunku Abdul Rahman, for UMNO and the MCA, it is immaterial whether the bill of rights is included or not. Meeting of the Alliance Party with the Reid Commission (27 September 1956) CO889/6.

[25] Jennings (n 11) para 165.

[26] Malaysia Agreement 1963, s 62.

the protections afforded by the Malaysian Constitution are thin. There are only nine provisions[27] covering – among others – the right to liberty, equality, freedom of religion, and the freedoms of speech, assembly, and association. However, these provisions are designed in ways that confer the legislature with broad powers to restrict the exercise of rights. This is particularly obvious with article 10, which deals with the freedom of speech, assembly, and association. Clause 2 of the provision provides that Parliament may impose restrictions as it 'deems necessary and expedient' in the interests of security, morality, and/or public order. In addition, the efficacy of constitutional rights protection is further diluted by provisions that allow the legislature to create laws: (1) violating fundamental rights guarantees in emergency situations (article 150); and (2) contradicting the right to liberty, freedom of movement, freedom of speech, assembly, and association, and property rights in order to combat subversion and threats to public order under normal circumstances (article 149).

There are at least two other features that are peculiar to the Malaysian Constitution and these are linked – or perhaps shaped by – the two most prominent sources of plurality in Malaysia: religion and ethnicity. The first relates to the parameters of the freedom of religion. Article 11 guarantees the right to profess, practise, and propagate one's religion, but the right to propagate is qualified by clause (4), which allows state legislatures to restrict the propagation of any religious doctrine or belief among Muslims. Following this provision, at least nine state legislatures in Malaysia have passed laws that criminalise acts to persuade, incite, or influence a Muslim to be a follower of another religion, or to distribute certain religious publications to Muslims. This restriction also covers unauthorised proselytising activities within the Muslim community in order to control the spread of doctrines deemed heretical or those that fall outside the mainstream Sunni Islam doctrine. Article 11 also carefully omits the explicit right to *choose* one's own religion. Although scholars suggest that article 11 can be construed broadly to include one's freedom to change his or her religious belief or to renounce a religion, whether this is possible in practice, especially for Muslims, is a different question altogether.

The second concerns the right to equality. Even though article 8 guarantees all persons the right to equality and equal protection under the law, there are important exemptions in matters implicating the special privileges accorded to certain sections of the society and personal law.[28] One consequence is that for persons professing the religion of Islam, Islamic laws govern their personal and family matters, as opposed to the civil law that governs such matters for non-Muslims. This is mandatory, in the sense that one could not choose to be governed by civil instead of Islamic law. Given this 'clawback' clause, it is arguable that the guarantees of equality under article 8 also may not necessarily invalidate policies enacted pursuant to article 153, which permits quotas in public service employment and in the award of business licences and scholarships for the Malays and natives of

---

[27] See arts 5 to 13 of the Federal Constitution of Malaysia.
[28] See ibid art 8(5).

Sabah and Sarawak. Indeed, this dispensation in article 153 has formed the legal basis for the New Economic Policy, where the *Bumiputras* enjoy preferential access to and quotas in the grant of – among others – business licences, permits, government contracts, scholarships, and university admissions.[29]

However, what has always been overlooked is that the creation of these 'special privileges' in article 153, however, was intended by the constitutional framers to be a temporary and transitional measure, in light of the then-prevailing social and economic conditions of the Malays.[30] In addition, the framers, having acknowledged the difficult task of reconciling articles 153 and 8, and the potential problems that could ensue in the ethnically plural society, constitutionalised safeguards in article 153. For instance, the *Yang di-Pertuan Agong* (YDPA) has a discretionary function under this provision, in that he may reserve such quotas as he deems 'reasonable'. As he discharges this discretion, he is also charged with the task of securing the 'legitimate interests of other communities'. Moreover, in safeguarding the special position under article 153, no person can be deprived of his/her continued enjoyment of the same public office, rights, grants, special facility or privileges.[31]

IV. Constitutional Ideas, Values, and Sources

The preceding sections have given us some sense of the constitutional ideas and values underpinning the Federal Constitution of Malaysia. The Constitution, unlike the Indonesian Constitution, does not contain a preamble setting out the fundamental values and philosophy underpinning constitutional law and governance in the country, such as the *Pancasila*. In fact, a set of national values (the *Rukun Negara*) – which is similar to the Pancasila, was only introduced 13 years after independence, as a response of sorts to the deadly May 13 racial riots in 1969. The Rukun Negara contains five principles: (1) the belief in God; (2) loyalty to the King and country; (3) the supremacy of the Constitution; (4) rule of law; and (5) courtesy and morality. Preceding these five principles in the Rukun Negara document is a set of aims, which include 'preserving a democratic way of life', 'guaranteeing a liberal approach' towards the country's diverse cultural traditions, and 'creating a just society'.

---

[29] Note that the New Economic Policy had a twenty-year time span, within which its objectives were to be achieved. See generally, Equal Rights Trust in partnership with Tenaganita, 'Washing the Tigers' (London, November 2012) www.equalrightstrust.org/ertdocumentbank/Malaysia%20CR%201.pdf accessed 18 September 2018.

[30] See Joseph M Fernando, 'Special Rights in the Malaysian Constitution and the Framers' Dilemma, 1956–57' (2015) 45 (3) The Journal of Imperial and Commonwealth History 535.

[31] See also Shad Saleem Faruqi, 'Affirmative Action Policies and the Constitution' (2003) 21 Kajian Malaysia 31, 36–40; Jaclyn L Neo, 'Malay Nationalism, Islamic Supremacy and the Constitutional Bargain in the Multi-ethnic Composition of Malaysia' (2006) 13 International Journal on Minority and Group Rights 95, 109.

All these ideas were of course not new, even though they were only formalised in the form of the Rukun Negara in the 1970s. The British government's terms of reference during the constitution-making process, as we have seen, laid out key constitutional ideas that should govern Malaya as an independent nation, including a parliamentary democracy and a centre-heavy federal structure. The Alliance – whose leaders were largely schooled in the British parliamentary tradition (Tunku Abdul Rahman was a Cambridge-trained lawyer) – also expressed explicit preference for 'a continuation of the British constitutional tradition'.[32] This, along with the leaders' political pragmatism, probably influenced the Alliance's initial resistance against incorporating a bill of rights into the Constitution. Despite this, the Alliance nevertheless emphasised that the emerging independent state should uphold the principle of separation of powers and an independent judiciary. With several lawyers within the ranks of the Alliance leadership, it was understood that the judiciary is an indispensable institution to check against legislative and executive excesses. Thus, the Alliance's memorandum to the Reid Commission not only declared that the judiciary should be 'independent of both the executive and the legislature', but also that a Supreme Court 'should be vested with powers to decide whether or not the action of both the Federal executives and the legislature are in accordance with the constitution.'[33]

In any case, the Malaysian Constitution, though rooted in Westminster constitutional values (and, to some extent, embodies Indian constitutional ideas), contains arrangements that depart from those values, taking into account not just the prevailing conditions at the time, but also local contexts and traditions as well as the Alliance's 'political and constitutional aspirations'.[34] For one, the principle of constitutional supremacy (as opposed to the British principle of parliamentary sovereignty) is firmly entrenched in article 4 of the Constitution. The Reid Commission report alluded to this, stating, for example, that the courts are duty-bound to enforce the fundamental rights guaranteed in the Constitution and to annul any legislative or administrative attempt to subvert these rights. In this respect, the Constitution incorporated constitutional ideas of the 1950s from India, who was also a former British colony.

The Constitution also establishes a federal system of government, unlike the UK's unitary state. However, as I mentioned previously, federalism is not a concept alien to Malaya. In 1895, the British government established the Federated Malay States – a federation of the protected states of Negeri Sembilan, Selangor, Perak, and Pahang – to centralise executive power in the hands of a Resident-General. The Malay Rulers (sultans) in these states thus relinquished substantial political power (although this did not mean that the sultans surrendered their sovereignty) and a division of federal-state powers was instituted, with the balance of power heavily tilted on the side of the federal authorities. These arrangements

---

[32] Fernando, *The Making of the Malayan Constitution* (n 8) 69.
[33] ibid 69–70.
[34] ibid 6.

significantly shaped not just the 1948 Federation of Malaya Agreement (which created a federation of all nine Malay states and two British Straits Settlements), but also the federalism that is practised today.[35]

Another key constitutional idea that was adopted by the constitution-makers in Malaya is the constitutional monarchy, but there are also important differences with the kind of constitutional monarchy that is practised in Britain. The Malay sultanate, as I mentioned earlier, has been a central feature of Malay society and governance. The constitutional practice of sultans acting on the advice of the executive (ie, the resident, and today, the ministers) continues along the lines of the British tradition, and this is also applied to the YDPA. The YDPA is the Supreme Head of the Federation (a position equivalent to a King or Queen in the UK), and he is elected and rotated every five years amongst the sultans from the nine Malay states. This election and rotation system was inspired by traditional systems in the states of Perak and Negeri Sembilan, where a sultan is rotated amongst three royal houses and elected by hereditary chiefs, respectively. The Constitution also provides the YDPA with some discretionary powers. Thus, the role of the YDPA is not merely 'symbolic' or 'ceremonial'; article 40(2) of the Constitution, for example, allows the YDPA to act on his personal discretion in at least three matters: (1) the appointment of a Prime Minister; (2) consent to a request for the dissolution of Parliament; and (3) the call for a Conference of Rulers meeting solely on issues concerning the privileges, position, honours, and dignities of the Rulers. There are similar arrangements in the state constitutions.

Given the good working relationship that has often been enjoyed between the YDPA and the federal government, controversies have been far and few in between. The same cannot be said, however, for the minister-sultan power dynamics at state level. For instance, although constitutional conventions, which are a key source of constitutional law in Malaysia, dictate that the sultan is to endorse a Chief Minister candidate proffered by the party that controls the state legislative assembly, this has not always been adhered to by the sultans. Two incidents are instructive. In Terengganu, the sultan rejected the *Barisan Nasional*'s (BN) candidate for Chief Minister and appointed his preferred candidate from the same party instead.[36] Similarly, in Selangor, the sultan unilaterally decided to interview three candidates (from the majority party in the legislative assembly), instead of appointing a candidate based on advice.[37] That the Rulers have been able to sidestep established conventions indicates, as Harding persuasively notes, that constitutional conventions are neither easily transplanted nor always followed, even when these conventions are explicitly expressed in federal and/or state constitutions.[38]

The place and role of the Malay monarchies in the constitutional order, now modified to meet the demands of modern-day constitutionalism, is not the only

---

[35] Harding, *The Constitution of Malaysia* (n 16) 20–21.
[36] Harding, '"Nazrinian" Monarchy in Malaysia' (n 5) 86.
[37] ibid 89.
[38] ibid 74.

manifestation of ethnic 'Malay' elements and traditions in the Constitution. The establishment of Islam as the religion of the Federation and the constitutional role of the sultans as the Heads of Islam in the nine Malay states, as I have explained previously, are crucial aspects of Malay governance traditions that have remained intact even during the British colonial period. Islamic law, therefore, is and has always been an important source of constitutional law, especially for the Muslims. During the British colonial period, Islamic law operated alongside British common law (which covered the general law) and was enforced through the *kadi* courts. Islamic law covered – as it does today, under the Ninth Schedule, List II of the Constitution – only personal and religious matters. It is important to note, however, that there was no single 'Islamic law' that applied throughout the country or the states on a particular issue because matters concerning Islam was under the prerogatives of the different sultans in their respective states. The content of the law invariably depended on the sultan's inclinations and the influence of Malay customs.[39] In Negeri Sembilan, for example, family and inheritance laws are shaped by the matrilineal *adat perpatih*, as opposed to the patrilineal traditional Islamic law. Today, however, Islamic laws on most matters are fairly standardised across different states. This is attributable to the role of the Malaysian Islamic Development Department (JAKIM – a federal body under the Prime Minister's office), which has been spearheading efforts at standardising Islamic laws throughout the country.

The range of constitutional sources available, and the adoption and adaptation of different constitutional traditions and ideas into what is now the Federal Constitution of Malaysia, exemplify efforts at managing pluralism in the country. A democratic form of government was undoubtedly foremost in the Alliance's mind,[40] but accommodating conflicting (and sometimes irreconcilable) demands was by no means an easy task. Under such circumstances, the Malaysian constitution-making experience showed that inter-group compromise was a fundamental element. It was needed to foster national unity and to manage the more extreme demands from radical factions within both the UMNO and the MCA. On the question of religion and the sultanate, for instance, it was recognised that establishing a constitution that completely disregards the centuries-long role of the Malay monarchies in the polity and position of Islam as the state religion was out of the question, for this would have triggered a destabilising socio-political conflict. Similarly, drawing up a document that left out Malay special privileges would have been unacceptable under prevailing conditions.[41] In return, it was agreed that the principle of jus soli would apply for citizenship (for the non-Malays);

---

[39] Harding, *The Constitution of Malaysia* (n 16) 227.

[40] In an election manifesto in 1955, for instance, the Tunku emphasised that 'The Alliance believes that the democratic form of government based on parliamentary institutions is ... best suited to Malaya.' Fernando, *The Making of the Malayan Constitution* (n 8) 69.

[41] The non-Malay representatives in the Alliance (ie the MCA) was not completely averse to the idea of affirmative action for the Malays. Their concern was that the privileges would be extended perpetually. ibid 85–86.

that the establishment of Islam shall not affect the religious freedom of non-Muslims; and while Malay would become the sole national language and the use of English for official purposes retained for 10 years, everyone retains the 'right to use their own languages'.[42]

V. Constitutional Institutions and Structure

Considering the controversies and difficulties in ironing out an agreement on communal issues, the constitutional drafters had a relatively easier task in deciding the structure and function of the government. In keeping with the terms of reference from the British government, the Constitution establishes three main branches of government – the executive, the legislature, and the judiciary.

Executive power is not only vested in the Westminster-model executive (ie, the Prime Minister and his Cabinet), but also in the YDPA, who is the Head of State. However, as I have explained in the preceding section, the establishment of a 'constitutional monarchy' meant that while the Malay rulers secured their positions and privileges within the constitutional order, the Constitution defines the parameters of their powers and functions. The office of the YDPA is also a reflection of efforts to respond to Malaysia's ethnic plurality – the YDPA is a symbol for unity and is bestowed the responsibility to safeguard the special position of the Malays and the natives of Sabah and Sarawak, as well as the legitimate interests of other communities.

The YDPA and the Rulers in their respective states are to act based on the advice of the government of the day, but there is also a specific list of matters where they may act in their discretion.[43] In nine states, the state constitutions extend the Rulers' discretionary powers to the exercise of their functions as the Heads of Islam; the appointment of heirs, consort, Regent or Council of Regency; the appointment of persons to customary ranks, titles, honours, and dignities; and the regulation of royal courts and palaces.[44] However, it would be misleading to suggest that the discretion is always absolute. In appointing the Prime Minister and the Chief Ministers (in various states), both federal and state constitutions require the YDPA and the Rulers to appoint a member of the legislative assembly who, in their judgment, commands the confidence of the majority of the assembly. In practice, as I have shown, this has not always been adhered to, and often, party leaders have relented to avoid a deadlock.

In line with the principles of parliamentary democracy that Malaysia has adopted, the Prime Minister and his Cabinet are the most important executive

---

[42] This was inspired by the language provisions in the Indian Constitution.
[43] See discussion above.
[44] Y A M Raja Azlan Shah, 'The Role of Constitutional Rulers in Malaysia' in F A Trindade & H P Lee (eds), *The Constitution of Malaysia: Further Perspectives and Developments, Essays in Honour of Tun Mohamed Suffian* (OUP 1986) 79–80.

Constitutionalising Multiple Pluralities in Malaysia 37

institutions. The prime ministerial office is especially powerful, particularly since the administration of the fourth Prime Minister – Mahathir Mohamad. Unlike his predecessors, Mahathir was a medical doctor by training and he was not always prepared to adhere to constitutional limitations on executive power.[45] The powers of the Prime Minister became virtually unchecked; he stifled political dissent; and engineered a constitutional amendment to place judicial power under the purview of the Parliament, among others. Although his premiership saw the country making great strides in modernisation and economic development, it also set the foundations for the more serious systemic problems in governance that Malaysia is experiencing today. Another important point to note with regard to the influence of ethnic and religious identities vis-à-vis constitutional practice and politics is that until the recent elections in May 2018, all Prime Ministers since independence have always been Malay-Muslim politicians from the UMNO party, which is the strongest and most dominant party in the multi-ethnic BN coalition. To be sure, the prime ministerial office is not an ethnically-reserved seat – it remains possible (in theory) that a non-Malay (and non-Muslim) could hold office. However, under current political conditions and as long as the BN remains the most dominant coalition, the 'tradition' of having a Malay-Muslim prime minister will continue, due to UMNO's dominant position and stature within the coalition.

The legislature consists of two houses – the Dewan Rakyat (House of Representatives) and the Dewan Negara (Senate). Members of the Dewan Rakyat represent single-member constituencies and are elected through the first-past-the-post system. The Dewan Negara, on the other hand, consists of 26 members elected by the 13 state legislative assemblies (each state thus gets two representatives in the Senate); four members appointed by the YDPA to represent the Federal Territories of Kuala Lumpur, Putrajaya, and Labuan; and 40 other YDPA-appointed members. The appointments made by the YDPA are based on the Prime Minister's advice. All this has undoubtedly affected the workings of the Parliament. That over 60% of the Senate membership are appointed on advice means that the ruling coalition is able to dominate the Senate. Therefore, although the Senate's approval is required to pass legislation, this does not operate as an effective check on the House of Representatives or the government, for that matter. Given BN's political dominance since independence (it has always held at least two-thirds of the seats in the lower house, except at the 1969 and 2008 elections), the Parliament has always operated as a rubber-stamp for the government's agenda. As Harding correctly notes, parliamentary process in Malaysia is only a 'formality'.[46] There is, of course, the YDPA, whose consent to a bill is also required before it could become law. However, the YDPA's role is limited – a bill automatically becomes law if he does not assent to it within thirty days.

All this, coupled with the BN coalition's ability to manipulate parliamentary proceedings to their advantage – for example, by 'bulldozing' bills through

---

[45] See Harding, *The Constitution of Malaysia* (n 16) 58.
[46] ibid 87.

Parliament at the eleventh hour – has allowed controversial laws to pass parliamentary scrutiny. One of the latest examples is the National Security Council Act 2016, which was introduced and rushed through the lower house in the final days of the parliamentary sitting in 2015, and then approved overwhelmingly by BN members at the Senate. This piece of legislation is very controversial as it provides the executive with broad and unchecked powers to declare a state of emergency, make arrests, and use lethal force during an emergency. Those empowered to act under the Act will not be held accountable; they are completely exempt from legal liability and prosecution. Under the law, constitutional guarantees of fundamental liberties are rendered meaningless. Shortly after the bill was passed through the Senate, the Conference of Rulers suggested that some provisions of the bill should be refined.[47] The YDPA never formally endorsed the bill and in the end, the bill became law upon the expiration of the thirty-day period. Given the government's penchant for utilising security laws to silence political dissent and buttress its position, academics and civil society groups have raised serious concerns about the potential abuse of the law, especially as the power of judicial review is expressly ousted. The constitutionality of the law remains extremely suspect, not just for encroachments against constitutional guarantees of fundamental liberties, but also against other constitutional provisions implicating the YDPA's powers vis-à-vis the armed forces and the proclamation of an emergency.[48] At the time of writing, however, the constitutionality of law has yet to be officially challenged.

In the face of such draconian laws, the role of the judiciary as a check and balance mechanism becomes important. The country's founding fathers recognised the importance of an independent judiciary and for a long time before the 1990s, the Malaysian judiciary enjoyed considerable prestige as an independent and competent institution. This began to change during the Mahathir administration, as the Prime Minister developed an antagonistic relationship with the judiciary. He was particularly annoyed by a string of court decisions at various levels challenging executive authority, especially on fundamental rights issues.[49] For Mahathir, such exercises of judicial power are undemocratic as judges had gone overboard by circumscribing parliamentary decisions and the policy-making

---

[47] 'Putrajaya's new security law now gazetted without royal assent', *The Malaymailonline* (Kuala Lumpur, 9 June 2016) www.themalaymailonline.com/malaysia/article/putrajayas-new-security-law-now-in-force-without-royal-assent accessed 18 September 2018.

[48] Malik Imtiaz Sarwar and Surendra Ananth, 'The National Security Council Bill: A Colorable Exercise of Power' (2016) 2 MLJ cxix.

[49] These decisions include a Supreme Court decision that upheld the quashing of an order to revoke the employment pass of a foreign journalist because he was deemed a threat to national security (*J.P. Berthelsen v. Director General of Immigration* [1987] 1 MLJ 134) and a High Court decision rejecting the Home Minister's reasons for refusing to grant a publication licence to *Aliran*, an NGO (*Persatuan Aliran v Minister for Home Affairs* [1988] 1 MLJ 440). For an overview of other decisions, see Chandra Kanagasabai, 'Malaysia: Limited and Intermittent Judicialization of Politics' in Bjorn Dressel (ed), *The Judicialization of Politics in Asia* (Routledge 2013) 206–7. See also, Harding, *The Constitution of Malaysia* (n 16) 142–44.

powers of the executive.[50] All this was exacerbated when a case on political infighting within UMNO (Mahathir's party) came before the courts. It involved a suit challenging the legality of UMNO's internal elections brought by a narrowly defeated faction within the party against the incumbents led by Mahathir. The High Court's ruling favoured Mahathir's faction, which then prompted the defeated faction to launch an appeal to the Supreme Court.[51] This controversy led to the suspension and eventual dismissal of the President of the Supreme Court (Chief Justice Salleh Abas) and the removal of two other judges.[52] It was also unsurprising that the reconstituted Supreme Court bench that heard the appeal held in favour of Mahathir's faction.

As all this unfolded, the executive also engineered a constitutional amendment to place judicial power under the purview of the legislature. Thus, whereas the original article 121(1) of the Constitution stated that '[t]he judicial power of the Federation shall be vested into High Courts of coordinate jurisdiction and status,' the proposed amendment provides that '[t]here shall be two High Courts of coordinate jurisdiction and status ... and the High Courts and inferior courts shall have such jurisdiction and *powers as may be conferred by or under federal law.*' (emphasis added) The bill was quickly passed and came into effect in June 1988, thus officially subordinating the judiciary to the executive-dominated legislature.

If we are to consider how institutions are set up or modified to respond to plurality, then the 1988 constitutional amendment exercise was significant. In particular, it had implications for religion and Islamic law. For the first time, under article 121(1A), the Constitution carves out an exclusive sphere of jurisdiction for the Syariah branch. The amendment emerged out of the concern that civil and Syariah courts were issuing conflicting decisions and that matters concerning Islamic law required the expertise of those trained in the field. It was thought that introducing a provision which explicitly states that the civil courts shall have no jurisdiction in matters that are *exclusively* within the Syariah jurisdiction would resolve these issues. However, as we shall see, the amendment has only served to amplify competing claims of final authority between the civil and Syariah jurisdictions.

The Constitution's Ninth Schedule, List II specifies a list of matters in which state legislatures are authorised to regulate, including issues that would fall under the Syariah jurisdiction. This covers, among others, Islamic personal and family laws that are only applicable to Muslims. State legislatures are also entitled to create and punish offences against precepts of Islam. However, there are specific constitutional limitations on this power: laws punishing offences against the

---

[50] See Ratna Rueben Balasubramaniam, 'Has Rule By Law Killed the Rule of Law in Malaysia?' (2008) 8 Oxford University CLJ 211, 213.

[51] The Supreme Court, which was the highest court in the country, became the Federal Court in 1994.

[52] The tribunal set up to investigate the President of the Supreme Court (Salleh Abas) was fraught with suspicions: it was chaired by a judge who would succeed Salleh Abas should he be dismissed, applied a civil standard of proof, and employed a broad test of judicial misbehaviour. See Harding, *The Constitution of Malaysia* (n 16) 146–47.

precepts of Islam are only applicable to Muslims and, in theory, state legislatures cannot legislate on matters that are exclusively within the federal jurisdiction.[53] Thus, crimes that are considered to be 'against the precepts of Islam' but are nonetheless under the federal list of legislative power, such as murder, theft, robbery, rape, and incest, are beyond state legislative power (and thus outside the Syariah jurisdiction). In practice, whether these limitations are always observed is debatable. For example, although the Penal Code criminalises 'carnal intercourse against the course of nature'[54] – a law inherited from the British colonial period – various state-level Syariah enactments also criminalise the offence of *liwat* (sodomy). The view that state legislatures do not possess the authority to enact just *any* laws concerning Islam, ie, that their legislative power is limited to matters specified in List II of the Ninth Schedule[55], is increasingly unpopular, if not ignored.

The relationship between Islam as the state religion, the 'civil' issue of religious freedom, and the Syariah jurisdictional autonomy is an uneasy one, and the consequence of article 121(1A) on the civil courts' review powers has been a subject of great debate. On the one hand, the amendment has been interpreted to prevent any form of review by ordinary civil courts. Others, however, argue that article 121(1A) does not strip the civil courts' constitutional review powers[56] and that it does not put the Syariah courts at an equal status with the ordinary civil courts. It also used to be the case that the jurisdiction of Syariah courts to adjudicate a matter falling within List II must be explicitly conferred by a statute.[57] However, the courts have also displayed an inclination towards a different approach – one that grants jurisdiction to the Syariah courts by *implication* in the absence of any explicit statute conferring jurisdiction on the Syariah courts.[58] All this veers from the dispensation in article 121(1A), which only safeguards the authority of the Syariah courts in matters exclusively within their jurisdiction and does not automatically strip the civil courts of jurisdiction, especially in matters involving constitutional interpretation.[59]

Another crucial feature of the Malaysian constitutional structure is federalism. As the previous sections illustrate, there is a great degree of federal-bias in

[53] Federal Constitution of Malaysia, arts 74 and 75.
[54] Under the Malaysian Penal Code, s 377A, 'carnal intercourse' refers to oral and anal sex between two individuals.
[55] Shad Saleem Faruqi, *Document of Destiny* (Star Publications 2008) 134.
[56] See *Lina Joy v Majlis Agama Islam Wilayah & Another* [2007] 4 MLJ 585, 630 (dissenting opinion of Justice Richard Malanjum); Faruqi (n 55); Harding, *The Constitution of Malaysia* (n 16) 203.
[57] *Dalip Kaur v Pegawai Polis Daerah, Balai Polis Daerah, Bukit Mertajam & Another* [1992] 1 MLJ 1.
[58] See *Lina Joy* (n 56); *Md Hakim Lee v Majlis Agama Islam Wilayah Persekutuan, Kuala Lumpur* [1998] 1 MLJ 681; *Soon Singh v Pertubuhan Kebajikan Islam Malaysia (PERKIM) Kedah* [1999] 1 MLJ 489.
[59] Harding argues, in reference to the *Lina Joy* case, that where crucial fundamental rights questions are at stake, express statutory authorisation is required: Harding, *The Constitution of Malaysia* (n 16) 243. See also the case of *Latifah bte Mat Zin v Rosmawati bte Sharibun & Another* [2007] 5 MLJ 101, 116–117 where Justice Abdul Hamid Mohamed, who delivered the Federal Court's judgment, argued that as courts (including the Syariah courts) are creatures of statutes (that is, state legislation in the case of Syariah courts), and therefore, Syariah courts should look to 'the relevant State laws' to determine whether they have jurisdiction over a particular matter.

federal-state division of power. The Constitution specifies three lists designating the executive and legislative powers that can be exercised by the federal authorities and state authorities, as well as concurrently by both federal and state authorities.[60] However, where state legislation and federal legislation conflicts, the latter will prevail. Similarly, even though state constitutions are a source of constitutional law in Malaysia, the Federal Constitution will prevail if there are any inconsistencies between state constitutions and the Federal Constitution. State powers are typically limited to matters involving Islamic law and Malay *adat*, land, forestry, agriculture, and natural resources. In Sabah and Sarawak, states have complete authority over immigration as well as native and customary law and this is another crucial feature of the Malaysian federal arrangement that takes into account divisions across territorial lines, which, to be sure, overlap in significant ways with ethnic, religious, cultural, and linguistic identities.

VI. Pluralistic Sources and Constitutional Law and Politics

Managing the pluralities in Malaysia requires addressing different and conflicting demands from different sections of the society and state actors. These demands are often grounded in important political, legal, and/or ideational arguments on what the constitution and the different constitutional sources mandate; or what best advances the nation's interests and shared values. Thus, the plurality of constitutional sources – each conceived and interpreted differently by different parties – has triggered a range of constitutional conflicts (and in some cases, constitutional crises) in the country, and the courts have been tasked to weigh and adjudicate these competing constitutional claims. Some of these cases involve competing claims of authority between 'secular' and religious institutions. In this section, I will highlight three key areas to illustrate the ways in which the key sources of plurality have informed and shaped constitutional law and politics in Malaysia.

The first concerns family law, where there have been important controversies on custody and child conversions. These cases raise questions not only about the boundaries of constitutional rights in the country, but also about the role and place of Islamic jurisprudence and institutions within Malaysia's constitutional order.[61] They also showcase crucial (and divisive) contestations around ethnic and religious identities. These cases typically involve non-Muslim women who were previously married to their spouses under a common law marriage (for non-Muslims) governed by the Law Reform (Marriage & Divorce) Act 1976.

---

[60] See the Ninth Schedule, Federal Constitution of Malaysia for the federal list, state list, and concurrent list.

[61] For a deeper analysis of these cases, see Dian A H Shah, 'Religion, Conversion, and Custody: Battles in The Malaysian Appellate Courts' in Andrew Harding and Dian A H Shah (eds), *Law and Society in Malaysia: Pluralism, Ethnicity and Religion* (Routledge 2018) 145–62.

At some point during the marriage, one spouse (usually the husband) would decide to convert to Islam and convert their children without the knowledge of the non-Muslim spouse. When the marriage is dissolved, a custody battle would emerge. The Muslim husband would apply for custody of the children at the Syariah court (which the court granted in favour of the husbands), but these would be done without the knowledge of the non-Muslim wife and despite the fact that the woman does not have *locus standi* to challenge the custody in the Syariah courts.

What remedies, then, do non-Muslim parents have and where do they turn to in order to challenge the unilateral conversion of their children and to secure custodial rights? Do such conversions violate a non-consenting parent's freedom of religion? What happens when the civil and Syariah courts – using different legal sources – deliver conflicting decisions and orders on the same issue?

These cases have presented competing interpretations of constitutional provisions implicating religious freedom. For instance, the non-Muslim spouse or parent may claim that the secret conversion of a child was not constitutionally valid.[62] It is argued that parents should have an equal say in crucial decisions relating to the children, and therefore, a minor's conversion should require the consent of *both* parents. The Constitution appears to support this contention. Articles 12(3) and 12(4), in particular, prohibits requiring a person to receive religious instruction or to participate in religious ceremony other than his/her own and provides that a minor's parent or guardian shall decide his/her religion. The constitution's Eleventh Schedule also stipulates that 'words in the singular include the plural'. For the Muslim parent, however, the consent of one parent is sufficient to convert a child to a different religion, and the other parent thus has no right to challenge the conversion. It is also imaginable that the Muslim parent felt that his decision to convert his children to Islam is also a manifestation of his right to religious freedom.

The appellate courts in Malaysia – the Court of Appeal and the Federal Court – have taken a very literal approach to the question of parental consent, by deciding that the term 'parent' is used in the singular.[63] The upshot is that in Malaysia, we are faced with a situation where either parent could repeatedly convert his or her children at will. In reality, this 'policy' is more disadvantageous to non-Muslims than Muslims for two reasons. First, given the realities of Syariah jurisprudence on conversion in Malaysia, it would be difficult for a Muslim to convert out of Islam. Second, once a child is officially a Muslim, he or she is subject to the jurisdiction of the Syariah courts. However, a non-Muslim parent does not have standing before the Syariah courts. The parent therefore cannot challenge the conversion in these courts and would potentially lose custodial rights over the child.

Aside from competing ideas on the meaning and parameters of constitutional rights, cases on child conversions and custody battles implicate the 'contest'

---

[62] See *Subashini a/p Rajasingam v Saravanan a/l Thangathoray and other appeals* [2008] 2 MLJ 147 and *Pathmanathan Krishnan v Indira Gandhi Mutho & Other Appeals* [2016] 1 CLJ 911.

[63] *Subashini* (n 62).

between the civil legal order and the religious legal order. Such contest, however, is also observable in a bigger set of religious freedom cases. The key problem here concerns jurisdictional overlaps: if a matter falls within the jurisdiction of the Syariah courts, but also involves a civil law (ie, constitutional law) question, which is the appropriate forum – the civil court or the Syariah court? The easiest way to illustrate this is by considering the right to change one's religion, which has become a particularly thorny issue for Muslims. If a Muslim decides to convert out of Islam, he or she may be deemed to have committed an 'offence against the precepts of Islam', which is under the exclusive jurisdiction of the Syariah court. At the same time, conversions raise important questions regarding the constitutional right to religious freedom.

Beyond questions on religion and ethnicity, these issues also inevitably implicate federal-state relations, because Syariah laws are products of individual state legislatures. Technically, each state may regulate a particular issue very differently from other states. Consider, for example, the regulations on Muslim apostasy. Some states such as Perak, Malacca, and Sabah have enacted laws identifying apostasy (or the act of expressing that one is no longer a Muslim) as an offence punishable by fine and/or imprisonment.[64] In conservative states such as Kelantan and Terengganu, apostasy is punishable by indefinite imprisonment or death, but these cannot be enforced under the existing constitutional framework and due to limitations imposed by federal law on the Syariah courts' punitive powers.[65] Nevertheless, for the most part, laws dealing with the administration of Islam, Islamic criminal laws and procedure, and Islamic family laws are now similar across state lines.

The case of *Lina Joy* has emerged as the classic example to illustrate the difficulties in the clash between the civil and Syariah jurisdictions. It involved a woman who had converted into Christianity and sought to remove the word 'Islam' (as her 'official' religious identification) from her national identity card. In its judgment, the Federal Court did not rule that Lina Joy had no right to change her religion. However, the majority opinion argued that Joy only needed to follow the right procedures to do so – those procedures required Joy to first present herself before the Syariah court to obtain the court's approval for the conversion.[66] The problem was that in the specific jurisdiction that Joy was in (the Federal Territories) there is no legislation dealing with conversion or which grants the Syariah courts with jurisdiction over conversion matters. Yet, the court still found it acceptable to defer to the Syariah court and declined to rule that the constitutional protection of religious freedom commands the right to change one's religion.

The (dominant) tendency of the civil courts to take their hands off sensitive issues concerning Islam (especially if conversions are involved) is evident in other

---

[64] See eg, Perak Crimes (Syariah) Enactment 1992 (Enactment No 3 of 1992), ss 12 and 13; Sabah Syariah Criminal Offences 1995 (Enactment No 3 of 1995), ss 55(1) and 55(2).
[65] Syariah Courts (Criminal Jurisdiction) Act 1965.
[66] *Lina Joy* (n 56) 618.

cases. In *Indira Gandhi*, a Hindu mother's attempt to challenge the conversion of her children also proved futile, as the Court of Appeal held that the Syariah court possesses exclusive jurisdiction in cases of Muslim conversion, even though there are crucial constitutional rights questions at stake.[67] The court deferred to the Syariah court, fully aware that Indira had no *locus standi* in the Syariah court and that the state law in question actually entrusts the duty of granting conversion certificates to the Registrar of *Muallaf* (as opposed to Syariah courts).[68] In *Shamala*, the High Court acknowledged that the Hindu mother could not challenge her children's conversion in the Syariah court. Its solution, instead, was that Shamala should seek 'assistance' from the Islamic Council of the Federal Territories.[69]

Although there have been a few rare occasions where courts emphasised the primacy of the right to religious freedom, a matter deemed solely under the jurisdiction of the civil courts,[70] the broad reading of the power of Syariah courts in religious freedom issues is the dominant view today. In doing so, not only have courts appeared to have taken for granted the injustice against non-Muslim parents, they have showcased the legal system's inability to provide relief where a non-Muslim's rights and interests are at stake.

Another area where the clash between different constitutional sources has significantly shaped constitutional law and politics in Malaysia concerns the role of the monarchy in government formation. Earlier in this chapter, I explained that state constitutions provide that sultans could exercise their discretion in appointing the chief ministers of their respective states. The discretion, however, is 'guided' in the sense that they may appoint a member of the state legislative assembly who (in their judgment) is 'likely to command the confidence of a majority of the members in the Assembly'.[71] Notwithstanding this constitutional provision, constitutional convention dictates that the sultan is to endorse chief ministerial candidates proffered by the party or coalition that has a mandate to form the government in a particular state. However, as we have seen, Malaysia has experienced several constitutional crises throughout its history, resulting

---

[67] *Indira Gandhi* (n 62) 928.
[68] ibid.
[69] *Shamala Sathiyaseelan v Dr Jeyaganesh C Mogarajah & Another* [2004] 2 MLJ 648, 658.
[70] In *Siti Hasnah Vangarama Abdullah v Tun Dr Mahathir Mohamad (as President of PERKIM)* [2012] 7 CLJ 845, the Court of Appeal was more careful not to automatically relinquish jurisdiction to the Syariah court, especially since the case involved an important constitutional rights question. The Court examined the evidence presented to it and concluded that the claimant had never been a Muslim. This case involved the conversion of a minor and in this respect, it was similar to *Subashini* and *Indira*. However, the case was rather unique in that it did not involve unilateral conversion of a minor by a converted parent. Instead, the claimant – who was born as a Hindu and was seven years old at the time of conversion – was brought before a Kadi in Penang (to go through a conversion ceremony) by an official of the Muslim Welfare Society of Malaysia (PERKIM) and officials from the Penang State Religious Council. See also *Azmi Mohamad Azam v Director of Jabatan Agama Islam Sarawak and Others* [2016] 6 CLJ 562.
[71] See eg, Constitution of Perak, art 16(2).

from sultans ignoring established conventions but deciding instead to exercise their discretion in appointing chief ministers of their own choice. But the Perak constitutional crisis in 2009 was perhaps one of the most significant cases in the history of Malaysian constitutional politics because the power of the sultan in matters concerning government formation now appears to have been expanded – with judicial recognition – beyond established constitutional conventions *and* constitutional provisions.

The Perak crisis began in the aftermath of the 2008 general elections, when the opposition coalition – *Pakatan Rakyat* (PR) – successfully wrestled the state of Perak from the governing coalition, BN. PR had a slim majority – it held only 31 out of the 59 seats in the state legislative assembly. Datuk Nizar Jamaluddin, a member of the Islamic opposition party, PAS, was appointed as the Chief Minister. A series of policies adopted by the Nizar administration marked the beginning of a sour relationship with the state monarchy. One case involved the transfer of the Director of the Perak Islamic Affairs Department to the State Secretariat without consulting the Sultan of Perak, which was seen as disrespectful given the position of the Sultan as the Head of Islam in the state. The Sultan then ordered the reinstatement of the Director. Nine months later, three legislative members from PR resigned, leaving the assembly deadlocked as both BN and PR now held equal number of seats. Nizar had an audience with the Sultan to request for a dissolution of the assembly, so a fresh round of elections could be called. The Sultan then met with 31 assemblymen (28 from the BN and the three former PR assemblymen) and shortly thereafter, he informed Nizar of his refusal to dissolve the assembly; issued a statement that Nizar had ceased to command the confidence of the majority of the assembly; and ordered Nizar and the state executive council to resign.[72] A new chief minister from BN was then appointed by the Sultan to fill the vacant office. A vote of confidence was never held in the assembly, but the Sultan invoked article 16(6) of the Perak Constitution to justify his decision.[73]

The three cases illustrated above illustrate that the different sources of pluralities in Malaysia – be they identity-based (ethnicity and religion) or institution-based (the monarchy and federalism) – have profoundly shaped constitutional development and politics in the country. Preservation of religious and ethnic interests has given rise to conflicting claims on the parameters of fundamental rights and the role of the dominant religion (Islam) in the constitutional order. A federalised arrangement on religion was to devolve autonomy to the states in matters involving Islam, and there is an element of path dependence and historical continuity in this arrangement. Relatedly, the introduction of article 121(1A) that carves out a

---

[72] See statement by Sultan Azlan Shah, reproduced in HP Lee, *Constitutional Conflicts in Contemporary Malaysia* (OUP 2017) 195.
[73] While the provision states that a Chief Minister who has ceased to command the confidence of the assembly shall tender his resignation, it does not empower the Sultan to order the Chief Minister's dismissal, especially without a vote of no confidence.

sphere of autonomy for the Syariah branch in specific matters spelled out in the Constitution appears to be an exercise in accommodating religious autonomy.[74] However, over time we have witnessed problems arising from competing claims of power between state and federal religious authorities, with the latter emerging as the driver of religious policies and discourses on Islam. With regard to the monarchy, the Perak crisis and other examples of royal assertions of power in state-level politics discussed in the preceding section demonstrate another facet of competing claims of power: between a traditional institution of authority versus a democratic government rooted in Westminster conventions.

How did the courts deal with pluralist constitutional sources pertaining to the boundaries of royal powers vis-à-vis government formation? In the Perak case, the High Court held in favour of Nizar, emphasising that a vote of no confidence must be held – as per usual democratic practice and convention – in order to force the resignation of the Chief Minister.[75] The Court of Appeal and the Federal Court, however, held otherwise.[76] The outcome of the Perak case, as well as other similar constitutional crises in other states, raises questions about the role and powers of the monarchy (as the head of state) vis-à-vis the effective head of government.[77] It would now appear that royal powers have expanded – in practice and with judicial approval – beyond what is expressly stipulated in the Constitution and existing constitutional conventions. All this has thus far only occurred at state level, and we have yet to witness such exercises of royal authority vis-à-vis the formation of the federal government.[78]

With regard to conceptions on the role of Islam, a dominant pattern appears to be that religious freedom (for Muslims and non-Muslims alike) is made to yield to Islam's special constitutional position or, more specifically, what the state deems to be in the interests of Islam and the Muslim community. Thus we see – in cases of Muslim apostasy – a normative convergence in the restrictive reading of religious freedom among secular and religious authorities.[79] In a similar vein, implicit in the cases concerning custody battles and child conversions is the desire to maintain the cohesion of the Malay-Muslim community and, by extension, the integrity and

---

[74] Jaclyn L Neo, 'Competing Imperatives: Conflicts and Convergences in State and Islam in Pluralist Malaysia' (2015) Oxford Journal of Law and Religion 1, 3.

[75] *Dato' Seri Ir Hj Mohammad Nizar Jamaluddin v Dato' Seri Dr Zambry Abdul Kadir* [2009] 5 MLJ 108 (High Court).

[76] *Dato' Seri Dr Zambry Abdul Kadir v Dato' Seri Ir Hj Mohammad Nizar Jamaluddin; Attorney General (Intervener)* [2009] 5 Current Law Journal 265 (Court of Appeal); *Dato' Seri Ir Hj Mohammad Nizar Jamaluddin v Dato' Seri Dr Zambry Abdul Kadir; Attorney General (Intervener)* [2010] 2 CLJ 925 (Federal Court).

[77] See Jaclyn L Neo, 'Change and Continuity: The Constitutional Head of State and Democratic Transitions in Malaysia' (2012) 5 MLJ i.

[78] See Harding, *The Constitution of Malaysia* (n 16) 127–29, discussing a 1985 constitutional crisis in Sabah, where the courts also intervened in a case concerning the role of the Head of State (not a sultan) in the appointment of the chief minister. Harding cites this case as 'evidence of the courts' willingness to enforce the spirit as well as the letter of the Constitution'.

[79] Neo (n 74) 15–16.

political superiority of Islam as the majority religion.[80] More explicitly, the case about the right of non-Muslims to use the word 'Allah' as part of their religious practice illustrates the ways in which the provision on Islam can be used as a justification to restrict religious practices of minority that are deemed 'threatening' to Islam and the Muslim community, and as a means of compelling policy-makers to prioritise Islamic interests in their decision-making.[81]

The patterns of convergence that I have described are – to be sure – not always continuous or consistent (hence, my use of the term *dominant*). On the issue of the role of constitutional heads of state and democratic change of government, a constitutional crisis in Sabah in 1985 illustrates that judicial intervention could yield outcomes consistent with the spirit of constitutional and Westminster democratic practices.[82] However, the real test will perhaps arise when a change of government occurs at the federal level. As Neo argues, transitions could be complicated either when the losing governing party forms a government anyway with only a minority of seats in Parliament, or when floor crossings tilt the balance of power in Parliament.[83] On the question of religion, while the federal authorities have – for the most part – flexed its authority over the states, there have been bouts of resistance from the states, often with royal involvement. The Sultan of Johor, in particular, has on several occasions questioned the authority of the federal-level department, JAKIM. In 2015, His Majesty questioned the budget afforded to JAKIM and demanded accountability in its expenditure.[84] More recently, the Sultan ordered the Johor state Islamic religious department to stop dealing with JAKIM, after a JAKIM-associated preacher criticised the Sultan in a controversy about a Muslim-only laundrette in the state.[85] In addition, the civil courts – depending on the type of case in question – has not always ceded jurisdiction to the Syariah branch in matters implicating Islam. In *Deepa*, for example, the Federal Court affirmed that the Syariah courts do not possess jurisdiction over a case if one party is a non-Muslim, even if the subject matter of the case is within its exclusive jurisdiction; and that the civil courts would continue to have exclusive jurisdiction over divorce and custody matters of a civil marriage, despite the conversion of one spouse.[86]

---

[80] Maznah Mohamed has written a compelling analysis on in cases concerning child conversions (or conversion more broadly) the state apparatus is engaged in 'making the majority'. See Mohamed (n 4).

[81] *Menteri Dalam Negeri & Others v Titular Roman Catholic Archbishop of Kuala Lumpur*, [2013] 6 MLJ468, 469, 511. See also Neo (n 74) 22–24; Dian A H Shah, 'The 'Allah' Case: Implications for Religious Practice and Expression in Malaysia' (2015) 4 Oxford Journal of Law and Religion 141.

[82] See n 78.

[83] Neo (n 77) xvii–xviii.

[84] 'Johor Sultan: Why does JAKIM need RM1b budget?', *The Malaymail Online* (Petaling Jaya, 27 December 2015) www.themalaymailonline.com/malaysia/article/johor-sultan-why-does-jakim-need-rm1b-budget#Ip0eq1tsK3oWmZES.97 accessed 18 September 2018.

[85] 'Johor Sultan order religious office to cut ties with Jakim', *The Straits Times* (Singapore, 15 October 2017) www.straitstimes.com/asia/se-asia/johor-sultan-orders-religious-office-to-cut-ties-with-jakim accessed 18 September 2018.

[86] *Viran Nagapan v Deepa Subramaniam & Other Appeals* [2016] 3 CLJ 505, 506. See also n 70.

VII. Conclusion

This chapter has illustrated that constitutional law and politics in Malaysia are not just shaped by the express provisions of the Federal Constitution, but also by a variety of constitutional sources ranging from Islamic law to state constitutions and constitutional conventions. The interaction amongst these different sources in the context of Malaysia's plural society is complex but equally fascinating. The Malaysian case study demonstrates that there are multiple competing claims of final authority between and within different institutions and legal orders. They manifest themselves in conflicting conceptions and interpretations of constitutional rights provisions; competing claims of supremacy between the civil and Syariah jurisdictions; and the contest between formal constitutions and constitutional conventions.

However, the complexities, as we have seen in the cases examined throughout this chapter, may produce uncertainties and adverse outcomes for constitutionalism and the rule of law. Context is key to understanding why and how things have unfolded the way they have. The growing assertion of Syariah power, for example, is not a recent phenomenon. However, this would have been unfamiliar (or unforeseen) to the Malaysian constitutional scheme at the time of constitution-making and in the first three to four decades after independence. State-led 'Islamisation' initiatives in the late 1980s – which was instituted both to buttress the ruling party's political dominance and to control the boundaries of the Islamic discourse in the country – were important game changers.

With regard to the monarchy, we have seen in the case cited above that governments (at the federal level and in various states) have tended to defer to royal pronouncements, even though they are constitutionally suspect. Prevailing political conditions and calculations are important, in this respect. A large section of the Malay community still holds the traditional sense of attachment to the Malay monarchy, which is seen as representing the pride and prestige of the Malay identity. In addition, as Harding argues, the Malays have an 'acute sense of protocol' in matters involving royal status. Going against the palace may thus be tantamount to a political suicide, particularly in situations where ruling parties or coalitions are politically vulnerable. A study of Malaysia's pluralist constitution, therefore, cannot be limited to an analysis of the text and practice (empirical evidence); it has to be evaluated in light of the unique historical, social, and political contexts of the country.

Bibliography

—— Constitution of Perak.
—— Federal Constitution of Malaysia.

—— 'Johor Sultan order religious office to cut ties with Jakim', *The Straits Times* (Singapore, 15 October 2017) www.straitstimes.com/asia/se-asia/johor-sultan-orders-religious-office-to-cut-ties-with-jakim accessed 18 September 2018.

—— 'Johor Sultan: Why does JAKIM need RM1b budget?', *The Malaymail Online* (Petaling Jaya, 27 December 2015) www.themalaymailonline.com/malaysia/article/johor-sultan-why-does-jakim-need-rm1b-budget#Ip0eq1tsK3oWmZES.97 accessed 18 September 2018.

—— Malaysia Agreement 1963.

—— Meeting of the Alliance Party with the Reid Commission (September 27, 1956) CO889/6.

—— Note on Pakistan and the Reid Commission Report, Constitutional Talks in London, May 1957 on the Future of Malaya (10 May 1957), DO35/6278.

—— Perak Crimes (Syariah) Enactment 1992 (Enactment No. 3 of 1992).

—— 'Putrajaya's new security law now gazetted without royal assent', *The Malaymailonline* (Kuala Lumpur, 9 June 2016) www.themalaymailonline.com/malaysia/article/putrajayas-new-security-law-now-in-force-without-royal-assent accessed 18 September 2018.

—— Report of the Federation of Malaya Constitutional Commission (21 February 1957), DO35/6282.

—— Sabah Syariah Criminal Offences 1995 (Enactment No. 3 of 1995).

—— Syariah Courts (Criminal Jurisdiction) Act 1965.

Balasubramaniam R R, 'Has Rule By Law Killed the Rule of Law in Malaysia?' (2008) 8 Oxford University Commonwealth Law Journal 211.

Equal Rights Trust in partnership with Tenaganita, 'Washing the Tigers' (London, November 2012) www.equalrightstrust.org/ertdocumentbank/Malaysia%20CR%201.pdf accessed 18 September 2018.

Faruqi S S, 'Affirmative Action Policies and the Constitution' (2003) 21 Kajian Malaysia 31.

—— *Document of Destiny* (Star Publications 2008).

Fernando J M, *The Making of the Malayan Constitution* (MBRAS 2002) 73.

—— 'Special Rights in the Malaysian Constitution and the Framers' Dilemma, 1956–57' (2015) 45(3) The Journal of Imperial and Commonwealth History 535.

Harding A, *Law, Government and the Constitution in Malaysia* (Kluwer Law International 1996) 13.

—— *The Constitution of Malaysia: A Contextual Analysis* (Hart Publishing 2012).

—— 'Nazrinian' Monarchy in Malaysia: The Resilience and Revival of a Traditional Institution' in Harding A and Shah D A H (eds), *Law and Society in Malaysia: Pluralism, Ethnicity and Religion* (Routledge 2018).

Jennings W I, 'Hearing of Counsel on Behalf of Their Highnesses the Rulers' (14–15 September 1956), in *Papers of Sir Ivor Jennings* B/X/2/iv 20.

—— 'Comments on the Reid Report' in *Papers of Sir Ivor Jennings* B/X/2/iv 20.

Kanagasabai C, 'Malaysia: Limited and Intermittent Judicialization of Politics' in Bjorn Dressel (ed), *The Judicialization of Politics in Asia* (Routledge 2013).

Lee H P, *Constitutional Conflicts in Contemporary Malaysia* (OUP 2017).

Maduro M P, 'Three Claims of Constitutional Pluralism' in Matej Avbelj & Jan Komarek (eds), *Constitutional Pluralism in Europe and Beyond* (Hart Publishing 2012).

Mohamed M, 'Making Majority, Undoing Family: Law, Religion and The Islamization Of The State In Malaysia' (2010) 39(3) Economy and Society 360.

Mohamad T H S b A, 'Traditional Elements of the Malaysian Constitution' in Trindade F A & Lee H P (eds), *The Constitution of Malaysia: Further Perspectives and Developments: Essays in Honour of Tun Mohamed Suffian* (OUP 1986).

Neo J L, 'Malay Nationalism, Islamic Supremacy and the Constitutional Bargain in the Multi-ethnic Composition of Malaysia' (2006) 13 International Journal on Minority and Group Rights.

—— 'Change and Continuity: The Constitutional Head of State and Democratic Transitions in Malaysia' (2012) 5 Malayan Law Journal i.

—— 'Competing Imperatives: Conflicts and Convergences in State and Islam in Pluralist Malaysia' (2015) Oxford Journal of Law and Religion 1.

Parkinson C O H, *Bills of Rights and Decolonization: The Emergence of Domestic Human Rights Instruments in Britain's Overseas Territories* (OUP 2007).

Sarwar M and Ananth S, 'The National Security Council Bill: A Colorable Exercise of Power' (2016) 2 Malayan Law Journal.

Shah D A H, 'Religion, Conversion, and Custody: Battles in The Malaysian Appellate Courts' in Harding A and Shah D A H (eds), *Law and Society in Malaysia: Pluralism, Ethnicity and Religion* (Routledge 2018).

—— 'The 'Allah' Case: Implications for Religious Practice and Expression in Malaysia' (2015) 4 Oxford Journal of Law and Religion 141.

Shah Y A M R A, 'The Role of Constitutional Rulers in Malaysia' in Trindade F A & Lee H P (eds), *The Constitution of Malaysia: Further Perspectives and Developments, Essays in Honour of Tun Mohamed Suffian* (OUP 1986).

Tan Y L K, 'The Creation of Greater Malaysia: Law, Politics, Ethnicity, and Religion' in Harding A and Shah D A H (eds), *Law and Society in Malaysia: Pluralism, Ethnicity and Religion* (Routledge 2018).

3

The Imperative of Integrative Pluralist Constitutionalism: Going Beyond Formal Equality, Eschewing Rights, and Accommodation of Differences in Singapore

EUGENE K B TAN

[T]he price for a more impressive genealogical table would be to turn Singapore into a bloody battleground for endless racial and communal conflicts and interventionist politics by the more powerful and bigger nations from which Singaporeans had emigrated.[1]

I. Introduction: Pluralism as Constitutional Reality

Pluralism is a fact of life and a way of life in Singapore. Race, religion, and language are the most constitutionally relevant types of plurality.[2] Plurality in fact is self-evident, and plurality in norm an organising principle of how society is governed, laws are made, and policies are designed. A result of its transformation from a colonial trading port to a modern economy and a cosmopolitan society, pluralism is reflected in the country's racial make-up and the fabric of society. This harmonious diversity is sustained as a facet of pragmatic governance. From a law and order perspective, pluralism is maintained and reinforced by the strict policing of ethnic markers of race, religion, and language, reflecting a state of affairs that views diversity as a source of inherent vulnerability even as Singapore and Singaporeans seem to embrace the diversity.

---

[1] Foreign Minister S. Rajaratnam quoted in Chan Heng Chee and Obaid ul Haq (eds), *The Prophetic & The Political: Selected Speeches & Writings of S. Rajaratnam* (Graham Brash 1987) 149. Rajaratnam was Singapore's Foreign Minister between 1965 and 1980.

[2] In this chapter, race is distinguished from and used in preference to ethnicity when referring to the group classifications assigned by the Singapore state to its citizens. Ethnicity is used to refer to the collective attributes of race, religion, language, and culture.

Pluralism is managed through an overarching policy known as multiracialism, a cornerstone of Singapore's state-building and nation-building that provides the foundation for stability, harmony, growth, development, and transformation. Multiracialism in Singapore is a governance ideology that accords equal status to the various races, and entails equal treatment of ethnic markers such as language (multi-lingualism) and religion (multi-religiosity).[3] Today, racial and religious harmony is enshrined as one of Singapore's five Shared Values, and very much aligned with the constitutional mores of the city-state where harmonious diversity is a watchword in regulating pluralism.

Although Singapore's plural society is often regarded as a colonial creation, European traders, merchants, and colonialists arrived in the early nineteenth century to an already plural society in the Malayo-Indonesian world. Colonial policies in Southeast Asia catalysed the mass movement of immigrants to Singapore, changing the fabric of society through a potpourri of peoples, cultures, languages, religions, and values.[4] Abetted by the colonial divide-and-rule policy, the colonial construct and distinction between the indigenous people and the non-indigenous people, with ethnic enclaves for distinct communities, further accentuated the pluralist features of a largely immigrant society. Such diversity enforced by bureaucratic separation could easily become divisive since there was no effort towards generating trust, confidence, and cohesion among the various communities who also saw themselves as sojourners in Singapore.

With decolonisation, the endeavour to break out of a racialised mode of government and governance gained ascendency. Singapore's steadfast commitment to the multiracial ethos contributed to its failed political merger with Malaysia between September 1963 and August 1965. Singapore's rigorous objections to the Kuala Lumpur-based federal government's goal of a race-based Malay-Malaysia translated into a tempestuous union marked by mutual suspicion and confrontation, political manoeuvring, and racial violence. On securing independence from Malaysia on 9 August 1965, the government consciously sought to develop a 'Singaporean Singapore' identity, an imperative for a new society,

---

[3] While multiracialism entails that each race is treated equally, it can reinforce ethnic essentialism by creating a greater consciousness of differences and boundaries by virtue of race as the lynchpin. Due to space constraints, I do not engage in the debate on the contested nature of multiracialism, often conflated with multiculturalism.

[4] As Singapore developed as a thriving entrepôt and a regional emporium, migration of people from other parts of Asia grew in tandem with the increased economic activity. By 1824, with the conclusion of the Anglo-Dutch Treaty and the Treaty of Cession which resulted in the British acquiring unchallenged sovereignty over Singapore, the population had reached 10,683 (comprising Malays 60%, Chinese 31%, Indians 7% and others 2%). By 1867, the Chinese community had increased to the extent that it was the majority with 65% of the population of 55,000. By 1959, when the British granted Singapore self-government, the racial composition had already long stabilised with the ethnic Chinese making up about three-quarters of the population, the Malays no larger than of one-sixth of the total population, and the Indians one-twelfth. The Malays were, however, momentarily the majority during the short-lived and tumultuous merger with Malaysia between 16 September 1963 and 9 August 1965. With government intervention on the demographic front, these racial ratios – seen as a prerequisite for Singapore's success – have more or less stayed the same since independence.

notwithstanding that the majority ethnic Chinese community comprised three-quarters of the city-state's 2 million people. At the same time, Singapore was committed to recognising the special position of the indigenous Malays.[5]

This nascent effort at pluralist constitutionalism was a domestic and geopolitical necessity for an accidental and improbable nation-state threatened by ethnic cleavages that could erupt into ethno-violence. With its sovereign survival precarious, if not under threat, for the fledgling nation-state to discriminate against the ethnic minorities would not only subject the fragile and unsettled polity to fresh waves of internal discord and strife but it would also invite interference from the ethnic minorities' co-ethnics in neighbouring countries. More fundamentally, it would be a cruel betrayal of the founding premise of independent Singapore.

This chapter argues that pluralism is a major influence in constitution-making and constitutional practice in Singapore. In fact, pluralism is consciously nurtured and scripted into the national discourse of nation-building. The form of pluralist constitutionalism practised in Singapore specifically recognises the reality of a plural society and seeks to ensure that the diversity does not become a structural weakness and a source of division. It is, however, one fraught with ironies and paradoxes. While the government recognises the importance of managing pluralism, there is also the conscious effort to avoid the development of an assertive rights-based legal regime in the management of pluralism in the post-colonial nation-building project. The Singapore Constitution has effectively structured the expectations of the majority and minority communities. It does this by consciously avoiding the provision of group rights while emphasising the formal equality of Singaporeans. The 1966 Constitutional Commission's rationale for proceeding on the basis of individual rights, rather than group rights, is cogently articulated in its report:

> We believe that a person, whether he is a citizen or not, who belongs to a racial or a linguistic or a religious minority in Singapore will have all his rights as a member of such racial or linguistic or religious minority safeguarded if his fundamental rights as an individual, and as a citizen if he is one, are entrenched in the Constitution, and if those fundamental rights are enforceable by the Courts.[6]

Rights and entitlement are accorded to individuals *qua* citizens. Substantive equality is relied upon to ensure that equality is not merely a procedural right and a rhetorical ritual only. Furthermore, the central importance of interests, duties, and responsibility – as the de facto language of citizenship – is clearly invoked in the constitutional discourse. This framework of pluralist constitutionalism is in

---

[5] Lee Kuan Yew, reflecting on this necessity, said: 'Because we, the Chinese majority in Singapore, suffered communal bullying and discrimination during the two years we were a part of Malaysia, the first-generation leaders vowed that we would never bully or discriminate our bullies': Speech by Lee Kuan Yew at the People's Action Party 50th anniversary celebrations, 21 November 2004. For a perspective from a protagonist in this pivotal constitutional moment, see, Lee Kuan Yew, *The Singapore Story: The Memoirs of Lee Kuan Yew* (Times Editions and The Straits Times Press 1998) 540–663.

[6] *Report of the Constitutional Commission* (Government Printer 1966) 3, para 12.

accord with and undergirded by the communitarian ethos of the larger good of the state and society taking precedence over sectarian ones. The Singapore Constitution recognises the Malays as Singapore's indigenous people. Yet, this constitutional recognition has not resulted in the provision of special rights to Malay-Singaporeans by virtue of their race, language, and religion. As such, there is no affirmative action in favour of the Malays or any minorities. Concessions, when provided, are carefully couched to avoid any sense of entitlement or legal rights.[7]

Singapore's ethnic minorities have embraced and adapted to the constitutional idea of civic citizenship as the overarching identity that unites Singaporeans regardless of their backgrounds. First, the tacit recognition of the ideal of an overarching Singaporean identity that is distinct from the sectarian and sub-national identities is vital in Singapore's search for its national identity. Secondly, citizenship is regarded as the most appropriate form of non-majoritarian, non-plebiscitarian accommodation. While Singapore adopts an ostensible civic conception of citizenship, it also urges a conscious formation and sustenance of distinctive ethnic identities of the majority and minority communities. The convergent civic and divergent ethnic identities naturally compete and conflict, giving rise to a variegated and rich discourse on belonging, identity, and citizenship denominated in terms of societal interests over sectarian ones. Similarly, the heterogeneity of Singapore requires careful attention be given to the design of institutions if multi-racialism is to be sustained. As John Ikenberry observes, 'Ethnic divisions put at risk the nation-state, but they also provide a powerful incentive for the designing and building of state institutions'.[8]

Constitutionalism is understood as the inter-connected set of principles, values, and norms that structure the state, shape public institutions, and nurture constitutional relationships among stakeholders in ways that promote the common good. Constitutionalism ultimately seeks to create effective institutions and to promote the rule of law, and not just constraints on the state. In recognising society's inherent diversity, pluralist constitutionalism can purposefully aid the nation-building quest if it promotes and advocates an overarching, common identity that unifies. This centripetal force is a *sine qua non* if pluralist constitutionalism is to give effect and purpose to constitutionalism and pluralism as distinct public goods.

The Singapore citizen's sense of belonging is aided by the ballast of healthy respect for pluralism in the overall constitutional structuring and ordering. In this scheme of things, the state does not require but instead enjoins Singaporeans of various racial communities not to forfeit their collective claim to recognition

---

[7] See Eugene K B Tan, 'Racial Politics and Imperatives and the Constitutional Special Position of the Indigenous Malays in a New Society: Asserting Interests and the Non-Contestation of Rights in Singapore's Communitarian Constitutionalism' in Marco Bünte & Björn Dressel (eds), *Politics and Constitutions in Southeast Asia* (Routledge 2017) 226.

[8] G. John Ikenberry, 'What States Can Do Now' in T V Paul, G John Ikenberry and John A Hall (eds), *The Nation-State in Question* (Princeton University Press 2003) 356.

of their distinctive communal identities. Neither do the communities demand national resources and concessions from the state to maintain their own identities in areas such as language, culture, and religion. This two-way street enables pluralist constitutionalism to thrive. Pluralist constitutionalism becomes a sociopolitical compact between the different racial groups and between these groups and the nation-state.

This chapter proceeds as follows. Part II attempts a brief discussion to contextualise the enduring debate on constitutional design as well as the approaches of integration and accommodation in conflict regulation. In Part III, I examine race as the central organising principle in Singapore and consider its application in various facets of life, including ethnic self-help. Part IV explores formal and substantive equality in Singapore as the engine of pluralist constitutionalism. In Part V, substantive equality is explored further through the lens of the special position of the Malays. The policy of religious accommodation and the symbolic value of Malay as the national language and its relationship to Singapore's bilingual policy are also discussed. Part VI dwells on another dimension of substantive equality – that of the political representation of racial minorities through electoral integration and reserved presidential election are important platforms in accommodating minority, especially Malay, representation in key political institutions. Part VII analyses the language of interests in constitutional accommodation. Part VIII concludes.

II. Integration and Accommodation in Constitutional Design Writ Large

The role of constitutional design in regulating conflict in divided societies is taking on greater importance. Constitutional regimes are conceived as providing a framework for the 'forging of a common political identity ... by creating the institutional spaces for shared decision making'.[9] This process of a shared experience of shared decision-making helps to engender a putative sense of shared identity and community. Put simply, a constitution that is able to provide a process of viable and sustainable governance in a divided society helps to engender trust and confidence in the institutions, the laws, and the policies. In turn, the rule of law is enhanced and the democratic process is given effect to.

Constitutional design and process for divided societies has broadly revolved around Arend Lijphart's consociational theory of power-sharing mechanisms and Donald Horowitz's model of constitutional and electoral arrangements that

---

[9] Sujit Choudhry, 'Bridging Comparative Politics and Comparative Constitutional Law: Constitutional Design in Divided Societies' in Sujit Choudhry (ed), *Constitutional Design for Divided Societies: Integration or Accommodation?* (OUP 2008) 6.

promote ethnic moderation.[10] To be clear, Lijphart's and Horowitz's approaches are not polar opposites. They cohere around the search for a framework to manage differences through constitutional arrangements that promote 'integration' and/or 'accommodation'.

Integration is fundamentally about equal citizenship, which entails turning 'a blind eye to difference for public purposes' or the privatisation of differences. Group-based partisanship in political institutions is frowned upon.[11] On the other hand, accommodation requires the recognition of multiple racial, religious, linguistic, cultural communities within a state. As such, co-existence is a powerful theme in accommodation given that identities are enduring and powerful mobilisers, if not primordial.

Flowing from the above starting points, the typical conflict regulation 'prescriptions' are of two general types: (1) 'Consociational democracy' incorporating an extensive regime of power-sharing and minority guarantees[12], and (2) a constitutional design that is geared towards making 'moderation pay' by nudging politicians to the moderate centre through incentivising moderation and the inculcation of cross-cutting ethnic support in politics. Thus, proponents of accommodation recognise differences and give it due regard in policies and laws and institutional design. On the other hand, integrationists prefer alternative strategies that seek to blur, transcend, and nurture crosscutting cleavages. Integrationists regard the accommodationist approach as having the propensity to entrench, perpetuate and exacerbate the very divisions they are designed to manage. On the other hand, accommodationists perceive integrationists as exaggerating the basis for unity and ignoring the ground reality of differences, divisions, and conflict. This longstanding debate between these two approaches is not just theoretical but is central to the political debates in many divided societies on how to regulate differences.

This chapter does not propose to elaborate on that debate as the Singapore city-state is not a deeply divided society. Singapore has achieved relative success in regulating differences based on ethnic markers like race, religion, and language. More importantly, the governance approach to regulating differences has been pragmatic with elements of both Lijphart's and Horowitz's approaches utilised. The regulatory approach is shorn of hardwired theoretical positions but instead nourished with practical experience, a deeply realist sense of societal

---

[10] See representative works of Arend Lijphart: *Democracy in Plural Societies: A Comparative Exploration* (YUP 1977); *Democracies: Patterns of Majoritarian and Consensus Government in Twenty-One Countries* (YUP 1984); *Patterns of Democracy: Government Forms & Performance in Thirty-Six Countries*, Second Edition (YUP 2012). See also Donald L Horowitz, *Ethnic Groups in Conflict* (University of California Press 1985).

[11] For a comprehensive discussion, see John McGarry, Brendan O'Leary, and Richard Simeon, 'Integration or Accommodation? The Enduring Debate in Conflict Regulation' in Sujit Choudhry (ed), *Constitutional Design for Divided Societies: Integration or Accommodation?* (OUP 2008).

[12] Specific arrangements include elections by proportional representation (especially closed-list proportional representation in not overly large districts), a parliamentary form of government, a cabinet in which power-sharing is prescribed in ethnic or partisan terms, a head of state elected by a legislature or whose office is combined with the Prime Minister's, federalism and decentralisation.

differences, and a constitutional design that is concerned with what works. This chapter proceeds on the basis of the Singaporean experience as being illustrative of melding both integration and accommodation.

III. Race as Core Organising Principle

Singapore's citizen population of 3.44 million as of June 2017 comprised 76.1% Chinese, 15.0% Malay, 7.4% Indian, and 1.5% Others.[13] The Singapore government treats race, language, and religion as fault lines in society that requires vigilant policing even as inter-racial trust and confidence is nurtured. Under Singapore's relatively rigid, largely state-assigned Chinese-Malay-Indian-Others (CMIO) racial classification, every Singaporean is racially designated at birth, primarily based on one's patrilineality.[14] This ascriptive racial identity is used for a variety of purposes including the choice of mother tongue language instruction in schools, ethnic quotas in public housing,[15] opportunities within military service (whether conscript or professional), and eligibility to contest as a Malay, Indian or other minority candidate in parliamentary and presidential elections.

The functional and organisational role of race persists in Singapore. In any plural society, it is inevitable that there is an ascriptive majority, and other minority communities. Majoritarianism will work against nation-building if it promotes exclusivity, privilege and preference for the majority, and facilitates or endorses discrimination against the minorities. However, Singapore was fortunate in that all key stakeholders in London and in Singapore embraced the idea and ideal of civic citizenship in the negotiations in 1958 for internal self-government.[16] This path dependence means that the aspiration of multiracialism and equal citizenship, however inchoately expressed in a nation-state's founding moment, makes it a non-starter to relegate the ethnic minorities to a subordinate status. It is instructive to bear in mind what the 1966 Constitutional Commission noted in its report of a non-racial approach in a polyglot society:

> We find also in the years succeeding the Second World War the growth of a national spirit amongst the many peoples of many races who now regard Singapore as their

---

[13] *Population in Brief 2017* (Prime Minister's Office, September 2017).
[14] On the CMIO classification, see Sharon Siddique, 'Singaporean Identity' in Kernial Singh Sandhu and Paul Wheatley (eds), *Management of Success: The Moulding of Modern Singapore* (Institute of Southeast Asian Studies 1989) 563. Limited racial self-definition, through 'double-barrelled race options,' was permitted from 2011. See Singapore's Immigration and Checkpoints Authority 'Greater Flexibility with Implementation of Double-Barrelled Race Option from 1 January 2011' (29 December 2010). For relevant Government policies and the collection of statistics, the first component of a double-barrelled race will be used. For example, a person who is classified as Chinese-Malay will be treated as Chinese for relevant official purposes and data gathering.
[15] The Ethnic Integration Policy provides for racial quotas at the apartment block and precinct levels in public housing estates.
[16] *Report of the Singapore Constitutional Conference held in London in March and April, 1957* (Cmnd 147, April 1957) paras 49–51.

home if not the home of their forefathers and we believe there is a growing awareness and acceptance amongst these peoples that in spite of their different origins, their destinies and that of their children are all inextricably intertwined, intermixed and interwoven and *that their future and the future of the nation lies in a non-racial approach to all problems under a form of government which would enable the growth of a united, multi-racial, free and democratic nation in which all its citizens have equal rights and equal opportunities.*[17]

This non-racial approach, ironically, requires the government to be very mindful of race as a core identity marker of Singaporeans, and how laws, policies and institutions have to be scrupulously impartial and yet recognise the differences among the races. Singapore's mode of regulating diversity is a veritable mix of integration and accommodation, which Prime Minister Lee Hsien Loong describes as:

> No race or culture in Singapore is coerced into conforming with other cultures or identities, let alone that of the majority. Ours is not a melting pot society, with every race shorn of its distinctiveness. Instead, we encourage each race to preserve its unique culture and traditions, while fostering mutual appreciation and respect among all of them. Being Singaporean has never been a matter of subtraction, but of addition; not of becoming less, but more; not of limitation and contraction, but of openness and expansion.[18]

But even this notion of being Singaporean has its limitations. Singapore's approach in managing the socio-economic and educational under-performance among the various races has a significant racial dimension. This is pragmatically illustrated in the government's policy of ethnic self-help. Ethnic self-help groups make up the main platform to uplift educational and economic performance among the major racial communities. Ethnic self-help groups reflect a degree of ethnic essentialism in the government's thinking, in particular that community self-help is far more effective in uplifting the disadvantaged members of the various races than a national, non-racial approach. It also seeks to promote equality in treatment through not according preferential treatment to any particular group, especially the Chinese majority. Ethnic self-help, it is argued, would also strengthen a community's sense of self-worth.

The Malay community has two ethnic self-help groups: MENDAKI (Council on Education for Muslim Children), the first ethnic self-help group created in 1982, and the Association of Muslim Professionals (AMP) set up in 1991. For Malays/Muslims, the religious dimension is also significant in their ethnic self-help groups.[19] In contrast, the identities of the other three self-help groups for

---

[17] *1966 Constitutional Commission Report* (n 6) 3, para 10. Emphasis mine.

[18] Speech by Prime Minister Lee Hsien Loong at the official opening of the Singapore Chinese Cultural Centre (19 May 2017).

[19] MENDAKI's logo incorporates a stylistic rendition of the Quranic term 'Iqra' which means 'Read': see MENDAKI, 'Our Logo' www.mendaki.org.sg/about-mendaki/our-logo accessed 22 September 2018.

the Chinese (Chinese Development Assistance Council or CDAC), Indians (Singapore Indian Development Association or SINDA), and Eurasians (Eurasian Association) are premised on race and are avowedly secular in outlook and disposition. Again, this fusion of race and religion elements in many Malay-Muslim organisations reflects the centrality of and recognition accorded to the Islamic identity as an integral part of the Malay identity in Singapore.

While naturally defensive about the role of such groups within the ethnic landscape, the government has been mindful of the criticisms against the ethnic self-help policy, chief being that it is detrimental to the building of a multiracial society as it accentuates racial and religious differences and separatism. Ethnic self-help groups, while helpful at the micro-level (within the ethnic group), may be detrimental at the macro-level (national integration). They remain a potentially potent symbol of distinctiveness, separateness and the lack of cohesion. The policy of ethnic self-help can also reduce ethnicity to a badge of honour in which ethnic commonality can be mistaken to be primary identifier for Singaporeans. The narrow ethnic identity would have gained precedence over the overarching, common civic and national identity.

IV. Sustaining Pluralist Constitutionalism: Formal and Substantive Equality

Pluralism is a feature found in Singapore's constitutional documents viz the Constitution of the Republic of Singapore, the Independence of Singapore Agreement 1965, and the Republic of Singapore Independence Act. In these founding documents, there is recognition of Singapore's plural make-up along racial, religious, and linguistic lines. The constitutional fact of pluralism is, more importantly, reflected in institutions and norms that the constitutional documents seek to engender. Taken together, they ensure that pluralist constitutionalism is not a mere constitutional fact but also a constitutional reality that is given effect to and consciously sustained. This entails ensuring formal equality in the constitutional provisions and various legislations. At another level, this requires the pursuit of substantive equality which may, at times, be at odds with formal equality.

Unsurprisingly, article 12 of the Singapore Constitution provides for equality before the law and equal protection of the law.[20] It has to be noted that the

---

[20] Article 12 reads as follows:

  (1) All persons are equal before the law and entitled to the equal protection of the law.
  (2) Except as expressly authorised by this Constitution, there shall be no discrimination against citizens of Singapore on the ground only of religion, race, descent or place of birth in any law or in the appointment to any office or employment under a public authority or in the administration of any law relating to the acquisition, holding or disposition of property or the establishing or carrying on of any trade, business, profession, vocation or employment.

framework of article 12 is premised on the individual, not a group, as the bearer of rights. In fact, the schema of the Singapore Constitution is premised on individual rights; group rights are neither explicitly provided for nor implicitly endorsed. This constitutional policy of formal non-discrimination is manifested in the core governing philosophy of meritocracy, a natural corollary of multiracialism, which seeks to promote equal opportunity for all citizens.

Formal equality is characterised most prominently by non-discrimination. To reiterate, equality before the law and equal protection of the law do not mean equal treatment of all persons. Rather, it only requires that like should be treated alike. An individual has a fundamental right to be treated the same as other individuals in like circumstances. Formal equality can be attained superficially either by depriving all persons being compared of a particular benefit, or by conferring the same benefit on all of them. Conversely, individuals in different circumstances are, by definition, not alike. Hence, their treatment, if different from others in different circumstances, does not necessarily run foul of article 12.[21]

The Singapore Constitution's commitment to non-discrimination, particularly on the basis of religion and race, is buttressed in article 12(2). This provision specifies that there shall be no discrimination against Singapore citizens 'on the ground only of religion, race, descent or place of birth' in any law, in any public office or employment, or in any law on the acquisition, holding or disposition of property or the establishing or carrying on of any trade, business, profession, vocation or employment. Put simply, discrimination on the basis of religion, race, descent or place or birth are strictly prohibited, unless expressly authorised by the Constitution. For a multiracial, multi-religious, and multilingual country, the clear lines against discrimination on these attributes are vital in ensuring that pluralism is not a source of division and discord. The provision of constitutionally recognised and protected pluralism cannot be underestimated.

Formal equality merely emphasises procedural fairness without guaranteeing any particular or even the same outcome from a course of equal treatment. On the other hand, substantive equality recognises that laws, policies, and institutional practices put in place in the name of formal equality may be non-discriminatory but may not address the specific needs of certain groups of people. In effect, such formal equality may be indirectly discriminatory, even perpetuating systemic discrimination. To be clear, substantive equality does not seek the equality of outcome but seeks to enhance the equality of opportunity by deliberately

(3) This Article does not invalidate or prohibit—
    (a) any provision regulating personal law; or
    (b) any provision or practice restricting office or employment connected with the affairs of any religion, or of an institution managed by a group professing any religion, to persons professing that religion.

[21] The equality concept has been heavily criticised for its emptiness. However, judicial pronouncements recognise that laws are consistent with formal equality where they embody an intelligible differentia and there is a rational nexus to the legislative object.

providing for better access. Substantive equality in the Singaporean context pays greater attention to the differences between groups and attempts to overcome those differences. It tacitly recognises that groups are in an unequal position because they either face current discrimination (real, apparent, or potential), or that they still bear the consequences of past discrimination. In short, members of the different races may not be able to compete on an equal footing.

So even if equality of opportunity is carefully observed from a procedural dimension, a group (and the individuals from or associated with the group) may not possess the ability or have the means to make use of the opportunity. In other words, the imperative for substantive equality is to promote and ensure the equality of access to opportunity. Substantive equality could also appear to contradict formal equality since the provisions, policies, and institutions created under its auspices would seem to detract from the parity of treatment demanded under formal equality. Substantive equality is, in essence, a broader approach to equality that recognises differences among groups due to prior disadvantages, systemic inequality, and historical developments. It seeks to take into account the contexts that had created inequality. This approach to equality focuses on the outcome and effects of a particular law or action rather than on their equality of the treatment.

Formal and substantive equality serve a complementary role in a multiracial society. For equality to be clothed with meaning and to serve a purposeful function in a heterogeneous society, formal equality alone is grossly inadequate. Pluralist constitutionalism in Singapore is not and cannot be a procedural end (ie, formal equality) in itself but it has to function as a means to a substantive end (substantive equality). Substantive equality may prescribe or permit differential, even apparently unequal treatment, across groups in order to procure the fair participation of their members in areas such as political representation, education, and socio-economic upliftment.

Both formal and substantive equality interrogate meritocracy, another cornerstone of Singapore's pluralist constitutionalism. Meritocracy, with its equal opportunities for all citizens regardless of race and religion, undergirds Singapore's model of multiracialism and the commitment to equality. In theory, meritocracy is indeed a noble principle of governance as it ensures that minorities' rights and interests will be safeguarded and that they would not be discriminated against on account of their ethnicities. However, this assumes that all races are able to take advantage of the equal opportunities which is not necessarily the case in reality.

While the Malay-Muslim community has made much socio-economic progress and now aspires to be a 'community of excellence', it continues to lag behind the other races. Indeed, the past perception of the Malay-Muslim community was a community characterised by weakness and backwardness. The government has been cautious about giving preferential treatment to Malay-Muslims to help the community level up with the other ethnic groups, as affirmative action of any kind could have a negative effect on a community's self-esteem and transmogrify into a debilitating crutch mentality. Yet, the persistence of socio-economic problems within the community can result in the community resorting to particularistic identities distinct from the national identity, which can be detrimental to inter-ethnic harmony and national cohesion. The danger is amplified when socio-economic differentials coincide significantly with ethnic cleavages and persist for generations.

The objective of levelling group differences necessitates treating groups unequally in order to realise substantive equality across the same. Intrinsic to substantive equality is the political judgment by the elected leaders on what substantive equality entails of the majority and minority communities.[22] While formal equality is necessary, there is also the need for societal consensus that it is not sufficient to sustain and nourish the raison d'etre of Singapore.

V. Multiracialism and Inclusive Citizenship

A. Special Position of the Malays

The centrepiece of Singapore's pluralist constitutionalism is encapsulated in article 152 of the Singapore Constitution, which ostensibly legitimises minority claims to ethno-cultural diversity and autonomy in Singapore. In particular, article 152 recognises the 'special position of the Malays' by virtue of their being the indigenous people of Singapore.[23] Article 152(1) states that: 'It shall be the responsibility of the Government constantly to care for the interests of the racial and religious minorities in Singapore'. Article 152(2) states that:

> The Government shall exercise its functions in such manner as to recognize the special position of the Malays, who are the indigenous people of Singapore, and accordingly it shall be the responsibility of the Government to protect, safeguard, support, foster and promote their political, educational, religious, economic, social and cultural interests and the Malay language.

This constitutional fact of the special position of the Malays with the commitment to equality manifested in the principle and requirement of the government of the day having a responsibility to care for the interests of racial and religious minorities predates Singapore's independence.[24] Nonetheless, it is in sync with Singapore's approach to the management of ethnic relations.

---

[22] There is certainly and always has been room for disagreement as to what substantive equality in Singapore entails.

[23] The Singapore Constitution does not define who a Malay is. In contrast, article 160(2) of the Malaysian Constitution defines a 'Malay' as '... a person who professes the religion of Islam, habitually speaks the Malay language, conforms to Malay custom'. On 'the Malays' and 'Malayness', see generally Anthony Milner, *The Malays* (Wiley-Blackwell 2008). See also, Syed Muhd Khairudin Aljunied, 'British Discourses and Malay Identity in Colonial Singapore' (2009) 37(107) *Indonesia and the Malay World* 1.

[24] This commitment to the special position of the Malays was agreed to between the colonial government and the All-Party delegation from Singapore, and incorporated into the preamble of

Singapore's Imperative of Integrative Pluralist Constitutionalism 63

Article 152(2) offers a framework for the development of substantive equality. This, in turn, requires the government through 'deliberate and conscious policy … take concrete steps to give meaning to the special position of the Malays by extending effective and adequate assistance to them' so that the Malay community may 'catch up in the fields of education and economy with [the] other peoples of Singapore'.[25] Substantive equality is also shaped by the need for social harmony, with article 152(2) reflecting the founding leaders' commitment to assuage the Malay minority's fear of dominance and discrimination by the Chinese majority.

In rebutting the notion of racial equality in the Singapore Constitution, Singapore's founding Prime Minister Lee Kuan Yew had stated with characteristic robustness that true racial equality was but an aspiration:

> We explicitly state in our Constitution a duty on behalf of the Government not to treat everybody as equal. It [racial equality] is not reality, it is not practical, it will lead to grave and irreparable damage if we work on that principle. So this was an aspiration. … You suggest to the Malays that we should abolish these provisions in the Constitution and you will have grave disquiet. … The American Constitution does not say that it will treat blacks differently but our Constitution spells out the duty of the Government to treat Malays and other minorities with extra care. … And I thought to myself, perhaps I should bring this House back to earth and remind everybody what is our starting point, what is our base, and if we do not recognise where we started from, and that these are our foundations, we will fail. … Today, 44 years later, we have a Malay community, I believe, at peace, convinced that we are not discriminating against them, convinced that we are including them in our society.[26]

Interpretations and expectations of article 152 differ. Some take the position that the provision requires the government of the day to do all that is necessary, including implementing an affirmation action policy. Others argue that privileged

---

the constitution of the colony of Singapore that granted internal self-government to Singapore. The relevant portion of the preamble of Singapore (Constitution) Order in Council, 1958 (SI No. 1956 of 1958) read:

> And … it is hereby expressly affirmed, that it shall be the responsibility of the Government of Singapore constantly to care for the interests of racial and religious minorities in Singapore, and in particular that it shall be the deliberate and conscious policy of the Government of Singapore at all times to recognise the special position of Malays, who are the indigenous people of the Island and are in most need of assistance, and accordingly, that it shall be the responsibility of the Government of Singapore to protect, safeguard, support, foster and promote their political, educational, religious, economic, social and cultural interests and the Malay language.

[25] Minister of State for Education Inche A. Rahim Ishak, parliamentary debate on the 'Report of Constitutional Commission, 1966,' *Parliamentary Debates Singapore Official Report*, vol 25 (16 March 1967) col 1331. Inche Rahim Ishak added that, 'in extending this assistance, I know that the non-Malays in Singapore are broad-minded enough to sympathise with their Malay brethren and big-hearted enough not to grudge them this assistance'.

[26] Minister Mentor Lee Kuan Yew, parliamentary debate on 'Nation-Building Tenets' motion, *Parliamentary Debates Singapore Official Report*, vol 86 (19 August 2009). This was also Mr Lee's last speech in Parliament.

treatment for the Malays has no place in Singapore's multiracialism as it undermines the meritocratic ideal, and foments a potentially debilitating crutch mentality within the Malay community.[27]

It is generally accepted that article 152 is directory and non-justiciable, rather than mandatory and rights bearing.[28] On its construction, article 152 does not confer any specific right and also precludes rights-based protection.[29] In extracurial remarks, then Chief Justice Chan Sek Keong likened article 152 to the Indian Constitution's Directive Principles of State Policy.[30] Such a provision elevates the principle of minority protection into one of salutary constitutional importance but not amounting to a constitutional guarantee with the force of law.[31] As such, article 152 is more of a symbolic shield, rather than a sword, that minorities can assert against the government of the day if it fails to care adequately for them.[32]

In the public discourse on race, the description of or reference to the Malays as the 'indigenous people' is hardly used. In comparison with Malaysia, Australia, Canada, or the US, there is little traction in Singapore for the indigeneity discourse. Indeed, that discourse holds little constitutional significance in right-sizing equality. The virtue of article 152 and related provisions in the Singapore Constitution is that they constitutionally recognise the ethnic minorities in Singapore, including their having distinct cultures, religions, and languages.[33] This recognition of minorities as equal citizens helps ensure that the basic substantive rights of citizenship are honoured. They include the right of membership in a nation-state expressed through the right to be recognised by others as an equal, treated by the same standards and values, and accorded the same level of respect and dignity as all other members of that community.

---

[27] SM Huang-Thio, 'Constitutional Discrimination under the Malaysian Constitution' (1964) 6 Malayan Law Review 1.

[28] Kevin YL Tan, 'The Legal and Institutional Framework and Issues of Multiculturalism in Singapore' in Lai Ah Eng (ed), *Beyond Rituals and Riots: Ethnic Pluralism and Social Cohesion in Singapore* (Institute of Policy Studies and Eastern Universities Press 2004) 102–104.

[29] See further Jaclyn Ling-Chien Neo, 'The Protection of Minorities and the Constitution: A Judicious Balance?' in Li-ann Thio and Kevin YL Tan (eds), *Evolution of a Revolution: Forty Years of the Singapore Constitution* (Routledge 2008).

[30] Chan Sek Keong, 'Culture and Legal Practice,' (Keynote speech by the Chief Justice at the International Bar Association Conference, Singapore, 15 October 2007). Singapore only signed on to the International Convention on the Elimination of All Forms of Racial Discrimination (CERD) in October 2015.

[31] Although the Directive Principles of State Policy are not enforceable by any Indian court, the Indian State is duty-bound to apply the principles in making laws: see art 37, and Pt IV generally of the Indian Constitution.

[32] Eugene K B Tan, '"Special position of the Malays": It's a shield, not a sword,' *The Straits Times* (Singapore, 25 August 2009) A18.

[33] Charles Taylor aptly puts it: 'Due recognition is not just a courtesy we owe people. It is a vital human need': See *Multiculturalism and 'The Politics of Recognition': An Essay* (Princeton University Press 1992) 26.

B. Limited Legal Pluralism and Sensitivity to Religious Equality and Pluralism

In April 2014, Pew Research Centre ranked Singapore as the world's most religiously diverse country or territory.[34] Public policy and legislation in a multi-religious society like Singapore must reflect the value – and belief – systems of citizens, including religious and secular ones. This task is fraught with difficulties, not least in ensuring that no particular set of religious beliefs is being discriminated or preferred.

Article 15 of the Constitution protects the freedom of religion. Article 15(1) guarantees that, 'Every person has the right to profess and practise his religion and to propagate it'. There is the implied equality of all religions in Singapore, and there is no official or state religion in Singapore. However, the separation of religion and state is not prescribed in the Singapore Constitution.

Given the religious plurality, secularism is a cardinal principle of political governance in Singapore. In Singapore's context, secularism is broadly understood as the governance principle of separating religion and state, and of the state being neutral vis-à-vis the various religious faiths and between religion and non-religion. However, secularism does not mandate metaphysical scepticism, and the Singapore government does not demonstrate such scepticism.

A corollary to article 152, article 153 of the Constitution provides for limited legal pluralism, applying specifically to the Muslim community. It states that, 'The Legislature shall by law make provision for regulating Muslim religious affairs and for constituting a Council to advise the President in matters relating to the Muslim religion'.[35] Subsequently, in 1966, Parliament enacted the Administration of Muslim Law Act (AMLA) to regulate Muslim religious affairs, including the establishment of *Majlis Ugama Islam Singapura* (MUIS, or the Islamic Religious Council of Singapore) to advise on matters relating to Islam in Singapore and to establish a Syariah Court.[36] Muslims in Singapore are governed by Islamic law in matters of personal law such as marriage, divorce, and succession. Such an arrangement is not afforded to the other religions.[37]

---

[34] Pew Research Centre, 'Global Religious Diversity: Half of the Most Religiously Diverse Countries are in Asia-Pacific Region' (*Pew Forum*, 4 April 2014) www.pewforum.org/2014/04/04/global-religious-diversity/ accessed 22 September 2018.
[35] Article 153 is the only constitutional provision where a religion is specifically mentioned.
[36] Administration of Muslim Law Act (Cap 3, 2009 Revised Edition) (hereinafter "AMLA").
[37] There are a number of primary and subsidiary legislative provisions relating to the personal law of other faith communities. For instance, the Prisons Regulations (Cap 247, Rg 2, 2002 Revised Edition) reg 103(2) provides that Jewish prisoners may not be compelled to work on Saturdays if they claim exemption and they may also keep such festival days as may be allowed by the government. Similarly, reg 103(3) of the Prisons Regulations allows Muslim prisoners to observe the fast of Ramadan and to labour at reduced task during the fast.

As highlighted earlier, although Singapore adopts a civic conception of citizenship, it also urges a conscious formation and sustenance of distinctive ethnic identities of the majority and minority communities. This is amplified by article 12(3)(a) of the Constitution, which states that article 12 (the equal protection provision) does not invalidate or prohibit any provision regulating personal law. There are a number of primary and subsidiary legislative provisions relating to personal law. While most of them relate to Islamic law, there is also recognition of the religious sensitivities and requirements of other minority communities. Indeed, the government cannot legislate against the interests of the racial and religious minorities without being subjected to scrutiny under either article 12 or Part VII of the Constitution.

Put simply, multiracialism is a de facto constitutionally entrenched obligation, manifested through pluralist constitutionalism that employs both formal and substantive equality. Formal equality serves to ensure that there is no overt discrimination. Substantive equality serves to endow equality with purpose and meaning and thus avoid formal equality becoming an unwitting agent or conduit for continued disparities between groups.

The various groups' ethnic identities, cultures and religions are neither explicitly encouraged nor are they suppressed. The vast majority of Malays (99.6%) are Muslims. The racial (Malay) and religious (Muslim) identities are often conflated and coterminous in official discourse, resulting in a top-down enforced reduction of individual and sub-group differences within the Malay-Muslim community, and the convenient tendency to treat Malays (a race) and Muslims (a religion) as a monolithic entity. In turn, this double bond of race and faith inevitably nurtures stronger Malay-Muslim community self-consciousness.

Although the linkage with article 152 of the Singapore Constitution was never asserted by the government, the (Malay-)Muslim community enjoys a semblance of preferential treatment which does not have any distorting effect on national policy. Besides being governed by Syariah law in personal matters,[38] the community enjoys free tertiary education (qualified through means-testing in 1989), state support for various aspects of its religious life, including the establishment of a statutory board to advise the government on matters relating to the Muslim religion in Singapore, a mosque-building programme[39] and the *haj* (pilgrimage to Mecca), and the appointment of a Minister-in-charge of Muslim Affairs in the Cabinet to assist in the governance of a significant and important minority.

---

[38] Since August 1999, following amendments to the Supreme Court of Judicature Act and AMLA (n 36), the (civil and secular) Family Court has concurrent jurisdiction in selected areas.

[39] The mosque-building programme provides for state land to be set aside for a mosque in every public housing estate, and for every Muslim working person in Singapore to make a monthly contribution to a central fund with the automatic payroll deduction done by a government agency (the Central Provident Fund Board). For more details, see Anthony Green, *Continuing the Legacy: 30 Years of the Mosque Building Fund in Singapore* (Majlis Ugama Islam Singapura 2007).

C. Giving Voice to Pluralist Constitutionalism: Malay as the National Language and the Bilingual Imperative

Given the various ascribed mother tongues in Singapore's linguistic landscape, Singapore's pluralist constitutional approach not only recognises this linguistic diversity but also gives a symbolic pride of place to the mother tongue of the indigenous Malay community.[40] This co-existence manifests both formal and substantive equality. More crucially, the co-existence also recognises the Malays as the indigenous people of Singapore, and making Malay the national language was a critical gesture of state affirmation of the Malay minority's place in a new society in the throes of independence and being sensitive to the geopolitical realities.

Although used by a minority of the population, Malay is the sole national language.[41] Article 153A of the Singapore Constitution prescribes the official languages (English, Malay, Mandarin, and Tamil) and national language, with Malay having the distinction of being both the national and one of the official languages.[42] Singapore's national anthem, *Majulah Singapura* ('Onward Singapore') is composed and renditioned in Malay. Similarly, Singapore's national motto, also Majulah Singapura, is rendered in Malay and incorporated into the national coat of arms. Further, the pre-independence practice of military parade commands in Malay continues. Making Malay the national language is a symbolic political gesture recognising the Malays as the indigenous people of Singapore and the geopolitical realities in Singapore's locale.[43] In a nod to substantive equality, since independence, English has been the language of education, commerce and government. English is the surrogate lingua franca of Singaporeans as it did not provide any racial group, including the ethnic Chinese majority, with any ostensible linguistic advantage.

Bilingualism is a cornerstone of Singapore's language ideology and policy; it gives effect to formal equality and substantive equality. Prior to the advent of an indigenous national school system, the education system was fragmented into English and the vernacular streams of Chinese, Malay, and Indian.[44] It was only

---

[40] For a fuller discussion, see Eugene K B Tan, 'The Multilingual State in Search of the Nation: The Language Discourse in Singapore's Nation-Building' in Lee Hock Guan and Leo Suryadinata (eds), *Language, Nation and Development in Southeast Asia* (Institute of Southeast Asian Studies 2007).

[41] Few non-Malay Singaporeans today can speak the Malay language. In his *Memoirs of a Mendicant Professor* (Chatto and Windus 1969), 120–121, DJ Enright described Malay in Singapore as the 'nominal' national language used as a 'linguistic red herring to distract attention from the real problem, or the real problem as reflected in the rivalry between the English and Chinese languages'. David Brown observes, '[T]he Malay minority [in Singapore] has been depicted as the symbolic ethnic core of the nation, but Malay culture continues to be marginal in the emergent Singaporean national culture': David Brown, 'Ethnic and Nationalist Politics in Southeast Asia' in Mark Beeson (ed), *Contemporary Southeast Asia* (Palgrave Macmillan 2009) 145.

[42] This provision reproduces s 7 of the Republic of Singapore Independence Act.

[43] Malay is, of course, the *lingua franca* of Singapore's immediate neighbours.

[44] The British colonial authorities left each community to structure their own education system. Colonial education policy in British Malaya resulted in 'different perceptions of these different groups

68 *Eugene K B Tan*

with self-government in 1959 and independence from Malaysia in 1965 that the political imperative to create an indigenous and integrated national school system united by a common language policy acquired added urgency.[45]

Rather than the common understanding of literacy in two languages, bilingualism in Singapore is configured on the study of the English language plus a mother tongue. Between 1959 and 1965, bilingualism often included the learning of Malay, with either English or Mandarin or Tamil depending the student's language stream. This was changed in 1966. Since then, 'mother tongue' has a particularistic definition: 'the symbolic language of the group of one's paternal ancestry, rather than the language of one's primary socialization, or one's "native speech".'[46] It is a formulaic definition, founded on the state's rigid CMIO racial classification.[47]

Bilingualism in Singapore seeks to enable students to maintain their cultural links while being equipped with skills to function in a knowledge-based economy.[48] The economic dimension looms large and is manifested in English being the first language in national schools. The political imperatives of social engineering ensure that meticulous and centralised language planning remains a focus of government's efforts in the governance of a multiracial, multilingual society.

Taken together, formal equality of the mother tongues is evident with substantive equality a key feature that ensures that the inherent linguistic diversity does not become a source of keenly-contested difference. These manifestations of recognition and accommodation help give credence to the multiracialism ethos as well as to secure popular support for Singapore's approach to pluralist constitutionalism. This is further demonstrated in the next Part through constitutional innovations that are aimed at ensuring plurality and representation of the major races in key public institutions such as the legislature and the presidency. Substantive equality is prioritised ahead of formal equality in ensuring that the electoral process contributes to ethnic integration.

---

towards each other'. See Keith Watson, 'Rulers and Ruled: Racial Perceptions, Curriculum and Schooling in Colonial Malaysia and Singapore' in JA Morgan (ed), *The Imperial Curriculum: Racial Images and Education in the British Colonial Experience* (Routledge 1993).

[45] This process started tentatively with the 1956 All-Party Committee on Chinese Education. In its report, it noted that 'Malay is important because of its regional importance …'. The committee went so far as to recommend bilingual education in the primary stage followed by trilingualism in the secondary stage: see the *Report of the All-Party Committee of the Singapore Legislative Assembly on Chinese Education* (Government Printing Office 1956).

[46] Nirmala Srirekam PuroShotam, *Negotiating Language, Constructing Race: Disciplining Race in Singapore* (Mouton de Gruyter 1998) 49–50.

[47] Indeed, the government's efforts to bond the heterogeneous Chinese community necessitated a radical remaking of the meaning of mother tongue. To enforce the invented pan-ethnic mother tongue for the Chinese community, the linguistic homogenisation of the ethnic Chinese was a prerequisite. This change required making Mandarin the mother tongue of the Chinese-Singaporeans and marginalising the Chinese 'dialects'. This mandated officially consigning the mother tongues of the various ethnic Chinese sub-groups such as Hokkien, Cantonese, Teochew, Hakka, etc, as 'dialects' and thus excluded from government support.

[48] *Education Statistics Digest 2002* (Singapore Ministry of Education 2002) v.

VI. Electoral Integration: Ensuring Political Representation of Racial Minorities

A. Group Representation Constituency

The Group Representation Constituency (GRC) is Singapore's legislative innovation at advancing pluralist constitutionalism in the political arena. This mode of electoral integration leverages on the concept of substantive equality. The overarching concern is that the political institutions must be and seen to be representative of Singapore's racial composition. Electoral integration operates by incentivising politicians, in the quest to secure as many votes as possible to win, to reach out and establish a broad-base appeal that transcends ethnic lines. Thus, electoral integration aims at designing a system of healthy political competition that facilitates the development of cross-cutting cleavages and encourages inter-ethnic cooperation while making racial chauvinism and extremism politically counter-productive. This approach lends critical support to and emphasises the virtues of moderation, racial non-partisanship, and the development of inter-ethnic trust and cooperation.

The GRC scheme was created 'to ensure the representation in Parliament of Members from the Malay, Indian and other minority communities.'[49] First implemented in the 1988 general election, the GRC ensures the adequate representation in Parliament of elected legislators from the Malay, Indian and other minority communities. The government had claimed that the electorate, especially young voters, voted along racial lines, preferring 'candidates who were best suited to their own needs without being sufficiently aware of the need to return a racially balanced slate of candidates'.[50] This supposed racial bias in the electoral process would particularly threaten the representation of the ethnic Malay community, the most significant minority race community. Hence, the law also prescribes that three-fifths of the total number of GRCs are to be designated constituencies where at least one of the candidates in every group shall be a person belonging to the Malay community.[51]

The government argued that the GRC system ensured that the minority races' needs, concerns, and views would not be ignored or neglected in a Chinese-majority polity. In January 1988, at the introduction of the GRC proposal, then First Deputy Prime Minister Goh Chok Tong disclosed that the then Prime Minister Lee Kuan Yew and he had first discussed in July 1982 the need to secure

---

[49] Art 39A(1), Singapore Constitution.
[50] *Singapore Parliament Reports*, vol 50, no 3 (11 January 1988) cols 181–192. Section 78D of the Parliamentary Elections Act (Cap 218, 2007 Revised Edition) also prohibits exit polls on polling day (hereinafter "PEA").
[51] See PEA (n 50) s 8A(3) read with s 8(1)(b)(i).

a multi-racial Parliament. The voting trend, if it continued, would result in the under-representation of Malays in Parliament. Goh Chok Tong explained:

> ... It is make-belief to pretend that race and language do not affect voter preferences ... Paradoxical as it may seem, to ensure that multi-racialism succeeds in Singapore, we have to openly recognize that race does play a part in politics. Loyalty to one's own community, to race, to one's religion and language is stronger than loyalty to the nation, particularly if that nation is a new one and has many races .... For Singapore to remain a beautiful, peaceful country for many more generations, it is wise of us to strengthen the political framework before it is weakened by disillusionment, despondency and despair when one community finds itself thrown out of Parliament by the electoral system.[52]

Under the GRC scheme, voters elect in a proportionately enlarged electoral district, on a 'one person, one vote' basis, a team of Members of Parliament (MPs) rather than an individual MP. A political party contesting in a GRC has to field a multi-member team of which at least one member must be from a designated minority race. The government argued that it had to take the lead in entrenching multiracialism. At the third reading of the Bill, First Deputy Prime Minister Goh remarked:

> [Our GRC/Team MPs concept] is benevolent. The constitutional change is initiated by the majority to directly benefit the minority communities without any direct benefit to itself. It is our way of sharing our future together, of giving Singaporeans, whether Malays, Indians, Chinese, Eurasians or Others, that feeling of belonging to a single nation ... On its own, it [the GRC] will not ensure success in building up or strengthening our multi-racial society. It is a formal institutional arrangement. For us to succeed, we must have the same spirit as the Swiss to search for consensus, to work through informal as much as formal arrangements, to make every citizen, whichever community, he belongs to, feel that he is a Singaporean.[53]

Given this apparent preferential treatment in favour of the minorities, Parliament explicitly provided for Article 39A(3) of the Constitution. This deeming provision states that no laws relating to the GRC scheme are invalid for being inconsistent with the equal protection clause under Article 12 or be considered a 'differentiating measure' under Article 68.[54]

Unsurprisingly, critics argue that the GRC scheme is designed to stem the ruling People's Action Party's electoral decline, and extend its electoral dominance.[55] In its idealised conception, the political parties competing in a GRC

---

[52] ibid.

[53] *Singapore Parliament Reports*, vol 51, no 1 (11 January 1988) cols 27–53.

[54] The GRC scheme is potentially inconsistent with art 12 on two counts: (1) That the scheme 'prefers' the minority races by giving them a designated number of parliamentary seats; (2) A vote cast in a multi-member electoral district is 'worth more' than that in a single-member constituency (SMC): A vote in a GRC could place up to six MPs while a vote in a SMC elects only one.

[55] Li-ann Thio, 'Choosing Representatives: Singapore Does it Her Way' in Graham Hassall and Cheryl Saunders (eds), *The People's Representatives: Electoral Systems in the Asia-Pacific Region* (Allen & Unwin 1997); Jinshan Li and Jørge Elklit, 'The Singapore General Election 1997: Campaigning Strategy, Results, and Analysis' (1999) 18(2) Electoral Studies 199; Li-ann Thio, 'Lex rex *or* rex lex? Competing Conceptions of the Rule of Law in Singapore' (2002) 20 UCLA Pacific Basin Law Journal 1.

have to portray a multi-racial orientation that appeals to the ethnic Chinese and non-Chinese voters alike in order to secure as many votes as possible. Taking an overtly racial line would risk alienating valuable vote banks within the electorate. Thus, the GRC scheme can actualise moderation in electoral politics if it successfully moulds electoral behaviour by the political parties, candidates and voters. However, while the GRC scheme ensures that there will be adequate parliamentary minority representation, it may well also 'institutionalise and rigidify divisions that have no substantive purpose other than formalising consciousness of "difference"'.[56,57]

GRCs are now the dominant electoral division, having expanded dramatically since its introduction. In 1988, each GRC team comprised three MPs, and just under half of all elected parliamentary seats was for the GRCs. By 1997, the size of a GRC team had increased to either five or six MPs, and the GRCs constituted almost 90% of parliamentary seats.[58] Table 1 shows the rapid pace at which GRCs became the majority of elected parliamentary seats although there has been a deliberate move to reduce the number of MPs per GRC since 2011.

Table 1 Distribution of SMC and GRC parliamentary seats, 1988–2015[59]

Date of General Election	Total No. of Parliamentary Seats	No. of SMC Seats (%)	No. of GRC Seats (%)	Make-up of GRCs / Average no. MPs per GRC
3 Sep 1988	81	42 (51.9%)	39 (48.1%)	Thirteen 3-member GRCs / 3.0
31 Aug 1991	81	21 (25.9)	60 (74.1)	Fifteen 4-member GRCs / 4.0
2 Jan 1997	83	9 (10.8)	74 (89.2)	Fifteen GRCs: five 4-member, six 5-member, and four 6-member / 4.93
3 Nov 2001	84	9 (10.7)	75 (89.3)	Fourteen GRCs: nine 5-member & five 6-member / 5.38

(continued)

---

[56] Graham Hassall, 'Systems of Representation in Asia-Pacific: A Comparative Analysis' in Graham Hassall and Cheryl Saunders (eds), *The People's Representatives: Electoral Systems in the Asia-Pacific Region* (Allen & Unwin 1997) 16.

[57] While the constitutional intent behind the GRC is praise-worthy, the manner in which the ruling party has sought to capitalise on the GRC scheme to maintain its political dominance can reinforce the perceived subordinate role of the minority races in the electoral process: see Eugene KB Tan, 'Multiracialism Engineered: The Limits of Electoral and Spatial Integration in Singapore' (2005) 4(4) Ethnopolitics 413.

[58] Section 8A(1A) of the PEA (n 50) mandates a minimum of eight SMCs.

[59] Source: Author's compilation based on information available at the Singapore Elections Department website.

Table 1 *(Continued)*

Date of General Election	Total No. of Parliamentary Seats	No. of SMC Seats (%)	No. of GRC Seats (%)	Make-up of GRCs / Average no. MPs per GRC
6 May 2006	84	9 (10.7)	75 (89.3)	Fourteen GRCs: nine 5-member & five 6-member / 5.38
7 May 2011	87	12 (13.8)	75 (86.2)	Fifteen GRCs: two 4-member, eleven 5-member & two 6-member / 5.0
11 Sep 2015	89	13 (14.6)	76 (85.4)	Sixteen GRCs: six 4-member, eight 5-member & two 6-member / 4.75

B. Reserved Presidential Elections

Proponents of electoral integration champion an electoral system that generates incentives for moderate behaviour and encourages crosscutting loyalties in a heterogeneous society.[60] As discussed above, the GRC system is a significant departure from the classic simple plurality electoral system that was the hallmark of Singapore's Westminster form of government. It was Singapore's sui generis attempt at sustaining multiracialism through electoral integration by overlaying formal equality with substantive equality in the electoral process. This approach to infuse substantive equality in the structure of political power was replicated in the reserved presidential election, which was conducted for the first time for candidates from the Malay community in September 2017. A citizen's positive identification with the nation-state follows from political representation. Individuals are more likely to embrace the nationalist narrative where they have meaningful exchange relationships with the nation-state. Conversely, there is less pride if a citizen's ethnic group lacks representation in the corridors of power.[61]

The reserved presidential election is the most significant re-engineering to Singapore's constitutional architecture since the introduction of the Elected Presidency (EP) in 1991. The institution of an elected president was born out of the fears of a popularly elected 'rogue government' that could send Singapore

---

[60] Donald L Horowitz, *Ethnic Groups in Conflict* (University of California Press 1985); Donald L Horowitz, 'Electoral Systems: A Primer for Decision Makers' (2003) 14(4) Journal of Democracy 115.

[61] Andreas Wimmer, 'Power and Pride: National Identity and Ethnopolitical Inequality around the World' (2017) 69(4) World Politics 605.

down the road to ruin through populist measures that are financially unsustainable and appointments of cronies to key leadership positions. In the context of Singapore's one-party dominant parliamentary system of government, this need for ample and robust checks and balances cannot be taken lightly. Introduced in 1991, the EP system does not, in any way, detract from the fact that executive power and responsibility resides with the Cabinet.[62] Under the Singapore Constitution, the EP is not a separate, countervailing power to the elected government. The EP's role has been likened to a 'second key,' a watchdog, and a custodian. Through his custodial powers, the EP provides an additional layer of checks and balances, which did not exist prior to 1991, in specifically defined critical areas including the drawdown of past national reserves, key appointments in the Public Service, corruption investigations, preventive detentions under the Internal Security Act, and restraining orders under the Maintenance of Religious Harmony Act. Where the EP institution does not fare as well as its ceremonial predecessor is for the office of the Head of State as a unifying institution in a polyglot society to be rotated among the different races.

In 2016, Prime Minister Lee Hsien Loong tasked the Constitutional Commission, chaired by Chief Justice Sundaresh Menon, with reviewing selected aspects of the elected presidency, including 'ensuring that minorities have the chance to be periodically elected to Presidential office'. After public consultations and hearings, the Commission proposed a hiatus-triggered reserved election mechanism to safeguard representation from minority racial groups. Starting from the premise that the presidency has a 'crucial symbolic role' and 'symbolises and embodies the nation itself,' the Commission stated in its report that there was a 'pressing need' to ensure that 'no ethnic group is shut out of the Presidency ... lest the office of President lose its vitality as a symbol of the nation's unity'.[63] The Commission was not in favour of making the office mechanically rotational among the major races, which can affect the legitimacy of the president's decisions in the exercise of his custodial powers. The government accepted the Commission's recommendation that the reserved election proviso be activated only after there has not been a president from a major racial community for five continual terms, or 30 years.[64] Singapore's first President Yusof Ishak, a Malay, died in office in 1970. There had been no Malay president until Halimah Yacob's election in 2017 where she was the only presidential aspirant eligible to contest in the first reserved election.[65]

The reserved election helps ensure that the presidency is not only accessible, but is seen to be accessible to persons from all the major racial communities.

---

[62] Prior to the EP, the President was appointed by Parliament and exercised mainly ceremonial powers.

[63] See *Report of the Constitutional Commission* (2016).

[64] White Paper, *The Review of Specific Aspects of the Elected Presidency: The Constitution of the Republic of Singapore (Amendment) Bill* (2016).

[65] President Halimah Yacob is also Singapore's first woman Head of State.

The Commission categorised the relevant racial groups into three: Chinese, Malay, and Indian and other communities. The mechanism works as follows: when a member from any racial group has not occupied the President's office after five continuous terms (each full term is six years), the next presidential election will be reserved for a candidate from that racial group.[66]

In its report, the Commission emphasised that candidates in a reserved election will also have to meet the stringent eligibility criteria, similar to an open election. However, as a reserved election is not open to candidates from other races, a legitimate argument can be made that the meritocratic principle is not exercised in its full measure.

The presidential election, with the open and reserved election mechanisms, is another attempt at making pluralist constitutionalism work meaningfully. It combines formal equality in open elections, where eligible candidates from any race can contest, with substantive equality in reserved elections where only eligible candidates from a specified racial community – which has not been represented for five electoral terms – can contest.

The reserved election proposal was never popular right from the outset. Prime Minister Lee Hsien Loong noted that the reserved election 'would be unpopular and cost us votes'.[67] For the government, their premise was that Singapore has 'not arrived at an ideal state of accepting people of a different race' even where progress have been made 'but it is a work in progress'. He added that Singaporeans 'should not be shy to acknowledge that in Singapore, the majority is making a special effort to ensure that minorities enjoy full and equal treatment'. In ensuring that minorities regularly have a chance to be the President, the reserved election would strengthen multiracialism: '[I]t is one important symbol of what Singapore stands for, and a declaration of what we aspire to be. It is a reminder to every citizen, especially the Chinese majority race, that there is a role for every community in Singapore'.

The reserved election can be regarded as an inter-generational safeguard for minority representation. It seeks to pre-emptively manage the potential issue of race marginalisation and to safeguard the outcome of having a person from every major race for the Head of State office. There is no doubt that having a minority President, elected through a popular mandate and exercising custodial powers, is a powerful statement of multiracialism for a Chinese-majority country. Similarly, Singapore would have attained racial nirvana if the ethnic Chinese community needs a reserved election to have one of their own become president. The reserved election mechanism could, however, lead to potential problems.

---

[66] In addition to obtaining from the Presidential Elections Committee a certificate of eligibility, a presidential hopeful must submit to the Community Committee a community declaration stating that he considers himself to be a member of a specified racial community.

[67] Quotes in this paragraph are taken from Prime Minister Lee Hsien Loong's remarks at the People's Association Kopi Talk at Ci Yuan Community Club, 23 September 2017. The title of his remarks was, 'Race, Multiracialism and Singapore's Place in the World'.

There is the need to guard against the reserved election being (or being seen as) a vehicle for affirmative action, which Singapore has strenuously avoided all these years. A race-based election can also give rise to the belief that a racial community has a legal entitlement or right for one of its own to be elected president. Will there be subsequent expectations that other public offices be rotated among the races?

The reserved election approach also presupposes that only a minority race President can be a symbol of Singapore's multiracialism. However, it is not their race that endowed past presidents as symbols of Singapore's multiracialism and national unity. Rather, it was their practice and promotion of multiracialism that infused into the presidency the spirit and soul of multiracialism.

Furthermore, a reserved election might just reinforce the alleged tendency of Singaporeans to vote along racial lines. Voters might see no necessity or urgency to vote for an electable minority candidate since the system will provide for a minority president in regular intervals if one is not elected in non-reserved elections. However, will Singaporeans compromise their own best interests and elect someone who is not deserving simply because they are of the same race?

The above discussion does not at all deny that race, religion, and language remain fault-lines in Singaporean society. Neither do the above arguments underestimate that these markers of ethnicity can induce and arouse primordial loyalties. But, as a principle of governance, these centrifugal forces should not be pandered to, especially when Singapore is not a deeply divided society in urgent need of symbolic approaches. If Singaporeans do vote along racial lines, then the urgent task is to sensitise Singaporeans to shed that behaviour so that minority candidates can compete on an even footing with ethnic Chinese candidates. The solution is not to give in to the racial discrimination.

No amount of constitutional engineering can remove a racial or even a racist electoral behaviour. Instead, nudges and 'incentives' can be provided for candidates and the electorate to think of how their electoral behaviour and their votes can entrench multiracialism and for their self-interest. Such a consideration should go into a voter's assessment of a candidate's overall merit. Values such as multiracialism, meritocracy, integrity, and the democratic engagement and active citizenry must continue to be nurtured so that they can stand Singapore in good stead as she strives to create a system of governance that is robust, relevant, and resilient. Pluralist constitutionalism, with substantive equality at its core, has to remain fit for purpose.

VII. Powering Pluralist Constitutionalism: Interests Rather than Rights

The Singapore State strives to scrupulously adhere to a non-racial orientation in governance. This is complemented by Singapore's pluralist constitutionalism eschewing a rights-based approach. As would be evident by now, constitutional safeguards for the ethnic minorities are structured on the basis of interests rather than rights. Thus, accommodations and preferences and the like, when provided, are carefully structured to avoid any sense of entitlement or legal rights. Nonetheless, the law is greatly relied upon to maintain a strict regime in matters of race and religion.[68] Furthermore, the government cannot legislate against the interests of the racial and religious minorities without being subjected to both judicial scrutiny under either article 12 or Part VII of the Constitution and strenuous political and societal opposition.

To reiterate, multiracialism is a constitutionally entrenched obligation. The Presidential Council of Minority Rights (PCMR), a constitutional organ, was also established as a commitment to the multiracial ethos.[69] While there are fundamental liberties provided for under the Constitution, these liberties proceed on the premise that the individual, rather than a community, is the bearer of such rights.[70] The Singapore Constitution is explicitly framed on the premise of individual rights. The 1966 Constitutional Commission's report noted:

> [T]he best way and most appropriate way of safeguarding the rights of the racial, linguistic and religious minorities in the Republic would be specially to entrench in the Constitution the fundamental rights of both the individual and the citizen (which would include prohibition against discriminatory treatment on the ground only of race, descent, place of origin or religion).[71]

Notably, even as article 152 seeks to protect the minorities, the provision does not use 'right' or 'rights', instead 'interest(s)' is adopted. While found in the Constitution no less, article 152 ought to be construed as being political, rather than legal, in substance. The special position of the Malays does not amount to the conferral of 'special rights' on them, as is the case in Malaysia. In addition, the constitutional exhortation to the government to care for racial and religious minorities is not regarded as providing the constitutional basis for affirmative action policies. As such, article 152 has not been a source of significant contestation or disaffection. In part, this even-handed and consistent approach in the management of ethnic relations in Singapore has not only managed the expectations of the various communities but has also set the tone for ethnic relations.

---

[68] There are many coercive legal instruments in the statute books allowing the government to act swiftly and strongly, and also pre-emptively, against real and apparent threats to ethnic stability.

[69] The PCMR has the general function of considering and reporting on 'matters affecting persons of any racial or religious community in Singapore' as may be referred to the Council by Parliament or the government. Its particular function is to draw attention to any Bill or to any subsidiary legislation if the Council deems them to be a differentiating measure. See, generally, Pt VII of the Constitution. A differentiating measure is 'any measure which is, or is likely in its practical application to be, disadvantageous to persons of any racial or religious community and not equally disadvantageous to persons of other such communities, either directly by prejudicing persons of that community or indirectly by giving advantage to persons of another community' (art 68, Singapore Constitution). To date, there has been no negative report by the PCMR.

[70] Part IV of the Singapore Constitution cf see discussion on Singapore in Joshua Castellino and Elvira Dominguez Redondo, *Minority Rights in Asia: A Comparative Legal Analysis* (OUP 2006) 193–236.

[71] *1966 Constitutional Commission Report* (n 6) para 11.

The management of ethnic relations pivots on the policy of balancing interests rather than an emphasis on rights entitlement. The interests of the minorities have to be balanced against the interests of the majority ethnic Chinese community, and vice-versa. In turn, this entails responsibility on the part of all key stakeholders in not pushing excessively for their community's interests, and for the government to always remain impartial vis-à-vis the different communities. Prime Minister Lee Hsien Loong noted that in Singapore, 'the minority community can live its own life, its own way of life, practice its faith to the maximum extent possible, and not be oppressed or to be marginalised by the majority community'. He also said:

> In fact, wherever possible, we lean in favour of the minority communities in order to give them an extra help, in order that they can participate in the success of the nation and to be integrated. So whether it is education with Mendaki, whether it is mosque building programme, whether it is through other social programmes which we have, where many of the beneficiaries are Malay Muslims, this is what the Government has done. ...
>
> But if we are going to do this [a multiracial society], we have to do this in a broad and informal way. We cannot take it issue by issue; *we cannot take it in terms of rights and entitlements*. We cannot go on basis of what is either the rules or the instruction manuals, or the laws or the Constitution, and try to find a legal interpretation on that issue and press that regardless, and to the possibility of detriment to the overall progress of the communities; of our harmony and of the overall space we have been able to carve out for the minority communities in Singapore, and create for the minority communities in Singapore. It's an approach which has worked for us. We are much more integrated than we were. I think compared to many other societies, we are doing much better. But it is an approach which we have to continue to work at maintaining. And if we are going to have anything happen which can change the status quo, we want to make sure that the change takes place gradually and for the better. ... So it's best that we evolve as we go forward, take it gradually, step by step.[72]

With the centrality of 'interests', the management of ethnic relations in Singapore has cohered around the careful policy of balancing interests without resorting to a language of rights entitlement.

VIII. Conclusion

> We have to know our blind spots, and make a special effort to ensure our minority communities feel welcomed and valued in Singapore.[73]

As part of the post-colonial nation-building project, pluralist constitutionalism in Singapore is sustained by the abiding and conscious avoidance of a group

---

[72] Prime Minister Lee Hsien Loong's remarks to the media after the closed-door dialogue with the Malay/Muslim community (25 January 2014) <www.pmo.gov.sg/newsroom/prime-minister-lee-hsien-loongs-remarks-media-malay-after-closed-door-dialogue> accessed 9 August 2018 (emphasis mine).

[73] HL Lee, 'Race, Multiculturalism and Singapore's Place' (n 67).

rights-based legal regime in the management of ethnic issues. Interests, duties and responsibility – rather than rights and entitlement – constitute the de facto language of citizenship, wherein the larger good of the state and society takes ultimate precedence. The goal of pluralist constitutionalism in Singapore is the mutual accommodation of the different races and the integration, but not the assimilation, of the component races.

This approach to the management of the ethnic relations has avoided affirmative action even in the quest to uplift the minorities. Pluralist constitutionalism has facilitated the commitment towards the imperative of racial equality at both the formal and substantive levels, wherein the national effort towards equal opportunity is part of the Singaporean multiracial ethos. Looking ahead, the effort has to cohere around increasing the access to opportunity for the minority groups. Singapore remains a work-in-progress as it seeks to attain the aspiration of 'one united people, regardless of race, language or religion,' an exhortation in the national pledge.

As society evolves, there will be more diversity of views as to how to ensure equality, formally and substantively, among the different races. The debates over the reserved presidential election indicate that efforts in Singapore at refreshing multiracialism, leavening meritocracy, and keeping pluralist constitutionalism relevant will have to be sensitive to public sentiments and be more inclusive.

Singapore's constitutional experience vis-a-vis a multi-ethnic polity highlights how pluralism is accommodated within the constitutional framework is very much a product of socio-legal and political recognition. Article 152 of the Singapore Constitution is a constitutional provision that is a shield (used reactively), as opposed to a sword (used proactively). Consequently, the constitutional posture and attitude towards the special position of the Malays establishes and facilitates the conscious avoidance of a rights-based legal regime in the management of ethnic issues in Singapore. In that regard, article 152 has paradoxically depoliticised, to some extent, the post-colonial nation-building project in Singapore.

In 1959, Singapore secured internal self-government with the promise to care for the interests of racial and religious minorities in Singapore. That promise took on greater meaning and importance when Singapore became independent in 1965. The path dependence on this promise remains, sustains and nourishes the nation-building endeavour, and is a core component of the PAP government's performance legitimacy. Notwithstanding the civic conception of citizenship in Singapore, nation-building is greatly aided by article 152 of the Singapore Constitution, which urges a conscious formation and sustenance of distinctive ethnic identities of the minority communities while recognising the imperative for an overarching identity. This recognition of a citizen's multiple identities and how they complement each other is critical in Singapore's pluralist constitutionalism.

Much faith is placed on constitutional engineering to reduce the imperfections of pluralism in Singapore. Pluralist constitutionalism is a powerful ideational tool for plural societies like Singapore. But is it also possible that too much is expected of pluralist constitutionalism? Pluralist constitutionalism alone does not enable governments and the citizenry to correctly choose from possible arrangements that promote inclusion and substantive equality. Instead, the norms of pluralist constitutionalism have to evolve in tandem with the changing complexion of society. In turn, this requires the internalisation of the pluralist ethos and given effect to through a constitutional framework that is conducive to trust- and confidence-building amid diversity.

The concept of pluralist constitutionalism is innately appealing to the point of seductiveness. The Singapore case demonstrates how pluralist constitutionalism can empower law and policy to drive governmental action for recognition, equality and inclusion. The challenge is to ensure the relevance and effectiveness of the various constitutional provisions, laws, institutions, and policies that seek to maintain pluralism on an even keel. Pluralist constitutionalism can be likened to a society's shared purpose. To reach that constitutional destination, it is imperative that the shared purpose is disciplined by shared values. Shared values inform, guide, and discipline what ought and what ought not to be done to attain the shared purpose. This is the challenge going forward: Imbibing values and generating norms and harnessing the centripetal forces that will sustain pluralist constitutionalism as a public good. Without shared values, pluralist constitutionalism can lead a society astray in the vain quest for constitutional unity.

Bibliography

—— Administration of Muslim Law Act (Cap 3, 2009 Revised Edition).
—— Constitution of the Republic of Singapore.
—— *Education Statistics Digest 2002* (Singapore Ministry of Education 2002) v.
—— Federal Constitution of Malaysia.
—— Parliamentary Elections Act (Cap 218, 2007 Revised Edition).
—— *Population in Brief 2017* (Prime Minister's Office, September 2017).
—— Prisons Regulations (Cap 247, Rg 2, 2002 Revised Edition) reg 103(2).
—— *Report of the All-Party Committee of the Singapore Legislative Assembly on Chinese Education* (Government Printing Office 1956).
—— *Report of the Constitutional Commission* (Government Printer 1966).
—— *Report of the Constitutional Commission* (2016).
—— *Report of the Singapore Constitutional Conference held in London in March and April, 1957* (Cmnd 147, April 1957).
—— Republic of Singapore Independence Act.
—— Singapore (Constitution) Order in Council, 1958 (SI No. 1956 of 1958).
—— *Singapore Parliament Reports*, vol 50, no 3 (11 January 1988) cols 181–192.
—— *Singapore Parliament Reports*, vol 51, no 1 (11 January 1988) cols 27–53.
—— The Constitution of India.

—— White Paper, *The Review of Specific Aspects of the Elected Presidency: The Constitution of the Republic of Singapore* (Amendment) Bill, 2016.

Aljunied S M K, 'British Discourses and Malay Identity in Colonial Singapore' (2009) 37(107) *Indonesia and the Malay World*. 1

Brown D, 'Ethnic and Nationalist Politics in Southeast Asia' in Beeson M (ed), *Contemporary Southeast Asia* (Palgrave Macmillan 2009).

Castellino J and Redondo E D, *Minority Rights in Asia: A Comparative Legal Analysis* (OUP 2006).

Chan H C and Obaid ul Haq (eds), *The Prophetic & The Political: Selected Speeches & Writings of S. Rajaratnam* (Graham Brash 1987).

Chan S K, 'Culture and Legal Practice' (Keynote speech by the Chief Justice at the International Bar Association Conference, Singapore, 15 October 2007).

Choudhry S, 'Bridging Comparative Politics and Comparative Constitutional Law: Constitutional Design in Divided Societies' in Choudhry S (ed), *Constitutional Design for Divided Societies: Integration or Accommodation?* (OUP 2008).

Enright D J, *Memoirs of a Mendicant Professor* (Chatto and Windus 1969).

Green A, *Continuing the Legacy: 30 Years of the Mosque Building Fund in Singapore* (Majlis Ugama Islam Singapura 2007).

Hassall G, 'Systems of Representation in Asia-Pacific: A Comparative Analysis' in Hassall G and Saunders C (eds), *The People's Representatives: Electoral Systems in the Asia-Pacific Region* (Allen & Unwin 1997).

Horowitz D L, *Ethnic Groups in Conflict* (University of California Press 1985).

—— 'Electoral Systems: A Primer for Decision Makers' (2003) 14(4) Journal of Democracy 115.

Huang-Thio S M, 'Constitutional Discrimination under the Malaysian Constitution' (1964) 6 Malayan Law Review 1.

Ikenberry G J, 'What States Can Do Now' in Paul T V, Ikenberry G J and Hall J A(eds), *The Nation-State in Question* (Princeton University Press 2003).

Immigration and Checkpoints Authority 'Greater Flexibility with Implementation of Double-Barrelled Race Option from 1 January 2011' (29 December 2010).

Inche A. Rahim Ishak, parliamentary debate on the 'Report of Constitutional Commission, 1966,' *Parliamentary Debates Singapore Official Report*, vol 25 (16 March 1967) col. 1331.

Li J and Jørge Elklit, 'The Singapore General Election 1997: Campaigning Strategy, Results, and Analysis' (1999) 18(2) Electoral Studies 199.

Lee Hsien Loong, Speech at the official opening of the Singapore Chinese Cultural Centre (19 May 2017).

—— 'Race, Multiracialism and Singapore's Place in the World', Remarks at the People's Association Kopi Talk at Ci Yuan Community Club (23 September 2017).

—— Remarks to the media after the closed-door dialogue with the Malay/Muslim community (25 January 2014) <www.pmo.gov.sg/newsroom/prime-minister-lee-hsien-loongs-remarks-media-malay-after-closed-door-dialogue> accessed 9 August 2018.

Lee Kuan Yew, parliamentary debate on 'Nation-Building Tenets' motion, *Parliamentary Debates Singapore Official Report*, vol 86 (19 August 2009).

—— *The Singapore Story: The Memoirs of Lee Kuan Yew* (Times Editions and The Straits Times Press 1998).

—— Speech at the People's Action Party 50th anniversary celebrations (21 November 2004).

Lijphart A, *Democracy in Plural Societies: A Comparative Exploration* (YUP 1977).

—— *Democracies: Patterns of Majoritarian and Consensus Government in Twenty-One Countries* (YUP 1984).

—— *Patterns of Democracy: Government Forms & Performance in Thirty-Six Countries, Second Edition* (YUP 2012).

McGarry J, O'Leary B, and Simeon R, 'Integration or Accommodation? The Enduring Debate in Conflict Regulation' in Choudhry S (ed), *Constitutional Design for Divided Societies: Integration or Accommodation?* (OUP 2008).

MENDAKI, 'Our Logo' <www.mendaki.org.sg/about-mendaki/our-logo> accessed 22 September 2018.

Milner A, *The Malays* (Wiley-Blackwell 2008).

Neo L C J, 'The Protection of Minorities and the Constitution: A Judicious Balance?' in Thio L A and Tan K YL (eds), *Evolution of a Revolution: Forty Years of the Singapore Constitution* (Routledge 2008).

Pew Research Centre, 'Global Religious Diversity: Half of the Most Religiously Diverse Countries are in Asia-Pacific Region' (*Pew Forum*, 4 April 2014) www.pewforum.org/2014/04/04/global-religious-diversity/ accessed 22 September 2018.

PuroShotam N S, *Negotiating Language, Constructing Race: Disciplining Race in Singapore* (Mouton de Gruyter 1998).

Siddique S, 'Singaporean Identity' in Sandhu K S and Wheatley P (eds), *Management of Success: The Moulding of Modern Singapore* (Institute of Southeast Asian Studies 1989).

Tan K B E, 'Multiracialism Engineered: The Limits of Electoral and Spatial Integration in Singapore' (2005) 4(4) Ethnopolitics 413.

—— 'The Multilingual State in Search of the Nation: The Language Discourse in Singapore's Nation-Building' in Lee H G and Suryadinata L (eds), *Language, Nation and Development in Southeast Asia* (Institute of Southeast Asian Studies 2007).

—— '"Special position of the Malays": It's a shield, not a sword,' *The Straits Times* (Singapore, 25 August 2009) A18.

—— 'Racial Politics and Imperatives and the Constitutional Special Position of the Indigenous Malays in a New Society: Asserting Interests and the Non-Contestation of Rights in Singapore's Communitarian Constitutionalism' in Bünte M & Dressel B (eds), *Politics and Constitutions in Southeast Asia* (Routledge 2017).

Tan Y L K, 'The Legal and Institutional Framework and Issues of Multiculturalism in Singapore' in Lai A E (ed), *Beyond Rituals and Riots: Ethnic Pluralism and*

Social Cohesion in Singapore (Institute of Policy Studies and Eastern Universities Press 2004).

Taylor C, *Multiculturalism and 'The Politics of Recognition': An Essay* (Princeton University Press 1992).

Thio L A, 'Choosing Representatives: Singapore Does it Her Way' in Hassall G and Saunders C (eds), *The People's Representatives: Electoral Systems in the Asia-Pacific Region* (Allen & Unwin 1997).

—— 'Lex rex *or* rex lex? Competing Conceptions of the Rule of Law in Singapore' (2002) 20 UCLA Pacific Basin Law Journal 1.

Watson K, 'Rulers and Ruled: Racial Perceptions, Curriculum and Schooling in Colonial Malaysia and Singapore' in Morgan J A (ed), *The Imperial Curriculum: Racial Images and Education in the British Colonial Experience* (Routledge 1993).

Wimmer A, 'Power and Pride: National Identity and Ethnopolitical Inequality around the World' (2017) 69(4) World Politics 605.

4

Pluralism in Brunei's Constitution? Ethnicity, Religion and the Absolute Monarchy

KERSTIN STEINER AND DOMINIK M MÜLLER

I. Introduction

Brunei Darussalam, also called Brunei, the 'Abode of Peace' or *Negara Brunei Darussalam* in Malay, is located on the north-west coast of Borneo in Southeast Asia. Brunei is an ethnically plural society with a majority of seven 'indigenous' ethnic groups, yet this classification has been considered difficult and needs to be understood vis-à-vis its political background.[1] In official government data the category of these 'original groups' (*puak jati*) is sub-divided into the Melayu Brunei (or Brunei), Kedayan, Tutong, Belait, Dusun, Bisaya, and Murut (or Lun Bawang). Yet all of these groups are also classified as 'Malay'.[2] Monoculturalism as enshrined in the political ideology is thus the goal, not multiculturalism.[3]

This is also evident in the official 2015 census: 66% of the population have been described as Malay, Chinese 10.1%, and the remaining catch-all category of 'Other' with 23.9%.[4] The ethnic classifier 'Malay' significantly differs from that in neighbouring countries such as Malaysia, where, for example, an ethnic Murut adhering to the Christian faith would not be considered 'Malay', which necessarily implies adherence to Islam there. Brunei's broadened classification, however,

---

[1] Donald E Brown, 'Brunei: The Structure and History of a Bornean Malay Sultanate' (1970) 2(2) Brunei Museum Monograph 3. See also Roger Kershaw, 'Marginality Then and Now: Shifting Patterns of Minority Status in Brunei Darussalam' (1998) 29(1–2) Internationales Asienforum: International Quarterly for Asian Studies 83. This ethnic classification system has been enshrined in the Constitution of 1959 and Nationality Enactment of 1961.
[2] Roger Kershaw, 'Brunei' in John Funston (ed), *Government and Politics in Southeast Asia* (Institute of Southeast Asian Studies 2001) 10.
[3] E Ann Black, 'Brunei Darussalam' in Ann Black & Gary Bell (eds), *Law and Legal Institutions of Asia: Traditions, Adaptations and Innovations* (CUP 2011) at 324.
[4] See Brunei Darussalam Prime Minister's Office, 'Population' www.depd.gov.bn/SitePages/Population.aspx accessed 18 September 2018.

enhances the breadth of the 'Malay' community, which has political implications considering the government's conceptualisation of Brunei as a 'Malay Islamic Monarchy' (*Melayu Islam Beraja* or MIB) requiring 'the Malays' to form a numerically sufficient majority.

The political system is even less pluralistic. According to the Constitution, the Sultan is the Head of State with full executive authority and thus one of the few absolute monarchs in the world.[5] The executive and legislative powers of the Sultan are neither separate nor independent but form a *Personaleinheit*.[6] The constitution explicitly stipulates that the Sultan 'can do no wrong', neither in 'his personal or any official capacity'.[7] Thus, according to the law, the Sultan stands above law, unlike any other political leader in Southeast Asia. In addition to his executive and legislative powers, the Sultan wields religious power as 'Head of the official religion' (*ketua ugama rasmi*, constitutionally defined as the Sunni Shafi'ite Islam, see below), and referred to in official religious government rhetoric as 'leader of (Muslim) believers' (*ulil amri*) and God's 'vice-regent on earth' (*khalifah*).[8] He holds the posts of Prime Minister, Minister of Finance, of Defense, of Foreign Affairs and Trade, commander of the army and police, and chancellor of the local universities. Accordingly, political and religious power is heavily centred in the person of the Sultan[9] in this tiny kingdom of 423,000 people (324,000 of whom are citizens) and only 5,765 square kilometres of territory.[10] In its own unique way, the leadership of Brunei operates based on the absolute monarchical principle of '*l'État c'est moi*' ('The State, That's Me'), while the population is expected to co-constitute state-power through absolute loyalty.[11]

Brunei is one of the few states in the world that formally styles itself 'Islamic'[12] and 'non-secular'[13] – it has maintained this framing consistently since its declaration of independence from the British in 1984. Utilising Islam to claim legitimacy

---

[5] The few states still ruled by absolute monarchies where the ruler claims full power as both Head of State and Head of government include Vatican City, Oman, Saudi Arabia, Qatar, and Swaziland.

[6] The German term 'Personaleinheit' refers to an amalgamation of roles and powers in one person. This is particularly the case for the executive and legislature. Technically the courts are independent, but the Sultan of Brunei appoints members of the judiciary and maintains wide latitude with regard to their discipline and dismissal.

[7] Art 84B of the Constitution of Brunei Darussalam 1959 (2011 Rev Ed) (hereinafter 'Constitution').

[8] Art 3(2) of the Constitution.

[9] ibid Art 4.

[10] Tim Lindsey & Kerstin Steiner, *Islam, Law and the State in Southeast Asia: Volume 3 Malaysia and Brunei* (I.B. Tauris 2012) 323.

[11] This has been also referred to as the sultan as the 'Grundnorm'; cf Tey Tsun Hang, 'Brunei's Revamped Constitution: The Sultan as the Grundnorm?' (2007) 9(2) Australian Journal of Asian Law 264.

[12] John Funston, 'Brunei' in Greg Fealy & Virginia Matheson Hooker (eds), *Voices of Islam in Southeast Asia – A Contemporary Sourcebook* (Institute of Southeast Asian Studies 2006) 19; Lindsey & Steiner (n 10); Dominik Müller, 'Sharia Law and the Politics of 'Faith Control' in Brunei Darussalam: Dynamics of Socio-Legal Change in a Southeast Asian Sultanate' (2015) 46(3) Internationales Asienforum 313, 326.

[13] 'Royal address (*titah*) of Sultan Hassanal Bolkiah 1991, Titah' (Department of Information, 14 January 1991) www.information.gov.bn/Malay%20Publication%20PDF/EDIT%20TITAH%201990-1991.pd> accessed 18 September 2018.

has a long-standing history in Southeast Asia. The British colonial authorities in Brunei, as elsewhere in their Malay possessions, relied on a conflation of Islamic identity and Malay sovereignty exercised by dependent local rulers, while those rulers in turn sought to consolidate their political and symbolic power particularly in the fields of religion, 'customary practices', and ethnic identity politics. Many of the authoritarian mechanisms of colonial rule that supported this trope not only survived the departure of the British and the end of their close control of local rulers, but also served as the basis of post-colonial nation-building. In the case of Brunei, the independent nation was to be defined on religious and ethnic grounds, presented in the primordialist logic of a centuries-old tradition of Malay monarchical governance.

Since independence in 1984 the Bruneian Sultanate has greatly expanded and deepened its domestic political power, building on political and ideological institutions it inherited from the British colonial system, including the conflation of royal power with Islam, which dates back to the Sultanate's pre-colonial era but acquired new meanings and institutional forms under British indirect rule. The authority of Brunei's absolute monarchy is formally enshrined in the official 'state ideology' of MIB, which explicitly equates sovereignty and political legitimacy with the Sultanate, Islam and 'Malay' identity.[14] These three pillars are 'sacrosanct'[15] insofar as they are considered unquestionable.

II. Historical Context: The State, Law and Islam in Brunei

According to official national historiography, the Sultanate of Brunei Darussalam had its birth as an Islamic nation in 1368, when its ruler Awang Alak Betatar[16] converted to Islam, taking the name Sultan Muhammad Shah.[17] Historical

---

[14] E Ann Black, 'Informed by Ideology: A Review of the Court Reforms in Brunei Darussalam' in Andrew Harding & Penelope Nicholson (eds), *New Courts in Asia* (Routledge 2011) 329; Lindsey & Steiner (n 10) 324.

[15] Human Rights Resource Centre, 'Brunei Darussalam' in David Cohen and Kevin Tan (eds), *Keeping the Faith: A Study of Freedom of Thought, Conscience and Religion in ASEAN* (Human Rights Resource Centre, 2014) 53, 75; Müller, 'Sharia Law' (n 12) 317.

[16] Although frequently referred to in narratives of the nation's origin, rarely anything appears to be known about Awang Alak Betatar or the nature, scope or history of the non-Muslim 'Bruneian' polity he was assumedly heading prior to his conversion to Islam, and this theme appears to be of little interest for national historiography. At the same time, national historiography does heavily emphasise reference to Brunei as 'puni' (or 'poli') in Chinese sources from the pre-Islamic era. Whether a continuity can be drawn (and if so of which kind) between 'puni' and 'Brunei', and how the polity of pre-colonial Brunei and the geographical entity of Borneo were linked (or even equal), remain contentious questions among local and international historians. Some historians also believe that a Muslim and a non-Muslim polity of 'Brunei' may have co-existed in its earliest period, but no published study has more systematically substantiated this assumption yet.

[17] For more details, see Ranjit Singh, *Brunei 1839-1983: The Problems of Political Survival* (OUP 1984). Several (non-Bruneian) historians argue that there is no clear evidence for the genealogy's

evidence pertaining to this time remains scarce, and one locally much-cited source – the famous poem and tale of origin *Syair Awang Semaun* (of which various versions exist) – is heavily mythical and supernatural in character. As in most Muslim communities across the Malay Archipelago (*Nusantara*) in what are today the States of Indonesia and Malaysia, *syariah*[18] jurisprudence in Brunei was historically drawn from the Shafi'i *madhhab*[19] of Sunni Islam.[20]

Law in pre-colonial Brunei, as elsewhere in Southeast Asia, was assumedly understood to emanate from the monarch, who was responsible for setting down, interpreting, and administering the law on behalf of his people,[21] although parallel to this, non-codified forms of normativity (some of which sources refer to as *Hukum Resam*, or customary law), have undoubtedly existed as well. The earliest-known Bruneian Islamic legal digest was the *Hukum Kanun Brunei* or 'Brunei Code', which Hooker has described as 'a rather corrupt version of the Malacca [i.e. the 15th century code *Hukum Kanun Melaka*] text or those parts of the text which seemed to a copyist to have some relevance to Brunei'.[22] An early copy of the Brunei Code is dated 1708, although it is likely that the full Malacca Codes were known in Brunei sometime from the fifteenth century onwards.[23] This code already established principles of governments providing explanations of the nature of the relationship between the ruler and his people, the conditions for becoming a ruler, and the responsibilities of the people to their ruler.[24] Although the Brunei Code's enforcement (about which little is known) ended in the pre-colonial era, the Code was rediscovered in the discursive framing of post-colonial legal Islamisation policies, discussed further below, with claims that a 'complete' Islamic legal order would have been in place only to have disappeared due to non-Muslim colonial interference.[25]

The colonial ambitions of Spain, Portugal and the Dutch impacted Brunei but it was Britain that was to decide Brunei's future. In 1888, Brunei – at the time having lost much of its previous influence in Borneo and facing existential economic problems – entered into a formal agreement to become a British Protectorate

---

historical accuracy particularly partaining to its earliest entries. See eg, Graham Saunders, *A History of Brunei* (Routledge 2002) 35–36.

[18] *Syariah* (Ar. *shari'a*, Islamic law). This is the standard spelling of this word used in Brunei.

[19] *Madhhab* (Ar., school of Islamic legal thought).

[20] See the three volumes series on *Islam, Law and the State in Southeast Asia*: Tim Lindsey, *Islam, Law and the State in Southeast Asia: Volume 1 Indonesia* (I.B. Tauris 2012); Tim Lindsey and Kerstin Steiner, *Islam, Law and the State in Southeast Asia: Volume 2 Singapore* (I.B. Tauris 2012) and the above-mentioned volume on Malaysia and Brunei in Lindsey and Steiner (n 10).

[21] An exceptional account of political and legal practices in the Sultanate as well as the royal court culture, authored in the late 16th century, has been the 'Boxer Codex'. For the latest transcription and translation, see George Bryan Souza & Jeffrey S Turley, *The Boxer Codex* (Brill 2016) 397.

[22] M B Hooker, *Islamic Law in Southeast Asia* (OUP 1984) 173.

[23] ibid.

[24] ASEAN Law Organisation, 'Legal Systems in ASEAN: Brunei – Historical Overview' <www.asean-lawassociation.org/papers/Brunei_chp1.pdf> accessed 18 September 2018.

[25] M S Othman, *Perlaksanaan dan Pentadbiran Undang-Undang Islam di Negara Brunei Darussalam* (Dewan Bahasa dan Pustaka Brunei 1996).

and in 1905 a British 'Resident' was appointed to 'advise' the Sultan under the Anglo-Brunei Treaty of 1905–06.[26] Throughout much of their sphere of influence in Malay Southeast Asia, the British governed through local rulers. In doing so, they typically inflated the prestige of the rulers while restricting their real power, which was instead exercised by the local British Resident.[27] The Resident in Brunei thus had significant authority and effectively acted as a kind of de facto governor until the outbreak of war in the Pacific in 1942. After the Japanese surrender in 1945, the British re-established their authority in Borneo, but gradually transferred their powers to the Sultanate – a process that occurred without violence but at times under highly contentious circumstances, particularly during the 'joint' (but de facto rather antagonistic) drafting of the Brunei Constitution from 1953 until 1959, when it was finally enforced and presented to the public.

One – political – result of British colonial policy was rulers who owed much of their prestige to their role as 'protectors' of their majority-Malay populations and their closely related role as the titular 'head' of Islam in their state. Brunei was no exception and this close conflation of sovereignty between both Islamic and Malay identities became the foundation of Brunei's modern absolute monarchy. This was made explicit very quickly, with the official MIB state ideology proclaimed as the central theme for post-colonial nation building when the British Protectorate came to an end and the Sultan declared Brunei's full independence on 1 January 1984.[28] The core elements of Malay supremacy, Islam, and the centrality of monarchical power were already present in the Constitution of 1959. The Constitution had been presented to the public 25 years before independence, parallel to a British guarantee of far-reaching domestic autonomy, except for security affairs and foreign policy, where Brunei accepted British support. The notion of MIB being a 'national philosophy' (*falsafah negara*), however, and the very propagation of MIB under that acronym as a *concept* in and of itself, only commenced in 1984 and started to become more institutionalised a few years later.

In his *titah* (royal speech) on the occasion of the Declaration of Independence, the Sultan established MIB as a 'national ideology' (*ideologi negara*) – upholding 'Islamic principles and values based on the Quran and Hadith as the basis of all activities concerning the racial necessity [sic], language, Malay culture and the monarchy institution as the governing system and administration[29] of Brunei

---

[26] E Ann Black, 'The Stronger Rule of the More Enlightened European: The Consequences of Colonialism on Dispute Resolution in the Sultanate of Brunei' (2009) 13(1) Legal History 91.

[27] ibid 101.

[28] Lindsey & Steiner (n 10) 324.

[29] So, eg, numerous key political positions have the requirement attached that the candidate must be of the 'Malay race' and profess Islam as his or her religion. For instance, Ministers and Deputy Ministers must be of the 'Malay race and professing the Islamic Religion, save where His Majesty the Sultan and Yang Di-Pertuan otherwise decide': Art 4(5) of the Constitution. In addition, art 84(A) of the Constitution states that no person 'shall be appointed to any office specified in the Third Schedule unless […] of the Malay race professing the Islamic religion'. The positions listed in the Third Schedule include key offices such as the Auditor General, the Attorney-General, the Chief Syariah Judge, the State Mufti, etc.

Darussalam', to be 'honoured and practiced by all people of Brunei'.[30] What followed was a process that was presented to the public as a 're-Islamisation',[31] with MIB being systematically propagated and established as national ideology. The MIB Concept Committee established in 1986, later transformed into the MIB Supreme Council, was tasked with overseeing the authorship and propagation of the contents of MIB until today.

III. Pluralism as a Constitutional Fact? Introduction to the Constitutional Framework: Absolute Monarchy and the State of Emergency

Following WWII, Sultan Omar Ali Saifuddin III (in office 1950–1967) initiated a 'slow programme designed to give Brunei internal self-government and a small measure of parliamentary democracy'.[32] The Constitution of 1959 was a result of his efforts towards achieving more autonomy vis-à-vis the British by establishing Brunei's first ever written constitution, while at the same time using that constitution also to cement royal power vis-à-vis possible domestic competitors.

The Constitution of 1959 did not provide for separation of powers, including the establishment, jurisdiction or independence of the judiciary, nor did it provide for the protection of human rights or individual freedoms.[33] Instead, full powers were vested in the Sultan under the terms of the Constitution of 1959, thereby replacing the colonial residency system. Unlike the case of any other former British colony in Southeast Asia, the Constitution 'granted internal *self-government to the Sultan, not to the people*. There was no elective majority on the Legislative Council and no direct elections [emphasis added]'.[34]

Elections were not held until 1961, and these were not general elections to form a national government, but only district council elections. This cautious experiment remained the first and last of its kind in Brunei history. In a dramatic victory, all electoral seats were won by the People's Party of Brunei (*Parti Rakyat Brunei* or PRB), which initially maintained relatively good personal relationships with the Sultan. However, only 16 seats of 33 were designated for elected members (all of which were won by the PRB), and no provisions existed that the district council delegates would be entitled to form a government. As tensions rose over the Sultan's considerations to merge with Malaya, while at the same time the PRB feeling side-lined by the Sultan, rebels of the PRB's military wing, calling themselves

---

[30] Speech by the Sultan at the proclamation of independence in 1984, as cited in Black, 'Brunei Darussalam' (n 3) 302.
[31] ibid 303.
[32] Singh (n 17) 129.
[33] Tey (n 11) 265.
[34] Graham Saunders, *A History of Brunei* (OUP 1994) 138.

the North Kalimantan National Army, staged a revolt against the government.[35] The Sultan proclaimed a state of emergency (which pro forma remains in force until today), and British troops from Singapore, aided by Gurkha soldiers, quelled the revolt within 12 days in December 1962. The PRB was banned, and the leaders were arrested or fled, while most of the average members and spontaneous supporters were pardoned by the Sultan and quickly re-integrated into society. The traumatic events surrounding the elections and rebellion, however, marked an end for any democratic experiments for many decades to come. No other opposition party or movement ever arose following the PRB's demise. A few largely loyalist parties briefly existed, but were either dissolved soon afterwards on formal grounds, or simply vanished for the lack of support – particularly, as civil servants were forbidden to join political parties. In any case, without elections, a parliament, or any other manoeuvring space – and considering the expectation of absolute loyalty – they had little, if anything, to do. Presently, one 'party' exists – the National Development Party (NDP), but it has no (and legally cannot have any) societal relevance or substantial following.

The absolute power of the Sultan has been legally cemented by the state of emergency declared following these events. The emergency powers in article 83(3) of the Constitution (and Section 3(1) of the Emergency Regulations Act, Cap. 21, 1984) grant the Sultan absolute discretion to issue Orders as long as the Sultan himself considers such Orders to be 'desirable in the public interest'. Thus, there are no external limits to these powers according to the Constitution.[36]

Technically, Brunei remains in the same state of emergency declared in 1962, with that declaration renewed every two years since then. Thus, in Bruneian legal terminology, 'Orders' are legislation instituted by the Sultan under his emergency powers in Section 83(3) of the Constitution, while 'Acts' are those enacted through normal processes involving the Legislative Council. The intention is that the Emergency Orders will be eventually promulgated as Acts over time.[37] However, Acts are also frequently replaced by Orders, so it is difficult to recognise any trends to these institutional changes.

In his role as both Head of government and Head of State, the Sultan is assisted and advised by five councils – the *Council of Cabinet Ministers*, the *Privy Council*,

---

[35] Notably, these tensions, the non-acceptance of the popular vote, and the Sultan's repeated postponing of setting up a date for the Legislative Council's meeting were only three of several interrelated factors and dynamics contributing to the PRB rebellion, the history of which is highly complex. For further details, see Harun Abdul Majid, *Rebellion in Brunei: The 1962 Revolt, Imperialism, Confrontation and Oil* (I.B. Tauris 2013). For a rare primary source from the PRB itself, available in some university library catalogues, see Ahmad Zaini, *The People's Party of Brunei: Selected Documents* (Institute of Social Analysis 1987).

[36] Kerstin Steiner, 'Brunei' in David Cohen, Kevin Tan, Aviva Nababan and Faith Suzzette Delos Reyes Kong (eds), *Update on the Rule of Law for Human Rights in ASEAN: The Path to Integration* (Human Rights Resource Centre 2016).

[37] Then-Attorney-General of Brunei Darussalam, Yang Berhormat, Dato Paduka Haji Kifrawi bin Paduka Haji Kifli, 'Opening of the Legal Year' (Attorney-General's Chambers, 18 March 2008) www.agc.gov.bn/AGC%20Site%20Pages/AGCspeechesview.aspx accessed 18 September 2018.

the *Legislative Council, Islamic Religious Council (Majlis Ugama Islam Brunei* or *MUIB*), and the *Council of Regency,* commonly also referred to as the Council of Succession.[38] The Council of Ministers forms the executive branch of government. As mentioned above, the Sultan holds key ministerial positions and naturally the other ministers are appointed by the Sultan according to articles 4(3) and 11 of the Constitution. In the course of the 2004 constitutional reforms, the function of this council has been severely limited. The Sultan is neither bound by the decision of the Council (article 19) nor are the decisions by the Council valid without the consent of the Sultan (article 19A).[39] It is thus relegated to an advisory function.

The Privy Council also only holds an advisory function in matters of constitutional reform and appointments of a person to Malay customary positions (article 6). Like other appointments, the members of this council are appointed by the Sultan and their tenure is held at the Sultan's pleasure (article 5).

According to article 39, the Sultan makes the law and while the Legislative Council may reject a bill, the Sultan can still pass the bill (article 43(3), (4) and (5)). The Legislative Council has a checkered past, having been suspended for two decades from 1984–2004.[40] Part of its members are directly appointed by the Sultan while there are provisions for a certain number of members to be elected. So far there is no timetable for the election of those members. The appointed members hold their position at the pleasure of the Sultan. When the Legislative Council was revived in September 2004, the Sultan appointed 21 members only to dissolve the Council a year later, before appointing 29 new members. This theme of disbanding and new appointments continued when in March 2011, a completely new Legislative Council was appointed by the Sultan.[41]

The power of MUIB, as provided in article 3(3), is similarly restricted. Despite its legal status as the 'chief authority' in 'all matters relating to religion'[42], it is only 'responsible for **advising** His Majesty the Sultan and Yang Di-Pertuan on all matters relating to the Islamic Religion [emphasis added]'.

The decisions, acts, etc of the Sultan are final with no judicial review available for them, with article 84C making this explicitly clear. Avenues of judicial reviews are very limited in general. For instance, the only judicial review of the Constitution can be carried out through an Interpretation Tribunal with members being appointed by the Sultan according to article 86. This Tribunal was established as a result of the 2004 constitutional reforms.

---

[38] The Council of Succession or Regency existed prior to the Constitution of 1959 and is formed whenever the Sultan is under the age of 18 when he ascends the throne. This happened for instance when Ahmad Tajuddin succeed his father Sultan Muhammad Jamal Alam in 1924. The Council of Regency temporarily held the reign until Ahmad Tajuddin reached the age of 18 in 1931. Jatswan S. Sidhu, *Historical Dictionary of Brunei Darussalam* (The Rowman & Littlefield 2010) 68.
[39] Steiner (n 36) 6.
[40] For details on this constitutional reform, see below.
[41] Steiner (n 36) 7.
[42] Section 38, Religious Council and Kadis Courts Act, Cap. 77 (1984).

The influence of the Sultan on the judiciary is also evident in the appointment process of members of the bench. The Sultan appoints the members of the judiciary and has far-reaching discretion on discipline and dismissal. The general laws provide for the necessary qualifications of the judges[43] and judicial commissioners[44] to the Supreme Court, the Intermediate Court[45] and the higher Syariah courts, yet the Sultan has the power to 'appoint any fit and proper person' as a judge in the subordinate courts.[46] In the case of the Syariah courts, this happens on the advice of the President of the Majlis and after consultation with the Majlis.[47]

In addition, the Constitution does not provide for any independence of the judiciary. Yet there is little to no evidence that the Sultan exerts undue influence on the judiciary.[48] The US Department of State's 2014 *Investment Climate Statement* reported that 'in practice the court system operates without government interference. Post has received no complaints from companies regarding the judicial system'.[49]

The above-made comments have to be taken in the context of Brunei as an absolute monarchy – the Sultan is the law or *Grundnorm* and at the same time above the law. This is even more pronounced due to the State of Emergency that Brunei has been under for more than five decades.

A. History of Constitution

The year 1959 marked a decisive shift in the history of Brunei, as the Sultanate succeeded in negotiating a new agreement with the British government replacing the previous residency system. Despite the global wave of popular and democratic movements following WWII and the global de-colonialisation process and the establishment of elected governments in the neighbouring Federation of Malaya and Singapore,[50] in Brunei the Sultan regained full executive authority.

---

[43] See s 7 Supreme Court Act, Cap. 5 (1984).

[44] Section 11(1) of the Supreme Court Act requires Judicial Commissioners to possess the same qualifications as Supreme Court Judges. Section 11(5) provides the powers of the Commissioners as follows:

> A Judicial Commissioner appointed under this section shall have power to act as a Judge and all things done by him in accordance with the terms of his appointment shall have the same validity and effect as if they had been done by a Judge and in respect thereof he shall have the same powers and enjoy the same immunities as if he had been a Judge.

[45] See s 10 Intermediate Courts Act, Cap. 162 (1999).

[46] See s 10(2) Intermediate Courts Act, Cap. 162 (1999).

[47] Sections 8, 9, 10 Syariah Courts Act, Cap. 184 (2000).

[48] Kershaw, 'Brunei' (n 2), describing the judiciary as the 'most independent institution in the State'.

[49] US Department of State, '*Department of State: 2014 Investment Climate Statement*' (June 2014) www.state.gov/documents/organization/226810.pdf accessed 18 September 2018.

[50] This is referred to as an 'anachromism in the age of democratic liberalism': Chang Wen-Chen, Thio Li-Ann, Kevin Y L Tan & Yeh Jiunn-Rong, *Constitutionalism in Asia: Cases and Materials* (Hart Publishing 2014) 37.

In the same year, Brunei presented its first (written) Constitution to the public. Its preparations had begun in 1953, followed by nearly six years of complicated contestations and power political maneuvers between Sultan Omar Ali Saifuddin III and the British side.[51] Only three years after the Constitution's promulgation, significant parts of the Constitution were suspended for decades following the state of emergency. Never again did Brunei witness anything like those early years that could be termed 'constitutional politics' or 'public debates' related to the constitution. This absence of constitutional politics or deliberations remains the status quo until today. Accordingly, the period from 1953 until 1959 was the only time in Brunei history when different actors negotiated over substantially competing, ie 'plural' constitutional visions and ideas.

In 1950, Anthony Foster Abell became governor of Sarawak and British High Commissioner for Brunei, following the assassination of his predecessor, the previous governor, in Sibu. In the same year, Sultan Omar Ali Saifuddin III was crowned as the twenty-eighth ruler of Brunei. While Abell aimed to maintain (or rather re-establish) British colonial order in turbulent times,[52] the new Sultan was equally determined to expand his powers and limit British influence.[53]

Sultan Omar Ali Saifuddin III's two predecessors had become sultans while they were still minors. Oil had been discovered in 1929, but the British refused to share the growing revenues in any serious manner and instead paid the Bruneian rulers very modest 'monthly allowances'.[54] While Sultan Ahmad Tajuddin (1913–1950, tenure 1924–1950, fully governing since 1932) spoke of oil revenues of annually 6,000,000 Malayan dollars, he received only 3,500 dollars per month in 1949, as he complained.[55] The British had also enacted personal and land reforms which stripped them of their entitlement to tribute payments from their subjects. Sultan Omar Ali Saifuddin III, however, was a different caliber to deal with, and his rule paradoxically benefited from the increasingly centralised and professionally managed state institution that the British had helped to establish. Crowned at the age of 35, he received a British-led elite education at the Malay College (1932–36) in Malaya. After graduation, he joined the British-led state administration and worked for the Forestry Department, where he closely interacted with 'average' Bruneians and, for example, reportedly lived among villagers for some time.

---

[51] The material on the historical development of the Constitution is extremely limited. For an unparalleled and authoritative account of constitution-making in Brunei in the 1950s which serves as the main source for the following section, see B A Hussainmiya, *The Brunei Constitution of 1959: An Inside History* (Brunei Press 2000), whose study is based on in-depth work with primary documents in British colonial archives.

[52] The turbulent times were partially shaped by anti-colonial secessionist movements in Sarawak, shortly after the brief Japanese occupation which ended in 1945.

[53] Hussainmiya, *The Brunei Constitution* (n 51) 10.

[54] ibid. For an account of the 'repeated local pressure to loosen its [British] purse strings', see B A Hussainmiya, '"Manufacturing Consensus": The Role of the State Council in Brunei Darussalam' (2000) 31(2) Journal of Southeast Asian Studies 335.

[55] Hussainmiya, *The Brunei Constitution* (n 51) 10.

Later he worked with the Judiciary Department in Kuala Belait, where he was trained by the British Assistant Resident, H. Hughes-Hallet, in law and state administration. Unlike his predecessors, he was well-equipped to become an increasingly challenging counter-part in negotiations with the British.

The then still Prince's increasing rejection of British domination may have been deepened when his application for a study program in the UK was rejected. He afterwards refused offers to continue working in the Bruneian state administration and instead, according to official historiography, devoted his time to the study of literature and religion.[56] He is officially remembered until today as an author of national poetry. He finally took up a new role in the administration in 1941. During the Japanese occupation (1941–1945), he cooperated and received further training from the Japanese administration. When the British had re-established their rule by 1946, he became more and more involved in their administration, and reportedly gained unprecedented respect from the British. When Sultan Tajuddin died in 1950, his brother Omar Ali Saifuddin III ascended to the throne. Among his first official acts was a pilgrimage (*haj*) to Mecca, Saudi-Arabia, which symbolically underlined the religious dimension of his office – a crucial element for his legitimation. The role previously exercised by the Resident shifted to the High Commissioner, Anthony Abell, who initially 'had high regard for the new Sultan' and 'needed the Brunei ruler's co-operation', and 'began to cultivate a personal friendship with the sultan in order to win his favor'.[57] Unlike the Resident, he closely interacted with the Sultan. Soon afterwards, however, the same Abell became the Sultan's opponent in the negotiation over the Constitution's six year-long drafting process, as the historian Hussainmiya (2000) describes in meticulous detail.

The influence of the Resident declined parallel to Abell's rising role. The Sultan began to convey his intention of securing a higher extent of autonomy in domestic affairs, and also to codify a fixed order for the royal succession. His demands culminated in increasingly detailed plans for drafting a constitution, which were in principle favoured by both sides. The British, however, at that time envisioned a constitution that would secure their own continuing influence. The British were, among other aspects, concerned about their colonial rule's legal status: they had realised that neither the protectorate agreement (1888) nor the supplementary treaty (1905–6) had given them legislative powers, although de facto they exerted them, thus posing questions of whether already enforced enactments were even valid.[58] The Sultans, in their acknowledged capacity as 'absolute sovereigns' and 'independent' rulers (as stipulated in the 1905–6 treaty), had never *formally* approved these laws, and there was no legal procedure in place for doing so.[59]

---

[56] ibid 12.
[57] ibid 13.
[58] ibid 14.
[59] Hussainmiya, '"Manufacturing Consensus"' (n 54) 342–343.

Another point of contention pertained to the State Council, which consisted of nobles (*Pengiran*) appointed by the Sultan. This 'traditional' political institution was increasingly seen as a counterforce against colonial interests. The Sultan had reportedly used the Council to counter British proposals, eg by turning down a British-envisioned State Treasurer (Incorporation) Enactment in 1953 through 'the Council's' objection'.[60] The British wanted to replace the Council and turn the Sultan into a 'constitutional monarch'.[61] Although both sides wanted to restructure Brunei's distribution of powers, resources, and law-making procedures in a 'modern', ie institutionally formalised way, and they agreed to jointly initiate the drafting of a constitution, their motivations could rarely have been more different.

As the treaty of 1905–06 defined the Sultan's powers as the 'absolute' and 'independent' sovereign and executive, the British were unable to enact a constitution simply on their own and depended on his willingness to enter into a substantial agreement. On 12 May 1953, the Sultan publicly declared in a royal address (*titah*) his 'consent to grant a constitution'.[62] They question now was, what should be its contents?

Sultan Omar Ali Saifuddin III established an Advisory Committee consisting of seven Brunei Malay representatives (called '*tujuh serangkai*', literally 'seven branches') to prepare a report on a future constitution. Its members were carefully chosen, as it included, among other members, Islamic officers from the mosque communities as well as a Malay group of influential school teachers (who had been trained in Malaya and were politically the most vocal group outside the palace). Among them was Haji Mohd Yusuf ('Yura Halim'), a key figure in Bruneian history who, among many other patriotic achievements, composed the royalist national anthem (*Allah Peliharakan Sultan*, Allah Save the Sultan) and also wrote the first (equally patriotic) Bruneian novels, including *Bendahara Menjadi Sultan* (The Chief Minister Becomes Sultan, 1951).[63] The committee's mission was to collect

---

[60] For details on the State Council, its role and political influence, including in the constitution making-process, see Hussainmiya, '"Manufacturing Consensus"' (n 54).

[61] For an account of the *1955 Memorandum of R.H Hickling* which indeed suggested that:

> [t]he Sultan was not an absolute monarch, but must consult his principal officers before making major decisions for the State. As Hickling concluded, "... in theory it will be clear that the Sultan has always been regarded as constitutional monarch, acting on the advice of his Ministers".

See B A Hussainmiya, 'Constitutional Practice in Brunei as highlighted in the 1955 Memorandum of R.H. Hickling' (2006) 79(2) *Journal of the Malaysian Branch of the Royal Asiatic Society* 32.

[62] Hussainmiya, *The Brunei Constitution* (n 51) 16.

[63] He had received degrees from University of Hiroshima in 1945 and an Honorary Doctorate in Law from the University of Vancouver, Canada, in 1961. He survived the American atomic attack on Japan and died in 2016, at the age of 92, as one of the most honoured members of the Bruneian State's senior elites, who held too many prestigious positions in Brunei and abroad to be listed here. He had also accompanied the Sultan for the constitutional negotiations in London. For more details, see 'YAM Pengiran Setia Negara Pengiran Dr. Haji Mohd Yusuf – Yura Halim' (*The Daily Brunei Resources*, 12 April 2016) http://bruneiresources.blogspot.de/2016/04/yam-pengiran-setia-negara-pengiran-dr.html accessed 18 September 2018.

Ethnicity, Religion and Absolute Monarchy in Brunei 95

views in Brunei society on a future constitution through interviews, to study other Malayan constitutions, and to prepare a final report. The *tujuh serangkai* are said to have gone to all sub-districts (*mukim*) to collect their data.[64] A 50-page report was submitted to the British High Commissioner in March 1954. Its recommendations were modelled largely after the 1948 Constitution of Kelantan and some elements from a draft of a constitution that was simultaneously proposed for Sarawak. The cited views from the public called for an improved education system, better living standards based on a better distribution of the oil wealth, employment, and nationalist sentiments with strong Malay ethno-nationalist undertones calling for a 'Brunei for Bruneians', while reaffirming 'friendship' with the British.[65] This to some extent resembled parallel Malay ethno-nationalist sentiments in neighbouring Malaysia. The 'Brunei for Bruneians' call may be read vis-à-vis British interference, but also in terms of 'migrant' populations such as the ethnic Chinese. The report called for the British Resident to be renamed as 'advisor' (*penasihat*) who must be 'eloquent in (the) Malay language', and who must not interfere in religious or customary matters.[66] It also called for the establishment of a Prime Minister (*menteri besar*) post, appointed by the Sultan, to be held by a Muslim 'Brunei Malay', among other proposed posts and institutions. Furthermore, only ethnic Malays should be allowed to work in the civil service, the educational sector should prioritize Malay needs, migration – read, the influx of non-Malays – should be limited, and the Constitution's official, first language should be Malay, which in cases of doubt would be superior to English. It also argued for freedom of expression and free 'assembly of religion', 'freedom from poverty and fear', and 'fair protection under the law'.[67] The draft which rejected any merger with neighbouring states, included details for handling the royal succession, and outlined citizenship rights. It also addressed possible elections, eg that voters must be Malays or other 'indigenous' Bruneians. In sum, the document put great emphasis on the Sultan's powers, the supremacy of ethnic Malays, the supremacy of Islam and Muslims, and a political role for customary elites (besides the Sultan, including eg the *wazir*, *cheteria*, and *mentri/pehin*) – all of which indeed became core themes for the MIB state as it exists today. Unsurprisingly, the British refused a constitutional vision that would change the status of their Resident and High Commissioner, even more so as the envisioned Malay Prime Minister would replace the High Commissioner as the highest-ranking administrative authority. Similarly, they found it unacceptable that their influence would be reduced to non-binding advice, amongst other disagreements. The Sultan faced diametrically contradicting expectations from two sides, namely his Bruneian elites and the British. For a start, he chose a strategic middle-stance.

---

[64] ibid.
[65] Hussainmiya, *The Brunei Constitution* (n 51) 19. For a more detailed account of the report see the same source.
[66] ibid.
[67] ibid 20.

Parallel to this report, the British High Commissioner had produced its own study which was completed in 1955 and led by an assistant attorney general from Sarawak, R.H. Hickling. Hickling had consulted with the ambitious Malay teachers[68] whom, he concluded, were inspired by anti-colonial developments in Malaya and Indonesia and were assumed to potentially become a politically influential group in a future Bruneian polity. He also assumed that Brunei already had a *non-written* constitution (reflecting debates in colonial legal anthropology about 'law' in non-Western societies),[69] and addressed the question of citizenship rights for foreigners and non-Malays, where the British position was hardly compatible with the *tujuh serangkai*'s. The report concluded that it would serve British interests best to keep the situation as it is, ie not having a written constitution for the time being. It also ascertained the legal interpretation according to which the British were not able to enforce a constitution of their own without the Sultan's consent through an 'order in council', as they did in Sarawak. Brunei had been a 'protected state', which would have allowed for an order-in-council solution, from 1888 until 1905–6, but the supplementary treaty stipulating the 'advice' clause and affirming the Sultan's independent 'sovereign' powers made any unilateral solution impossible.

The Sultan, for his part, then requested the British to advise him on technical matters for the drafting of a constitution. In late 1954, the British had provided him with a first draft. The Bruneian Constitutional Advisory Committee members, however, felt that their recommendations had not sufficiently been considered. The Sultan, again taking a middle-stance, first gave his approval to the draft before withdrawing it again and demanding the High Commissioner Abell to explain why the Bruneian recommendations had not been incorporated. The draft, the Sultan and British side agreed, would thus only be a starting point.[70] Abell, however, had sent Hickling's Report and the draft to the Colonial Office in London in March 1955 to consider preparations for the legislative procedure, without consent from the Sultan, much to the latter's displeasure. The Sultan asked Abell to submit to him the full report and related documents. As Hussainmiya's (2000: 25) research in the colonial archives reveals, Abell had indeed sent *two* documents to London, only one of which the Sultan had approved. The Sultan therefore had every reason to be suspicious. The secret second document declared Abell's intention to maintain British political control and addressed 'the details of the legal instruments designed to bring' the draft constitution 'into effect', which Abell explicitly considered unnecessary to be discussed with the Sultan or his *wazir* at this stage.

The British draft distinguished between legislative and executive branches, which would be overseen by a colonial governor. The Bruneian State Council, in contrast, which as mentioned above served as an important political instrument

---

[68] Labelled 'young turks' by Hussainmiya, *The Brunei Constitution* (n 51).
[69] Hussainmiya, 'Constitutional Practice in Brunei' (n 61) 33.
[70] Hussainmiya, *The Brunei Constitution* (n 51) 23.

for the Sultan, would have to be rearranged into separate bodies. Brunei Malay key functionaries (the two principal wazir, *pemancha* and *pengiran bendahara*) and the other *pengirans* would be stripped of their influence, whereas the High Commissioner and Resident would enjoy constitutionally guaranteed supreme veto powers. Both of these conditions were neither discussed with the Sultan, nor would he have accepted them.

In September 1954, Brunei established district advisory councils in the four districts (*daerah*), following the British-led constitutional committee's advice, which, unlike the Sultan and his elites, wanted to establish representative Western-style democratic institutions. The councils' members came from diverse backgrounds: Malay school teachers, religious teachers, and even Chinese traders. The dominating force, however, were the 'young turk' teachers.[71] The Councils were supposed to send 'observers' to State Council meetings. They were not supposed to speak there, except with permission from the Sultan requested two weeks in advance, but some ignored this and acted as a de facto opposition, provocatively undermining both the Council's and the High Commissioner's authority. The Sultan, it is said, saw advantages in this, 'waiting to deal a final blow to the high commissioner's ambitions to enshrine British powers in the constitution'.[72]

Abell realised the need to make further concessions. He made certain promises to the Sultan, including abolishing the 'advice' clause and returning of the island of Labuan to Brunei's territory. However, those suggestions were turned down by the Colonial Office in London resulting in a further loss of Abell's credibility.

The first constitutional proposal envisioned three bodies to replace the state council, a legislative council (headed by the resident), a policy-making executive council, and a privy council (headed by the Sultan), backed by up to six local councils. The Sultan had, once again ambiguously, initially been agreeable to this structure, but realising that this framework would keep the High Commissioner's supreme powers in place and maintain British control over finance, royal succession, the public service and the judiciary, afterwards withdrew his agreement again. Abell offered new concessions in the fields of finances, security, and external defence. The Sultan responded positively, but started to make further demands, for example regarding the political status of his nobles (*pengiran*) for whom he wanted to have guaranteed seats in each council. Such demands strengthened the Sultan's support among his royal court's traditional elites. Throughout 1955, he refused to ratify any British drafts and instead made further demands, especially targeting at the High Commissioner's powers, much to the latter's frustration. The Colonial Office in London simultaneously put increased pressure on Abell to ensure that the constitution would serve their interests, although the style of negotiation should not alienate the Monarch. As of 1956, this situation was not going anywhere, with the three forces – the Colonial Office, High Commissioner

[71] ibid 27.
[72] ibid 28.

Abell, and the Sultan – being unable to come to terms. Things became even more complicated when a fourth force entered the scene, namely the newly formed first political party in Bruneian history, the earlier mentioned PRB, which had begun to organise itself since the early 1950s with growing popularity and 10,000 followers by the time of its registration (10% of the population).

The PRB entered the stage of constitutional politics with full force and sought to exploit the constitution-making negotiations for its own purposes.[73] Inspired by the rising powers of like-minded nationalist anti- and post-colonial movements elsewhere in the Malay world, it wanted to influence the formation of a post-colonial political and legal order. Initially, the British may even have secretly supported the PRB on this matter to some extent, although officially, they exclusively negotiated with the Sultan.[74] Leaving aside any details on the complex agitation between the PRB, traditional royal and village elites, and the Sultan, the British mood and that of the Sultan soon turned against the PRB, which was increasingly seen as an aggressive force and hindrance, rather than as a constructive participant in the constitutional negotiations.

Following the original plan, a constitution should be enforced two years after the Sultan's earlier mentioned royal speech of 1953. In 1956, there were still no tangible results. One point of contention was the Sultan's demand that at least the post of a Prime Minister should be established now, for which the British insisted that no Brunei Malay was presently qualified, whereas the Sultan insisted that *only* a Brunei Malay should fill that post (a position shared by the PRB). As this would have implied the de facto replacement of the British Resident by a Malay, and the Sultan defined it as a red line for negotiations, no agreement was reached until 1959.

As of mid-1957, the British had given up their insistence on the 'advisory' clause, and also softened their stance on citizenship and immigration matters. The Sultan grew in confidence through the increasingly successful negotiations and continued his strategy of maximum demands. The Monarch later wrote a poem about these negotiations – the *Syair Perlembagaan Brunei*. One section of it, cited by Hussainmiya, reads: 'As his (Abell's) proposals change constantly … he no more holds faith or credibility … The entire (constitution) draft needs review … To assume new and appropriate meaning'.[75]

In 1957, the British presented a new draft. The Sultan expressed 'general agreement' but, following discussions with the state council,[76] insisted on further changes. The High Commissioner was in a difficult position; neither was he able to convince London of the concessions he personally favoured, nor was he able to convince the Sultan of London's or alternatively his own proposals.

---

[73] ibid 31.
[74] ibid.
[75] Translation as cited in ibid 37.
[76] ibid 38.

Ethnicity, Religion and Absolute Monarchy in Brunei 99

The PRB, for its part, made an unsuccessful attempt of having their own negotiations with the British by submitting a 'memorandum' to the Colonial Office through the High Commission (after consulting a British lawyer) and even making an uninvited travel to London in 1957. The Sultan was not amused, and knowing this, the British sought to discourage the PRB's travel plans. The Sultan, too, was travelling to London in September 1957, with the intention to personally negotiate a constitution that would reserve his and his elite's unrestricted powers. While the Sultan and the British were still unable to agree on the Prime Minister post, the PRB further complicated things by calling for an *elected* office, as opposed to one *appointed* by the Sultan.

The Sultan held three discussion meetings with the Colonial Office in London, in which the British made important *symbolic* concessions: They affirmed their 'support' for the Sultan and the royal family and acknowledged Brunei's status as a Muslim Malay Sultanate – the later MIB state's core themes. However, they also wanted the Sultan to develop an inclusive government politically accommodating the entire population and wanted him to work together with Sarawak and Northern Borneo under a proposal called 'Closer Association'. The Sultan, for his part, insisted on the abandonment of the High Commissioner's reserve powers and the immediate replacement of the Resident through a Malay Prime Minister. After all, he left London 'deeply disappointed'.[77] The PRB's visit was even less successful, as the British expressed their unwillingness to accept them as a negotiation party without the Sultan's consent.

The Sultan had agreed in London to the British demand of holding elections for the district councils, but, remaining consistent to the earlier pattern of unpredictable ambiguity, withdrew this position shortly afterwards.[78] As of 1958, the mood in Brunei became increasingly heated, with groups supporting the Sultan, the PRB, and the Brunei Malay Teachers' Association all emphasising their rejection of the British position. At a state council meeting, a delegate publicly tore apart a copy of the newest British draft. The district councils, too, were now working on their own draft proposals, some of which also wanted to limit the Sultan's executive powers. All Bruneian parties, however, agreed on the establishment of a Prime Minister's post to replace the Resident. As of March 1958, the state council presented its own draft calling for an independent, post-colonial order that would disadvantage any 'non-indigenous' population.[79] The British, again, refused to accept the Bruneian position.

The Sultan then tried to split the British side: When the state council's draft was presented, the High Commissioner was present, but his comments were left out of the protocol – instead, the Sultan ordered these comments to be sent to the Secretary of State for the British colonies, which infuriated Abell. He was also

---

[77] ibid 41.
[78] ibid 44.
[79] On the details, see ibid 45.

disappointed by the Bruneian side's categorical rejection of the Closer Association agreement for Borneo. Brunei indicated it would rather cooperate with the Muslim-dominated Malay Federation. Making things worse for Abell, the Colonial Office sent a high-ranking officer to study the situation in Brunei first-hand. This study resulted in a position that differed from Abell's but emphasised understanding for the Sultan's side. The intra-British splits deepened. The Sultan's relationship with the Resident, Gilbert, had turned so bad that Gilbert became a 'persona non-grata',[80] and London withdrew him. For the farewell reception held for Gilbert, the Sultan excused himself for 'health' reasons, to the anger of Abell, who viewed this as a show of disrespect. The Sultan's side celebrated Gilbert's departure. The new Resident, D.C. White, showed even greater understanding of the Sultan's refusal to accept a 'Western'-imposed constitution, thus contradicting Abell's tireless efforts to protect British powers even further.

As of 1958, the British finally gave up their insistence on retaining the High Commissioner's reserve powers – a final defeat for Abell. Over the years, Abell had made one concession after the other, while the Sultan's side gradually increased its demands. He finally resigned from the negotiations, without prior discussion with the Colonial Office. Abell suggested that all involved parties should continue their negotiations directly with London.[81]

Finally, a Bruneian delegation left for London, although the Colonial Office had not been pleased by Abell's self-chosen withdrawal from the process. Abell and White also travelled to London to prepare the British side for their negotiation. The final negotiations between the Bruneians and the Colonial Office lasted from 23 March until 6 April 1959. The results entirely contradicted Abell's and the Colonial Office's long-held positions. The Resident's post was given up, and the details for a takeover to a Bruneian Malay Prime Minister were determined. Brunei achieved its complete separation from Northern Borneo and Sarawak. Only one major point of Brunei's demands was not conceded, which ironically, ensured the monarchy's survival – namely that Britain would retain total control over defence matters. In this capacity, British military forces, aided by Gurkha soldiers, ended the PRB rebellion in December 1962.

The treaties of 1888 and 1905–6 were abrogated, and the British-Brunei Agreement (Treaty) of 1959 came into force. The new Agreement still included a weakened 'advise' clause, excluding religious and customary affairs, but unlike pre-1959, the High Commissioner did not have any executive powers anymore.[82] Follow-up letters exchanged between the British Secretary of State and the Sultan ensured that despite this clause, the Sultan would de facto be autonomous in law and foreign relations.[83] Effectively, Brunei was given the right to self-governance

---

[80] ibid 48.
[81] ibid 51.
[82] Saunders, *A History of Brunei* (n 17) 137.
[83] Hussainmiya, *The Brunei Constitution* (n 51) 56.

by the British on 29 September 1959 and Brunei's Constitution of 1959 came into force, although the Sultanate was, to a limited extent, still formally under British colonial rule. Through the Constitution, the Sultan became the supreme executive authority, a position that his office enjoys until today. The outcome of these negotiations therefore provided the very foundations on which much of the absolute monarchy's powers today, and its principle of Muslim-Malay domination in state and society, are grounded.

The PRB dismissed the Constitution as (neo-)colonial[84] and not going far enough, also in terms of establishing democratic structures. It made some public declarations, but was unable to trigger a larger, or sustaining, constitutional debate – indeed, no such debate has publicly taken place since then. The royal and traditional elites, and the Brunei Malay Teachers' Association, however, reportedly supported the Constitution of 1959.[85]

As much of the Constitution of 1959's provisions were abandoned following the PRB rebellion of 1962, we will not discuss here the detailed provisions pertaining to the different councils (Religious Council, Privy Council, Council of Ministers, Legislative Council, and Council of Succession, all of whom would advise the Monarch holding absolute executive powers), or the short-lived politics surrounding their initial inauguration. It suffices to say that the Sultan's initial status as a powerful 'constitutional monarch' remained in place for only three years and has never been re-established. Under the contemporary constitutional provisions, he stands above the Constitution and explicitly 'can do no wrong', as discussed above.

Parallel to the Emergency Rule, Sultan Hassanal Bolkiah has ordered amendments to be made to the constitution in 1971, 1984, and 2004–2006. The amendment of 1971 further reduced the remaining British influence of foreign affairs, whereas defence became a joint responsibility. The next amendment, made in the year of Independence, 1984, finally removed the last remaining pieces of British colonial influence from the Constitution. In the wake of the 1984 constitutional reform, the Legislative Council was suspended and was only re-instated in the constitutional reforms 20 years later, that is in 2004. The newly added article 84(2) of the Constitution made the limitations of this Council clear, stating that 'nothing in this Constitution shall be deemed to derogate from the prerogative

---

[84] ibid 66.

[85] At least according to Hussainmiya's account: Hussainmiya, *The Brunei Constitution* (n 51). Locating other resources has proven futile and to the authors' knowledge, neither the PRB nor the teachers have produced publications on these matters that are still publicly accessible. It might, however, be an exciting task for constitutional historians to search for such documents possibly among elderly ex-PRB members. The pioneering Brunei anthropologist Donald E Brown had access to 'copies of the defunct and outlawed Parti Rakyat's newspaper' at the Brunei Museum during a research stay there in 1966, as he notes in the preface of forthcoming edited volume to be published in his honour, edited by Victor King and Stephen Druce. Future research may also seek access to the Museum's archives to see whether the PRB newspaper, or possible publications of the Teachers Association from that time, might still exist and possibly be made available for research now, more than five decades afterwards. Through such sources, an 'alternative history' of Brunei's constitutional politics of the 1950s could possibly be derived.

powers and jurisdiction of [… the Sultan who …] retains the power to make laws and to proclaim a further Part or Parts of the law of this Constitution as [… the Sultan …] may seem expedient'. Tey (2007) commented on these reforms stating that they:

> provided for the Sultan's unfettered legislative authority, rendered the Legislative Council a meaningless rubber stamp chamber, centralized and accentuated the executive authority in the person of the Sultan, enhanced protection of the Sultan's status as an absolute sovereign and ousted judicial review. The Sultan was now clearly made 'above the law', with the effect that the Constitution is certainly not a superior law in Brunei. Instead, the Sultan has become the state's *Grundnorm*.

Other important changes in the 2004–2006 constitutional amendment process are the establishment of the new Interpretation Tribunal, mentioned above, and the Council of Adat Istiadat, discussed below.

It is difficult to imagine for uninitiated outside observers, and therefore cannot be stressed enough, that these later constitutional developments were not accompanied by any public or otherwise documented deliberation over competing modes of constitutional interpretations, or public constitutional politics of any kind. The only interpretation put forward in the Bruneian public is that of the government, and more than anything else, it emphasises the fact that the Brunei Constitution would underline the country's character of being a Malay Islamic Monarchy (*Melayu Islam Beraja* or *MIB*). The notion of public 'constitutional politics', in this particular context, has become a contradiction in terms, and remains so until today.

According to Kershaw, since the 1970s, the Constitution had for decades even not been available for sale locally, and the Constitution Day (29 September) had been replaced by Teachers' Day.[86] This clearly reflects the government's intention to keep the issue of constitutionalism out of public speech and thought, at least until the 1990s. Only more recently, in the 2000s, has the Constitution again been made publicly available through government webpages and book publications, but again not accompanied by any public discussion consisting of differing views on it. The continuing absence of such discussions has to do with the absence of space for non-state political deliberations of any kind. Where today references are made to the Constitution by official Bruneian sources, it is for purposes of legitimation, never contestation.

B. Constitutional Ideas, Values and Sources: The Constitution and Melayu Islam Beraja (MIB)

The key cornerstones of Brunei's Constitution are the absolute monarchy and the 'Malay Islamic Monarchy' (*Melayu Islam Beraja*). Those motives are not

[86] See Roger Kershaw, *Monarchy in Southeast Asia: The Faces of Tradition in Transition* (Routledge 2001) 124.

exclusive and indeed as will be seen, the 'B' in MIB does take the theme of absolute monarchy and combines the other two themes.

In his *titah* on the occasion of independence on 1 January 1984, the Sultan announced that MIB would be the nation's national ideology, and that it 'must be honoured and practiced by all people of Brunei'.[87] On 2 October 1990 in a speech commemorating the birth of the Prophet Muhammad, the Sultan even went one step further by declaring MIB to be 'God's Will'.[88]

The roots of this ideology are debated,[89] with official Bruneian discourse asserting that it encapsulates the continuity of a six-centuries-old tradition. Mohd Zain (1996: 45)[90] for instance claims that MIB might be a new acronym but refers to and sums up the essence of the nation's centuries old character. According to the Brunei government, MIB is:

> a blend of Malay language, culture and Malay customs, the teachings of Islamic laws and values and the monarchy system which must be esteemed and practiced by all.[91]

Other, non-Bruneian, scholars are more sceptical and consider this more of an invented tradition used as a nation-building tool and to further legitimise the absolute power of the Monarch.[92] Indeed, these two positions might not be as mutually exclusive as they appear. Yet local scholars have been criticising foreign analyses as ignorant, orientalist and possibly malicious misrepresentations of Brunei.[93] The official publications themselves state that 'Brunei officially acknowledged MIB as the hallmark of the Brunei identity on January 1, 1984'.[94] May as it be, the term MIB entered political discourse in the 1980s and was propagated with 'an unprecedented commitment'.[95] The standing or prominence of MIB is also constitutionally enshrined with article 42(1)(e) prohibiting members of the Legislative Council from introducing or proposing a bill without the approval of the Sultan that 'may have the effect of lowering or adversely affect directly or indirectly the standing or prominence of the National Philosophy of Melayu Islam Beraja (known in English as Malay Islamic Monarchy)'.

---

[87] As cited in Black, 'Brunei Darussalam' (n 3) 302.
[88] Saunders, *A History of Brunei* (n 17) 187.
[89] For a short summary of this discussion, see Müller, 'Sharia Law' (n 12) 73.
[90] Mohd Zain Serudin, *Melayu Islam Beraja: Suatu Pendekatan* (Dewan Bahasa dan Pustaka 1996).
[91] Cited in Gary Bouma, Rodney Ling and Douglas Powell, *Religious Diversity in Southeast Asia and the Pacific* (Springer 2010) 48.
[92] G Braighlinn, *Ideological Innovation Under Monarchy: Aspects of Legitimation Activity in Contemporary Brunei* (VU Press 1992); Geoffrey C Gunn, *Language, Power and Ideology in Brunei Darussalam* (Ohio University Press 1997); Lindsey and Steiner (n 10); Frank Fanselow, 'The Anthropology of the State and the State of Anthropology in Brunei' (2014) 45(1) Journal of Southeast Asian Studies 90.
[93] See e.g., Abdul Latif Ibrahim, *Issues in Brunei Studies* (Akademi Pengajian Brunei 2003); Abdul Latif Ibrahim, *Melayu Islam Beraja: Suatu Pemahaman* (Pentagram 2013).
[94] Musa Mohidin, 'Brunei Darussalam Annual Report 2005–2009' (Department of Information 2013) www.information.gov.bn/Publication%20listsPDF/Annual_Report_BruneiDarussalam_2005-2009(Part_One).pdf accessed 18 September 2018.
[95] Kershaw, *Monarchy in Southeast Asia* (n 86) 127.

i. The Malay Element in the Constitution

In Brunei, Malay-Muslims form a larger percentage of the kingdom's tiny population than in neighbouring Malaysia, probably because of counting various 'indigenous' ethnic groups as 'Malay' as mentioned above. Malays are the ruling elite and benefit from the huge wealth the kingdom has enjoyed by virtue of its vast oil reserves. So, for example, in addition to providing free healthcare (except in private clinics) and elaborate infrastructure, the government also heavily subsidises rice and housing and even offers significant economic incentives to *mu'allaf* (Ar., a person newly converted to Islam or whose conversion is imminent).[96]

Only Malays are allowed to hold certain key positions in the government with article 84(A) providing that no person 'shall be appointed to any office specified in the Third Schedule unless ... of the Malay race professing the Islamic religion'. Positions that are reserved for Malays include the Auditor-General, Attorney-General, Chief Syariah Judge, Chairman of the Public Service Commission, Speaker of the Legislative Council, Clerk of the Privy Council and Legislative Council, and Secretary to the Council of Ministers. In addition, persons appointed as Ministers or Deputy Ministers have to be from the 'Malay race professing the Islamic religion' unless the Sultan makes an exception (article 4(5)).

ii. Islam in the Constitution

Reflecting the centrality given to the role of Islam in the Constitution and a non-secular conception of the nation, the Constitution begins with an 'Invocation' (Malay version: *Ucapan Doa*, literally a 'prayer recitation'), namely the Muslim expression (in the English version) '*In the name of ALLAH, the Compassionate, the Merciful, PRAISE be to ALLAH, the Lord of the Universe, and may the benediction and peace of ALLAH be upon Our Leader Muhammad and upon all his Relations and Friends*'.[97] Any prayer, and according to a wide-spread norm in orthodox Muslim discourse also any *deed* or writing, should be started 'in the name of God'. This is justified by the fact that the Qur'an's opening similarly begins 'In the name of God, the Compassionate, the Merciful'[98] (*Bismillahir Rahmanir Raheem*, as a

---

[96] Lindsey & Steiner (n 10) 326.

[97] Notably, this invocation was slightly altered in the English version vis-à-vis the first version of the Constitution of 1959, where the Invocation had been called 'Recital' and read: 'In the name of GOD, the Compassionate, the Merciful, PRAISE be to GOD, the Lord of the Universe, and may the benediction and peace of God be upon Our Leader Muhammad and upon all his Relations and Friends'. The original translated wording 'God' has been changed to *Allah*. In the Malay version of it, there have been no changes. The Malay version reads: 'Bismillahhir Rahmanir Rahim, Alhamdulillahi Rabbil 'Alamin, Wassalatu Wassalamu 'Ala Saiyidina Muhammad Wa'ala Alihi Wasahbihi Ajma'in'.

[98] There are also several slightly different (and possibly more precise) translations into English, such as 'Praise be to Allah the Almighty, the Most Gracious and Most Merciful' (which is also used in other Brunei government documents and the Sultan's speeches), but for the sake of consistency, we have chosen the version here that is used in the English version of the Brunei Constitution.

noun also called 'the *basmallah*'). In the context of Muslim-majority countries in Southeast Asia, Brunei is the only state that has placed this invocation of faith at the beginning of its Constitution. It is further noteworthy that the Constitution's Preliminary Part I from the outset stresses that 'Islamic Religion' in the constitutional documents exclusively refers to 'the Shafeite sect of Ahlis Sunnah Waljamaah', ie a state-brand of Sunni Islam adhering to the Shafi'ite Islamic legal school (*maddhab*), and not any other interpretation.

The Constitution, in *Part II: Religion and Adat Istiadat*, declares that the official religion of Brunei is Islam. This part also establishes the Adat Istiadat Council. Obviously, this structural order of the Constitution symbolically manifests that Islam should stand before and above anything else in the country's political sphere. It also reaffirms that within the 'triangle' of MIB, 'Islam' is consistently stressed to be superior vis-à-vis the other two elements. Against this backdrop, it is also noteworthy that the second part of the 'Recital', following the above-cited invocation of God, makes reference to another part of the MIB triangle, namely the monarchy ('B'), at that time represented 'By the Grace of God' by '(Sultan) Omar Ali Saifuddin (III)'.

Institutionally, there are three key agencies that share the mandate to preserve 'Islamic principles and Malay culture'.[99] These are the Ministry of Religious Affairs; the MUIB with its Legal Committees; and the State Mufti's Office.[100] Complemented by this is the Adat Istiadat Council which was introduced in the 2004 constitutional reform and is responsible for royal traditions and protocol.

The Ministry of Religious Affairs has bureaucratic responsibility for matters relating to Islam and the implementation of Islamic policy. Initially, this institution was only a department (Jabatan Hal Ehwal Ugama) within the Prime Minister's Office. In 1986, however, the Jabatan was elevated to become a State Ministry, with the first appointment of the first Minister of Religious Affairs on 21 October that year. Since then, the Ministry has been one of the politically most influential bureaucratic institutions in Brunei.[101]

The relationship between the Religious Council and the Ministry of Religious Affairs is, in principle, clear. The Council, by virtue of its capacity to issue legally binding *fatawa* and policy recommendations that carry significant religious weight, is a sort of de facto legislative body for the administration of Islam in Brunei. The Ministry, by contrast, is a bureaucratic body – an arm of the executive. Thus, the implementation of any decision or policy adopted by the Religious Council or approved by the Sultan is usually left to the Department of Religious Affairs.

---

[99] Ismail Duraman and Abdul Amin Hj Hashim, 'Brunei Darussalam: Developing Within its Own Paradigm' in Derek da Cunha and John Funston (eds), *Southeast Asian Affairs 1998* (Institute of Southeast Asian Studies 1998).
[100] See Religious Council and Kadis Court Act, Cap. 77 (1984).
[101] David Leake, *Brunei: The Modern Southeast-Asian Islamic Sultanate* (N. C. McFarland 1989) 141; Müller, 'Sharia Law' (n 12).

The Islamic Religious Council is responsible for advising the Sultan on Islamic religious matters in Brunei and reports directly to him.[102] It thus operates on the same level as other key organs of state, including the Council of Cabinet Ministers, the Legislative Council, Privy Council, and the Council of Succession. Its role as 'Religious Adviser' to the Sultan is acknowledged in article 3(3) of Brunei's Constitution of 1959, which states that 'the principal officers responsible to His Majesty the Sultan and Yang Di-Pertuan for Religion, Custom and Welfare shall be the Religious Adviser, the Adat Isti'adat Officer and the Welfare [sic] respectively'.

iii. Beraja (Monarchy) and the Constitution

The element *Beraja* of course contains some aspects of Islam with the Sultan being the official 'guardian and protector' of Islam and tradition in Brunei. Government literature also describes him as 'Allah's vice-regent on earth' (Khalifah) and 'leader of Muslim believers' (*ulil amri*), although 'sovereignty is in Allah alone'.[103]

The Constitution of Brunei Darussalam does not limit the power of the Sultan, Hj Hassanal Bolkiah Mu'izzuddin Waddaulah, instead providing the foundation and justification for his absolute power. The above mentioned 'Personaleinheit' of the Sultan and the state is, for instance, evident in the provisions of *Part VIII: Finance* of the Constitution. This part provides rules regarding the finance of the state, called the 'consolidated fund', and the Sultan and his family, titled the 'civil list'. While there is a distinction between government funds and the funds and expenditure of the Sultan and his family, 'Brunei has been described as being in the early Tudor period somewhere between Henry VII and Henry VIII. There is no clear separation between the privy purse and the public treasury'.[104] Indeed accountability of public finance has been a contentious issue in Brunei in the past.[105]

In addition, the Constitution grants the Sultan the exclusive power to amend the Constitution. Based on the amendments made in 2004 to the Constitution, the Sultan has to submit the draft of the constitutional amendment to the Privy Council but is not bound to act in accordance with the given advice of that Council (article 85(3) and (4)). The interpretation of the Constitution is in the hands of the Interpretation Tribunal, with its members being appointed by the Sultan (article 86).

---

[102] John Halligan and Mark Turner, *Profiles of Government Administration in Asia: Brunei Darussalam, Indonesia, Malaysia, Philippines, Singapore, Thailand* (Australian Government Publication Service 1995) 13.

[103] Abdul Latif (n 93) 205, 210.

[104] Richard Behar, 'The Fairy Tale's Over for the Kingdom of Brunei' *Fortune Magazine* (1 February 1999) 62.

[105] See, ie, the costly legal and rather public dispute between the Sultan and his brother Prince Jefri Bolkiah, who was chief of the Brunei Investment Agency and Minister of Finance in the late 1990s before he was sacked from both positions for misuse of funds. For a detailed account, see Saunders, *A History of Brunei* (n 17) 194–195.

Last but not least, under the provisions in *Part XI Miscellaneous*, the Sultan has immunity in either personal or official capacity (article 84B). The same immunity is granted to officials working on behalf of the Sultan; immunity is granted for actions conducted in their official capacity, although provisions can be made by written law against these officials to initiate proceedings against them (article 84B(2)). In addition, their actions are also not subject to judicial review (article 84C(2)).[106]

iv. Interaction between the Different Elements of MIB

Starting from the late 1980s, MIB was transformed into a more systematised and institutionalised 'national ideology'. For instance, while being a compulsory subject since the early 1990s, the new Education Order 2003 was 'inaugurated with the aim of achieving an effective, efficient and equitable system of education that was both consonant with the national philosophy of a Malay Islamic Monarchy or Melayu Islam Beraja (MIB)'.[107] Today, Brunei's literacy rate of 92.5% is the highest among the ASEAN states. By positioning Islamic studies and MIB at the core of Brunei's education and national development efforts, the Sultan's stated aim is to produce citizens with 'high morals' as well as a sound basic education.[108] The policy also acts, however, to shore up the conflation between Islam, Malay identity, and the monarchy that is the political foundation of the state.

The trends of an increasing emphasis of MIB developed parallel to an increasing emphasis of Islam. The government's MIB literature, as well as the Sultan's related statements, unambiguously stress that the three elements should be viewed as inseparable but do not enjoy equal status: within what the former Head of the MIB Supreme Council's Secretariat Abdul Latif Ibrahim (2003: 206) calls the 'triangle' of 'MIB', Islam is by definition superior to the other two elements (this had similarly been stressed in the earlier conceptualisation of MIB in the highly influential publication by the late former Minister of Religious Affairs Mohd Zain Serudin 1996: xi).

The relationship between the 'M' and 'I' is also peculiar. Whereas in neighbouring Malaysia, Malays are by constitutional definition Muslims, the government's definition of Malays in Brunei also includes non-Muslims, namely the small group of members of the officially-acknowledged 'indigenous tribes' (*puak jati*) who continue to resist the government's intense efforts in converting them to Islam. These persons can consider themselves ethnically fulfilling the characteristics

---

[106] Those provisions were included following the 2004 constitutional reform.
[107] Ministry of Education, *Education for All 2015 National Review Report: Brunei Darussalam* (UNESCO 2015), http://unesdoc.unesco.org/images/0023/002305/230503e.pdf accessed 18 September 2018.
[108] Khairunnisa Ibrahim, 'Religious Teaching, High Morals Key to Nation's Progress, Says Sermon' *The Brunei Times* (Brunei, 23 February 2008).

of the governmentally prescribed national identity, whereas in religious terms, they are excluded from it. The de facto equation of 'Malay culture' with 'Muslim culture' in public discourse, however, further complicates the picture. A non-Muslim member of the Murut community, for example, has shared with one of the authors his perceived alienation from MIB-framed national identity, despite being declared as a 'Malay' by the government in the official census – a classification with which he personally disagreed.

C. Constitutional Rights

The Constitution does not contain any fundamental or civic rights. The only provision that can be constructed in such a manner is article 3(1), which states that the official religion of Brunei is Islam and that 'other religions may be practised in peace and harmony by the persons professing them'. This is a provision that is similar to neighbouring Malaysia, albeit less controversial in the Bruneian context.

In relation to international human rights treaties in general, Brunei has been described as the 'most reluctant ratifiers' of the Asian countries, together with Singapore and Myanmar.[109] This might be because MIB has been elevated to the official state ideology and, since independence, the government consistently rejects in particular ideas of liberalism which are arguably closely connected to international human rights and related civic liberties.[110] The MIB-state's discourse strongly opposes calls for an expansion of democratic rights and civic liberties, while these restrictions are flexibly justified on traditional, cultural/ethnic, and religious grounds.[111] For example, MIB ideology limits freedom of expression and speech in regard to the criticism of either Islam or the Sultan, the 'I' and 'B' in MIB as discussed above. The new Syariah Penal Code Order 2013 (SPCO) provides a recent example of how these restrictions play out in legislative measures. For instance, the SPCO has various sections prohibiting acts – committed by Muslims and non-Muslims alike – that disrespect Islam or encourage Muslims to act in an anti-Islamic manner. Section 207(1) SPCO makes it a criminal offence to teach or expound 'any doctrine relating to the religion of Islam in a manner contrary to Hukum Syara' [syariah law] or carry out, perform or practise 'a ceremony or act contrary to Hukum Syara', while Subsection 2 expands its

---

[109] Riccardo A Sunga, 'Judicial Training in Brunei' in Aviva Nabadan, Christopher Sperfeldt, Faith Suzzette de Ios Reyes and Michelle Staggs-Kelsall (eds), *Judicial Training in ASEAN: A Comparative Overview of Systems and Programs* (Human Rights Resource Centre 2014) 29.

[110] Speech of Sultan Hassanal Bolkiah (1 Jan 1984), quoted in 'Brunei Seeks To Uphold 'Correct' Islamic Teachings' *Borneo Bulletin* (Borneo, 10 Sep 2013); see also Anthony Reid, 'Understanding Melayu (Malay) as a Source of Diverse Modern Identities' (2001) 32(3) Journal of Southeast Asian Studies 295. For the nexus of MIB and freedom of religion, see Human Rights Resource Centre (n 15) 57.

[111] Müller, 'Sharia Law' (n 12) 319; cf Kershaw, *Monarchy in Southeast Asia* (n 86).

application to non-Muslims. In both cases the punishment is a fine not exceeding $20,000 BND and/or imprisonment for a term not exceeding five years. In addition, non-Muslims who contempt the Prophet Muhammad or deride verses of the Qur'an face the death penalty if evidence is presented that satisfies Islamic law, that is by confession or by two male Muslim or one male and two female Muslim witnesses (sections 221(1) and 222(1) SPCO). If such evidence cannot be provided, the punishment will be up to 40 strokes and up to 30 years' imprisonment (sections 221(2) and 222(2) SPCO). Attempting to commit these offences carries the same punishment as actually committing it (section 223 SPCO), while abetting it carries a sentence of up to 40 strokes and up to 30 years' imprisonment (section 224 SPCO).

The new SPCO does not only include offences against the tenets of Islam but also 'religious' authorities. Section 230 SPCO exposes a person who 'contempts, neglects, contravenes, opposes or insults' [sic] a titah or decree of the Sultan and Yang Di-Pertuan to a prison term of up to five years. In the case of a person who 'contempts, neglects, contravenes, opposes or insults' the Islamic Religious Council, its members, its sub-committees or members, the Syariah Courts or the administration of the Syariah justice, the fine is $2,000 BND and/or up to six months' imprisonment. This provision is applicable to Muslims and non-Muslims alike.[112] No similar provision existed in the civil Penal Code, Cap. 22 (1951).

The paramountcy of the Sultan is also reflected in the strict *lèse majesté* provisions of article 53(1A)(a) of the Constitution, limiting the freedom of speech of members of the Legislative Council stating that no member:

> directly or indirectly derogatory of the rights, status, position, powers, privileges, sovereignty or prerogatives of His Majesty the Sultan and Yang Di-Pertuan, his Successors, His Consort or other members of the Royal Family or the National Philosophy of Malay Islamic Monarchy.

Indeed, the relationship between the ruler and the people of Brunei is based on a patron-client relationship of mutually binding duties between a 'just ruler' and his 'loyal subjects', which is framed on local discourse with reference to a paradigm ascribed to Malay monarchical tradition. In a locally well-known saying, it states that a 'ruler must be just and the people must be loyal' (*Raja wajib adil, rakyat wajib taat*), or, in another wording, a 'ruler must not be oppressive and the people must not betray the ruler' (*raja tidak zalim, rakyat pantang menderhaka kepada rakyat*). In return to the provision of order and security as well as the generous benefits of the oil- and gas-funded Bruneian welfare state, which is presented as the Sultan's gifts to his people, the society is expected to be strictly loyal and never question the Sultan and his government's policies.[113]

---

[112] Section 3(1) Syariah Penal Code Order 2013.
[113] Tim Lindsey & Kerstin Steiner, 'Islam, the Monarchy and Criminal Law in Brunei: The Syariah Penal Code Order, 2013' (2017) 25(4) *Griffith Law Review* 552.

IV. Conclusion

Brunei is one of the few absolute monarchies in the world as such the Sultan wields substantial power combining the authorities of the executive and legislative in a *Personaleinheit*. The Sultan does not only stand above the law but has become the *Grundnorm*. The conflation of the Sultanate, Malayness, and Islam in the MIB ideology further strengthens the absolute monarchy. The exceptional status of the Sultan is also evident in the Constitution which provides the regulatory framework for his absolute power. Even more so, the Constitution elevates the Sultan above the Constitution itself.

When the Constitution was first negotiated in the 1950s, this outcome was not pre-destined, indeed the colonial powers had different regimes in mind, initially more aligned to a constitutional monarchy rather than an absolute monarchy. Yet once the British handed over the political power to the successor regime, Brunei experienced a consolidation and expansion of the power in the hand of the Sultan, both through the Constitution and, to an even larger extent, through the emergency legislation that followed the rebellion of 1962. This consolidation of power is clearly evident in the development of the Legislative Council which was supposed to be elected and to have far-reaching powers, such as the exercise of financial control, pass laws, and criticise the actions of the government.[114] This institution was arguably supposed to provide some form of check and balance to the monarchy. This 'key' institution was quickly sidelined by the previous Sultan and his current successor – disbanded and once it was re-established, tightly controlled by the Sultan with its powers limited.

This streamlining of political power is complemented by a political and legal 'Islamisation'[115] process which strengthens the sacrosanct power and divine legitimisation of the Sultan. The above-discussed SPCO is just one stepping stone in the Islamisation of law in Brunei. Noteworthy in it is the applicability of Islamic law to non-Muslims and Muslims alike, so far a unique development in Southeast Asia. In addition, it criminalised questioning religious authorities, in particular in regard to the Sultan as the head of the religion.

Bibliography

—— 'Brunei Seeks To Uphold 'Correct' Islamic Teachings' *Borneo Bulletin* (Borneo, 10 September 2013).

—— Constitution of Brunei Darussalam 1959 (2011 Rev Ed).

---

[114] Saunders, *A History of Brunei* (n 17) 139.

[115] However, on problems related to scholarly usages of that term in the Bruneian and other contexts, see Dominik M. Müller, 'The Bureaucratization of Islam and its Socio-Legal Dimensions in Southeast Asia: Conceptual Contours of a Research Project' (2017) 187 Max Planck Institute for Social Anthropology Working Paper 6.

—— Intermediate Courts Act, Cap. 162 (1999).
—— Religious Council and Kadis Court Act, Cap. 77 (1984).
—— 'Royal address (*titah*) of Sultan Hassanal Bolkiah 1991, Titah' (Department of Information 14 January 1991) <www.information.gov.bn/Malay%20Publication%20PDF/EDIT%20TITAH%201990-1991.pdf> accessed 18 September 2018.
—— Supreme Court Act, Cap. 5 (1984).
—— Syariah Courts Act, Cap. 184 (2000).
—— Syariah Penal Code Order 2013.
—— 'YAM Pengiran Setia Negara Pengiran Dr. Haji Mohd Yusuf – Yura Halim' (*The Daily Brunei Resources*, 12 April 2016) http://bruneiresources.blogspot.de/2016/04/yam-pengiran-setia-negara-pengiran-dr.html accessed 18 September 2018.
ASEAN Law Organisation, 'Legal Systems in ASEAN: Brunei – Historical Overview' www.aseanlawassociation.org/papers/Brunei_chp1.pdf accessed 18 September 2018.
Behar R, 'The Fairy Tale's Over for the Kingdom of Brunei' *Fortune Magazine* (1 February 1999) 62.
Black A, 'The Stronger Rule of the More Enlightened European: The Consequences of Colonialism on Dispute Resolution in the Sultanate of Brunei' (2009) 13(1) Legal History 91.
—— 'Brunei Darussalam' in Black A & Bell G (eds), *Law and Legal Institutions of Asia: Traditions, Adaptations and Innovations* (CUP 2011).
—— 'Informed by Ideology: A Review of the Court Reforms in Brunei Darussalam' in Harding A & Nicholson P (eds), *New Courts in Asia* (Routledge, 2011).
Bouma G D, Ling R & Pratt D, *Religious Diversity on Southeast Asia and the Pacific: National Case Studies* (Springer 2009).
Braighlinn G, *Ideological Innovation Under Monarchy: Aspects of Legitimation Activity in Contemporary Brunei* (VU Press 1992).
Brown D E, 'Brunei: The Structure and History of a Bornean Malay Sultanate' (1970) 2(2) Brunei Museum Monograph 3.
Brunei Darussalam Prime Minister's Office, 'Population' www.depd.gov.bn/SitePages/Population.aspx accessed 18 September 2018.
Chang W C, Thio L A, Tan K Y L & Yeh J R, *Constitutionalism in Asia: Cases and Materials* (Hart Publishing, 2014).
Cohen D and Tan K (eds), *Keeping the Faith: A Study of Freedom of Thought, Conscience and Religion in ASEAN* (Human Rights Resource Centre 2015).
Duraman I and Hashim A A H, 'Brunei Darussalam: Developing Within its Own Paradigm' in C D d and Funston H (eds), *Southeast Asian Affairs 1998* (Institute of Southeast Asian Studies 1998).
Fanselow F, 'The Anthropology of the State and the State of Anthropology in Brunei' (2014) 45(1) Journal of Southeast Asian Studies.
Funston J, 'Brunei' in Fealy G & Hooker V M (eds), *Voices of Islam in Southeast Asia – A Contemporary Sourcebook* (Institute of Southeast Asian Studies 2006) 19.

Human Rights Resource Centre, 'Brunei Darussalam' in Cohen D and Tan K (eds), *Keeping the Faith: A Study of Freedom of Thought, Conscience and Religion in ASEAN* (Jakarta: Human Rights Resource Centre, 2014).

Hussainmiya B A, '"Manufacturing Consensus": The Role of the State Council in Brunei Darussalam' (2000) 31(2) Journal of Southeast Asian Studies 335.

—— 'Constitutional Practice in Brunei as highlighted in the 1955 Memorandum of R.H. Hickling' (2006) 79(2) Journal of the Malaysian Branch of the Royal Asiatic Society.

—— *The Brunei Constitution of 1959: An Inside History* (Brunei Press 2000).

Hooker M B, *Islamic Law in Southeast Asia* (OUP 1984).

Ibrahim A L, *Issues in Brunei Studies* (Akademi Pengajian Brunei 2003).

—— *Melayu Islam Beraja: Suatu Pemahaman* (Pentagram 2013).

Ibrahim K., 'Religious Teaching, High Morals Key to Nation's Progress, Says Sermon' *The Brunei Times* (Brunei, 23 February 2008).

Kershaw R, 'Marginality Then and Now: Shifting Patterns of Minority Status in Brunei Darussalam' (1998) 29(1) Internationales Asienforum: International Quarterly for Asian Studies 83.

—— 'Brunei' in Funston J (ed), *Government and Politics in Southeast Asia* (Institute of Southeast Asian Studies 2001).

—— *Monarchy in Southeast Asia: The Faces of Tradition in Transition* (Routledge 2001).

Leake, D, *Brunei: The Modern Southeast-Asian Islamic Sultanate* (N. C. McFarland 1989).

Lindsey T *Islam, Law and the State in Southeast Asia: Volume 1 Indonesia* (I.B. Tauris 2012).

—— & Steiner K, *Islam, Law and the State in Southeast Asia: Volume 2 Singapore* (I.B. Tauris 2012).

—— & Steiner K, *Islam, Law and the State in Southeast Asia: Volume 3 Malaysia and Brunei* (I.B. Tauris 2012).

—— & Steiner K, 'Islam, the Monarchy and Criminal Law in Brunei: The Syariah Penal Code Order, 2013' (2017) 25(4) *Griffith Law Review* 552.

Majid H A, *Rebellion in Brunei: The 1962 Revolt, Imperialism, Confrontation and Oil* (I.B. Tauris 2013).

Mohidin M, *Brunei Darussalam Annual Report 2005–2009* (Department of Information 2013) www.information.gov.bn/Publication%20listsPDF/Annual_Report_BruneiDarussalam_2005-2009(Part_One).pdf accessed 18 September 2018.

Müller D M, 'Sharia Law and the Politics of 'Faith Control' in Brunei Darussalam: Dynamics of Socio-Legal Change in a Southeast Asian Sultanate (2015) 46(3) Internationales Asienforum 313, 326.

—— 'The Bureaucratization of Islam and its Socio-Legal Dimensions in Southeast Asia: Conceptual Contours of a Research Project' (2017) 187 Max Planck Institute for Social Anthropology Working Paper 6.

Othman M S, *Perlaksanaan dan Pentadbiran Undang-Undang Islam di Negara Brunei Darussalam* (Dewan Bahasa dan Pustaka Brunei 1996).

Paduka Haji Kifli P H K b, 'Opening of the Legal Year' (Attorney-General's Chambers, 18 March 2008) www.agc.gov.bn/AGC%20Site%20Pages/AGCspeechesview.aspx accessed 18 September 2018.

Reid A, 'Understanding Melayu (Malay) as a Source of Diverse Modern Identities' (2001) 32(3) Journal of Southeast Asian Studies 295.

Saunders G, *A History of Brunei* (OUP 1994).

——, *A History of Brunei* (London: Routledge 2002).

Sidhu J S, *Historical Dictionary of Brunei Darussalam* (The Rowman & Littlefield 2010).

Singh R, *Brunei 1839–1983: The Problems of Political Survival* (OUP 1984).

Souza G B & Turley J S, *The Boxer Codex* (Leiden: Brill 2016).

Steiner K, 'Brunei' in Cohen D, Tan K, Nababan A and Kong F S D R (eds), *Update on the Rule of Law for Human Rights in ASEAN: The Path to Integration* (Human Rights Resource Centre 2012).

Sunga R A, 'Judicial Training in Brunei' in Nabadan A, Sperfeldt C, Reyes F S d I and Staggs-Kelsall M (eds), *Judicial Training in ASEAN: A Comparative Overview of Systems and Programs* (Human Rights Resource Centre 2014) 29.

Tey T H, 'Brunei's Revamped Constitution: The Sultan as the Grundnorm?' (2007) 9 Australian Journal of Asian Law 2.

Halligan J and Turner M, *Profiles of Government Administration in Asia: Brunei Darussalam, Indonesia, Malaysia, Philippines, Singapore, Thailand* (Australian Government Publication Service 1995).

US Department of State, 'Department of State: 2014 Investment Climate Statement' (June 2014) www.state.gov/documents/organization/226810.pdf accessed 18 September 2018.

Zaini A, *The People's Party of Brunei: Selected Documents* (Institute of Social Analysis 1987).

5

Indonesia's Constitutional Responses to Plurality

HERLAMBANG P. WIRATRAMAN AND DIAN A. H. SHAH

I. Introduction

The national emblem of Indonesia is the '*Garuda Pancasila*' – it depicts the claws of the Garuda bird gripping a white ribbon scroll inscribed with the national motto '*Bhinneka Tunggal Ika*' (Unity in Diversity). This motto captures the founding fathers' desire to ensure that Indonesia's plural society is appreciated and celebrated – they were of the view that in Indonesia's incredibly diverse society, the development of a common national culture for the whole nation is necessary and inevitable.

At the same time, Indonesia's founding fathers envisioned the '*Negara Hukum Indonesia*' (that is, a state that upholds the rule of law). Although this foundational idea underpinning the national legal system is often seen as a remnant of the Dutch civil law tradition,[1] Soepomo (the chief architect of Indonesia's independence constitution) had also propounded the idea of Indonesia as a *rechtstaat* (a state based on law), not *machtstaat* (a power-state). The political reality at the time, however, was far from Soepomo's imagination and, over time, the philosophical ideas underpinning modern Indonesia was subverted to serve the political interests of different regimes, with adverse consequences on Indonesia's plural social and political fabric.

Indeed, the history of the rule of law in Indonesia has been fueled by many contradictions, especially during Soekarno's Guided Democracy era until Soeharto's New Order regime. An authoritarian system dominated and shaped law and governance during these periods – this was manifested in policies that repressed fundamental rights[2] and restricted press freedom.[3] Extra-judicial dissolution of

---

[1] Daniel S Lev, *Legal Evolution and Political Authority in Indonesia: Selected Essays* (Kluwer Law International 2000).

[2] Todung Mulya Lubis, *In Search of Human Rights: Legal Political Dillemas of Indonesia's New Order, 1960–1996* (Gramedia 1993).

[3] See Herlambang P Wiratraman, *Press Freedom, Law and Politics in Indonesia: A Socio-Legal Study* (EM Meijers Institute-Wohrmann 2014).

dissident political movements was also a common practice. Therefore, law and the legal system as a whole were tools to serve the interest of political regime rather than safeguarding constitutional values and the plurality of ideas, cultures, and ethnic as well as religious identities in the archipelago.

The departure of Soeharto in 1998 offered hopes for a breakaway from Indonesia's authoritarian past. The post-Soeharto transition to democracy brought about growing political participation amongst civil society groups, political parties, and the press, which provided conditions for promising reforms. Centralised power was shifted to a decentralised model of politics, and this allowed local governments to develop a degree of authority in making local-based policies. This signaled, in some respect, a recognition of Indonesia's pluralistic nature, as a multiplicity of ethnic, religious, and linguistic groups – each with their own cultures and traditions – are geographically spread across over 30 provinces and 17,000 islands. In addition, the establishment of the Constitutional Court signaled a break away from the judiciary's troubled (and heavily politicised) past, while an anti-graft strategy was institutionalised into the broader system of governance. The idea of separation of powers became prominent in constitutional politics, underpinned by a relatively more accountable, free, and fair election. The birth of the Constitutional Court – whose role includes examining the constitutionality of laws, the impeachment of the president, the dissolution of political parties, and political conflicts among state institutions – has also been seen as a positive step towards democratisation and improving the rule of law.

More importantly, a comprehensive catalogue of human rights is adopted in the constitution. Hence, unlike the Soekarno and Soeharto administrations, politics and governance in the post-Soeharto period are framed by a constitutional commitment to securing rights of the people as well as restricting any potential abuse of power.

Notwithstanding the recent 'democratic backsliding',[4] Indonesia's democratic transition and development has been deemed as the most progressive amongst Southeast Asian countries. However, the spirit of the Pancasila's five pillars, which is considered as the backbone of the nation, is the most crucial driving force in contemporary law and politics. These five pillars or principles are embedded in the Constitution's Preamble, which also provides that the Indonesian state 'shall protect all the people of Indonesia and their entire native land' and that the five principles will guide the nation in 'improv[ing] the public welfare, advanc[ing] the intellectual life of the people and contribut[ing] to the establishment of a world order based on freedom, abiding peace and social justice.'

Against this background, this chapter is aimed at reconciling the various discourses on constitutional law and politics in Indonesia, by highlighting the

---

[4] See Edward Aspinall, 'Twenty years of Indonesian democracy – how many more?' (*New Mandala*, 24 May 2018) www.newmandala.org/20-years-reformasi/ accessed 22 September 2018.

importance of values and the ideal position of state constitutionalism, ranging from diverse political-cultural expressions of societies to the accepted governance system, to the ideal purpose of the country as stated in the Constitution's Preamble. In light of the growing dissonance in Indonesia about the nature of the Indonesian state and the principles underpinning it – in part fueled by radical groups seeking to re-enforce the 'Jakarta Charter', which would constitutionalise the implementation of *sharia* law in the country – an analysis of the plurality of constitutional understandings and sources in Indonesia is timely.

II. Historical Context

Indonesian society is incredibly diverse. There are over 300 ethnic groups spread across more than 30 provinces in the archipelago, but ethnic cleavages overlap with other important identity markers including language, territory, and religion. These pluralities shape, and are reflected in the constitutional order. It is beyond the scope of this chapter to discuss every aspect of such pluralities, but here we focus on three aspects that have been central to the practice of law and constitutional development in Indonesia.

First, religious laws operate alongside 'secular' laws, and this contributes to the plurality of laws that exist in Indonesia. Religious laws operate not only in Aceh, but also in several other regions and districts in the country. Second, this plurality of laws is enhanced by *adat* law (indigenous law), which reflects Indonesia's extremely diverse social fabric. Third, decentralisation is important to post-Soeharto law and governance in Indonesia. The clash between local laws and the national legal system is not solely related to adat law controversies, but also relates to the prevailing politics and other socio-cultural factors that are shaped by the country's overlapping pluralities. The following sections will highlight how these three issues have played out in the constitution-making debates in Indonesia, which will, in turn, illuminate an understanding of the context underpinning Indonesia's constitutional responses to plurality.

A. Managing Plurality in the 1945 Constitution and the First Fifteen Years of Independence

Since independence, Indonesia has had four constitutions. However, to understand constitutionalism and the constitutional responses to plurality in Indonesian legal history, one needs to track more than four periods of constitutional drafting processes: (1) the 1945 process (1945 Constitution, or UUD 1945), (2) the 1949 process (Federal Constitution, or *Konstitusi RIS*), (3) the 1950 process (Provisional

Constitution, UUDS 1950), (4) the 1956–1959 process (draft of Constitution),[5] and (5) the 1999–2002 process (Amendment of 1945 Constitution). The first four constitution-making processes are best understood within the contexts of decolonisation and a country in search of its national identity, while the last constitutional amendment is primarily shaped by the country's experiences with authoritarianism and the move toward democratisation and decentralisation.

The 1945 constitution-making process began with the formation of the BPUPKI (The Investigating Committee for Preparatory Works for Indonesian Independence) or *Dokuritsu Zjunbi Tyoosakai*, which was a Japanese-formed body inaugurated on 1 March 1945. The task of the BPUPKI was to investigate the readiness of the Indonesian nation to embrace independence and self-govern. In that committee, the Japanese authority appointed Radjiman Wediodiningrat as the chairman of BPUPKI.

The session, which took place from 29 May to 1 June 1945, featured 46 speakers who submitted their views on what should be the soon-to-be-independent country's foundational principles. Of the many speakers, three stood out, ie, Moh Yamin, Soepomo, and Soekarno. Yamin proposed five basic national principles, namely: nationhood, humanity, divinity, deliberation, and people's welfare. Soepomo, too, proposed five principles: unity, kinship, balance of body and soul, deliberation, and justice of the people. On 1 June 1945, Soekarno (who would later become Indonesia's first president) submitted his own iteration of the five principles, which he called 'Pancasila' (the five pillars).[6] It is Soekarno's version, as we shall see, which survives to this day. The five principles include: first, divinity; second, a just and civilised humanity; third, the national unity of Indonesia; fourth, deliberative consensus among popularly-elected representatives with inherent wisdom (which is considered as a form of representative democracy); and fifth, social welfare for all Indonesian people. For Soekarno, these philosophical principles were consistent with Indonesia's underlying values and its multiethnic, multireligious, and multicultural society. They were also deemed appropriate to achieve unity in a deeply fractured polity.

However, these ideas – particularly the first pillar on divinity (*Ketuhanan*) – were opposed by an 'Islamic' faction within the BPUPKI who wished to emphasise the predominance of religious (ie Islamic) values as the state's foundation. The debates were especially vociferous during the PPKI session (*Dokuritsu Junbi Inkkai*), or the Indonesian Independence Preparation Committee.[7] The most crucial issue

---

[5] Many constitutional law studies in Indonesia did not consider this period as an important political process of in making Indonesia's identity. If there is discussion on that period, mostly refers to the work of Adnan Buyung Nasution, *The Aspiration for Constitutional Government in Indonesia: A Socio-Legal Study of the Indonesian Konstituante 1956-1959* (Sinar Harapan 1992). Also, it refers to the work of Daniel S Lev, 'Colonial Law and The Genesis of the Indonesian State' (1985) 40 Indonesia 57.

[6] The word of *Pancasila* is adopted from Malay: [pantʃaˈsila]), considered as foundational philosophical theory of the Indonesian state. *Pancasila* comprises two Old Javanese words originally derived from Sanskrit: '*pañca*' (five) and '*sīla*' (principles).

[7] The PPKI was chaired by Ir.Soekarno and Vice Chairman Drs. Muhammad Hatta. The task of PPKI was to discuss the basis of the state foundation and everything related to the preparation of

discussed was whether or not Islam should be the basis of the state. In the end, the religious group relented, but sought, instead, a constitutional preamble containing a set of 'seven words' to accompany Soekarno's first pillar of the Pancasila: '... *dengan kewajiban menjalankan syariat Islam bagi pemeluknya*' (with the obligation of carrying out Islamic sharia for its adherents).[8] This proposal was eventually incorporated into the Pancasila through the Jakarta Charter – an agreement struck between the 'nationalist' and 'Islamic' factions after a long and protracted debate.

Yet, in the end, the Jakarta Charter fell through. The PPKI approved (unanimously) an eleventh-hour removal of the 'seven words' due to threats of secession by Christian nationalists from the eastern islands of Indonesia, who thought that the 'seven words' only served the interests of the Muslim majority.[9] The PPKI members, who represented a variety of ideological leanings (including those from the 'Islamic' faction), agreed to remove the 'seven words' to ensure that independence remained on track and that the young nation – in spite of all its cleavages – could be united under a common, 'Indonesian' identity.

In the early years of independence, the new Indonesian state – the Republic of Indonesia – was politically unstable. The Dutch government persisted in claiming authority and control over Indonesia, despite the proclamation of independence in 1945. Part of its strategy was to support the creation of a federal government,[10] and this motivated nationalists to negotiate with the Dutch government in developing a new draft of the Constitution.

Accounts on the constitution-making debates for the 1949 Federal Constitution is rather limited, but Drooglever's *The Genesis of the Indonesian Constitution of 1949* represents one of the most comprehensive works on the 1949 Constitution thus far.[11] Federalism was one of the key issues debated – a direct challenge to the 1945 Constitution that established a unitary state, which was seen as a solution for national unity and to safeguard the territorial integrity of the country. To be sure, the idea of constituting a federal arrangement had emerged years before the 1949 Constitution was drawn up. In November 1946, The Netherlands and the Republic of Indonesia agreed on a Netherlands-Indonesia Union that was to be established according to the federal principle.[12] Prime Minister Hatta (a Republican) was nevertheless quite open on this issue – he argued that 'only

Indonesian independence. Although the PPKI was formed 7 days before Japan came to its knees on allies, the PPKI was considered the most meritorious of preparing the Basic Bill of the State.

[8] For a full account, see Arskal Salim, *Challenging the Secular State: The Islamization of Law in Modern Indonesia* (University of Hawai'i Press 2008).

[9] Dian A H Shah, *Constitutions, Religion and Politics in Asia: Indonesia, Malaysia and Sri Lanka* (CUP 2017) 38.

[10] Audrey Kahin. *Rebellion to Integration. West Sumatra and the Indonesian Polity 1926–1998* (Amsterdam University Press 1999). See also P J Drooglever, 'The genesis of the Indonesian constitution of 1949' (1997) 153(1) Bijdragen tot de Taal-, Land- en Volkenkunde 65.

[11] See also the works of Solly Lubis in explaining 1949 Federal Constitution and 1950 Provisional Constitution Solly Lubis, *Konstitusi Republik Indonesia Serikat* (Graha Pustaka 2010) and Solly Lubis, *Undang-Undang Dasar Sementara Tahun 1950* (Graha Pustaka 2010).

[12] Drooglever (n 10) 69. This agreement was entrenched in the Linggarjati Agreement. The territories of this Union would 'coincide with that of the former Netherlands East Indies'.

through democratic government could Indonesia achieve steady progress and prosperity' and described federalism as an expression of democracy.[13]

For the Dutch, the federal solution appears to have been motivated by reasons of principle and practicality. Apart from concerns about self-determination and minority rights, they knew that Christian minorities in the northeastern islands were not keen on separating from the Dutch Crown.[14] The 1949 Constitution that finally took shape upon the formal transfer of sovereignty from the Dutch colonial power to the Unites States of Indonesia contained several features of a federal system. After a period of protracted negotiations between the Federalists and the Republicans, they agreed, for instance, to establish a Senate with legislative powers in all matters involving the federation's member state or center-state relations.[15]

The enactment of the Provisional Constitution of 1950 (*Undang-Undang Dasar Sementara* 1950 or UUDS 1950) was also coloured by tensions about federalism. The formation of the United States (ie the federation arrangement) in 1949 was not based on the will of the people, but it was instead a political ploy by the then ruling elites to gain recognition of sovereignty from the Dutch government.[16] It did not take too long before they realised that the federal arrangement was not sustainable for Indonesia. From the early days of negotiations leading to the Roundtable Conference on 27 December 1949, where a settlement to establish the federation was finally reached, Indonesian nationalists saw the arrangement as an imposed colonial structure. The federal arrangement was thought to link the core of the republic to Dutch-sponsored states.

Less than a month later, an abortive anti-Republic coup in Bandung on 23 January 1950 resulted in the dissolution of the populous Pasudan state in West Java, thereby accelerating the dissolution of the federal structure.[17] Violence and unrest spread to other parts of the archipelago – in Makassar, colonial soldiers (who were largely Ambonese Christians) clashed with Republican troops in April 1950. Shortly thereafter, an independent Republic of South Maluku (RMS) was proclaimed in Ambon, but this was suppressed by Republican troops during a campaign from July to November.[18] These events precipitated a joint decision – the RIS-RI Agreement Charter of 19 May 1950, according to which Indonesia would return to the form of a unitary state as per the 1945 Constitution. On 17 August 1950, Soekarno proclaimed the Republic of Indonesia as a unitary state.

In the next phase of constitutional debates, which took place during the *Konstituante* Council (1956–1959),[19] religion emerged again as one of the key

---

[13] ibid 82.
[14] ibid 70.
[15] ibid 80.
[16] Solly Lubis, *Ketatanegaraan Republik Indonesia* (Mandar Maju 1993) 48.
[17] Adrian Vickers, *A History of Modern Indonesia* (CUP 2005) 115.
[18] Anthony Reid, *The Indonesian National Revolution 1945–1950* (Longman 1974) 170–172
[19] The *Konstituante* Council, or Constitutional Council, was officially formed on 10 November 1956 and held meetings for almost two and a half years. As mandated by art 134 of the 1950 Constitution, the *Konstituante* together with the government, were in charge of drafting a new constitution. It was elected at the same time as Parliament during the general elections of 1955.

points of contention. This was particularly marked in the discussions about the ideological foundation of the state (*dasar negara*). It is worth nothing the majority of the parties constituting the Council represented different ideological leanings, but they could be broadly categorised into three groups:[20] those who formed the religion faction;[21] those who were proponents of socialism;[22] and those who advocated 'indigenous nationalism'.[23] All this more or less corresponded to what was proposed as the *dasar negara* – Islam (and, by extension, Islamic principles and values); social welfare; and the Pancasila.[24] With regard to Islam, the proposal to include the 'Jakarta Charter', which almost led to a deadlock in the 1945 constitution-making process, re-emerged in the *Konstituante*. As with the 1945 process, the idea of an 'Islamic State' was pitted against the 'integralistic state' concept that comprised the Pancasila values.

This time, the *Konstituante* failed to agree on the ideological foundation of the state, prompting Soekarno to decree a 'return' to the 1945 constitution. Although the constitution-making process fell through, it is worth noting that the *Konstituante* actually made significant strides with respect to fundamental rights. It was agreed that the Constitution would contain 24 provisions on human rights and 18 provisions on 'citizen rights'. There were 13 pending provisions that were to be adopted as human rights or citizen rights after further consideration by the Preparatory Committee. What was even more momentous – as far as Indonesian constitutional history was concerned – was the fact that this was the only draft Constitution that explicitly protected press freedom, including the right to print and publish freely (*hak kebebasan tjetak-mentjetak*).[25] Unfortunately, Soekarno's decree dashed any hopes for a new constitution and paved the way for an authoritarian regime.[26]

---

[20] Other scholars have distinguished different categories, such as Feith and Castles who divided Indonesia's political thinking into five groups: (1) radical nationalism; (2) Javanese traditionalism; (3) Islam; (4) democratic socialism; (5) communism. See generally Herbert Feith and Lance Castles (eds), *Indonesian Political Thinking, 1945–1965* (Cornell University Press 1970).

[21] These were members of the *Nahdlatul Ulama, Masyumi, Pergerakan Tarbiyah Islamiyah (Perti)*, and *Partai Syarikat Islam Indonesia (PSII)*.

[22] These were members of the Indonesian Communist Party (PKI) and Indonesian Socialist Party (PSI).

[23] These were members of the PNI, *Partai Indonesia Raya* (PIR), and *Partai Rakyat Nasional* (PRN). See Robert Cribb and Collin Brown, *Modern Indonesia: A History since 1945* (Longman 1995) 52.

[24] Yusril Ihza Mahendra, *Dinamika tatanegara Indonesia: kompilasi aktual masalah konstitusi, dewan perwakilan, dan sistem kepartaian* (Gema Insani Press, 1996). See also a study of Nasution (n 5).

[25] See Risalah, 1958/IV: 1881 in Wiratraman (n 3).

[26] Nasution (n 5). The *Konstituante* did not succeed in completing its task due to not merely the failed in agreeing ideology foundation of the State, but also the account the social and political context during *Konstituante* sessions. Nasution wrote that the failing of *Konstituante* is caused by several reasons, first, the deteriorating situation of economic and political conditions, while general elections in 1955 had no resulted in a stable majority government. Secondly, the role of Army was strong, while it was aloof from the *Konstituante*. Soekarno gained popular support, especially when he tried to return to the 1945 constitution back, while the army harnessed Soekarno's popular support. See Nasution's PhD thesis for complete account on this event.

B. 1999–2002: Post-Authoritarian Constitutional Reforms

The most recent constitutional amendment process began after the fall of Soeharto in 1998. The considerably 'freer' political space during the *Reformasi* ('reformation') era opened doors for access to justice, the establishment of democratic principles and practices, and greater citizen participation in political life and decision-making. It is therefore unsurprising that constitutional reforms were high on the agenda and became a matter of widespread concern. This was bolstered by the Asian economic crisis which resulted in dissatisfied citizens and the rapid growth of social movements supporting constitutional reforms.

The constitutional amendment spread over four years from 1999 to 2002, which coincided with the four stages of constitutional debates and deliberations. There were 21 matters listed for amendments[27] and the changes were radical and substantial, particularly those that concerned issues regarding the balance of power among the main organs of the state, judicial reforms, human rights provisions, and safeguards against abuses of power. There was great consciousness and ambition within the constituent assembly to emerge with a constitution that could prevent a recurrence of (or at least one that could remedy) the transgressions of the New Order period.

The constitutional reform process was led by the People's Consultative Assembly (*Majelis Permusyawaratan Rakyat*, or MPR). The MPR comprised 695 members, 500 of whom were national legislators of the People Representative Council (DPR), including 38 appointed military members. The remainder of the MPR consisted of 130 regional delegates elected by the Provincial Parliament and 65 representatives of Functional Delegates chose by the Election Commission. In the post-Soeharto era, this was the first opportunity for the political leaders to address constitutional reforms because the MPR is the sole body empowered by the 1945 Constitution to amend the Constitution. The primary actors in the constitutional reform were the political 'factions' (*fraksi*) – there were five main factions divided along party lines: the PDI-P (the Indonesian Democratic Party-Struggle), Golkar (the dominant party during Soeharto's regime), the PPP (United Development Party – an Islamic party), the PKB (the National Awakening Party), and *Reformasi* (a faction made up of the National Mandate Party, PAN and the Justice Party, PK). In addition, the military and police comprised a single faction (TNI-Polri) and there were four other factions made up of smaller parties in the legislature. Thus, unlike the New Order era where the Golkar party was the centre for Indonesia's political and economic gravity, the post-Soeharto era saw the emergence of political pluralism. In the MPR, each faction had its own agenda and preferences with regard to the substance of the Constitution, although those preferences were not always mutually exclusive.

---

[27] Denny Indrayana, *Indonesian Constitutional Reform 1999–2002: An Evaluation of Constitution-making in Transition* (Kompas 2008).

Consider, for instance, the Preamble of the Constitution. The constituent assembly – comprising the nationalist (such as PDI-P and Golkar) and Islamic-oriented (such as the PPP and *Reformasi*) factions agreed at the outset that the Constitution's Preamble (which contains the Pancasila) would remain 'untouched' throughout the amendment process. This was significant because it meant that the 'seven words' central to the Jakarta Charter in 1945 could not be introduced in the Preamble. However, the controversy on the role of Islam in the Constitution emerged again, but this time it was manifested in the debates on article 29 on religion (and religious freedom). The initiative to reintroduce the seven words was led by the PPP and the PBB. Factions such as the PDI-P, TNI-Polri, and Golkar resisted the effort as they were concerned about the prospect of an Islamic state.[28]

The debate on the role of Islam in the constitutional order was unavoidable for several reasons. First, the Islamic faction and advocates of political Islam, who were relatively silenced during Soeharto's New Order administration, have now found a platform to reintroduce Islamic elements into the Constitution. Second, the post-Soeharto period was deemed as a 'golden period' in which advocates of democracy, personal liberties, and human rights could articulate their views and visions for the country. Third, while Islam is the religion of the majority in Indonesia (over 85% of the population), there are a variety of perspectives on the role of sharia in the state and its place in relation to secular laws.[29]

In any case, to understand how and why the recent constitutional amendment exercise turned out the way it did, one must appreciate the different contexts in which the 1945 and the 1999–2002 constitution-making processes and debates took place. The pre-independence process was shaped by decolonisation and efforts at attaining independence, while the recent amendments were significantly influenced by the desire to deconstruct the legacies of authoritarianism. Both nationalist and Islamic factions who comprised the constituent assembly were themselves victims under Soeharto's New Order politics, and while they had different objectives (especially on questions regarding Islam and religion), they were eventually able to iron out – albeit not neatly – their differences on many issues.

---

[28] For a more detailed discussion of the different positions of the factions, see Shah (n 9) 40–42. See also Nadirsyah Hosen, *Sharia & Constitutional Reform in Indonesia* (Institute of Southeast Asian Studies, 2007) 199–204.

[29] Hosen (n 28) 255. Hosen observed that there is a group that believes that sharia is incompatible with constitutionalism. This group is divided into two camps: authoritarian/fundamentalist and secularist. On the other hand, there is a second group that holds the view that sharia can walk together with constitutionalism. This position rejects both the views of authoritarians and the secularists on this subject. He also found this second group is also divided into two approaches: formal sharia and substantive sharia. The formal sharia attempts to use sharia as a source or the primary source of law–which makes their position closer to the authoritarian/fundamentalists views. This suggests that human rights protection, checks and balances mechanisms, independence of judiciary and separation of powers are accepted in their constitutional theory as long as these elements of constitutionalism are in line with their formal interpretation of sharia.

In the end, the outcomes provided the foundations for the kind of constitutional democracy that is practised and lived in Indonesia today. The philosophical foundation of the country as stipulated in the Preamble and the idea of a unitary state survive in their original (ie, 1945) form. However, the amendments greatly enhanced separation of powers by entrenching the principles of constitutional supremacy (as opposed to the previous practice where the MPR reigned supreme) and judicial independence, and limiting presidential power. The commitment to democracy is evident through instituting a system of direct election of members of the DPR, regional representatives, and the president; provisions for decentralisation and the greater autonomy for regions, including the respect for indigenous peoples and their traditional rights; ending the established practice of *dwifungsi* which saw the military playing a prominent role in socio-political life; expanding the protection of human rights; establishing a Constitutional Court; and establishing several state auxiliary bodies to strengthen the balance of power amongst state institutions.

III. Pancasila's Unity in Diversity and Constitutionalising Indonesia's Plural Society

A. Ideational Plurality and the 'Source of All Legal Sources'

The constitution-making processes throughout Indonesia's history resulted in an amalgam of constitutional ideas and values that have shaped, and continue to shape, the development of Indonesian constitutional law. As we have seen, there were several values that have emerged and persisted throughout these constitution-making exercises. The Pancasila (five principles: 'believe in God', 'civilized and just humanity', 'nationalism', 'democracy' and 'social justice'), in particular, has persisted as the Nation-state's underlying philosophy. It is expressed in the Preamble, which also sets out the four aims of the Indonesian state: (1) the protection of the people of Indonesia and their native lands; (2) the improvement of public welfare; (3) the advancement of the intellectual life of the people; and (4) contributing to the establishment of a world order based on freedom, abiding peace, and social justice. In addition, the founding fathers recognised the importance of societal integration in the development of post-colonial and post-independent Indonesia. This awareness is reflected in paragraph 32 of the Constitution which states that 'the Government promotes National Culture'. The elucidation to the Constitution, drafted by Soepomo, provides that the national culture should be based on the 'old and genuine' cultures as manifested in the paramount cultures of the 'regions'.[30]

---

[30] In the context of the establishment of Indonesia's independence, as written by Darmaputera, there were facts that a great number of religious, ideological, ethnical, racial, provincial, etc. conflicts and tensions. Given the facts of diversity and heterogeneity, but there is also underlying unity. Some

Given its importance in the Indonesian constitutional context, the Preamble is known as the 'source of all legal sources' (*sumber dari segala sumber hukum*).[31] The position and function of Pancasila as a fundamental basis of the state and the source of all legal sources are rooted in the Provisional People Representative Assembly's decrees.[32] The Pancasila is essentially considered as a distinct Indonesian worldview, comprising legal and moral ideals that capture the 'spirit and character of the Indonesian nation'.[33] In the post-Soeharto period, the idea of the Pancasila as the source of all legal sources is engrained in MPR Decree No.III/MPR/2000, which provides the sources of law and the hierarchy of the rule of law in Indonesia.[34] Then, this MPR Decree is replaced by Law No.10 of 2004 on the Making of Laws and Regulations.[35] All this fortifies the view that no legislation could contravene the Constitution (including the values expressed in the Preamble) and the Pancasila.[36]

Nevertheless, the interpretation and implementation of the Pancasila vary across different regimes and different time periods. On the one hand, this may reflect the existence of plural interpretation of constitutional ideals and values, but what the Pancasila means in a given period of time has also been dependent on the prevailing regime's political interests. This was evident, for example, in Soeharto's speech regarding press freedom:

> In a democratic society that we wish to develop, there is no doubt whatsoever among us, about the right to have a different opinion, including having a different opinion from that of the government. Nevertheless, such difference must grow out of the pure desire to improve oneself ... [and any efforts] to express different opinions ... should be done in a democratic manner, based on the Pancasila and the 1945 Constitution.[37]

During Soeharto's administration, the Pancasila was enforced with an iron fist and used as a tool to pursue the regime's political (and mostly authoritarian) objectives. Therefore, any activity – be they political, social, economic, or cultural – which is

---

generalisations can be made that Indonesia is also unity. First, although diverse in linguistic as well as from the racial point of view, but Indonesia has linguistic unity which effectively applied as national language. This is *bahasa Indonesia*, which is based on Malay language, the *bahasa Melayu*. Racially it can be said that most of the Indonesian people, except Papua and adjacent islands, belong to the same racial root, namely the Deutero-Malay group. See Eka Darmaputera, *Pancasila and the Search for Identity and Modernity in Indonesian Society: A Cultural and Ethical Analysis* (E.J. Brill 1988).

[31] RM A B Kusuma, *Lahirnya Undang-Undang Dasar 1945: Memuat Salinan Dokumen Otentik Badan Oentoek Menyelidiki Oesaha-Oesaha Persiapan Kemerdekaan* (Badan Penerbit Fakultas Hukum Universitas Indonesia 2004) 28; K Kurnisar, 'Pancasila Sumber dari Segala Sumber Hukum di Indonesia' (2012) 11(3) Jurnal Ilmiah Ilmu Sosial 243.

[32] MPRS Decree No.XX/MPRS/1966, MPR Decree No.V/MPR/1973, and MPR Decree No. IX/MPR/1978.

[33] Darmaputera (n 30).

[34] Article 1 para (3) of MPR Decree No.III/MPR/2000 states that 'the source of national basic law is *Pancasila*'.

[35] Article 2 of Law No. 10 of 2004 states that '*Pancasila* is the source of all sources of state law'.

[36] Kurnisar (n 31).

[37] 'Pers Pembawa Panji-Panji Demokrasi' [Press as Carrier of the Banner of Democracy], Opening remarks for Indonesia's chief editors' meeting in Jakarta (26 March 1975).

deemed contrary to the state's visions of the Pancasila and 'democracy' were labelled as 'anti-Pancasila'.[38] The state apparatuses were given full authority to arbitrarily determine the kinds of activities and practices that were anti-Pancasila. In the realm of religion, the Soeharto administration prohibited any advocacy for sharia; civil society organisations – including religious ones – must make the Pancasila as their only underlying ideology; and every citizen must adopt one of the five officially recognised religions in the country.[39] The state's propagation of its peculiar interpretation of the Pancasila also entailed embedding the term 'Pancasila' in a range of social, political, and economic discourses, such as 'Pancasila Economics', 'Pancasila Mosque', 'Pancasila Industrial Relationships', 'Pancasila Democracy', and 'Pancasila Press'.[40]

In a similar vein, under Soekarno's 'Guided Democracy' era, the Pancasila was also utilised in ways that supported the administration's rigid philosophies, visions, and objectives. In this regard, it is important to understand that Soekarno was deeply suspicious of liberal democratic ideas, which he associated with the imperialistic motives of the West. Consider, for example, his views about the Pancasila in relation to press freedom: the Indonesian press – for Soekarno – is a tool of the Indonesian 'revolution' and it thus had to reflect and defend the ideals of the 'revolution' unconditionally. The press is thus obligated to support the Pancasila as the basis of the state (*dasar negara*), work to strengthen national unity, and subscribe to Soekarno's *Nasakom* (an abbreviation for 'Nationalism, Religion, and Communism') ideology.[41] *Nasakom* stressed the importance of three ideals: nationalism, Islam, and Marxism. For Soekarno, *Nasakom* embodied a unity among the three revolutionary forces that drove the Indonesian people's movement to remove the shackles of colonialism.[42] Interestingly, although communism and religion are often seen in antagonistic terms, the idea of *Nasakom* has been accepted by the largest Islamic organisation of Nahdlatul Ulama (NU) in the beginning.[43]

What all this shows is that the Pancasila can become a double-edged sword – on the one hand, it embodies values that are important for driving and sustaining Indonesia's plural society; on the other, as history has shown, it can be (mis)used as a tool to buttress a regime's political dominance and control over the society.

---

[38] Donald E Weatherbee, 'Indonesia in 1984: Pancasila, Politics, and Power' (1985) 25(2) Asian Survey 187; Douglas E Ramage, *Politics in Indonesia: Democracy, Islam and the Ideology of Tolerance* (Routledge 2002); Aris Arif Mundayat, 'Ritual and Politics in New Order Indonesia: A Study of Discourse and Counter-Discourse in Indonesia' (PhD Thesis, School of Social and Life Sciences, Swinburne University of Technology, February 2005).

[39] The five officially recognised religions during the Soeharto period are: Islam, Catholicism, Protestantism, Buddhism, and Hinduism. This list was later expanded during President Abdurrahman Wahid's administration to include Confucianism.

[40] Sulfikar Amir, *The Technological State in Indonesia: The Co-constitution of High Technology and Authoritarian Politics* (Routledge 2013) 27; Wiratraman (n 3).

[41] Wiratraman (n 3) 80.

[42] Soekarno, *Dibawah Bendera Revolusi* (Jakarta 1964) 1–23.

[43] Jan S Aritonang, *Sejarah Perjumpaan Kristen dan Islam di Indonesia* (BPK Gunung Mulia 2004) 332–333.

B. A Plurality of Sources and Approaches in Designing and Implementing Constitutional Rights

One of the ways in which the 1999–2002 constitutional amendments ushered in greater prospects for constitutionalism in Indonesia is reflected in human rights reforms. Previously, the original 1945 Constitution only contained a thin set of rights guarantees. There were five articles related to 'human rights': the right to work and livelihoods worthy of humanity; freedom of association and assembly and thought; freedom of religion and belief; the right to education; and the right to access natural resources.

The amendment introduced a comprehensive and impressive catalogue of human rights guarantees (Chapter XIA on Human Rights), covering various civil and political rights as well as economic, social, and cultural rights, indicating the acceptance (at least on paper) of universal human rights norms. Today, the Constitution provides at least 17 articles on human rights.[44] Most provisions mirror those found in the Universal Declaration of Human Rights (UDHR) and the International Covenant on Civil and Political Rights (ICCPR). There are also provisions similar to the human rights guarantees in the 1949 Federal Constitution and 1950 Provisional Constitution, both of which were heavily influenced by the provisions in the UDHR.[45]

Yet, the debates in the constituent assembly indicate that there was no wholesale and unanimous acceptance of principle of universalism (indeed, nowhere in the Constitution is this principle expressly recognised or endorsed). During the debates, there were many statements and arguments emphasising Indonesia's distinct character and circumstances, and these eventually shaped the outcomes for particular provisions, such as the limitation clause in article 28J(2). The clause provides a list of justifications to restrict human rights that largely mirror comparable provisions in the UDHR and the ICCPR, but there is one exception – 'religious values' is also included in the list. What this means is that 'religious values' could be invoked to restrict the exercise of rights, in line with the values of a Pancasila state that is based on the 'belief in the one and only God' and consistent with the 'religious' character of the Indonesian people.[46] Indeed, one of the

---

[44] See n 26. The human rights provisions under present Constitution is comparable to what the *Konstituante* has drafted 1956–1959. In the *Konstituante* session of 12 August 1958, a Drafting Committee was established to wrap up the debate about human rights and to formulate a decision about the human rights discussed in the plenary session An important distinction made by the *Konstituante* was between 'human rights', which applied to all human beings, and 'citizen rights', which only applied to those with the Indonesian nationality. The drafting report, submitted one week later, contained 24 human rights articles, which were agreed upon, 18 citizen rights, and 13 additional rights, which were to be adopted as human rights or citizen rights, but which still had to be further considered by the Preparatory Committee. This last group included the right to freedom of expression and opinion.

[45] See Koentjoro Poerbopranoto, Hak-hak Manusia dan Pancasila Dasar Negara Republik Indonesia [HumanRights and Pancasila as the Republic of Indonesia's Foundation] (J B Wolters 1953) 92.

[46] For a detailed account of the inclusion of the 'religious values' limitation and the motivation behind it, see Shah (n 9) 56–57.

justifications proffered for including 'religious values' was that it would prevent unrestrained exercises of rights.[47] In short, the quest to accommodate both universalism and particularism resulted in the creation of a bill of rights that is pluralist and – by any standards of a modern constitution – comprehensive,[48] but at the same time provides avenues for rights restrictions in ways that purportedly reflect the values of the society.

Context is thus important in understanding the differences in constitutional rights protection in Indonesia's constitutional history. The original 1945 constitution was promulgated before the UDHR existed, and Soekarno and Soepomo were deeply skeptical of Western-inspired liberal rights discourse. Nonetheless, conceptually, there was some element of progressive thought behind the 1945 constitution. The first paragraph of the Preamble, for example, states: 'Whereas independence is the inalienable right of all nations, therefore, all colonialism must be abolished in this world, for it is incompatible with humanity and justice'. When Soeharto ousted Soekarno and came into power in 1965, the already thin set of guarantees became virtually meaningless. The freedom of association and assembly and the freedom of thought were restricted under the guise of advancing political and economic stability. Soeharto's disregard for human rights and disdain toward political and ideological dissent was most notably evident in the mass killings of those who were allegedly Communists or Communist sympathisers in 1965–1967.[49]

The 1999–2002 constitutional amendments were thus informed and shaped by the experience with Soeharto's brutal violations of human rights, as well as the religious, ethnic, and regional-based violence that erupted in the country following the fall of Soeharto. There was a sense that Indonesia should work to rebuild its image in the international community. Therefore, in the year following Soeharto's resignation in May 1998, the MPR already began initiatives to promote greater human rights protection by adopting Law No. 39 of 1999 on Human Rights. This law then became one of the bases for human rights reforms in the constitutional amendment process in 2000. During that amendment process, the government also demonstrated its commitment to human rights protection by establishing a special Human Rights Court to prosecute those who were involved in gross violation of human rights during the *Reformasi* period.[50] In 2005, the government ratified the ICCPR. These initiatives were welcomed, but the public began to demand greater accountability. In particular, activists had hoped that Soeharto and his associates (namely, Prabowo Subianto, who was his son-in-law and a Commander General of the Indonesian Army's Special Forces Unit) would be prosecuted for human

---

[47] ibid.
[48] See Tim Lindsey, 'Indonesia: Devaluing Asian Values, Rewriting Rule of Law' in Randall Peerenboom (ed), *Asian Discourses of Rule of Law: Theories and Implementation of Rule of Law in Twelve Asian Countries, France and the U.S.* (Routledge 2004).
[49] Cribb and Brown (n 23).
[50] David Cohen, *Intended to Fail: The Trials before the Ad Hoc Human Rights Court in Jakarta* (International Centre for Transitional Justice 2003).

rights violations during the New Order era. Until today, no prosecution has been initiated by the state.

In any case, there is no guarantee that a comprehensive set of human rights protections on paper would secure the practice and enjoyment of rights. Much would also depend on the prevailing legal, social, and political dynamics in the country. For instance, although article 28I(1) of the Constitution protects the right to life and states that this 'cannot be limited under any circumstances', capital punishment is still being enforced in the country for drugs and terrorism offences. In 2007, the Constitutional Court was called upon to examine the constitutionality of capital punishment provided in Law No. 22 of 1997 on Narcotics. It held that such punishment was consistent with the Constitution, which did not have any explicit prohibition for capital punishment.[51] The principle of universalism continues to be sparsely acknowledged and applied in the courts, with judges preferring to provide an 'Indonesianised' interpretation of the parameters of constitutional rights that is measured against the principles and values of the Pancasila).

Another example of this contextualised approach to interpreting human rights protection concerns the Constitutional Court's decision on the constitutionality of the Blasphemy Law.[52] In deciding that the law – problematic though it might be – was constitutional, the court reasoned that as a nation that upholds the principle of the 'belief in one and only God' and is based on religious values, the Indonesian Constitution does not protect the freedom *from* religion, nor does it endorse antireligious ideas or the desecration of religious teachings and doctrines.[53] The court was also concerned about the prospect of widespread religious conflict if religious interpretations are left unregulated and if religious sensitivities are not protected.[54] It would appear that from the court's perspective, outlawing religious practices or expressions that could be deemed (by certain sections of the society) defamatory or blasphemous is justified in order to prevent public disorder in a divided and fragile society. There was no explanation of what 'religious values' entail or who would decide what those values are; instead, the court merely stated that religious interpretations must follow the correct methodology and that a religion's 'internal authorities' would determine the fundamental doctrines of that religion.[55]

In other cases, however, the court has demonstrated a greater degree of judicial creativity and activism in protecting human rights, to the extent that it effectively 'created' rights that are not explicitly provided in the constitution. This was evident in a petition for judicial review against Law No. 18 of 2003 on Advocates,

---

[51] Constitutional Court Decision No. 2-3/PUU-V/2007 on Judicial Review of Law No. 22 of 1997 on Narcotics. The case was filed by Edith Yunita Sianturi, Rani Andriani (Melisa Aprilia), Myuran Sukumaran, Andrew Chan, Scott Anthony Rush.

[52] Constitutional Court of Indonesia, Decision No. 140/PUU-VII/2009, Examination of Law No. 1, Year 1965 on the Prevention from Abuse of and/or Desecration of Religion (Arts 1, 2(1), 2(2), 3 and 4(a)) (19 April 2010).

[53] ibid 275.

[54] ibid 287.

[55] ibid 289. For further discussion on this point, see Shah (n 9) 150.

which prohibited non-advocates (ie non-lawyers) from providing legal services and legal advice. The court, in that case, declared that the concept of *negara hukum* (*rechtstaat*) implies 'the right to legal assistance', which is a part of human rights and must therefore 'be considered a constitutional right of citizens, even though the Constitution does not explicitly regulate or mention it.'[56] What all this seems to indicate is that the court's approach to resolving human rights questions could well be influenced by a plurality of factors, legal and extra-legal.

IV. Constitutional Structure and Institutional Arrangements for a Plural Society

The original 1945 Constitution has undergone substantial changes during the four constitutional amendment processes from 1999 to 2002. Where the original manuscript of the 1945 Constitution contained only 71 provisions and sub-provisions, now the amended 1945 Constitution comprises 199 provisions and sub-provisions.

Constitutional and democratic reforms after the fall of Soeharto have paved the way for the establishment and development of new institutions, especially those with important check and balance functions that were missing during the New Order and Guided Democracy era. The Constitutional Court and the Supreme Court are separate from the other branches of state powers (executive and legislative power). The amended 1945 Constitution of the State of the Republic of Indonesia establishes at least nine institutions of governance: (1) the People's Legislative Assembly (DPR); (2) the Regional Representative Council (DPD); (3) the People's Consultative Assembly (MPR); (4) the Supreme Audit Board; (5) the President; (6) the Vice President; (7) the Supreme Court; (8) the Constitutional Court; and (9) the Judicial Commission.

With these nine institutions, there is a clearer structure for separation of powers in Indonesia, but it also illustrates the plurality of political power and the ways in which it is dispersed. Previously, the MPR sat at the apex of the constitutional structure, with other institutions such as the Supreme Court, the DPR, and the President placed under it. As a result of the reforms, the Constitutional Court is placed on par with the Supreme Court, the President/Vice President, and the MPR (which consists of both the DPR and the DPD). The Constitutional Court – whose role is not just limited to examining the constitutionality of laws passed by the DPR, but who is also entrusted to adjudicate political conflicts among state institutions and electoral disputes – is not organised like the Supreme Court, which oversees the high courts (*pengadilan tinggi*) and district courts (*pengadilan negeri*) and operates as a final court of appeal for cases from the lower courts. The high courts are further divided into four branches: the general courts; the

---

[56] Constitutional Court Decision No. 006/PUU-II/2004.

state administrative courts; the religious courts; and the military court. Notably, the military is out of the political equation – prior to the the fall of Soeharto, they played a role in socio-political affairs (under the *dwifungsi* doctrine) and occupied seats in the legislature. Now, they are completely absent from the legislature and the *dwifungsi*, as well as the policy permitting active military officers to occupy state bureaucracies, were abolished in 2000.

In addition to the nine institutions, there are also several other institutions that are recognised in the constitution, namely: (1) the Indonesian National Army; (2) the Indonesian National Police; (3) the regional government; and (4) Political Parties. In addition, there are also specific bodies (though not explicitly named in the Constitution) whose authority is to be regulated by law, namely: (1) a central bank (now called 'Bank Indonesia'); and (ii) an election commission (now called the *Komisi Pemilihan Umum*, or General Election Commission). Both institutions are independent institutions that derive their authority from the specific legislations promulgated by the DPR.[57]

Therefore, one must distinguish between state organs that are regulated by and derive their authority from the constitution on the one hand, and those that are regulated by and derive their authority from ordinary legislation on the other. There are also state institutions or organs whose authority is derived from a Presidential Decree. Some examples include the National Ombudsman Commission[58] and the National Law Commission.[59] Examples of institutions whose authorities are granted by law include the National Commission on Human Rights, the Indonesian Broadcasting Commission, the Financial and Development Audit Body, and the Financial Transaction Reports and Analysis Centre (PPATK).

The recognition of Indonesia's plural character is also manifested in the commitment to decentralisation initiatives, which led to the establishment of the DPD and the recognition of special autonomous regions, such as Aceh (based on Islamic values in the society), Yogyakarta (based on the significance of the sultanate), and Papua (based on the existence of plural indigenous communities). The DPD, together with the DPR, serves as the second chamber of the Indonesian Parliament (the MPR). This bicameral legislative system is peculiar in the sense that it does not provide both the DPD and DPR with equal stature or similar functions. The DPD's authority is limited to matters such as centre-local relations and regional autonomy and governance; it has no other law-making capacity and it can only provide advice to the DPR on any given bill.

The post-Soeharto constitutional reforms retained the presidential system of government in Indonesia, but various check-and-balance mechanisms were

---

[57] Since 1998, there are many changes of law, in relation to the central bank or Bank Indonesia (23 of 1999, 3 of 2004, Lieu of Law 2 of 2008 and 6 of 2009) and General Election Commission (32 of 2004, 12 of 2008, 42 of 2008, 15 of 2011 and 8 of 2012).

[58] This is changed to ORI (Ombudsman Republic of Indonesia), based on Law No. 37 of 2008.

[59] The commission is dissolved by President Joko Widodo, by enacting Presidential Regulation No. 176 of 2014, 4 December 2014.

introduced to prevent the rampant abuse of power experienced under the New Order regime. For Asshiddiqie, the post-Soeharto presidential system in Indonesia embodies five important principles.[60] The first is that the President and Vice President are the highest state executive authority under the Constitution, thus obviating the need to distinguish between the Head of State and head of government.

Second, the President and Vice President are directly elected by the people and therefore they are not directly accountable to the MPR or the parliamentary body. It is worth noting that the electoral mechanism for the presidential and vice-presidential offices is designed to take into account Indonesia's plural character. Candidates are elected by an absolute majority. Where there are more than two pairs of candidates running for office, the winning pair must secure 50% plus one of the total votes and obtain at least 20% of the popular votes in at least 17 of the 33 provinces in Indonesia. The territorial distribution requirement is a mechanism to encourage multi-ethnic appeals and ensure that minority votes matter, especially since non-Muslims tend to be territorially concentrated in the islands outside of Java.[61]

Third, the President and/or Vice President may be held legally accountable if the President and/or Vice President violate the constitution. In such cases, the President and/or Vice President may be held accountable before the MPR, but allegations of violation must first be proven legally through the judicial process in the Constitutional Court. The MPR will then convene and determine the President and/or Vice President's dismissal (impeachment) after such judicial process. Fourth, ministers are considered 'assistants' of the President. They are appointed and dismissed by the President and are accountable only to the President. Their positions do not depend on the will of the Parliament. In addition, these Ministers are essentially government leaders in their respective fields. Finally, to limit the powers of the President, it is also determined that the five-year term of the President shall not be held by the same person for more than two terms.

V. Responding to Plurality

A. The Courts and the Plural Legal System

The Indonesian constitution provides some recognition of the existence of a plurality of legal orders in the country, as well as recognition of Indonesia's territorial and ethnic pluralities. Article 18B of the Constitution provides that

---

[60] Jimly Asshiddiqie, 'Struktur Ketatanegaraan Indonesia Setelah Perubahan Keempat UUD Tahun 1945 [Structure of Indonesian Governance After the Fourth Amendment to the Constitution Year 1945]' (Seminar Pembangunan Hukum Nasional VIII, Denpasar, Bali, July 2003) 8–9.
[61] Shah (n 9).

'[t]he State recognises and respects units of regional authorities that are special and distinct, which shall be regulated by law'. Subsection 2 then cements the recognition of respect for traditional communities and their customary rights, 'as long as these remain in existence and are in accordance with the societal development and the principles of the Unitary State of the Republic of Indonesia'. This provision – placed in the Constitution's chapter on 'Regional Authorities' – and other provisions under that chapter, thus opens the door not only for regional government autonomy in matters of 'local' significance, but also for the establishment of mechanisms to protect traditional customary rights. In addition, the Preamble – apart from setting out the meaning and essence of Indonesia's independence and the Pancasila – contains the four aims of the Indonesian state, one of which is the protection of the Indonesian people and their native lands.

We have previously alluded to the fact that ordinary laws regulate the operation of religious courts and adat courts, with the former placed under the purview of the Supreme Court. In some measure, these different institutional arrangements reflect the respect for the plurality of legal orders in Indonesia. The Supreme Court institutionally accommodates the existence of the plural legal system, such as the sharia Court in Aceh (*Mahkamah Syariah*) and Papua Special Court, while the Constitutional Court – with its authority to review legislation – changes the position and relation of state law when it comes to customary law.[62] Interestingly, beside these judicial institutions, the state also recognises numerous customary courts (or adat courts), which are formally regulated under regional laws.[63]

In light of the foregoing account, it is unsurprising that the role of the state in unifying the plural judicial systems that exist in Indonesia has been a consistent topic of concern. As Lev argued, in post-colonial countries like Indonesia, judicial unification is a 'necessary step' towards political integration and modernisation.[64] Yet, there were Indonesian leaders who opposed adat courts in favour of modern, secular courts for they considered these courts as 'backward' institutions.[65] In Lev's study, at the centre of the debates on judicial unification and pluralism are two courts – the customary (adat) courts and the religious (Islamic) courts – and for him, unification raises important functional questions, ie, how courts could better serve the 'legal needs of the people'.[66] For Lev, the answer to this question was dependent on one's own perspective and that perspective may often be dictated by one's ideological leanings.[67] There is also the question of legitimate authority,

---

[62] See the Constitutional Court Decision No. 47-81/PHPU.A-VII /2009 in relation to the recognition of Noken as accepted model to local representation in General Election, or the Constitutional Court Decision No. 35/PUU-X/2012 in relation to the recognition of customary forest which override state forest status.

[63] Herlambang P Wiratraman, 'Adat Court in Indonesia's Judicial System A Constitutional Pluralism Analysis' ('Adat Law 100 years on: towards a new interpretation?' conference, Leiden, May 2017).

[64] Daniel S Lev, 'Judicial Unification in Post-Colonial Indonesia' (1973) 16 Indonesia 1.

[65] ibid 4.

[66] ibid 36.

[67] ibid.

which pits different classes of elites (local, regional, and national elites) against each other in a struggle for institutional power and symbols.

Regardless of these issues, today we see the retention and accommodation of traditional legal systems in Indonesia. The special autonomy for Aceh and Papua – mandated by the Constitution as a result of the post-Soeharto amendments – provides an excellent example of arrangements instituted to respond to the ethnic and religious plurality that exists in Indonesia. These arrangements then opened the doors for the establishment of the sharia Court and the Papuan Adat Court – both of which are special courts within the Supreme Court structure and are distinct from the general courts. The existence of these courts signals the state's recognition of the importance of the distinct legal systems that are – in practice – still turned to in order to resolve legal issues within particular indigenous and religious communities. In both examples, the courts derive their authority from laws promulgated by the legislature: Law No. 21 of 2001 on Special Autonomy Law for the Province of Papua (Articles 50(2) and 51), Special Regional Regulation (*Perdasus*) Papua No. 20 of 2008 on the Adat Court in Papua, and Law No. 11 of 2006 on Aceh government.

In the case of Aceh, the implementation of sharia law is effected through local regulations and the *Qanun* (religiously-inspired regulations) enacted by the local government. In other provinces, the existence of the customary court is also regulated through the regional regulations or governor regulations enacted by local government. One example is the Central Kalimantan Provincial Regulation No. 16 of 2008, which regulates the adat institution in Central Kalimantan. What all this demonstrates is that although the existence and authority of customary courts are not explicitly provided for in the constitution, they are nonetheless accommodated (and thus allowed to operate) through other formal state avenues (ie through local regulations and ordinary laws).

There are other encouraging developments. For one, the Constitutional Court now acknowledges the plurality of legal systems in Indonesia through its decision in 2012 which affirmed the recognition of indigenous peoples over the forest lands.[68] In that case, the Alliance of Indigenous Peoples of the Archipelago (AMAN) and two indigenous communities (*Kanegerian Kuntu* and *Kasepuhan Cisitu*) petitioned the court to review the constitutionality of Law No. 41 of 1999 on Forestry, as they sought rights over the forests (customary land) in which they lived. The law had designated customary forests or lands as 'state forests' under the purview and control of the government. The court ruled in favour of the petitioners, granting them rights and control over those areas and declaring that 'customary forests are no longer state forests'. As a result, tens of millions of hectares of indigenous forest that was claimed as state forests are recognised as belonging to, and can be managed by, the indigenous peoples who occupy them. This landmark decision not only strengthens the rights and position of indigenous

---

[68] Constitutional Court Decision No. 35/PUU-X/2012 (n 62).

people in the Indonesian constitutional order; it also has significant impact on the protection of and access to natural resources in Indonesia.

More recently, President Joko Widodo (Jokowi) issued a Decree on the Recognition of Adat Forest to nine Adat Law Communities (*Masyarakat Hukum Adat*) scattered in several areas in the country.[69] According to the President, the recognition will be extended throughout Indonesia as there are many other indigenous and/or adat communities and the Decree is only the beginning of a broader recognition initiative by the government. For the President, the recognition of customary forests and the traditional rights of indigenous and tribal peoples reflects the recognition of indigenous values in Indonesia. This not only represents a crucial shift in state policy, as the previous administration's policies in relation to land and natural resources had largely benefited private corporations; it also showcases the importance of political will in managing pluralism in Indonesia.

B. The '*Noken*' Electoral System

The state's growing recognition and protection of indigenous rights is also manifested in universal suffrage. The Constitutional Court has again played an important role in this through its decision in a case involving a dispute over election results in Papua.[70] It is worth noting, as a starting point, that elections in many electoral districts Papua are unique compared to other provinces in Indonesia, in that the voting customs and practices differ from the standard voting procedures established by state law. In Papua, the Noken system (a colloquial term to describe the voting custom) is employed. This entails voting by consensus – voters do not cast their votes individually; instead, they apportion their votes through consensus, and an indigenous (adat) leader then 'casts' those votes at the polling stations. The rationale behind such voting by acclamation custom was to prevent conflict, but there is also a geographical factor. In the Papuan highlands (such as the Yahukimo district), residents live in the mountains, making it difficult for all of them to participate in the electoral process.

The case before the Constitutional Court concerned allegations of electoral fraud and electoral law violations in the Yahukimo district. Elion Numberi, a candidate who contested for a seat in Papua's DPD (Regional Representative Council), argued – among other things – that there was a 'fictitious acquisition

---

[69] The nine communities of Indigenous People who obtained the Decision Letter of *Adat* Forest Recognition are: The *Adat* law community of Marga Serampas; the *Adat* law community of Ammatoa Kajang; the *Adat* law community of Lipu Wana Posangke; the *Adat* law community of Kasepuhan Karang; the *Adat* law community of Air Terjun; the *Adat* law community of Suangai Deras); the *Adat* law community of Tigo Luhah Permenti; the *Adat* law community of Tigo Luhah Kemantan; and the *Adat* law community of Pandumaan Sipituhuta.
[70] Constitutional Court Decision No. 47-81/PHPU.A-VII /2009 (n 62).

of votes' (*perolehan suara fiktif*)[71] in Yahukimo that advantaged another candidate (Paulus Yohannes Sumino). This was significant because it meant that – in a system where only the four candidates with the four highest total votes would be elected as DPD representatives – Elion Numberi came in fifth and thus failed to be elected to the DPD.[72]

It is beyond the scope of this chapter to examine in great detail Elion Numberi's specific claims with regard to the discrepancies in the number of votes he obtained. What is more important, however, is the question of the recognition of the voting by acclamation procedure. Critics argue that such procedure – though central to Papuan customs – calls into question the principle of one-person-one-vote and the individual right to universal suffrage. In fact, in 2016, the Election Supervisory Agency (*Badan Pengawas Pemilihan Umum* or *Bawaslu*) called for the Noken system, which is not provided for by any state laws or regulations, to be abolished on the ground that it violates principles of democracy.[73] Others have argued that the system is against the foundations of an election and prone to manipulation and distortion.[74]

The Constitutional Court ruled in favour of Elion Numberi because it deemed the elections to be fraudulent. However, what is significant from this case is not the court's approval of a fresh round of elections, but rather its acceptance of local (Papua) customs and practices in local elections (ie the Noken system).[75] For the court, there was some values in the acclamation system practised by the Papuan community – the court 'accepted' the significance of this practice, noting that if existing electoral regulations were 'forced' upon the Papuans, a conflict might ensue within the community.[76] The court's approach, which was driven by the realities of the Papuan community, has enabled alternative (indigenous) systems of electing political representatives to legally and constitutionally exist alongside the conventional one-person-one-vote principle.

---

[71] ibid 5.
[72] ibid 6.
[73] 'Bawaslu calls for abolition of 'noken' voting system in Papua', *The Jakarta Post* (Jakarta, 15 March 2016) www.thejakartapost.com/news/2016/03/15/bawaslu-calls-abolition-noken-voting-system-papua.html accessed 22 September 2018.
[74] See Cillian Nolan, 'Votes in the bag? The noken system and conflict in Indonesian Papua' (International Crisis Group Commentary, 11 September 2012) www.crisisgroup.org/asia/south-east-asia/indonesia/votes-bag-noken-system-and-conflict-indonesian-papua accessed 22 September 2018; 'Pemerintah Anggap Sistem Noken Bertentangan dengan Asas Pemilu' (*Hukumonline*, 6 May 2014) www.hukumonline.com/berita/baca/lt5368d22e8f65a/pemerintah-anggap-sistem-noken-bertentangan-dengan-asas-pemilu accessed 22 September 2018; ''Noken' voting system may lead to vote distortion: Commission' *The Jakarta Post* (Jakarta, 24 April 2018) www.thejakartapost.com/news/2018/04/24/noken-voting-system-may-lead-to-vote-distortion-commission.html accessed 22 September 2018.
[75] Ahmad Sodiki, 'Konstitusionalitas Pemilihan Umum Model Masyarakat Yahukimo' (2009) 6(2) Jurnal Konstitusi [Constitution Journal]; Yance Arizona, 'Konstitusionalitas Noken: Pengakuan model pemilihan masyarakat adat dalam sistem pemilihan umum di Indonesia' (2010) 3(1) Jurnal Konstitusi [Constitution Journal] 109.
[76] Constitutional Court Decision No. 47-81/PHPU.A-VII /2009 (n 62) 46.

This was, of course, not the first time that the Constitutional Court has upheld traditional voting customs. The court has recognized the validity of the Noken system in at least two other high profile cases – one involving gubernatorial elections and another involving a challenge by Prabowo Subianto and Hatta Rajasa against the results of the 2014 presidential elections.[77] More crucially, 7 years after the decision on the Papua DPD elections case, the General Elections Commission – previously critical of the *Noken* procedure – announced improvements to the Noken voting system in preparation for the 2017 regional elections, despite the clear absence of the recognition of such system in the latest amendment to the Regional Elections Law.[78]

C. Federalising a Decentralised Indonesia?

In the early years of the post-Soeharto *Reformasi* period, one of the most significant demands for political reforms revolved around the question of regional autonomy. Soeharto's obsession with centralised power, order, and control made Jakarta the centre of political gravity, much to the chagrin of those living in over 30 other provinces (covering more than 17,000 islands) throughout Indonesia. Some saw a less center-heavy federal system as a solution; while others demanded complete secession from the Unitary State of the Republic of Indonesia. For example, the Irian Province (Papua), the Special Territory of Aceh, and Riau explicitly demanded a separation from the Republic, while the East Kalimantan Province also sought the application of federal system.[79]

During the transitional administration immediately after Soeharto's resignation, President B.J. Habibie (who replaced Soeharto) took serious notice of these competing demands. For Habibie, any lack of urgency in addressing the calls for decentralisation would risk a bigger problem – a complete disintegration of the Republic. To complicate matters further, a crisis was brewing in East Timor since 1997, and by the time Habibie took office, calls for an independent East Timor were growing. Habibie assured the East Timorese that a plan for special autonomy was in the works. The government and the DPR then responded by formulating Law No. 22 of 1999 on Regional Governments, which replaced Law No. 5 of 1974 on the Principles of Government in the Region.

---

[77] See Simon Butt, *The Constitutional Court and Democracy in Indonesia* (Brill-Njihoff 2015) 169–170.
[78] See Law No. 10 of 2016 on the Second Amendment to Law No. 1 of 2015 on the Enactment of Government Regulation in Lieu of Law No. 1 of 2014 on the Election of Governors, Regents, and Mayors into Law.
[79] Tabrani Rab, 'Kemerdekaan, Otonomi, atau Negara Federal: Suara Rakyat Daerah, in Ikrar Nusa Bhakti' in Ikrar Nusa Bhakti and Irine H. Gayatri (eds), *Kontroversi Negara Federal: Mencari Bentuk Negara Ideal Indonesia Masa Depan* (Mizan Media Utama 2002) 175; Sadu Wasistiono, 'Desentralisasi dan Otonomi Daerah Masa Reformasi (1999–2004)' in Anhar Gonggong (ed), *Pasang Surut Otonomi Daerah – Sketsa Perjalanan 100 Tahun* (Institute for Local Development & Yayasan Tifa 2005).

East Timor eventually seceded from Indonesia in 2002, but this only triggered further instability as demands for autonomy grew in other provinces.[80] In response, the government granted special autonomy status to two areas with the highest possible risk of disintegration: Aceh (Law No. 18 of 2001 on Special Autonomy for the Province of Nanggroe Aceh Darussalam (NAD)) and Papua (Law No. 21 of 2001 on Special Autonomy for Papua Province). At the end of the crisis, Indonesia was still able to retain its unitary character but managing pluralism necessitated some compromises. Those compromises came in the form of arrangements for special autonomy for two provinces, and a new policy for regional autonomy (by devolving central government power to local governments in all government administrative sectors, except for security and defence, foreign policy, monetary and fiscal matters, justice, and religious affairs).[81] In effect, as some scholars noted, a federal system of government emerged in Indonesia.[82]

VI. Conclusion

A Constitution – as a highest law – reflects a country's social and political realities. These realities include the existence of multiple and overlapping pluralities that must be carefully addressed and managed. And in doing so, such pluralities will, in turn, inevitably shape constitutional law, politics, and development of the country. The attempt to integrate and unify different ideas, aspirations, values and other aspects of 'diversity' (including legal systems) into the 1945 Constitution began before independence, and it has continued after independence.

The existence of plural legal systems in Indonesia has significantly influenced constitutional law and development, whether at the point of constitution-making, the final constitution document, or the implementation of the constitution. The current legal recognition of adat court within the national judicial system, the adoption adat law values into Constitutional Court decisions, Noken electoral system, and the policy of land recognition of indigenous peoples in Indonesia provide strong evidence that non-hierarchical rules have played a role in the constitutional order.

The ideas and values of the Pancasila that underpin constitutional law in Indonesia have also been shaped by the dynamics of the pluralities in the country. Yet, despite historical records on the founding fathers' visions on the Pancasila, over

---

[80] Rab (n 79).
[81] Law No. 22 of 1999 on Local Government.
[82] Jimly Asshiddiqie, *Pengaturan Pemikiran Undang-Undang Dasar Negara Kesatuan Republik Indonesia* (The Habibie Centre 2001) 28; Faisal H. Basri, 'Tantangan dan Peluang Otonomi Daerah' in Indra J. Pilliang, Dendi Ramdani and Agung Pribadi (eds), *Otonomi Daerah: Evaluasi dan Proyeksi* (Divisi Kajian Demokrasi Lokal 2003) xiv-xv; Samad Thahir, *Otonomi Daerah, Pemilu, dan Pembangunan Politik Bangsa* [Regional Autonomy, Elections, and the Nation's Political Development] (Pusat Pengkajian Etika Politik dan Pemerintahan 2002) 112; Ryaas Rasyid, 'Indonesia Mengarah Federalisme' Media Indonesia (22 August 2005).

time, what the Pancasila means and how it should drive Indonesia's constitutional order and consciousness have become a contested discourse. A clear example is the ways in which the Pancasila was propagated and enforced during Soeharto's New Order regime. This – although authoritarian and offensive to fundamental rights – is a manifestation and consequence of how the Pancasila engages with pluralist ideas and approaches to governance.

The plurality of constitutional norms, values, and sources thus creates a practical dilemma. For one, it raises the question of supreme and final authority. The idea of the Constitutional Court as the sole and final interpreter of the constitution, for instance, has been recognised by influential legal scholars such as Asshiddiqie and Mahfud (both of whom served as Chief Justices of the Constitutional Court).[83] Indeed, the formal interpretation of constitutionality under the 1945 Constitution is carried by the Constitutional Court, in order to resolve any given constitutional question. However, in practice, constitutional interpretation is not the exclusive province of the judiciary; other state or non-state institutions constantly engage in constitutional interpretation in policy- and decision-making exercises.[84] All this is ultimately linked to political power-play within the constitutional order. Indonesia's experience in interpreting and realising the values and ideals of the Pancasila – as we have explained throughout this chapter – is again instructive in showcasing the power dynamics in constitutional interpretation and development.

Bibliography

—— Constitutional Court Decision No. 006/PUU-II/2004.
—— Constitutional Court Decision No. 2-3/PUU-V/2007 on Judicial Review of Law No. 22 of 1997 on Narcotics.
—— Constitutional Court Decision No. 35/PUU-X/2012.
—— Constitutional Court Decision No. 47-81/PHPU.A-VII /2009.
—— Constitutional Court of Indonesia, Decision No. 140/PUU-VII/2009, Examination of Law No. 1, Year 1965 on the Prevention from Abuse of and/or Desecration of Religion (Arts. 1, 2(1), 2(2), 3 and 4(a)) (19 April 2010).
—— Law No. 10 of 2004.

---

[83] Jimly Asshiddiqie, *Pokok-Pokok Hukum Tata Negara Indonesia Pasca Reformasi* (Bhuana Ilmu Populer 2007); Mahfud MD, *Perdebatan hukum tata negara: pasca amandemen konstitusi* (LP3ES 2007) 97.

[84] eg, the President and the House (DPR) often to sit and discuss together for a consultation, either for proposing a particular provision (in the case of revision plan of Anti Graft Commission Law) or proposing a legal solution (in the case of Setya Novanto – the chairperson of the House who was on a travel ban imposed by the Anti Graft Commission). 'Setya Novanto Travel Ban, Kalla: KPK have initial evidence' (*Tempo*, 11 April 2017) https://nasional.tempo.co/read/news/2017/04/11/055864948/setya-novanto-travel-ban-kalla-kpk-have-initial-evidence.

—— Law No. 10 of 2016 on the Second Amendment to Law <u>No. 1 of 2015</u> on the Enactment of Government Regulation in Lieu of Law <u>No. 1 of 2014</u>.
—— Law No. 22 of 1999.
—— Law No. 23 of 1999, 3 of 2004, Lieu of Law 2 of 2008 and 6 of 2009.
—— Law No. 32 of 2004, 12 of 2008, 42 of 2008, 15 of 2011 and 8 of 2012.
—— Law No. 37 of 2008.
—— MPR Decree No.III/MPR/2000.
—— MPR Decree No.V/MPR/1973.
—— MPR Decree No. IX/MPR/1978.
—— MPRS Decree No.XX/MPRS/1966.
—— 'Bawaslu calls for abolition of 'noken' voting system in Papua', *The Jakarta Post*, (Indonesia, 15 March 2016) www.thejakartapost.com/news/2016/03/15/bawaslu-calls-abolition-noken-voting-system-papua.html accessed 22 September 2018.
—— "Noken' voting system may lead to vote distortion: Commission' *The Jakarta Post* (Indonesia, 24 April 2018) www.thejakartapost.com/news/2018/04/24/noken-voting-system-may-lead-to-vote-distortion-commission.html accessed 22 September 2018.
—— 'Pemerintah Anggap Sistem Noken Bertentangan dengan Asas Pemilu' [Government Deems Noken System Against the Foundation of Elections] (*Hukumonline*, 6 May 2014) www.hukumonline.com/berita/baca/lt5368d22e8f65a/pemerintah-anggap-sistem-noken-bertentangan-dengan-asas-pemilu accessed 22 September 2018.
—— 'Pers Pembawa Panji-Panji Demokrasi' [Press as Carrier of the Banner of Democracy], Opening remarks for Indonesia's chief editors' meeting in Jakarta, 26 March 1975.
—— Presidential Regulation No. 176 of 2014, 4 December 2014.
—— 'Setya Novanto Travel Ban, Kalla: KPK have initial evidence' (*Tempo*, 11 April 2017) https://nasional.tempo.co/read/news/2017/04/11/055864948/setya-novanto-travel-ban-kalla-kpk-have-initial-evidence accessed 22 September 2018.
Amir S, *The Technological State in Indonesia: The Co-constitution of High Technology and Authoritarian Politics* (Routledge 2013).
Aritonang J S, *Sejarah Perjumpaan Kristen dan Islam di Indonesia* (BPK Gunung Mulia 2004).
Arizona Y, 'Konstitusionalitas Noken: Pengakuan model pemilihan masyarakat adat dalam sistem pemilihan umum di Indonesia' (2010) 3(1) Jurnal Konstitusi [Constitution Journal] 109.
Aspinall E, 'Twenty years of Indonesian democracy – how many more?' (*New Mandala*, 24 May 2018) www.newmandala.org/20-years-reformasi/ accessed 22 September 2018.
Asshiddiqie J, *Pengaturan Pemikiran Undang-Undang Dasar Negara Kesatuan Republik Indonesia* (The Habibie Centre 2001) 28.

―― 'Struktur Ketatanegaraan Indonesia Setelah Perubahan Keempat UUD Tahun 1945 [Structure of Indonesian Governance After the Fourth Amendment to the Constitution Year 1945]' (Seminar Pembangunan Hukum Nasional VIII, Denpasar, Bali, July 2003) 8–9.
―― *Pokok-Pokok Hukum Tata Negara Indonesia Pasca Reformasi* (Bhuana Ilmu Populer 2007).
Basri F H, 'Tantangan dan Peluang Otonomi Daerah' in Pilliang I J, Ramdani D and Pribadi A (eds), *Otonomi Daerah: Evaluasi dan Proyeksi* (Divisi Kajian Demokrasi Lokal 2003).
Butt S, *The Constitutional Court and Democracy in Indonesia* (Brill-Njihoff 2015).
Cohen D, *Intended to Fail: The Trials before the Ad Hoc Human Rights Court in Jakarta* (International Centre for Transitional Justice 2003).
Cribb R and Brown C, *Modern Indonesia: A History since 1945* (Longman 1995).
Darmaputera, *Pancasila and the Search for Identity and Modernity in Indonesian Society: A Cultural and Ethical Analysis* (E.J. Brill 1988).
Drooglever P J, 'The genesis of the Indonesian constitution of 1949' (1997) 153(1) Bijdragen tot de Taal-, Land- en Volkenkunde 65.
Hosen N, *Shari'a & Constitutional Reform in Indonesia* (Institute of Southeast Asian Studies, 2007).
Feith H and Castles L (eds), *Indonesian political Thinking, 1945–1965* (Cornell University Press 1970).
Indrayana D, *Indonesian Constitutional Reform 1999–2002: An Evaluation of Constitution-making in Transition* (Kompas 2008).
Kahin A, *Rebellion to Integration. West Sumatra and the Indonesian Polity 1926–1998* (Amsterdam University Press 1999).
Kurnisar K, 'Pancasila Sumber dari Segala Sumber Hukum di Indonesia' (2012) 11(3) Jurnal Ilmiah Ilmu Sosial 243.
Kusuma A B, *Lahirnya Undang-Undang Dasar 1945: Memuat Salinan Dokumen Otentik Badan Oentoek Menyelidiki Oesaha-Oesaha Persiapan Kemerdekaan* (Badan Penerbit Fakultas Hukum Universitas Indonesia 2004).
Lev D S, 'Judicial Unification in Post-Colonial Indonesia' (1973) 16 Indonesia 1.
―― 'Colonial Law and The Genesis of the Indonesian State' (1985) 40 Indonesia 57.
―― *Legal Evolution and Political Authority in Indonesia: Selected Essays* (Kluwer Law International 2000).
Lindsey T, 'Indonesia: Devaluing Asian Values, Rewriting Rule of Law' in Peerenboom R (ed), *Asian Discourses of Rule of Law: Theories and Implementation of Rule of Law in Twelve Asian Countries, France and the U.S.* (Routledge 2004).
Lubis S, *Ketatanegaraan Republik Indonesia* (Mandar Maju 1993).
―― *Konstitusi Republik Indonesia Serikat* (Graha Pustaka 2010).
―― *Undang-Undang Dasar Sementara Tahun 1950* (Graha Pustaka 2010).
Lubis T M, *In Search of Human Rights: Legal Political Dillemas of Indonesia's New Order, 1960–1996* (Gramedia 1993).

Mahendra Y I, *Dinamika tatanegara Indonesia: kompilasi aktual masalah konstitusi, dewan perwakilan, dan sistem kepartaian* (Gema Insani Press 1996).

Mahfud MD, *Perdebatan hukum tata negara: pasca amandemen konstitusi* (LP3ES 2007) 97.

Mundayat A A, 'Ritual and Politics in New Order Indonesia: A Study of Discourse and Counter-Discourse in Indonesia' (PhD Thesis, School of Social and Life Sciences, Swinburne University of Technology, February 2005).

Nasution A B, *The Aspiration for Constitutional Government in Indonesia: A Socio-Legal Study of the Indonesian Konstituante 1956–1959* (Sinar Harapan 1992).

Nolan C, 'Votes in the bag? The noken system and conflict in Indonesian Papua' (International Crisis Group Commentary, 11 September 2012) www.crisisgroup.org/asia/south-east-asia/indonesia/votes-bag-noken-system-and-conflict-indonesian-papua accessed 22 September 2018.

Poerbopranoto K, Hak-hak Manusia dan Pancasila Dasar Negara Republik Indonesia [HumanRights and Pancasila as the Republic of Indonesia's Foundation] (J B Wolters 1953) 92.

Rab T, 'Kemerdekaan, Otonomi, atau Negara Federal: Suara Rakyat Daerah, in Bhakti I N and Gayatri I H(eds), *Kontroversi Negara Federal: Mencari Bentuk Negara Ideal Indonesia Masa Depan* (Mizan Media Utama 2002).

Ramage D E, *Politics in Indonesia: Democracy, Islam and the Ideology of Tolerance* (Routledge 2002).

Rasyid R, 'Indonesia Mengarah Federalisme' *Media Indonesia* (22 August 2005).

Reid A, *The Indonesian National Revolution 1945–1950* (Longman 1974).

Salim A, *Challenging the Secular State: The Islamization of Law in Modern Indonesia* (University of Hawai'i Press 2008).

Shah D A, *Constitutions, Religion and Politics in Asia: Indonesia, Malaysia and Sri Lanka* (CUP 2017).

Sodiki, A 'Konstitusionalitas Pemilihan Umum Model Masyarakat Yahukimo' (2009) 6(2) Jurnal Konstitusi [Constitution Journal].

Soekarno, *Dibawah Bendera Revolusi* (Jakarta 1964).

Thahir S, *Otonomi Daerah, Pemilu, dan Pembangunan Politik Bangsa* (Pusat Pengkajian Etika Politik dan Pemerintahan 2002).

Vickers A, *A History of Modern Indonesia* (CUP 2005).

Wasistiono S, 'Desentralisasi dan Otonomi Daerah Masa Reformasi (1999–2004)' in Gonggong A (ed), *Pasang Surut Otonomi Daerah – Sketsa Perjalanan 100 Tahun* (Institute for Local Development & Yayasan Tifa 2005).

Weatherbee D E, 'Indonesia in 1984: Pancasila, Politics, and Power' (1985) 25(2) Asian Survey 187.

Wiratraman H P, *Press Freedom, Law and Politics in Indonesia: A Socio-Legal Study* (EM Meijers Institute-Wohrmann 2014).

—— 'Adat Court in Indonesia's Judicial System A Constitutional Pluralism Analysis' ('Adat Law 100 years on: towards a new interpretation?' conference, Leiden, May 2017).

6

Myanmar's Pluralist Constitution: Nation-Building versus State-Building

NYI NYI KYAW

I. Introduction

Constitution-making in ethnically diverse and politically contentious Myanmar has been pluralist or made to be so since before the founding of the independent Union of Burma in 1948 when independence was obtained from the British. Having lived under military (known as *Tatmadaw* in Burmese) or military-dominated authoritarian regimes from 1962 to 2011, constitution-making has been authoritarian and the state constituted unpopular. Likewise, several ethnic minorities who altogether constitute about a quarter of the total population have generally found themselves marginalised by the Bamar majority whose population is 69% of the total.[1]

Hence, the nation of Myanmar that is perceived as equally shared by the majority and minorities has not been successfully and completely built whereas the state of Myanmar mostly dominated by the military has been constantly challenged by the people. Myanmar's pluralist constitutionalism, however 'authoritarian',[2] 'unpopular',[3] 'top-down elite',[4] and 'hybrid'[5] from the 1960s through the 2000s, therefore, has espoused two foundational ideas of multi-ethnic unity and republicanism. Even during two extended periods in which the country was ruled by

---

[1] These ethnic demographic statistics are taken from the second last census conducted in 1983. It took 31 years to conduct another in 2014. Yet, due to perceptions of conflicts that may arise from updated ethnic demographic data, the latest census data on ethnic groups and their respective numbers have not been announced yet. For details, see M Callahan, 'Distorted, Dangerous Data? *Lumyo* in the 2014 Myanmar Population and Housing Census' (2017) 32 Sojourn: Journal of Social Issues in Southeast Asia 452.

[2] M Tushnet, 'Authoritarian Constitutionalism' in T Ginsburg and A Simpser (eds), *Constitutions in Authoritarian Regimes* (CUP 2013).

[3] M Versteeg, 'Unpopular Constitutionalism' (2014) 89 Indiana Law Journal 1133.

[4] TA Eisenstadt, AC LeVan, and T Maboudi, *Constituents Before Assembly: Participation, Deliberation, and Representation in the Crafting of New Constitutions* (CUP 2017) ch 4.

[5] V Hsueh, *Hybrid Constitutions: Challenging Legacies of Law, Privilege, and Culture in Colonial America* (Duke University Press 2010).

the military coup juntas *without* a Constitution in operation, those two ideas continued to be held and expressed – however superficially – by the military in the constitution-making processes under their guidance. Military coup regimes would claim that they had taken power amid political chaos and/or threats to multi-ethnic unity with the sole intention of defending the multi-ethnic union and returning power to the people as soon as possible. Hence, the political interest, interference and role of the military must be and is considered here as a feature of political pluralities in Myanmar.

A mainland Southeast Asian country, Myanmar exhibits ethnic, racial, national, linguistic and ideational pluralities. This chapter looks at how plurality has been constitutionalised in Myanmar in the past seven decades – textualised in three Constitutions[6] so far, ie Constitution of the Union of Burma (known as the 1947 Constitution after the year of its adoption and in operation from 1948 through 1962); Constitution of the Socialist Republic of the Union of Burma (known as the 1974 Constitution after the year of its adoption and in operation from 1974 through 1988); and Constitution of the Republic of the Union of Myanmar (known as the 2008 Constitution after the year of its adoption and in operation since 2011).

The trajectory of Myanmar's constitutionalism has been a fragmented one since 1947. The founding and making of each of the three Constitutions in Myanmar has been preceded by a critical juncture or 'a period of significant change, which typically occurs in distinct ways in different countries … [and] is hypothesized to produce distinct legacies'.[7] As much as the three constitutions have produced distinct legacies – the third or present one is now in the midst of producing its own legacy, they have also been divorced from one another by two extended periods in which Myanmar was ruled not by a Constitution but by decree of military juntas. The 1947 Constitution and the 1974 Constitution were suspended from 1962 to 1974 and from 1988 to 2008 respectively. In 70 years since independence in 1948, the country lived without a Constitution for 32 years whereas it only had a somewhat *operational* constitution for 37 years. It means that Myanmar has only lived under a constitution for a little more than half of the post-independence period. In other words, the country has only had a fifty-fifty chance of generally operational constitutional rule because it has been subjected to two eons of constitution-less rule by decree.

Hence, I view these constitutional paths of Myanmar as constitutional cycles. By cycles, I mean all three of them have undergone periods or stages of expansion and contraction or peaks and troughs.[8] Upon closer look, Myanmar's

---

[6] It must be stated that there were previously two Constitution or constitution-like documents in colonial Burma drawn up by the British and Japanese respectively when they ruled Burma although the focus of this chapter is on three Constitutions of independent Myanmar.

[7] RB Collier and D Collier, *Shaping the Political Arena: Critical Junctures, the Labor Movement, and Regime Dynamics in Latin America* (Princeton University Press 1991) 29.

[8] The theory of constitutional cycles is descriptively and analytically distinct from Bruce Ackerman's popular theory of constitutional moments that argues that American constitutional development

constitutionalism in general exhibits a need-based – not merit-based – nature. The first constitution was written in haste to obtain independence as soon as possible and the latter two to formalise or constitutionalise the continued rule of the two military coup juntas in different forms and to differing degrees. Hence, once a constitution was adopted and became operational, its peaks and troughs were usually seen in the early years and in the later years respectively.

I highlight two types of pluralities in Myanmar that have been both politically and constitutionally relevant. They are ethnic pluralities and political pluralities with which design of all three constitutions of Myanmar have grappled to differing degrees. Ethnic pluralities mainly refer to eight major ethnic groups – the Bamar, Kachin, Kayah, Kayin, Chin, Mon, Rakhine, and Shan – and several other sub-groups grouped under each of the eight. Now, the government-recognised number of these groups is 135. Since the political transition began in 2010 and a peace process between the central government, military, and ethnic armed groups was initiated in August 2011,[9] a few sub-groups such as the Pa-O and Wa have expressed resentment against their sub-status and demanded stand-alone positions.

Political pluralities refer to the diversity of these groups – mainly represented by the military and broader democratic opposition in the post-1988 context – that have vied for political legitimacy and power throughout the post-independence period. Ideationally and discursively influenced by two foundational ideas of republicanism and multi-ethnic unity, the military would then constitutionalise itself as an essential player in politics in both post-coup contexts to safeguard themselves and protect further political chaos. In this way, the military and its role in formal, constitutionalised politics would become an extremely important political reality. However, I take 1988 as a turning point in Myanmar politics that have so far progressed or regressed to the present political context. Also, I focus on what has happened since 1988 and what is textually stated in the 2008 Constitution regarding ethnic and political pluralities and what has been seen in action. However, I will also discuss pre-1988 contexts insofar as it is relevant and necessary in line with my focus on contemporary pluralist constitutionalism in Myanmar.

Below, I will discuss and analyse how an electoral democratic system is constituted and how power and resources are shared between the centre dominated by the Bamar and peripheral ethnic minority states are two key aspects of Myanmar's pluralist constitutionalism under the 2008 Constitution. At the outset, four facts about this are worth noting. Firstly, not all diversities or pluralities in Myanmar have been constitutionalised. Only when a plurality is defined as part

---

has had significant moments of change or transformation: Bruce Ackerman, *We the People: Transformations* (Harvard University Press 2001). But Ackerman's theory is only applicable to American constitutional development that has occurred within a *single* constitution, however it has been changed or transformed.

[9] Government of the Republic of the Union of Myanmar Announcement No. 1/2011, *Invitation to Peace Talks*, dated 18 August 2011, *New Light of Myanmar* (Yangon, 19 August 2011) 1.

of a political settlement, negotiated or imposed by a higher power, and written into a Constitution, can it be said to be related to the focus of the paper, ie pluralist Constitution in Myanmar. So, I will only look at those types of pluralities that have been constitutionalised and/or are constitutionally relevant. Secondly, certain constitutionalised pluralities, especially those which have political ambitions and are politically empowered by a Constitution, tend to be more contentious and power-loaded than other types of constitutionalised pluralities. For example, the issue of ethnic minority languages vis-à-vis Burmese/Myanmar[10] as the *only* official language of Myanmar, can be subsumed – for convenience of description and analysis – under the heading of ethnic pluralities. Likewise, although religion was a constitutionally contentious issue in the early 1960s that resulted in Buddhism being recognised for a few months as the State Religion and again amid religiously motivated violence in 2012–2014, the issue of constitutional prerogatives relating to religion has not – again – been broached by the Buddhist majority or by ethnic minorities some among whom are predominantly or sizeably Christian. Hence, the constitutional question of 'religion' is not discussed at length from a pluralist perspective here.[11]

Thirdly, Myanmar's pluralist constitution has been a discontinuous project with three Constitutions that textualised pluralities in diverse ways and to differing degrees. That said, contestations over constitutional prerogatives of political and ethnic pluralities have been defined by two broader, never-ending projects of state building and nation building. Finally, pluralities and their constitutionalisation are not static, but dynamic. There are two parts to this. First, those pluralities in Myanmar at the times of contemplating and writing each of the three Constitutions had become politically important so they needed to be constitutionalised. Second, constitutionalisation can never be complete. Once particular pluralities are written into a constitution, ie constitutionalism in books, it becomes a live document. *Lived* experiences of the pluralist Constitution, ie constitutionalism in action,[12] may never be optimal or satisfactory for everyone. That may, in theory,

---

[10] Burmese is officially called 'Myanmar.' The word 'Myanmar' is used not only as a noun for the name of the country, that of a person or persons from Myanmar, and that of the official language but also as an adjective to mean 'belonging to or relating to Myanmar.' Hence, its usage in confusing. Therefore, 'Burmese' is used to refer to the official language of Myanmar.

[11] It does not mean that the question is neither presently nor potentially important. Nyi Nyi Kyaw has focused on the issue of textual and contextual constitutionalism relating to Buddhism and other minority religions, especially Islam. For more details, see Nyi Nyi Kyaw, 'Alienation, Discrimination, and Securitization: Legal Personhood and Cultural Personhood of Muslims in Myanmar' (2015) 13 Review of Faith & International Affairs 50.

[12] I borrow this distinction from legal realism that basically claims that how law is adopted, enacted, passed, interpreted, enforced, upheld, obeyed, observed, broken, flouted, violated, annulled, and repealed, ie law in action, is no less important than law in the books. The tendencies for non-conformity between law in books and law in action was famously pointed out by Roscoe Pound more than one hundred years ago: Roscoe Pound, 'Law in the Books and Law in Action' (1910) 44 American Law Review 12. Similarly, Kim Scheppele coined another term 'constitutional ethnography' that suggests that the socio-legal researcher pay attention to 'the logics of particular contexts as a way of illuminating complex interrelationships among political, legal, historical, social, economic, and cultural

require a Constitution in operation in the present to undergo further pluralist constitutionalisation.

After this brief introduction of the overall nature of pluralities and their constitutionalism so far in Myanmar, this chapter is structured as follows: first, it will trace and present the drafting history of the constitution of Myanmar and the constitutional rights relating to political and ethnic pluralities; second, it will then discuss those ideas, values, and sources that have animated Myanmar's constitutionalism; third, an analysis of how constitutionalised institutions and structures have meant for pluralities naturally follows; and finally, it will go backward and see how pluralities have impacted and are expected to continue to affect constitutional law and politics of Myanmar.

II. Drafting History and Constitutional Rights for Pluralities

A. Drafting History

Let us now take a close look at each of the three constitutional paths Myanmar has pursued. I will focus on the 1947 and 2008 Constitutions because they are more similar in terms of responding to political and ethnic pluralities. In contrast, the 1974 Constitution only established a one-party socialist state[13] that did not allow any substantial pluralist political expressions and representations although it did contain some pluralist content. However, the extent to which the rights and demands of ethnic pluralities was accorded constitutional recognition can be said to be nominal and superficial simply because political and economic power was concentrated in the center and not shared with the periphery. Political plurality was also non-existent because it was a one-party socialist state. People that belong to both the ethnic majority and minorities regardless of their political interests and stance largely lost political and ethnic pluralist rights. That said, it is undeniable that the formation of a socialist state from 1962 that was finalised in the 1974 Constitution largely built upon what had happened before – a point I shall turn to below.

Now, we will look back at the constitution-making of the 1947 Constitution that originated in the British colonisation of the Konbaung Dynasty (1752–1885) that had ruled Burma. Dynastic Burma became a British colony in 1885 after it lost its sovereignty to the British in the immediate aftermath of the third

---

elements' and 'better understand how constitutional systems operate by identifying the mechanisms through which governance is accomplished and the strategies through which governance is attempted, experienced, resisted and revised, taken in historical depth and cultural context.' See Kim Scheppele, 'Constitutional Ethnography: An Introduction' (2004) 38 Law & Society Review 389, 390–1.

[13] Constitution of the Socialist Republic of the Union of Burma s 11.

Anglo-Burmese War that lasted less than a month.[14] At the end of the previous two wars, the kingdom was not *fully* colonised although the British took the Burmese territories of Arakan and Lower Burma. The third war completed the British colonisation project over Burma. There were sporadic rebellions in the early years of colonial rule against the foreign rulers but these were never united and therefore not very successful.[15]

It was only at the beginning of the twentieth century that we saw a nationalist seed that would gradually germinate into a full-blown movement by the 1930s. Shocked by rule by a foreign Christian coloniser whose language was English, the earliest nationalists of colonial Burma started out by mobilising themselves to promote Buddhist education and donations. They *only* aimed at preservation and perpetuation of their *indigenous* Buddhist beliefs and practices and the Burmese language. This reached a climax with the establishment of the Young Men's Buddhist Association (YMBA) in 1906, which in turn paved the way for more organised nationalism.[16] Concurrently, we saw the emergence of the '*political monk*' who worked in close cooperation with lay nationalists.[17] That early politics did not last long was due to schism and disunity within the General Council of Burmese Associations (GCBA) that grew out of YMBA and was established in 1920 as a more overtly anti-colonial nationalist organisation. Schism within lay nationalists consequently led to that within their respective monk supporters. The people by and large had lost trust in religiously motivated or expressed nationalists and their monastic gurus by the early 1930s.[18]

By the 1930s, a new generation of secular-oriented university graduates and students had joined political activism who viewed their plight not in religious and racial terms but from the lenses of coloniser-colonised and class divide. Among these young politicians was Aung San,[19] who emerged as arguably the most popular due to his strong will and legendary honesty. He and his team agitated for independence, demanded political concessions and founded the Burmese Independence Army (BIA) with Japanese assistance. The BIA later fought against the British and later against the Japanese that had broken its promise to liberate Burma

---

[14] The British invaded and colonised Burma in stages by waging three wars with the Burmese in 1824–26, 1852, and 1885 after which Arakan (now Rakhine), Lower Burma, and Upper Burma were acceded to the British by the Burmese respectively. But the year 1885 is usually taken as the culmination or start of British colonization because the Burmese king Thibaw was only overthrown then.

[15] Thant Myint-U, *The Making of Modern Burma* (CUP 2001).

[16] E Sarkisyanz, *Buddhist Backgrounds of the Burmese Revolution* (Martinus Nijhoff 1965); AM Turner, *Saving Buddhism: The Impermanence of Religion in Colonial Burma* (University of Hawaii Press 2014).

[17] J Schober, *Modern Buddhist Conjunctures in Myanmar: Cultural Narratives, Colonial Legacies, and Civil Society* (University of Hawaii Press 2011).

[18] U Maung Maung, *From Sangha to Laity: Nationalist Movements of Burma, 1920–40* (Manohar 1980).

[19] Aung San is regarded as the father of modern Burma who was unfortunately assassinated on the eve of independence and did not see the fruits of his nationalist toil for almost a decade. For details of Aung San's political legacy, see Maung Maung, *Aung San of Burma* (Martinus Nijhoff 1962); Josef Silverstein, *The Political Legacy of Aung San* (Southeast Asia Program, Cornell University 1972).

upon the British retreat in 1942.[20] The British came back to rule Burma in 1945 after the Burmese and British joined hands to fight against the Japanese regime that had repressively ruled Burma for three years. In the face of the pro-independence campaign led by Aung San and changing post-World War II international politics, the British eventually promised to restore Burma's independence on two conditions set out in the Aung San-Atlee Agreement signed on 27 January 1947.[21] Firstly, an election needs to be held to convene a legislative assembly at which a constitution for independent Burma would be drafted and passed. Secondly, Aung San and the political alliance known as the Anti-Fascist People's Freedom League (AFPFL) that he led needed to seek the opinion of minorities – called peoples of Frontier Areas – whether they would want to join the Bamar majority – called peoples in Ministerial Burma – in forming a Union of Burma.[22]

Two weeks after the Aung San-Atlee Agreement was signed, Aung San as the *only* representative of the Interim Burmese government and 22 representatives of three Frontier peoples – the Shan (thirteen), Kachin (six) and Chin (three) – signed an historic agreement known as the Panglong Agreement on 12 February. The agreement expressly states that the signees believe that 'freedom will be more speedily achieved by the Shans, the Kachins and the Chins by their immediate co-operation with the Interim Burmese Government.' Relating to the rights of those Frontier peoples, the agreement asserts: 'Full autonomy in internal administration for the Frontier Areas is accepted in principle,' and 'Citizens of the Frontier Areas shall enjoy rights and privileges which are regarded as fundamental in democratic countries.' Despite its symbolic value as a milestone of majority-minority cooperation, the now-ritualistic agreement[23] was only meant as a *transitional* one to be further developed into a more detailed arrangement later. It did not specify any territorial boundaries and power-sharing arrangements whatsoever. These were to be further discussed and later written into the Constitution. The agreement was extremely short – that could be the main reason why there was consensus – with nine paragraphs with no more than six lines each. More importantly, so-called full autonomy and democratic rights and privileges for the three minorities were only agreed in principle. Most importantly, other significant ethnic minorities such as the Mon, Rakhine, and Kayin were not part of the agreement that would turn problematic after independence.

The following constitutional process was so quick that it only took three days – from 20 to 23 May – for the 111-member committee formed by the AFPFL that

---

[20] In 1942, BIA that had been trained by the Japanese fought with the Japanese imperial forces against the British who later withdrew from Burma. But the Japanese broke its independence promise and ruled Burma from 1942 to 1945 that is known as the Japanese Interregnum, see DM Seekins, *Burma and Japan since 1940: From 'Co-prosperity' to 'Quiet Dialogue'* (Nordic Institute of Asian Studies 2007).

[21] Maung Maung, *Burma's Constitution* (Springer Netherlands 1961).

[22] ibid.

[23] The Union Peace Conference that has been held twice by State Counselor Aung San Suu Kyi and her National League for Democracy (NLD) government since August 2016 is also symbolically called the 21st Century Panglong. Also, the 12th of February is annually celebrated as Union Day.

had won in the legislative assembly elections held on 9 April. It was later revised by a 127-member committee formed on 18 June by the Legislative Assembly after it met on 9 June.[24] In the meantime, Aung San and almost all his cabinet members were assassinated on 19 July by a gang of armed men tasked by U Saw who was a prominent pre-World War II politician and Prime Minister from 1940 to 1942, supposedly held grudges against the young rising star Aung San, and was allegedly supported by the British.[25] However, this event of widespread national mourning did not stop the constitution-founding and -making process; the final draft was already ready before the third session of the assembly resumed on 15 September.[26] It was consequently adopted on 24 September.[27]

Due to jubilation in the early years of independence that was regained in 1948, the Constitution and its content at its peak was not problematised by AFPFL's political and ethnic rivals. Communist[28] and other ethnic insurgencies[29] were mostly caused by elitist disagreements and motivations for *complete* independence or more substantial concessions from the allegedly Bamar-dominated central state under AFPFL.[30] Young independent Burma and its brand-new government headed by U Nu – Aung San's trusted deputy – found itself surrounded by a multitude of politically and ethnically inspired insurgencies. At one point, the central government was even called the 'Rangoon Government' because of its extreme lack of reach of power out of the capital then.[31] After suffering an internal split in July 1958 between Prime Minister U Nu and Thakhin Tin on one side as the *Clean AFPFL* and Kyaw Nyein and Ba Swe on the other side as the *Stable AFPFL*, the AFPFL government even had to *constitutionally* give power to the military in 1958, which then governed the war-torn country as a care-taker government for two years.[32]

Although the military returned power to U Nu who again won in the elections held in 1960,[33] the AFPFL split and consequent military care-taker governance 'shook the very foundations of the State and perturbed the people.'[34] Most importantly, those two years set an example – good for the army but bad for the

---

Matthew J Walton problematises the assumed symbolic value of the agreement and calls it a myth: Matthew J Walton, 'Ethnicity, Conflict, and History in Burma: The Myths of Panglong' (2008) 48 Asian Survey 889.

[24] Maung Maung, *Burma's Constitution* (n 21).

[25] Maung Maung, *A Trial in Burma: The Assassination of Aung San* (Springer Netherlands 1962); Kin Oung, *Eliminate the Elite: Assassination of Burma's General Aung San and His Six Cabinet Colleagues* (Print, Post, Plus (p3) Design 2011).

[26] Maung Maung, *Burma's Constitution* (n 21).

[27] ibid.

[28] Martin Smith, *Burma: Insurgency and the Politics of Ethnicity* (Zed Books 1991).

[29] ibid.

[30] ibid.

[31] ibid.

[32] Sein Win, *The Split Story* (Guardian Ltd 1959).

[33] Robert Taylor, *The State in Myanmar* (2nd edn, NUS Press 2009).

[34] Sein Win (n 32) 1.

people – for military intervention under the pretext of need and urgency in times of political crisis among civilians. The care-taker Ne Win successfully encouraged, or forced, 25 Shan and Kayah Saophas or Sawbwas to give up their hereditary feudal powers on 29 April 1959. However, due to declining trust in the centre, the fire of old insurgencies continued to burn and was further fuelled by new ones, most significantly being the rebellion of the Kachin Independence Army (KIA) in 1961.[35]

Ethnic dissention grew stronger and by the early 1960s the Shan were on the verge of invoking the 'secession' clause in the 1947 Constitution that allows breaking away from the union after ten years post-independence, ie from 1958 onwards.[36] Other ethnic peoples such as the Rakhine, Mon, and Kayin had already started demanding self-autonomy and/or statehood as early as 1947 which only grew more intense in the 1950s.[37] Political conflicts had become explicitly constitutional. The military saw ethnic political and constitutional demands excessive and became concerned – at least in their rhetoric – about possible disintegration of the union.[38] The same rhetoric was notably used by the second coup junta in 1988.[39]

Having tasted power and governance in the two-year apprenticeship as the care-taker government, the military would come back twice to the political stage as the saviour of the state and of the nation as well – in 1962 and 1988. Whereas the first take-over was constitutional and meant for restoring law and order for a brief period of two years, the latter two annihilated the pre-existing political architecture and suspended the Constitutions in operation. Hence, the second and third constitutional foundings originated in military dictatorship. In both situations, the 1974 and 2008 Constitutions were simply written at the behest of the military.

The Revolutionary Council (RC) led by General Ne Win took power in a coup on 2 March 1962 from the U Nu-led government that was democratically elected in 1960. RC ruled by decree after suspending the 1947 Constitution. But as early as November 1969, Ne Win started talking about transferring power back to the people and having a Constitution in line with socialist ideals.[40] The second Constitution was drafted by a 97-member committee from September 1971 to October 1973. The 1974 Constitution was consequently adopted on 4 January 1974 that created a one-party socialist state to be ruled by the Burma Socialist

---

[35] For a good background of the Kachin identity and their contracted ethnic insurgency, see Edmund R Leach, *Political Systems of Highland Burma: A Study of Kachin Social Structure* (Harvard University Press 1954); Mandy Sadan, *Being and Becoming Kachin: Histories Beyond the State in the Borderworlds of Burma* (British Academy 2013).
[36] Constitution of the Union of Burma ss 201, 202.
[37] Taylor, *The State in Myanmar* (n 33).
[38] ibid.
[39] ibid.
[40] Albert D Moscotti, *Burma's Constitution and Elections of 1974: A Source Book* (Institute of Southeast Asian Studies 1977) 3.

Programme Party (BSPP) that was founded by the RC on 4 July 1962, four months after the coup.[41]

Centralised power and command economy instituted by the 1974 Constitution turned out to be problematic for socialist Burma. Amid the all-out Cold War spreading into Southeast Asia, Ne Win closed Burma's doors and adopted isolationism.[42] Whereas open-door economic policies handsomely paid neighbouring authoritarian countries such as Malaysia, Burma with its incessant political and economic problems gradually became poor. Ne Win became increasingly mercurial along the road to poverty that fell to a trough in 1987 when Burma was designated as a Least-Developed Country by the United Nations.[43] The poverty was deeply felt by the people who eventually came out to the streets to protest. The whole society was chaotic.[44] It again prompted Burma's political saviour to come back with an express promise of republicanism that power would be returned to the people.[45]

The second and third military take-overs were different at least in three ways. Firstly, political agents in 1962 Burma were almost decimated after the coup whereas dissidents led by future Nobel Prize winner Aung San Suu Kyi supported by the West emerged and constantly challenged the military in the 1990s and 2000s. Secondly, Burma's doors were shut to the outside world after the 1962 coup whereas they had to be opened after the 1988 coup. Thirdly, the 1962 coup was launched to protect the socialist ideal – however it was defined and understood by both the elites and people then – whereas the next coup was meant for a democratic transition *the military way* that was expressly guided by republicanism and multi-ethnic unity.

Despite these three differences, there is one important similarity between the two military coup regimes. It was that both juntas took a long time just to start a constitution-making process. It took 12 and 20 years to have a new Constitution drafted and adopted in the first and second instances respectively. Compared to the smooth process in the first instance, the second junta-led process constituted a contentious constitutional cycle with a series of peaks and troughs. It took almost five years just to start a National Convention to formulate constitutional principles, let alone finalise them. Therefore, the process is the most controversial and conflictual among the three Myanmar has had. The entire process was effectively 'imposed constitutionalism'[46] because it was imposed by the military regime as a

---

[41] The coincidence of the date of Burma's Independence Day and that of the adoption of the second constitution is noteworthy and seems to carry symbolic value behind the choice of the date.

[42] Mya Maung, *The Burma Road to Poverty* (Praeger 1991). For Ne Win years and his legacy, see Maung Maung, *Burma and General Ne Win* (Asia Publishing House 1969); Robert Taylor, *General Ne Win: A Political Biography* (Institute of Southeast Asian Studies 2015).

[43] Mya Maung (n 42).

[44] U Maung Maung, *The 1988 Uprising in Burma* (Yale University, Southeast Asia Studies 1999).

[45] Taylor, *The State in Myanmar* (n 33).

[46] Noah Feldman, 'Imposed Constitutionalism' (2004–2005) 37 Connecticut Law Review 857.

state structure on the people of Myanmar. It was simply 'drafted and adopted in the shadow of the gun.'[47]

Once it started, the process took a period of 14 more years from 1993 to 2007 with a long hiatus of eight years from 1996 to 2004. Not only did the State Law and Order Restoration Council/State Peace and Development Council (SLORC/SPDC)[48] take several years to start a constitution-making process but it also had a long break. The National Convention (NC) formed in July 1992 by the SLORC mostly comprised delegates hand-picked by the junta. Only 99 out of 702 delegates had won in the general elections of 1990. The result of the election was initially accepted by the SLORC that would later break its promise to transfer power to the National League for Democracy (NLD) with its secretary-general Aung San Suu Kyi that had won in a landslide victory. Instead, the SLORC – interestingly – used the lack of an operational constitution as the reason behind its delay in transferring power. The junta was adamant that the elected representatives were supposed not to take up the reins of government but to draw up a Constitution.[49]

Due to several problems over the process and content of the junta-led constitution-making, 86 NLD delegates had already walked out of the NC by November 1995, leaving only 14 election-winning delegates in the convention. The NC resumed in 2004 again with hand-picked delegates and ended on 3 September 2007 adopting the Fundamental Principles and Detailed Basic Principles.[50] Those principles became the blueprint for the 54-member Commission for Drafting State Constitution formed by the junta on 18 October[51] – another entity hand-picked by the junta – which finished the final draft of the 2008 Constitution in February 2008.[52] It was adopted on 29 May through a referendum.[53] The third constitution has been in operation since 31 January 2011 when the first parliament was convened.[54]

B. Constitutional Rights for Pluralities

This history of constitutional moments, events, and processes in Myanmar seems to have encouraged the formation of two important foundational ideas of

---

[47] Feldman (n 46) 858.

[48] SLORC changed its name into SPDC in 1997. 'SLORC' is then used here to refer to the junta before 1997 and 'SPDC' to that after 1997. 'SLORC/SPDC' is used to denote the junta in both periods from 1988 until 2011.

[49] David C Williams, 'Constitutionalism Before Constitutions: Burma's Struggle to Build a New Order' (2009) 87 Texas Law Review 1657.

[50] ibid.

[51] State Peace and Development Council Announcement No. (2/2007) on Formation and Assignment of Commission for Drafting State Constitution (18 October 2007), *New Light of Myanmar* (Yangon, 19 October 2007) 1, 3 & 4.

[52] Donald M Seekins, 'Myanmar in 2008: Hardship, Compounded' (2009) 49 Asian Survey 170.

[53] ibid.

[54] Constitution of the Republic of the Union of Myanmar s 441.

constitutionalism that have been discussed above. The first idea or philosophy that the state or union of Burma/Myanmar has been a republic has been reproduced by both civilian and military regimes through its post-independence history, regardless of the nature of the state that is formed according to each of the three Constitutions. The second idea that Burma/Myanmar is a multi-ethnic nation-state composed of the Bamar majority and several other minorities that have pledged to come together as a union or were forced to do so has also prominently figured in all the three Constitutions.

Constitutional rights for pluralities may therefore be said to emanate from these two foundational ideas. It does not mean that these two grand ideas have been constitutionalised in an optimal way that has satisfied interests and aspirations of politically and ethnically plural groups in Myanmar. The nature of the state that has been constituted by the 2008 constitution and the process of making it is among the most contentious issues relating to Myanmar's constitutionalism to date.[55] Common opinion among democrats and ethnic minorities nowadays is that the ways in which the 2008 Constitution has responded to pluralist political and ethnic demands and aspirations fall short of optimum standards of democracy and federalism. Whereas the people in general still view the 2008 Constitution as a democratically deficient social contract imposed upon them by the SLORC/SPDC, ethnic minorities feel that power- and resource-sharing between the Bamar-dominated centre and them disproportionately favours the centre.[56]

Although Myanmar's constitutional history has been traced above to pre-independence and post-independence years and decades, I will focus on the content of the 2008 Constitution from now on. But before doing that, I must state that depending on the nature of the state that is formed by each Constitution, constitutional rights have been differently recognised to differing degrees. For example, the right to secession of ethnic minority states from the Union of Burma in ten years after independence is only given in the 1947 Constitution[57] compared to the subsequent two Constitutions that lack such a provision and expressly prohibit secession respectively.[58] Likewise, the role of the military in formal politics was minimal in the first and second Constitutions but extensive in the third that affects constitutional rights of citizens and minorities. That said, it is not wrong to state that republicanism and multi-ethnic unity have constantly been two foundational ideas behind Burma/Myanmar's constitutionalism. In the present Constitution as well, the two ideas are operationalised into

---

[55] J Saffin, 'Seeking Constitutional Settlement in Myanmar' in A Harding (ed), *Constitutionalism and Legal Change in Myanmar* (Hart 2017); Williams, 'Constitutionalism Before Constitutions' (n 49).

[56] D Williams, 'What's So Bad about Burma's 2008 Constitution? A Guide for the Perplexed' in M Crouch and T Lindsey (eds), *Law, Society, and Transition in Myanmar* (Hart 2017).

[57] Constitution of the Union of Burma ss 201, 202.

[58] Constitution of the Republic of the Union of Myanmar s 10. For constitutional politics around the issue of secession in the 1950s, see J Silverstein, 'Politics in the Shan State: The Question of Secession from the Union of Burma' (1958) 18 The Journal of Asian Studies 43.

a wide range of constitutional rights meant for the demos and for members of ethnic minorities that are discussed in detail below.

III. Constitutional Ideas, Values, and Sources

Besides two grand ideas of multi-ethnic unity and republicanism, another controversial constitutional idea or feature – the constitutionalised role of the military – was added to the 2008 constitution[59] (hereafter the constitution) that was written at the behest of the SLORC/SPDC. As stated at the start of this chapter, the role of the military has been a feature of Myanmar's political pluralities since at least 1962 that has been written into the Constitution. These two or three – if we count the military as a standalone constitutional idea – ideas or objectives are explicitly stated in Section 6 of the Constitution. Firstly, since independent Myanmar has been constructed as a united, multi-ethnic nation-state, constructed union hood and multi-ethnic unity must not be harmed.[60] For that purpose, the constitution prohibits secession of any 'part of the territory constituted in the Union.'[61] Secondly, the type of republicanism or democracy envisioned by the constitution is 'a genuine, disciplined multi-party democratic system'[62] however it is understood and has been implemented so far by the constitution-making military in the 1990s and 2000s and two transitional governments of President Thein Sein (2011–16) and State Counselor Aung San Suu Kyi (2016 onwards).

Thirdly and most importantly, the military or defence services *must* have a role of political *leadership*.[63] The first two foundational ideas are not new. Yet, the prohibition against secession is new because the 1947 Constitution allowed it and the 1974 Constitution did not mention it at all. The third idea among them is entirely unprecedented. It is true that as head of the military General Ne Win launched a *military* coup in 1962. It is also true that the socialist BSPP regime was headed by Ne Win and his cabinet were mostly composed of active or ex-military officers. Yet, the military as an institution did not play any leadership role whatsoever because the RC only built a one-party socialist state in both pre- and post-1974 years – before and after building of socialist Burma was eventually constitutionalised. Authority was constituted in the BSPP and its party units downward along the chain of command while the military was supposed to be concerned with defence alone. In other words, the RC and BSPP were not military regimes per se

---

[59] Myanmar's official language is Myanmar/Burmese *alone* and interpretation of the text of the 2008 constitution must be based on the Burmese text *alone*, Constitution of the Republic of the Union of Myanmar ss 450, 452. But, interestingly, an unofficial English translation accompanied the Burmese text when it was first published in 2007. This section is based on the English version and the Burmese text will be discussed as necessary.
[60] Constitution of the Republic of the Union of Myanmar ss 6(a), 6(b).
[61] ibid s 10.
[62] ibid s 6(d).
[63] ibid s 6(f).

but military-dominated regimes. More importantly, they were not concerned with development and preparation of the military for a future political leadership role like the SLORC/SPDC did in the 1990s and 2000s.[64]

To create such a political leadership role for themselves, the SLORC/SPDC did three things. First, they modernised and developed the military that had been poorly manned and funded[65] but grew united in combat against communist and ethnic insurgencies for half a century[66] – they are 'a solidly united organization that had never had a mutiny within its Ranks.'[67] Second, they established, organised, and lavishly funded a mass association known as Union Solidarity and Development Association (USDA) in September 1993 that would later be transformed into a political party in June 2010 – a few months before the general elections.[68] Third, they crushed the NLD and other political dissidents throughout the 1990s and 2000s by imprisoning most, if not all, prominent dissidents and putting Aung San Suu Kyi under house arrest. By the late 2000s, the opposition had been largely decapitated and annihilated.[69] The SLORC/SPDC also made sure that the Nobel peace laureate with two sons who are British citizens could not become President of Myanmar by 'inserting' a section in the constitution – notorious Section 59 (f) that prevented her from assuming presidency after winning in the 2015 general elections.[70]

Again, I must emphasise that all three ideas or sources have not been constructed and constitutionalised through a proper negotiation and pact-making process between elites themselves and consultation with the people. However, it represents the constitutional reality now in Myanmar. Now, let us look at the rights provided in the Constitution for ethnic and political pluralities. The latter includes both ordinary citizens and non-military political elites and groups on one hand, and the military on the other hand.

A. Constitutional Rights for Ethnic Pluralities

Although Myanmar has been criticised for being a polity that is dominated by the ethnic Bamar majority both constitutionally and politically, nothing is found in

---

[64] Y Nakanishi, *Strong Soldiers, Failed Revolution: The State and Military in Burma, 1962–1988* (NUS Press 2013).

[65] Andrew Selth, *Burma's Armed Forces: Power without Glory* (EastBridge 2002); Maung Aung Myoe, *Building the Tatmadaw: Myanmar Armed Forces since 1948* (Institute of Southeast Asian Studies 2009).

[66] Mary Callahan, *Making Enemies: War and State Building in Burma* (Cornell University Press 2003).

[67] Zoltan Barany, *How Armies Respond to Revolutions and Why* (Princeton University Press 2016) 83.

[68] Taylor, *The State in Myanmar* (n 33).

[69] Monique Skidmore, *Karaoke Fascism: Burma and the Politics of Fear* (University of Pennsylvania Press 2004); Christina Fink, *Living Silence in Burma: Surviving Under Military Rule* (2nd edn, Silkworm Books and Zed Books 2009).

[70] A Harding, 'Editorial Note: The Debate Concerning Section 59 (f) of Myanmar's 2008 Constitution: A Gordian Knot of Rule of Law, Democracy, and the Application of Problematical Constitutional Provisions' in A Harding (ed), *Constitutionalism and Legal Change in Myanmar* (Hart 2017).

Myanmar's Pluralist Constitution: Nation-Building versus State-Building   157

the text of the Constitution that majoritises the Bamar. Neither does it minoritise non-Bamar groups.[71] Instead, the Constitution uses 'national races'(called *taingyintha* in Burmese) that includes both the Bamar majority and other minorities as a collective multi-ethnic identity. The Constitution states: 'The state is where where multi-National races collectively reside.'[72] This provision effectively views the state of Myanmar as constituted by descendants from one or more of 135 races *alone*. But, the following section asserts: 'The Sovereign power of the Union is derived from the citizens.'[73] It seems to imply that this section makes amends for the lack of the notion of democratic citizenship and legal egalitarianism.

Ethnic rights provided for in the Constitution can be categorised in numerous ways depending on how one looks at and analyses them. Ethnic minorities or 'national races' as they are called in the unofficial English version of the Constitution are often named ethnic groups and ethnic nationalities as well – I interchangeably use all of them. Despite those different names, they have a common feature, ie they all refer to group identity. Once a group of people is called an ethnic minority or national race or ethnic group or ethnic nationality, it follows that that group of people becomes a group with members who share common ascriptive or constructed traits different from other groups. Therefore, it is reasonable to identify and analyse constitutional rights for ethnic minorities at two levels: individual rights and group rights. However, constitutional rights for them are entirely geared towards their group identity, rather than their individuality.

Yet, there is an important constitutional right given to individual members of national races, ie citizenship. Despite their special status as native races, their individual members are concurrently citizens. It then requires one to explore how citizenship of those national races' members and of other citizens operate. On a superficial level, the Constitution does not distinguish between the two types of citizens; rather, it predominantly uses 'citizens' which includes both types throughout. But it does state that there are two types of citizenship: the first given to descendants of national races and the second to others.[74] It then stops short of defining who citizens are but only states that 'citizenship, naturalization and revocation of citizenship shall be as prescribed by law,'[75] implicitly referring to the *Myanmar Citizenship Law* (1982). The controversial law, commonly believed to be a root cause of the *de jure* statelessness of the Rohingya,[76] effectively creates

---

[71] Only one constitutional section (s 361) could be said to majoritise Buddhists – not the Bamar – that states: 'The Union recognizes special position of Buddhism as the faith professed by the great majority of the citizens of the Union.' But it does not have any ethnic or racial connotation. The section can even be said to create a Buddhist majority that includes several ethnic peoples such as the Bamar, Mon, Shan, and Rakhine.

[72] Constitution of the Republic of the Union of Myanmar s 3.

[73] ibid s 4.

[74] ibid s 345.

[75] ibid s 346.

[76] Contrary to this common assumption, Nick Cheesman and Nyi Nyi Kyaw have shown how the Rohingya have been arbitrarily and intentionally deprived of their Myanmar citizenship by successive Myanmar governments since the late 1980s. See Nick Cheesman, 'How in Myanmar "National Races"

two classes of native-race citizens and non-native citizens with different rights. The most radical difference between the two is that the former may never be revoked except when such native-race citizens become citizens of foreign countries, permanently leave Myanmar, or obtain passports or similar documents of foreign countries all because Myanmar does not recognise dual citizenship.[77] The latter may be revoked[78] and never be acquired again once revoked.[79] This is why Nick Cheesman calls belonging to national races 'the gold standard for citizenship'.[80]

In contrast to the 'permanent legal limbo'[81] of non-native citizenship that is not suffered by native citizenship, Chapter 8 of the Constitution is titled 'Citizen, Fundamental Rights and Duties of the Citizens' and is dedicated to rights, and duties, of citizens. The chapter does not distinguish between the two classes of citizens. Yet, there exists another radical difference between native-race citizens and non-native citizens that is constitutionalised. The highest office of Myanmar, ie presidency and vice-presidency, is only reserved for native-race citizens.[82] So, legally and constitutionally, demos and ethnos are different in terms of rights.

Besides citizenship and presidency/vice-presidency, the constitution provides ethnic minorities with several other rights. Political (and civil to some extent) rights of the minorities shall be discussed below. Social, economic, and cultural rights constitutionally accorded to minorities include general provisions for state assistance in 'language, literature, fine arts and culture'.[83] Again, the state pledges to 'assist development, consolidation and preservation of National [minorities'] culture,'[84] and to 'promote socio-economic development including education, health, economy, transport and communication, so forth, of less-developed National races."[85] Also, the state is committed to make laws to "enable National people to participate in matters of their education and health'.[86]

As we can see, all these provisions are very general and do not possess much substance. However, for realisation of these general constitutional rights, the Parliament passed a dedicated law in 2015, namely the *Ethnic Rights Protection Law*. The law is effectively an ethnic bill of group – not individual – rights and it lists several rights. Importantly, the enjoyment of one or more of those rights is subject to existing law, national security, community peace and tranquility, public order, and morality.[87] The rights are: free profession of their language, literature,

---

Came to Surpass Citizenship and Exclude Rohingya' (2017) 47 Journal of Contemporary Asia 461; Nyi Nyi Kyaw, 'Unpacking the Presumed Statelessness of Rohingyas' (2017) 15 Journal of Immigrant and Refugee Studies 269.

[77] Myanmar Citizenship Law 1982 ss 16, 17.
[78] ibid ss 18, 35, 58.
[79] ibid s 22.
[80] Cheesman (n 76) 471.
[81] Nyi Nyi Kyaw (n 11) 55.
[82] Constitution of the Republic of the Union of Myanmar s 59(b).
[83] ibid s 22(a).
[84] ibid s 27.
[85] ibid s 22(c).
[86] ibid s 28(b).
[87] Ethnic Rights Protection Law 2015 s 4.

fine art, culture, custom, and religion; teaching and learning of their language and literature; freedom to hold cultural and customary ceremonies and special days; development of literature and fine art and research on culture; equality in education, health care, employment, and business; preservation and development of traditional medicine; revelation of ethnic histories and preservation of heritage.[88] Moreover, a dedicated ethnic affairs ministry whose chief is a cabinet minister is established.[89]

B. Constitutional Rights for Political Pluralities

As stated above, constitutional rights for political pluralities need to be seen at least in two ways: rights of individual citizens and that of political groups, especially the military. Chapter 8 of the Constitution lists several rights for citizens that include but are not limited to: 'equal rights before the law;'[90] non-discrimination 'based on race, birth, religion, official position, status, culture, sex and wealth;'[91] equal opportunities in work and vocation;[92] women's rights and child rights;[93] personal integrity rights;[94] freedoms of conviction and opinion, assembly, association and organisation, development of language, literature, culture, religion, and customs;[95] freedom of residence and settlement anywhere in Myanmar;[96] property rights;[97] right to education;[98] right to health care;[99] and freedom of conducting business.[100] In addition to these *individual* rights of citizens that are more socially, economically, and culturally oriented, there are several constitutional rights for citizens for the realisation of their civil and political rights. Most important among them is the right to elect and be elected.[101] Likewise, the rights to have political representation,[102] form political parties,[103] and assume public office[104] are also provided.

---

[88] ibid.
[89] ibid s 6.
[90] Constitution of the Republic of the Union of Myanmar s 347.
[91] ibid ss 348, 352.
[92] ibid s 349.
[93] ibid ss 350–351.
[94] ibid s 353.
[95] ibid s 354.
[96] ibid s 355.
[97] ibid s 356.
[98] ibid s 366.
[99] ibid s 367.
[100] ibid s 370.
[101] ibid s 38.
[102] ibid s 391.
[103] ibid ss 404, 405, 406.
[104] There exist several sections in the constitution relating to nomination and appointment of public officials from among citizens in the constitution, eg, s 59 that is concerned with qualifications of the President and Vice-Presidents.

The other political group that has been accorded special constitutional rights is the military simply because it supervised the whole process of constitution-making. In breach of military professionalism[105] and standard civil-military relations in which civilian authority has oversight on the military,[106] the Constitution creates a somewhat permanent political leadership role for the military as an institution and its members as well. The Myanmar military – called Defence Services in the constitution – assumes political leadership[107] and is under its own control or that of the commander-in-chief.[108]

Besides its constitutionally provided right of political leadership in general terms, the military has made sure that the Constitution contains specific terms to give itself a guardian role in the legislature that elects and/or nominates the executive and the judiciary. For that purpose, the unelected military representatives nominated by the Commander-in-Chief automatically takes a quarter of the seats of the Union Parliament that constitutes a lower house and an upper house.[109] It effectively serves as a veto over any amendments – significant or otherwise – to the Constitution that require Yes votes of more than 75% of members of Parliament.[110]

To militarise the executive branch, the commander-in-chief nominates three cabinet ministers for defence, border affairs, and home affairs[111] who are then appointed by the President. Also, the military representatives in Parliament nominates one of the three vice-presidents[112] under the guidance of the commander-in-chief[113] – the other two are nominated by the lower and upper houses[114] – who may become President if elected in order of the number of votes obtained by the Presidential Electoral College[115] composed of *all* members of parliaments including military ones.[116] The Vice-President nominated by the military bloc may at least remain to be one of the two Vice-Presidents if unelected by the college.

The other constitutional prerogative given to the military is the formation of a National Defence and Security Council (NDSC) composed of eleven persons: President; two Vice-Presidents; speakers of the two houses; Commander-in-Chief and his deputy; and four cabinet ministers for defence, foreign affairs, home affairs, and border affairs. The council has extensive powers whose approval or

---

[105] For a good overview of the doctrine of military professionalism, see M Alagappa (ed), *Military Professionalism in Asia: Conceptual and Empirical Perspectives* (East-West Center 2001).
[106] For a good overview of the theory of civil-military relations and its contours during democratisation in Asia, see A Croissant, D Kuehn, P Lorenz and PW Chambers (eds), *Democratization and Civilian Control in Asia* (Palgrave Macmillan 2013).
[107] Constitution of the Republic of the Union of Myanmar s 6(f).
[108] ibid s 338.
[109] ibid ss 109(b), 141(b).
[110] ibid s 436.
[111] ibid s 232(b)(ii).
[112] ibid s 60(c).
[113] President and Vice-Presidents Election Law (2010) s 5(b)(iii).
[114] Constitution of the Republic of the Union of Myanmar s 60(c).
[115] ibid s 60(a).
[116] ibid s 60(e).

recommendation is required by the President to grant amnesty,[117] urgently sever foreign relations,[118] wage wars against aggression towards Myanmar;[119] appoint the Commander-in-Chief;[120] declare an emergency[121] and transfer executive, legislative, and judiciary powers to the Commander-in-Chief who will deal with emergencies.[122] Upon declaration of emergencies, the Commander-in-Chief may 'restrict or suspend' citizens' fundamental rights.[123] All these constitutional rights of the military lend strong support to a view of continued militarisation of politics in Myanmar or of the military 'caretaking' democratisation[124] even in the context of a so-called transition that was ongoing from 2011 until 2016 after President Thein Sein came to power.

IV. Constitutional Institutions and Structure

The political system of Myanmar is now a mixed one in which the Parliament is elected by citizens and the former elects a President. That said, the President is by no means ceremonial but has strong powers. However, his/her powers to appoint and remove public officials from top to bottom that are in all other aspects absolute are curtailed by that of the Commander-in-Chief who holds sway over the executive and legislature. The state is composed of seven ethnically designated states – Kachin, Kayah, Kayin, Chin, Mon, Rakhine, and Shan – and seven regions (formerly called divisions) – Sagaing, Magway, Tanintharyi, Mandalay, Ayeyarwady, Bago, and Yangon regions – plus the capital of Nay Pyi Taw designated as Union territories.[125]

All these three constitutional arrangements – parliamentary elections, formation of ethnic states, and military's prerogatives – reflect political realities of Myanmar at least from the late 1980s when incremental militarisation has been seen since. Also, they apparently originate in constitutional ideas of republicanism, multi-ethnic statehood, and the military's role in politics. The way that unelected military representatives sit in Parliament and three internal and external security-related cabinet positions are taken by the military shows how the institution has constitutionalised its dominant political role. That said, as seen above, the Constitution has several provisions for the roles of the people and ethnic minorities in the state, however imperfect and disproportionate they are. What has happened in

---

[117] ibid s 204(b).
[118] ibid s 206.
[119] ibid s 213(a).
[120] ibid s 342.
[121] ibid s 410.
[122] ibid s 418(a).
[123] ibid s 420.
[124] R Egreteau, *Caretaking Democratization: The Military and Political Change in Myanmar* (OUP 2016).
[125] Constitution of the Republic of the Union of Myanmar s 49.

the past eight years after the transition beginning in 2010 shows a clear progression from militarised dictatorship in the 1990s and 2000s when the military reigned supreme over the people who did not exert considerable influence upon the state. The first five years of the transition was basically staged because the Union Solidarity and Development Party (USDP) that evolved from USDA won in the unfree and unfair 2010 general election in which the key opposition party NLD did not participate. It then becomes more visible after the NLD chaired by Aung San Suu Kyi won by a landslide in the next general election held in November 2015 and came to power.

Now, let us look closely at constitutional institutions or structures created to respond to ethnic pluralities in Myanmar. As stated above, the seven-ethnic-state and seven-non-ethnic-region/division structure has been maintained at least since 1974. They have been nominally or symbolically included in the second and third constitutions. The giving of statehood by name to the Kachin, etc may have been aimed at creating a sense of equality between and among different ethnic groups. However, the right is given *only* to seven out of 135 government-recognised national races and it has proven tantamount to the constitutional creation of an ethnocratic, majoritarian state structure that neglects other nested minorities within individual ethnic states. That is why five self-administered zones – namely, Naga, Danu, Pa-O, Palaung, and Kokang – and one self-administered division – namely Wa – have been created in the 2008 Constitution that is unprecedented.[126] These zones stem from ceasefire agreements between the SLORC/SPDC and those ethnic groups except for the Danu that would later demand creation of the zones/divisions.[127]

Another key constitutional structure newly created in the 2008 constitution is the office of ministers for national races affairs at the region/state/self-administered area levels.[128] Such ministers are appointed as special representatives of national races as long as the population of a national race constitutes at least 0.1% of the total population of the respective region/state/self-administered area.[129] There were 29 national races affairs ministers during President Thein Sein's government (2011–16).[130] Interestingly, due to decisions made on population figures, five among them were ministers that represented 'Bamar' minorities who constitute the ethnic majority in Myanmar as a whole in five ethnic states – Kachin, Kayah, Kayin, Mon, and Shan.[131] Also, a ministry of ethnic affairs has

[126] ibid s 56.
[127] For detailed history of the creation of the six administered areas, see M Crouch, 'Ethnic Rights and Constitutional Change: The Recognition of Ethnic Nationalities in Myanmar/Burma' in AJ Harding and M Sidel (eds), *Central-local Relations in Asian Constitutional Systems* (Hart 2015).
[128] Constitution of the Republic of the Union of Myanmar s 15.
[129] ibid ss 161(b), (c).
[130] This number remained unchanged in the general election held in November 2015. For a study on those 29 ministers in 2011–16, see AM Thawnhmung and Yadana, 'Citizenship and Minority Rights: The Role of 'National Race Affairs' Ministers in Myanmar's 2008 Constitution' in A South and M Lall (eds), *Citizenship in Myanmar: Ways of Being in and from Burma* (Singapore, Institute of Southeast Asian Studies 2017).
[131] ibid.

been created and ethnic Mon leader Naing Thet Lwin appointed as minister by the NLD government although the new ministry has so far only been able to work for education, health, language, culture, and infrastructure of ethnic peoples in ethnic states.[132] Therefore, it is not wrong to state that actual power is still in the hands of the central government despite these constitutional institutions and structures.

The two most contentious issues between the government and ethnic minorities are the appointment of chief ministers of their states by the President[133] and the unequal distribution of powers between the union government and states/regions/self-administered areas as outlined in Schedules One, Two, and Three of the constitution. The first issue was evidenced in appointment of Nyi Pu – a central executive committee member of the NLD – by the party after it won in the 2015 general elections as Chief Minister of Rakhine state in which the Arakan National Party (ANP) obtained more seats at the state level than the national electoral winner did. The NLD appointed Nyi Pu without heeding to the calls by ANP to appoint one of its members or negotiate with it.[134] Hence, there was an earlier unsuccessful attempt in 2015 by ethnic members of Parliament to amend this constitutional provision so that they would assign and remove their respective chief ministers.[135] Unequal center-periphery relations between the Bamar-dominated Union government and Parliament and regional governments and parliaments in ethnic states have also been pointed out.[136]

The other often-overlooked issue relating to ethnic minorities is their representation in the Upper House – called the *Amyotha Hluttaw* – that is composed of 168 elected representatives (12 each from 14 states and regions including one representative each from six self-administered areas) and 56 military representatives.[137] Seven regions are believed to be dominated by the Bamar majority although we do not have demographic data by ethnicity; hence, it follows that the Bamar possess at least half of the voting power at the upper house. The Lower House – called the *Pyithu Hluttaw* – is composed of 330 elected representatives (one from each township of all regions/states/self-administered areas/Union territories) and 110 military representatives.[138] Bamar-dominated regions

---

[132] Han Hmway and Lin Naing, 'The government's roadmap for national reconciliation and union peace' *Global New Light of Myanmar* (Yangon, 22 May 2018) 11–12.

[133] Constitution of the Republic of the Union of Myanmar s 261(b).

[134] Kyaw Phone Kyaw, 'NLD Goes It Alone, Raising Ethnic Party Ire' *Frontier Myanmar* (Yangon, 2 May 2016) <https://frontiermyanmar.net/en/nld-goes-it-alone-raising-ethnic-party-ire> accessed 19 September 2018.

[135] Htoo Thant, 'Military Opposes Chief Minister Selection Reform' *Myanmar Times* (Yangon, 2 July 2015) <www.mmtimes.com/national-news/15306-military-opposes-chief-minister-selection-reform.html> accessed 19 September 2018.

[136] I Holliday, Maw Htun Aung, and C Joelene, 'Institution Building in Myanmar: The Establishment of Regional and State Assemblies' (2015) 55 Asian Survey 641; Hamish Nixon, Cindy Joelene, Kyi Pyar Chit Saw, Thet Aung Lynn, and Matthew Arnold, *Region and State Governments in Myanmar* (Myanmar Development Resource Institute-Centre for Economic and Social Development and Asia Foundation 2013).

[137] Constitution of the Republic of the Union of Myanmar s 141.

[138] ibid s 109.

have 207 townships or constituencies whereas ethnic states only 123. Therefore, the Bamar also dominates the voting power in the lower house. This dominance becomes more overwhelming when there is disagreement between the lower and upper houses over legislation. Such cases will be decided at the combined Union Parliament[139] – called the *Pyidaungsu Hluttaw* – at which the Bamar representatives from both houses will dominate. Bamar dominance will reach its maximum if we consider the voting power of a quarter of the total representatives of the Union Parliament, ie military representatives. The military is believed to be a Bamar-dominated institution, so its voting preference may, in theory, be oriented towards the Bamar when there is debate and voting over critical matters relating to majority-minority issues.

Now, let's briefly turn again to the case of the two most important political groups, ie the military and the people. We have seen in the previous section how the military has written their own constitutional rights into the 2008 Constitution but still had to guarantee citizens' rights as well. That said, since the political transition was meant for transferring power back to the people, the Constitution has several institutions and structures to reflect the political pluralities. Although the military occupies a quarter of the parliamentary seats, the Constitution still allows the people to elect their representatives through a regular parliamentary election. Likewise, leadership positions of the judiciary, legislature, and executive branches of the government are nominated by the President who is now a civilian. Although the military has a veto over constitutional amendments, the civilian representatives of the parliament may still make, repeal, or revise non-constitutional legislation through a simple majority vote as long as it is in accord with the constitution.

V. Conclusion

To sum up, Myanmar has always been and remains plural since before independence was obtained from the British and the 1947 Constitution was written. However, this constitutional pluralism has not been optimal. The people have not fully regained their power that was usurped and monopolised by the military in 1962. Likewise, ethnic minorities are not fully satisfied because power- and resource-sharing between them and the central state is found to be superficial or inadequate. These pluralities and how they have been so far constitutionally accommodated may also be seen in terms of state-building and nation-building. By state-building, it is meant that the central government, civilian or military, has always tried to control power and build a state in the ethnically and politically diverse society of Myanmar. Concurrently, the state has had to build a nation in which all diverse ethnic groups have faith in and feel affiliated with. Unfortunately, despite prolonged military rule to monopolise power from 1962 through 2011

---

[139] ibid s 95(b).

that could be said to be an improper militarised state-building exercise, nation-building has largely failed. Ethnic plurality and its consequent constitutional demands remain to be critical issues that bogs down any serious state- and nation-building project.

President Thein Sein offered the olive branch to ethnic armed groups (EAGs) on 18 August 2011.[140] In almost seven years, ten EAGs have signed a nation-wide ceasefire agreement (NCA) – eight signed it in October 2015 during the Thein Sein administration and two more joined in February 2018 with the NLD led by Aung San Suu Kyi in power. However, armed conflict between the military and those EAGs who have not signed the NCA has resumed since 2011 and intensified in recent years. State Counselor Aung San Suu Kyi and the NLD seem bitterly aware of their limitations to amend the constitution at the Parliament where the military may block any untoward moves by the democrats to limit and remove its power. Also, with the military running the show in security-related matters, Aung San Suu Kyi cannot do much. That is most probably the reason why she announced a seven-step roadmap on the first anniversary of NCA on 15 October 2016. The roadmap outlines that principles for future democratic federal changes would be discussed and agreed at the Union Peace Conference-21st Century Panglong (UPC) that the NLD has held twice since it came to power in March 2016. Then, the current constitution would be amended in line with the agreed principles.[141]

Hence, the 2008 constitution remains insufficiently democratic and federalist for the people and ethnic minorities in Myanmar. The military still maintains and jealously guards its political leadership. However, another constitutional process has been ongoing at the UPC with strong expectations on the part of the people/democrats led by the NLD and ethnic minorities. How and when the process will end and what concrete constitutional results will be produced remains to be seen. But, one thing is certain. Myanmar's plurality continues to evolve and demands further constitutionalisation, whether in the form of an amended constitution or a new one.

Bibliography

—— Constitution of the Union of Burma.
—— Constitution of the Socialist Republic of the Union of Burma.
—— Constitution of the Republic of the Union of Myanmar.
—— Ethnic Rights Protection Law 2015.
—— Government of the Republic of the Union of Myanmar Announcement No. 1/2011, *Invitation to Peace Talks*, dated 18 August 2011, *New Light of Myanmar* (Yangon, 19 August 2011) 1.

---

[140] New Light of Myanmar, *Announcement No. 1/2011* (n 9).
[141] 'The government's roadmap for national reconciliation and union peace' *Global New Light of Myanmar* (Yangon, 16 October 2016) 1.

—— Myanmar Citizenship Law 1982.
—— President and Vice-Presidents Election Law (2010).
—— State Peace and Development Council Announcement No. (2/2007) on Formation and Assignment of Commission for Drafting State Constitution (18 October 2007), *New Light of Myanmar* (Yangon, 19 October 2007).
—— 'The government's roadmap for national reconciliation and union peace' *Global New Light of Myanmar* (Yangon, 16 October 2016).
Ackerman B, *We the People: Transformations* (Harvard University Press 2001).
Alagappa M (ed), *Military Professionalism in Asia: Conceptual and Empirical Perspectives* (East-West Center 2001).
Barany Z, *How Armies Respond to Revolutions and Why* (Princeton University Press 2016).
Callahan M, *Making Enemies: War and State Building in Burma* (Cornell University Press 2003).
—— 'Distorted, Dangerous Data? *Lumyo* in the 2014 Myanmar Population and Housing Census' (2017) 32 Sojourn: Journal of Social Issues in Southeast Asia 452.
Cheesman N, 'How in Myanmar "National Races" Came to Surpass Citizenship and Exclude Rohingya' (2017) 47 Journal of Contemporary Asia 461.
Collier RB and Collier D, *Shaping the Political Arena: Critical Junctures, the Labor Movement, and Regime Dynamics in Latin America* (Princeton University Press 1991).
Croissant A, Kuehn D, Lorenz P and Chambers PW (eds), *Democratization and Civilian Control in Asia* (Palgrave Macmillan 2013).
Crouch M, 'Ethnic Rights and Constitutional Change: The Recognition of Ethnic Nationalities in Myanmar/Burma' in Harding A J and Sidel M (eds), *Central-local Relations in Asian Constitutional Systems* (Hart 2015).
Egreteau R, *Caretaking Democratization: The Military and Political Change in Myanmar* (OUP 2016).
Eisenstadt TA, LeVan AC, and Maboudi TF, *Constituents Before Assembly: Participation, Deliberation, and Representation in the Crafting of New Constitutions* (CUP 2017).
Feldman N, 'Imposed Constitutionalism' (2004–2005) 37 Connecticut Law Review 857.
Fink C, *Living Silence in Burma: Surviving Under Military Rule* (2nd edn, Silkworm Books and Zed Books 2009).
Han Hmway and Lin Naing, 'The government's roadmap for national reconciliation and union peace' *Global New Light of Myanmar* (Yangon, 22 May 2018) 11–12.
Harding A, 'Editorial Note: The Debate Concerning Section 59 (f) of Myanmar's 2008 Constitution: A Gordian Knot of Rule of Law, Democracy, and the Application of Problematical Constitutional Provisions' in Harding A (ed), *Constitutionalism and Legal Change in Myanmar* (Hart 2017).
Holliday I, Maw Htun Aung, and C Joelene, 'Institution Building in Myanmar: The Establishment of Regional and State Assemblies' (2015) 55 Asian Survey 641.

Hsueh V, *Hybrid Constitutions: Challenging Legacies of Law, Privilege, and Culture in Colonial America* (Duke University Press 2010).

Htoo Thant, 'Military Opposes Chief Minister Selection Reform' *Myanmar Times* (Yangon, 2 July 2015) www.mmtimes.com/national-news/15306-military-opposes-chief-minister-selection-reform.html accessed 19 September 2018.

Kin Oung, *Eliminate the Elite: Assassination of Burma's General Aung San and His Six Cabinet Colleagues* (Print, Post, Plus (p3) Design 2011).

Kyaw Phone Kyaw, 'NLD Goes It Alone, Raising Ethnic Party Ire' *Frontier Myanmar* (Yangon, 2 May 2016) https://frontiermyanmar.net/en/nld-goes-it-alone-raising-ethnic-party-ire accessed 19 September 2018.

Leach E R, *Political Systems of Highland Burma: A Study of Kachin Social Structure* (Harvard University Press 1954).

Maung Aung Myoe, *Building the Tatmadaw: Myanmar Armed Forces since 1948* (Institute of Southeast Asian Studies 2009).

Maung Maung, *Burma's Constitution* (Springer Netherlands 1961).

—— *A Trial in Burma: The Assassination of Aung San* (Springer Netherlands 1961).

—— *Aung San of Burma* (Martinus Nijhoff 1962).

—— *Burma and General Ne Win* (Asia Publishing House 1969).

—— *The 1988 Uprising in Burma* (Yale University, Southeast Asia Studies 1999)

Mya Maung, *The Burma Road to Poverty* (Praeger 1991).

Moscotti A D, *Burma's Constitution and Elections of 1974: A Source Book* (Institute of Southeast Asian Studies 1977).

Nakanishi Y, *Strong Soldiers, Failed Revolution: The State and Military in Burma, 1962-1988* (National University of Singapore Press 2013).

Nixon H, C Joelene, Kyi Pyar Chit Saw, Thet Aung Lynn, and Arnold M, *Region and State Governments in Myanmar* (Myanmar Development Resource Institute-Centre for Economic and Social Development and Asia Foundation 2013).

Nyi Nyi Kyaw, 'Alienation, Discrimination, and Securitization: Legal Personhood and Cultural Personhood of Muslims in Myanmar' (2015) 13 Review of Faith & International Affairs 50.

——'Unpacking the Presumed Statelessness of Rohingyas' (2017) 15 Journal of Immigrant and Refugee Studies 269.

Pound R, 'Law in the Books and Law in Action' (1910) 44 American Law Review 12.

Sadan M, *Being and Becoming Kachin: Histories Beyond the State in the Borderworlds of Burma* (British Academy 2013).

Saffin J, 'Seeking Constitutional Settlement in Myanmar' in Harding A (ed), *Constitutionalism and Legal Change in Myanmar* (Hart 2017).

Sarkisyanz E, *Buddhist Backgrounds of the Burmese Revolution* (Martinus Nijhoff 1965).

Scheppele K, 'Constitutional Ethnography: An Introduction' (2004) 38 Law & Society Review 389, 390-1.

Schober J, *Modern Buddhist Conjunctures in Myanmar: Cultural Narratives, Colonial Legacies, and Civil Society* (University of Hawaii Press 2011).

Seekins D M, *Burma and Japan since 1940: From 'Co-prosperity' to 'Quiet Dialogue'* (Nordic Institute of Asian Studies 2007).

—— 'Myanmar in 2008: Hardship, Compounded' (2009) 49 Asian Survey 170.

Sein Win, *The Split Story* (Guardian Ltd 1959).

Selth A, *Burma's Armed Forces: Power without Glory* (EastBridge 2002).

Silverstein J, 'Politics in the Shan State: The Question of Secession from the Union of Burma' (1958) 18 The Journal of Asian Studies 43.

—— *The Political Legacy of Aung San* (Southeast Asia Program, Cornell University 1972).

Skidmore M, *Karaoke Fascism: Burma and the Politics of Fear* (University of Pennsylvania Press 2004).

Smith M, *Burma: Insurgency and the Politics of Ethnicity* (Zed Books 1991).

Taylor R, *The State in Myanmar* (2nd edn, NUS Press 2009).

—— *General Ne Win: A Political Biography* (Institute of Southeast Asian Studies 2015).

Thant Myint-U, *The Making of Modern Burma* (CUP 2001).

Thawnhmung AM and Yadana, 'Citizenship and Minority Rights: The Role of "National Race Affairs" Ministers in Myanmar's 2008 Constitution' in South A and Lall M (eds), *Citizenship in Myanmar: Ways of Being in and from Burma* (Singapore, Institute of Southeast Asian Studies 2017).

Turner AM, *Saving Buddhism: The Impermanence of Religion in Colonial Burma* (University of Hawaii Press 2014).

Tushnet M, 'Authoritarian Constitutionalism' in Ginsburg T and Simpser A (eds), *Constitutions in Authoritarian Regimes* (Cambridge University Press 2013).

U Maung Maung, *From Sangha to Laity: Nationalist Movements of Burma, 1920–40* (Manohar 1980).

—— *The 1988 Uprising in Burma* (Yale University, Southeast Asia Studies 1999).

Versteeg M, 'Unpopular Constitutionalism' (2014) 89 Indiana Law Journal 1133.

Walton M J, 'Ethnicity, Conflict, and History in Burma: The Myths of Panglong' (2008) 48 Asian Survey 889.

Williams D C, 'Constitutionalism Before Constitutions: Burma's Struggle to Build a New Order' (2009) 87 Texas Law Review 1657.

—— 'What's So Bad about Burma's 2008 Constitution? A Guide for the Perplexed' in Crouch M and Lindsey T (eds), *Law, Society, and Transition in Myanmar* (Hart 2017).

7
Pluralist Constitution in Cambodia

TAING RATANA

I. Introduction

The pluralist constitution is an interesting analytical concept to be applied to the context of the Cambodian Constitution. Using this analytical concept, this chapter covers three main points: (i) the historical context that provides a brief understanding of the history of the nation's founding, a brief account of the plurality of the country, and a brief account of the drafting and adoption of the constitutional text; (ii) pluralism as a fact of constitutional ideas and values, and sources of constitutional norms, structures, and rights; and (iii) key observations on how pluralistic sources shape or affect constitutional law and politics in Cambodia. This chapter can be beneficial for further understanding and research on other related topics of pluralist constitutionalism in Cambodia.

II. Historical Context

Cambodia is known to be one of the oldest countries in Asia. It was a civilised and prosperous nation for centuries before falling into destruction over the last few centuries. In his writings about Angkor, George Cedès[1] came to the conclusion that a territory with large numbers of Khmer temples, stretching from the gulf of Siam to Vientiane and *Prey Nokor* (Saigon) and finally to the river of *Me Nam*, formed the territory of today's Cambodia. This large territory also formed the *Khmer Empire* from the ninth to the thirteenth centuries. Cambodia has experienced a long walk of change: from prosperity and great civilisation to destruction; absolute monarchy to constitutional monarchy; constitutional monarchy to republic; republic to communism; communism to socialism; and again from socialism to constitutional monarchy.

---

[1] George Cedès wrote the book *Pour Mieux Comprendre Angkor* (Jouve 1947), which was translated from French into Khmer by Prof. Minh Nakry in 1998.

170   Taing Ratana

Interestingly, Cambodia is an unpredictable nation in terms of its natural, socio-political, and legal contexts. In terms of its natural context, the waters of the *Tonle Sap* lake twist and turn with annual reversals in its flow. In terms of its political regime, monarchism collapsed in 1970 and was re-installed in 1993, while the nation went through the trauma of auto-genocide from 1975 to 1979 before grappling with new forms of administration such as the co-prime minister formation in 1993. In terms of the legal context, new legal norms have been formed through additions to the Constitution in 2004. These contexts set the backdrop for plurality in this kingdom. These kinds of plurality also shape this kingdom, which is also known as *'The Kingdom of Wonder'*.

A. Brief History of the Founding of the Nation

The Cambodian people have been told from generation to generation that the land of Cambodia is intertwined with a very interesting legend of the princess *Soma*, a female dragon (*Nagi*), and a prince from India, *Kaundinya* – both of whom are known as *Preah Thong-Neang Neak* by the Khmer people. This legend explains the creation of the territory and administration of this nation.

In the beginning, this land was a small island called *Koh Kok Thlork*,[2] after the symbolic *Thlork* tree. The island was thought to belong to *Naga Raja* (the dragon king of the ocean). Princess *Nagi*, who often transformed herself and her followers into beautiful ladies, came to play at *Koh Kok Thlork*. It so happened that prince *Kaundinya*, who was sailing from India with hundreds of followers, stopped at *Koh Kok Thlork* at night and saw Princess *Nagi* playing on the beach in the moonlight. The prince fell in love with the princess and asked her for her hand in marriage. The princess accepted but asked him to obtain the consent of her father, *Naga Raja*, who lived in a palace in the deep ocean. The prince promised, and Princess *Nagi* then brought the prince to meet her royal father. As a human being, Kaundinya, or *Preah Thong* as he was later called, could not travel like a dragon to the palace of the *Naga Raja* in the deep sea. Hence, *Nagi* asked him to carry her tail and so brought him to meet her father.[3] The *Naga Raja* had no objections to this proposal because he found *Preah Thong* very suitable for his beloved daughter. The *Naga Raja* then agreed to preside over the marriage of Princess *Nagi* and Prince *Preah Thong*, even using his magical powers to reclaim a larger *Koh Kok Thlork* from

---

[2] *Koh* means Island, *Kok* means dry land, and *Thlork* is a type of a tree that produces edible nuts and oil used for waterproofing.

[3] *Preah Thong*'s act of carrying the tail of the *Nagi* has been preserved until today in a Khmer wedding tradition that honours this love story. The groom must carry the *Chong Phahom or Sbai (the end of the long train of the bride's dress, which falls from her shoulder)* of his bride when entering the honeymoon room. The act of *Preah Thong* also marks the start of matriarchy in Cambodia. Khmer ladies are considered the Head of the Family.

the ocean. This land thus became a territory ruled over by the newly-wed couple, who became the King and Queen of a new nation named *Nokor Kok Thlok* – the Cambodia of today.

The Cambodian people have believed for generations that they are descended from Princess *Nagi* and Prince *Preah Thong*. Thus, they believe that the first ruler of *Nokor Kok Thlork* was the Queen *Neang Neak* (*Nagi*), the owner of the land. This tradition explains the custom of replies that is observed, even today, by members of the Khmer royal family. Normally, 'yes' in the Khmer language is '*Bat*' for the males, and '*Cha*' for the females. However, the Khmer King and all princes of the royal family say '*Cha*' when they are saying 'yes' in reply to someone, following the response of the Queen and the princesses. This tradition is strong evidence that the Khmer ladies were very powerful in the past. Even though Prince *Preah Thong* married Princess *Nagi*, he has never been regarded as being more powerful than his queen. The lasting influence of the legend of *Nagi*, who is believed to be the *Queen Mother* of all Cambodian people, can also be seen in the Khmer silk dress called *Hol*[4] which resembles the *Krala Neak* (snake skin). When Khmer ladies wear the *Hol*, their seated position, *Bort Cheung*,[5] is called *Neak Paen* (coiled like a snake). The history of Cambodia can be traced back to this legend, though it has since evolved through many notable periods marked by changes in administration.

The history of Cambodia can be divided into the following periods: (i) the *Funan* period; (ii) the *Chenla* period; (iii) the *Angkor* period; (iv) the *Longvek* period; (v) the *Oudong* period; (vi) the French Colony period; and (vii) the *Chaktumuk* period. As more details of these historical periods can be found in many interesting books by both local and international historians, this chapter will not detail them. Instead, this chapter will focus on some points relating to the legal background and legal conceptions that have led to constitutional pluralism in Cambodia. It is important to note that while Cambodia inherited its modern legal system from the French, the historical legal background and legal conceptions in question have existed for thousands of years.

Still, there were notable social, political, economic, and cultural changes in Cambodia during its time as a French colony (1863–1953). These have all had an impact on the development of today's Cambodia. One key change is the legal system, which transformed from an old-fashioned system into a modern one by adopting the French civil law tradition and other western legal concepts, thus allowing Cambodia and her citizens to enter the modern, civilised world.

Cambodia was also caught in the wave of change and globalisation that swept through the world after World War II (1939–1945). Cambodian citizens hoped to

---

[4] Retold by Mr. Chea Neang in 2008 according to his research on the history of Khmer traditional dresses.
[5] Sitting while bending the legs backwards.

number their nation among the ranks of modern states by attaining the status of a sovereign state. This was done through the creation of the first Constitution of 1947, marking the formation of a constitutional monarchy for the first time in the history of this kingdom.

B. Brief Account of the Plurality of the Country

The plurality in term of languages, ethnicity, and religion can be found in the land of Cambodia. The Cambodian people and language are known as 'Khmer', which means 'people who are living in Cambodia'.[6] Cambodia is also known as *Cambodge* or *Cambojia* in different languages. The Khmer people themselves call this country *Kampuchea*, which is derived from *Kambuja*. *Kampuja* means 'golden land'.[7] *Kampuchea* or *Khmer* is also called *Khemara*. Regardless of these linguistic variations, the Cambodian people have never lost their country name on the world map. This is a big source of pride for the people of this golden land, *Suvarna Bhumi*.[8] There are many discussions of the origin of the Khmer people. Troeung Ngea said in his book, which is based on the research of Berard Philippe Groslier and Mercel Talabot, that the Khmer people belong to the *Khmer-Mon*[9] group. The Khmer-Mon can trace their roots to the *Mélanésiens* and *Indonésiens* who lived in the geographical area ranging from the South China Sea to the borders of India.[10] The traditions and culture of the *Khmer-Mon* can still be found in many aspects of today's Cambodian society, such as languages and beliefs. After the collapse of the Angkor Empire, the Khmer people and their associated territories can be divided into three groups: (i) the *Khmer Loeu*,[11] whose lands once belonged to the Khmer empire but are now part of today's Thailand; (ii) the *Khmer Kandal*,[12] who live in today's Cambodia; and (iii) the *Khmer Krom*,[13] who live in the area that was lost during French colonisation (forming the southern part of today's Vietnam). The country of the *Khmer Kandal* is thus today's Cambodia. Notable groups

---

[6] Chuon Nath, *Khmer Dictionary* (Buddhist Institution Press 1967).

[7] ibid.

[8] *Suvarna Bhumi* is a Pali term meaning 'land of gold'. The Cambodian people claim this name for themselves because they feel that their land is rich with natural resources and culture, as proven by the civilisation of Angkor. However, *Suvanna Bhumi* should also span Myanmar, Thailand, and Laos, where used to be parts of Khmer Empire.

[9] *Mon* is a state in today's Myanmar that used to be very civilised in the past.

[10] Troeung Ngea, *Khmer History: From the Beginning to Abandon of Angkor* (1st ed, Phnom Penh 1973) 5.

[11] *Khmer Loeu* refers to the Khmer people living in the 'upper land', or the plateau that reaches the *Dangrek* mountain.

[12] *Khmer Kandal* refers to the Khmer people living in the 'middle land', which forms the territory of today's Cambodia.

[13] *Khmer Krom* refers to the Khmer people living in the 'lower land (down to the sea)', which is now South Vietnam.

of foreigners that migrated to Cambodia were the Chinese,[14] Vietnamese,[15] and Cham.[16] Besides these three groups, Cambodia also contains many ethnic groups, which are mainly hill tribes such as the *Krung, Kachok, Brao, Kavet, Kraol, Kuy, Phnong, Tampuan, Stieng, Mnong, Samre, Chong, Sa'och, Somray, Suoy, Jarai ... etc.* These ethnic groups have their own languages and lifestyles. Yet, the diversity of these ethnic groups has not produced any notable conflict in this Kingdom. They all live peacefully and harmoniously in today's Cambodia.

Hinduism and Buddhism are the two main religions which have shaped Cambodian culture, social values, lifestyle, morality, and legal background. The religious leaders of both religions – the *Purohita* (Brahman priests) and the *Sangha* (Buddhist monks) – have greatly influenced the systems of administration and legal concepts in Cambodia. Religious leaders have in the past been regarded as *Gurus* (Professors/Advisors) to the Khmer monarch and his high-ranking officers. If the Khmer King practised Hinduism, the *Purohita* would be most powerful; but if the King practised Buddhism, the *Sangha* would be the most influential. While Cambodia is today a *Theravada Buddhism* country, as enshrined in article 43 of the Constitution of 1993,[17] believers of Hinduism and other religions such as the traditional Khmer faith still exist. Hinduism and Buddhism have thus produced plurality in Cambodia's cultural values, traditions, society, political ideals, and national identities.

Both religions have been practised harmoniously and respectfully by the Khmer people for thousands of years. Even though Hinduism is no longer officially practised in Cambodia, the traditions and beliefs of this religion have co-existed alongside those of Buddhism and the traditional Khmer faith. There is no doubt that the harmony between Hinduism and Buddhism in Cambodia is a legacy of the political ideals of King Jayavarman VII the Great (1125–1218 AD),[18] who cleverly integrated both religions during his reign. His successful integration resulted in socio-political stability and development. Temples constructed during his reign are unique in that they feature towers with the four faces of *Brahma*.[19] They include temples such as *Bayon, Ta Prom, Preah Khan, Banteay Chhmar*, and *Banteay Kdey*.

Besides these two main religions, Christianity, Islam, and other religions can be found in Cambodia as well. In spite of the religious diversity, there have been

---

[14] The Chinese have migrated to Cambodia for centuries, but the migration peaked when the Communists took power in China.

[15] The Vietnamese people have migrated to Cambodia for centuries.

[16] The Cham are Muslims who lost their territory ('*Champa*') to Vietnam during the 17th century. They have been migrating to Cambodia since then. They are now known as *Khmer Islam*, or Khmer nationals originating from *Champa*.

[17] Para 3, art 43 of the Constitution of Cambodia states: 'Buddhism is the State Religion'.

[18] George Cedès's research shows that King Jayavarman VII was born in 1120, or 1125 at the latest, and died in 1218.

[19] *Brahma* is one of three main gods in Hinduism; who are Brahma, Shiva, and Vishnu. But within the concept of combination of Hinduism and Buddhism, four faces of Brahma were known as *Lokeshvara's* in Mahayana Buddhism.

no notable religious conflicts in the history of Cambodia. Thus, Cambodia can be said to be a peaceful land in Asia which upholds the freedom to worship and religious harmony.

C. Brief Account as to the Drafting and Adoption of the Constitutional Text

Before discussing the drafting and adoption of the constitutional text of 1993, it is necessary to first briefly summarise the constitutional history of Cambodia via its six Constitutions.

i. *The Constitution of 1947 of the Kingdom of Cambodia*

This Constitution was promulgated on 6 May 1947 by His Majesty the King Norodom Sihanouk and was modified several times from then to 1964.[20] It transformed Cambodia into a constitutional monarchy for the first time in Cambodian history. After independence in 1953, this Constitution was amended many times due to the political situation at the time. There were nine amendments in all: 8 March 1957, 7 January 1958, 30 April 1958, 13 February 1959, 21 April 1959, 28 July 1959, 5 April 1960, 14 June 1960, and 13 January 1964.[21]

According to the amendment of 1964, this Constitution consists of 122 articles in 12 Titles (Chapters), which are as follows: Title I on the Nature and Form of the State; Title II on Freedoms, Rights, and Duties of Cambodians; Title III on Law and Powers; Title IV on the King; Title V on National Assembly; Title VI on the Council of the Kingdom; Title VII on the Popular Assemblies of the Khet and the Capital; Title VIII on the National congress; Title IX on the Ministers; Title X on Judicial Power; Title XI on general provisions; and Title XII on special provisions.

As a constitutional monarchy under the Constitution of 1947, Cambodia was said to be a nation that was an 'Oasis of Peace'. This ended with the coup d' etat of 18 March 1970,[22] which pushed Cambodia into war and political conflict for more than three decades.

---

[20] The General Presentation of Constitutional Council of the Kingdom of Cambodia.
[21] Raoul M Jennar, *The Cambodian Constitutions (1953–1993)* (Phnom Penh 1995) 36.
[22] The Coup d'Etat was led by General *Lon Nol* and his military clan, which included prince Sisowath Sirik Matak, H.E. In Tam, and H.E. Cheng Heng, while the Head of State Samdach Preah Norodom Sihanouk was abroad. This Coup d'Etat was believed to be supported by the United States of America. In a famous letter dated 16 April 1975 from prince Sirik Matak to the Ambassador of the United States of America, the prince declined to leave Cambodia with the US embassy's staff a few days before the arrival of Khmer Rouge troops, before concluding: "I committed this mistake of believing in you, the Americans." Prince Sirik Matak was killed by Khmer Rouge once they seized Phnom Penh.

ii. The Constitution of 1972 of the Khmer Republic

Following the coup, the Khmer Republic was declared, thereby replacing the nearly 2000-year-old Kingdom of Cambodia. The Constitution of 1972 of the Khmer Republic was promulgated on 10 May 1972.[23] According to the translation by G. Thomas Bowen,[24] this Constitution consists of 121 articles in 11 Chapters, which are as follows: Chapter I on Fundamental Provisions; Chapter II on Rights and Duties of Citizens; Chapter III on The President of the Republic; Chapter IV on The Cabinet, Chapter V on Parliament; Chapter VI on Relations between Parliament and the Executive; Chapter VII on The Judicial Authority; Chapter VIII on Other Institutions of the Republic; Chapter IX on The Territorial Administrative Divisions; Chapter X on Revision and Amendment; and Chapter XI on Transition Provisions.

iii. The Constitution of 1976 of Democratic Kampuchea

The Khmer Republic did not last for a thousand years as planned. The *Khmer Rouge*[25] seized Phnom Penh on 17 April 1975 and Cambodia immediately became a communist state. The Constitution of 1972 was then dissolved with the promulgation of the new Constitution of 1976 on 5 January 1976.[26] According to the unofficial English translation by David Chandler,[27] this Constitution consists of only 21 articles in 16 Chapters, which are as follows: Chapter I on the State; Chapter II on the Economy; Chapter III on Culture; Chapter IV on the Principle of Leadership and Work; Chapter V on Legislative Power; Chapter VI on the Executive Body; Chapter VII on Justice, Chapter VIII on the State President; Chapter IX on the Rights and Duties of the Individual; Chapter X on the Capital; Chapter XI on the National Flag; Chapter XII on the National Emblem; Chapter XIII on the National Anthem; Chapter XIV on the Kampuchean Revolutionary Army; Chapter XV on Worship and Religion; and Chapter XVI on Foreign Policy.

iv. The Constitution of 1981 of The People's Republic of Kampuchea

Democratic Kampuchea collapsed on 7 January 1979. A new regime known as *The People's Republic of Kampuchea* was then formed with support from Vietnam and the Soviet Union. Thus, the Constitution of 1976 was dissolved and a new one was made. This Constitution was adopted on 27 June and was

---

[23] Jennar (n 21) 57.
[24] G Thomas Bowen, 'Khmer Republic' in A P Blaustein and G H Flanz (eds), *Constitutions of the Countries of the World* (New York, Oceana Publication 1972).
[25] A Khmer Communist group that fought against Lon Nol's regime, which was backed by the US.
[26] Jennar (n 21) 81.
[27] David Chandler, 'The Constitution of Democratic Kampuchea: The Semantics of Revolutionary Changes' (1976) 49(3) Pacific Affairs 506.

printed and released on 9 July 1981.[28] According to an unofficial translation by G. Thomas Bowen and Scott Sheldon,[29] this Constitution consists of 93 articles in 10 Chapters: Chapter I on the Political System; Chapter II on the Economic System and the Political-Cultural-Social Line; Chapter III on Rights and Duties of Citizens; Chapter IV on the National Assembly; Chapter V on the Council of State; Chapter VI on the Council of Ministers; Chapter VII on the Local People's Revolutionary Committees; Chapter VIII on Jurisdictions and Courts; Chapter IX on the National Emblem, National Flag, National Anthem, and Capital; and Chapter X on the Effects and Amendments to the Constitution.

v. The Constitution of 1989 of the State of Cambodia

The People's Republic of Kampuchea was not recognised widely by that time. The four Khmer parties made claims for their right to recognition on the international stage. The first meeting between HRH *Sihanouk* and *Hun Sen* marked the beginning of the peace building process in Cambodia.[30] This meeting was held in *Fer en Tardenois*, France, on 2 December 1987.[31] Both personalities have been recognised as peace founders for Cambodia today. Following a series of negotiations, *The People's Republic of Kampuchea* decided to adjust the Constitution of 1981 – an adjustment which has been viewed as a major reform that effectively created a new Constitution. This Constitution was adopted in 1989. According to the translation by the Foreign Broadcast Information Service (US government) and the United Nations,[32] this Constitution consists of 93 articles in 10 Chapters: Chapter I on the Political System; Chapter II on the Economic System and Socio-Cultural Policies; Chapter III on the Rights and Duties of Citizens; Chapter IV on the National Assembly; Chapter V on the Council of State; Chapter VI on the Council of Ministers; Chapter VII on the Local People's Committees; Chapter VIII on the Courts and the Offices of the Prosecutor-General; Chapter IX on the National Emblem, National Flag, National Anthem, and Capital; and Chapter X on the Legal Status and Amendment of the Constitution.

vi. The Constitution of 1993 of the Kingdom of Cambodia

This Constitution arose from the strong will of all Cambodian political factions and the Cambodian people, as expressed in its preamble: '*We, the Khmer people, in virtue of this unshakable will, we inscribe in the Constitution of the Kingdom of*

---

[28] Jennar (n 21) 90.
[29] G Thomas Bowen and Scott Sheldon, 'Cambodia' in A P Blaustein and G H Flanz (eds), *Constitutions of the Countries of the World* (New York, Oceana Publication 1982).
[30] David Chandler, *Cambodia's Historical Legacy* (1998) 5 Conciliation Resources 19.
[31] HE Ouch Borith, 'Cambodia's Peace-building Experience' (Presentation at 'Tokyo Peace-builder Symposium 2008', Tokyo, 24–25 March 2008).
[32] Jennar (n 21).

Cambodia, as follows.[33] This Constitution subsequently took on the elevated status of a holy legal text for all Khmer people.

This Constitution was made in accordance with the Paris Peace Accords of 1991, which put an end to decades of internal conflict within the nation. Before the making of this Constitution, it was decided that the Cambodian people would elect their representatives in a universal and free election. The election of 1993 was organised by the United Nations Transitional Authority in Cambodia (UNTAC) and was held from 23 to 28 May 1993. Amongst the 4,764,439 registered voters, 4,276,192 – or 89.56% of electors[34] – cast their ballots. In that election, the FUNCINPEC Party won 58 seats, the Cambodian People's Party (CPP) won 51 seats, the Buddhist Liberal Democratic Party (BLDP) won 10 seats, and the MOULINAKA Party won 1 seat.[35]

Annex 5 of the Paris Peace Accord is one of the core values for the 1993 Constitution drafting. There are six main principles required by Paris Peace Accord to be included in this drafting:

(1) The Constitution shall be the supreme law of Cambodia, which is stated in article 152 new-two (former article 150 new) of the Constitution.
(2) The principles in universal declaration on human rights and basic rights, which are stated in from article 31 to article 50 of the Constitution.
(3) The principle of sovereignty, independence, neutrality, and national unity; which are stated in article 1, article 2, article 3, and article 52 of the Constitution.
(4) The principle of liberal-multi-party democracy, which is stated in article 1, article 34 (new), article 51 (new), and article 76 (new) of the Constitution.
(5) The principle of independence of judiciary, which is stated in article 51 (new), article 128 new (former article 109) of the Constitution.
(6) The principle of two-third majority for adopting the Constitution, which is stated in article 153 new (two) of the Constitution.

Moreover, the Paris Peace Accord required respect from foreign countries. All foreign countries and parties to this accord were not to interfere in Cambodia's internal affairs, as is stated in Article 8 and Article 18 of the accord. Article 1 (point 2-c), Article 2 (point 1 and point 2-b), and Article 4 of Paris Peace Accord also required the respect of sovereignty, independence, integrity; and inviolability of Cambodia's territory, neutrality, and national unity. These principles are included in article 53 of the Constitution: oath for the National Assembly as stated in Annex 5, oath for the government as stated in Annex 6, and oath for the senate as stated in Annex 7 of the Constitution.

---

[33] Constitutional Council, The Constitution of the Kingdom of Cambodia (published March 2010).
[34] Statistics of the National Election Committee (NEC).
[35] HE Ieng Moly, 'The Making of the Cambodian Constitution' (Presentation at the 10th Konrad Adenauer Stiftung Law Talk, Sihanoukville, 11 October 2013).

The 1993 Constitution was drafted by the Constitutional Assembly and promulgated by the King of Cambodia through a procedure established in it.

a. The Constitutional Assembly

Following the election of 1993, the Constitutional Assembly was formed and began functioning on 14 June 1993.[36] On 30 June 1993, the Constitutional Assembly held its first session where it established a permanent constitution-drafting commission to be led by the President of the Constitutional Assembly, or by the Vice President in the absence of the President.[37] Samdach *Son San* from the Buddhist Liberal Democracy Party (BLDP) was the President; H.E. *Chem Snguon* from the Cambodian People's Party was the Vice President, while another dignitary from the FUNCINPEC Party, H.E. *Tao Seng Hour*, was appointed the Rapporteur.[38] Besides the President and Vice President, the Constitutional Assembly's permanent commission also comprised five members from the FUNCINPEC Party, four from the Cambodian People's Party (CPP), and one from the Buddhist Liberal Democratic Party (BLDP) as well as alternate members and experts from other elected political parties. The United Nations also supported Cambodia by providing legal experts who acted as advisers to the constitution-drafting commission. It was hoped that the new constitution would conform with the principles of the Paris Peace Accords. The different background of personalities in this commission shaped pluralistic sources and ideas for this Constitution, which can be found in the provisions of the Constitution.

b. The Adoption and Promulgation of the Constitution of 1993

After spending months to draft the Constitution and following six days of debate from 15 to 21 September 1993, the Constitutional Assembly cast secret ballots on 21 September 1993 and voted overwhelmingly in favour of adopting the Constitution. There were 113 votes in favour, five against, and two abstentions.[39] This adoption was considered to be a big step in Cambodian politics as it allowed state institutions to carry out their functions at last. Three days later, on 24 November 1993, *Samdach Preah Norodom Sihanouk* signed the *Royal Kram* at the *Maha Prasat Devavinichhaya*[40] of the Royal Palace, thereby promulgating this Constitution urgently and in accordance with articles 135 and 136 of Chapter XIV on the Transitional Provisions of this Constitution. The Constitutional Assembly then automatically became the National Assembly.

---

[36] ibid.
[37] ibid.
[38] ibid.
[39] ibid.
[40] The great pavilion for serving the meeting of Deva (deities).

III. Pluralism as a Constitutional Fact

A. Constitutional Ideas and Values

i. *The Shared Common Goals the Nation Adopts*

As stipulated in the preamble of the Constitution of 1993, the shared common goals of the nation are: (i) to unite and strengthen national unity; (ii) to defend the Cambodian territory; (iii) to preserve the precious sovereignty and the marvellous civilisation of ANGKOR; (iv) to re-build the country and become once again an '*Oasis of Peace*' based on the system of a liberal multi-party democracy; (v) to guarantee human rights; (vi) to ensure respect for the law; and (vii) to be highly responsible for the destiny of the nation, which should forever move towards progress, development, and prosperity.

Those aforesaid respective points are the shared common goals that Cambodia adopts in creating the following provisions of the Constitution. All aforesaid values stated in the preamble are the *State Ideology* of Cambodia. This ideation is priceless for all persons in the nation.

Following the collapse of the Angkor Empire in the late twelfth century, Cambodia had been broken into war and suffered. Cambodia was known as a place of power competition by using weapons and violence, hence national unity was broken for centuries until the late twentieth century (*1998*). For this reason, the ideation of the first 'TO' – *to unite and strengthen national unity* [...] – was used in the preamble.

Cambodia had lost a large amount of territory many times throughout its history. The rich resource of this land is one reason, amongst others, for territory aggression. Thus, in order to protect the land that remains today, the second 'TO' was formed as a common value in this Constitution.

The sovereignty and civilisation of Cambodia had faced suffering and destruction many times in its history. The period of French colonisation (1863–1953) is one such example. During the seventeenth and eighteenth centuries, Cambodia almost disappeared from the world map due to invasion. Such history awoke the authors of the 1993 Constitution to enshrine the third 'TO' into its preamble.

Cambodia was declared by the former King *Norodom Sihanouk* in 1955 in *Bandung*, Indonesia, to be a non-aligned state along with other states in Asia and Africa. This status of Cambodia prevented the spreading of the Vietnam War into this land. It was a great opportunity during this period for Cambodia to develop its economy. Within 10 years of its real neutrality, Cambodia occupied the status of an 'Oasis of Peace' state in Southeast Asia. Unfortunately, the Coup of 1970 by General *Lon Nol* broke the peace and development in Cambodia, and led the country into war and internal conflict for more than two decades. The trail of this history is another reason to include the fourth 'TO' into the Constitution.

When the Khmer Rouge ruled Cambodia from 17 April 1975 to 7 January 1979, the Cambodian people were living in a place which was called the '*9th level of deep hell',* where their rights and freedom were totally uprooted. During the period of three years, eight months, and 20 days under the Khmer Rouge Administration, millions of lives were killed. To prevent Cambodia's relapse into such a situation, the fifth and sixth 'TO' in the preamble were made in order to remind the Cambodian people to pay high respect towards human rights and the rule of law.

The last 'TO' – to *be highly responsible for the destiny of the nation* [...] – is consistent with the provision in the last paragraph of article 52 (new), that *'Khmer citizens are the masters of their Country's destiny'*. This provision is among the priceless provisions to be highly regarded in the Cambodian Constitution. This provision was established for two main purposes: for all Khmer citizens to (i) remind themselves of the history of Cambodia during the last five centuries, where Khmer citizens had no longer time to be real masters of their country's destiny; and (ii) to awaken today's Khmer citizen to strengthen themselves to be real masters of Cambodia presently and in the future, for strong virtues (1) to guarantee independence, sovereignty, national integrity, and national unity and (2) to not, totally, allow interference in the internal affairs of Cambodia, or to order Cambodia's national policy or international policy, and (3) to not, absolutely, serve for foreign benefit to destroy the benefits of the Khmer and national benefits of Cambodia.

ii. The Fundamental Ideas and Values that Inform the Constitutional Practices of the Nation

As mentioned above, Cambodia has experienced various forms of constitutional orders for more than half a century through its six constitutions. The first Constitution of 1947 led to constitutional monarchism; the second Constitution of 1972 created an American-style presidential system; the third Constitution of 1976 was an extremist communist constitution; while the fourth Constitution of 1981 and the fifth Constitution of 1989 were socialist constitutions.

The following section explores in greater detail the current Constitution of 1993 of the Kingdom of Cambodia:

a. Main Values of the 1993 Constitution

The Constitution of 1993 of the Kingdom of Cambodia is influenced by general principles of western constitutional law as well as Khmer values. Thus, some common constitutional characteristics can be found in this Constitution, such as (i) Constitutional Monarchy; (ii) Fundamental Rights; (iii) Liberal Multi-Party Democracy; (iv) Separation of Powers; (v) Rule of Law; (vi) Conditio Sine Quanon; and (vii) Additional Constitutional Law. The constitutional values and ideas in Cambodia can be classified into three types:

(1) **Universalist values** that are derived from following texts:
   (i) The United Nations Charter;

(ii) The Universal Declaration of Human rights; and
(iii) All the treaties and conventions related to human rights, women's rights and children's rights.

(2) **Western liberalist values**:
   (i) *Fundamental Rights*: found from the idea of western philosopher *John Locke*'s social contract of three important rights: rights to life, rights to property, and rights to freedom.
   (ii) *Liberal Multi-Party Democracy*: The Kingdom of Cambodia is a Liberal Multi-Party Democracy, as stipulated in paragraph 1 of article 51 (New): 'The Kingdom of Cambodia adopts a policy of liberal multi-party democracy'. This idea was influenced from the western concept of democracy.
   (iii) *Separation of Powers*: The Kingdom of Cambodia follows the doctrine of separation of powers, as stipulated in paragraph 4 of article 51 (New): 'The powers shall be separated between the legislative power, the executive power and the judicial power'. This idea is from the famous 'separation of powers' theory of *Montesquieu*, a French social commentator and political thinker who lived during the Enlightenment period of the West.

(3) **Localist-Cambodian values**:
   (i) *Constitutional Monarchy*: The Constitutional Monarchical regime of Cambodia is affirmed in Paragraph 1, article 1 of the Constitution: 'Cambodia is a Kingdom where the King shall fulfil His functions according to the Constitution and the principles of liberal multi-party democracy'. This idea is consistent with Cambodia's local values on monarchism, a style of the state that most Cambodian people prefer. Monarchism has been found as a core value in promoting national symbolism, culture, tradition, and also the life-style of Cambodian people.
   (ii) *Conditio sine qua non*: There are three circumstances in which revision or amendment of the Constitution is absolutely prohibited: (a) when Cambodia is in a state of emergency; (b) when the proposed revision or amendment affects the liberal multi-party democracy system; and (c) when the proposed revision or amendment affects the constitutional monarchy regime. These three prohibited principles are found as Cambodia's local ideas in preserving its monarchism and democracy system, which are believed to be beneficial to the process of building peace and prosperity in this nation.
   (iii) *Additional Constitutional Law*: This is an exceptional law in the constitutional law-making process. It provides for the creation of a package vote, which allows for the election of the President, Vice Presidents, as well as the Chairpersons and Vice Chairpersons of the Commissions; while at the same time granting confidence to the Royal government.

This is a rare norm in parliamentary systems. However, it has been very beneficial for the political stability in Cambodia.

(iv) *Oath*: the provisions of oath for the King is stated in Annex 4; oath for the President, Vice Presidents, and all Members of the National Assembly are stated in Annex 5; oath for the Prime Minister and all Members of the Royal government are stated in Annex 6, and oath of the President, Vice Presidents, and all Members of the Senate are stated in Annex 7. These oaths is a tradition in Cambodia since the past time. Once the high ranking officials come to the position; they have to take oath.

The constitutional ideas and values in the Constitution of Cambodia are correlated and indivisible. Thus, all the aforesaid fundamental ideas and values are interlinked as follows.

The idea of reinstating the constitutional monarchy in Cambodia is consistent with the historical values and traditions of Khmer society. Even though there have been many changes in political regimes, the monarchy has retained its popularity among the Khmer people. As a well-known Cambodian proverb goes, 'People with no monarch, hence they walk erratically'. This encapsulates the attitude towards monarchism here. As a result, the reinstatement of the monarchy in Cambodia through the Constitution of 1993 was considered the best choice for the nation and an expression of the common will of Khmer citizens.

The ideals of human rights, democracy, separation of powers, and rule of law are very closely related to the values of Cambodian society. Cambodia has been a Buddhist state for centuries, and the values of '*respect for rights*' and '*respect for dignity*' have existed in Khmer society. Examples of these values can be found in the precepts of *Buddha Sāsanā* and in the codes of social morality, or '*Cpāp*',[41] followed by various scholars.

The establishment of *Additional Constitutional Law* is unique in the Cambodian context. The idea behind this innovation was to ensure the regular functioning of national institutions after Cambodia entered a political deadlock following the 2003 election. While additional constitutional law may appear to be a strange model of constitution-making, this idea and the values behind it should be assessed according to the impact on Cambodian society as a whole.

B. Sources of Constitutional Norms

i. *The Sources of Constitutional Law in Cambodia*

There are two main sources of constitutional law in Cambodia:

(i) *Written Sources*: The Constitution of 1993 of the Kingdom of Cambodia can be considered a sibling to Western constitutionalism tradition, particularly that

---

[41] *Cpāp* is a code of social morality created by many scholars in the past. One famous *Cpāp* is *Cpāp Krom Gnoy* written by Preah Pirom Pheasa OU (alias *Krom Ngoy*), who was a great scholar of social morality.

of French constitutional law. Thus, western written constitutions are important sources of the Cambodian Constitution. Besides these models, general principles of constitutional law and other constitutional theories played very important roles in shaping the values of the Cambodian constitution. The United Nations Charter, the Universal Declaration of Human Rights, and other international instruments relating to human rights, women's rights, and children's rights are among the important written sources of this constitution. Another source that cannot be excluded is the *Agreement on a Comprehensive Political Settlement of the Cambodia Conflict*, made at the Paris Conference of 23 October 1991, which resolved the political conflict at the time. This text is a core document that led to the creation of the Constitution of 1993. These international instruments are important to the Cambodian Constitution and laws. For instance, in Decision N° 092 /003/2007 CC.D of July 10, 2007 concerning the 20 June 2007 Royal Message of His Majesty *Preah Bath Samdech Preah Boromneath Norodom Sihamoni*, King of Cambodia – requesting the Constitutional Council to review the constitutionality of the article 8 of the Law on the Aggravating Circumstances of Felonies – the Constitutional Council clearly defines:

'[…]

Whereas in principle, during the trial the judge does not only rely on the Article 8 of the Law on the Aggravating Circumstances of Felonies to convict the criminal, but also on the laws. The term "Laws" as above referred to means the national laws, including the Constitution, which is the supreme law, all the laws that remain in force, and the international laws already recognized by the Kingdom of Cambodia, in particular the Convention on the Children's Rights.

[…]'

(ii) *Unwritten Sources*: Among the unwritten sources of the Constitution, Buddhist philosophy was crucial in forming some of the constitutional provisions. The influence of Buddhism can be found in Cambodia's constitutional monarchy and religious practices. Khmer customary law, including family values, also played an important role in shaping the constitution. The unwritten sources have influenced the 'Virtuous Awareness' of the Khmer people, who have experienced both great civilisation and suffering throughout their history, as enshrined in the preamble of Cambodia's Constitution. Buddhism plays a very important role in Cambodian society. It closely links to the practical behaviour of people. For instance, in Decision N° 107/003/2009 CC.D of 23 December 2009, which concerned a request from the President of the National Assembly – requesting the Constitutional Council to interpret article 4 and article 43 of the Constitution, in reference to the 13 December 2009 request from *Sangha Nayaka* of the Theravada Buddhist Order of the Kingdom of Cambodia – the Constitutional Council interpreted:

'[…]

Whereas Buddhism being the State's religion, therefore:
- In the Kingdom of Cambodia, the State assists, supports and elevates Buddhism to be worthy of a State's religion, by being developed, grand, glorious. That is the reason why, in the Royal Ceremony of the coronation of the King of Cambodia, there is the presence of Supreme Patriarchs of the two Buddhist Orders in accordance with the Royal Rites. Moreover, the main Buddhist festivities, in particular those of the *Meak Bochea* and *Visak Bochea* days are made national holidays.
- The *Mahānikāya* Supreme Patriarch and the *Dhammayutikanikaya* Supreme Patriarch are members of the Crown Council as stipulated in the Article 13(New) of the Constitution. Besides the Supreme Patriarchs of both Orders preside over the important oath ceremonies as stipulated in the annexes of the Constitution, and moreover in the national anthem the third verse says that "In all the temples echoing the voice of the Dharma, chanting with joy, remembering Buddhism with gratitude, may we as true and sincere believers follow the path of our ancestors, so that the *Tevadas* may assist and grant prosperity to the Khmer Land as a Great Nation."
- The paragraph 3 of Article 68 of the Constitution stipulates "The State shall help propagate and promote the Pālī schools and the Buddhist education."
- And the great majority of the Khmer people in the Kingdom of Cambodia have raised the National flag, the Buddhist flag, and the Royal Emblem side by side, with the conscience in the belief that the wheel of the State and the wheel of Buddhism must turn evenly, and then the Nation can prosper and be glorious

[…]'

ii. Some of the Distinctive Norms of these Different Sources of Laws

Some distinctive norms of the written and unwritten sources of the Cambodian Constitution are as follows:

(i) *The norm of respect for rights*: The Khmer tradition also respects the basic rights found in international human rights instruments. However, the Khmer style of respect for rights is based on hierarchical respect rather than respect between equals. The elder person shall be more respected than the younger one. Ladies shall be more respected than men. High-ranking persons shall be more respected than normal people. For instance, if a younger person challenges an elder, he will be criticised.

(ii) *The norm of separation of powers*: Currently, the norm of separation of powers in Cambodian constitutionalism is based on the separation of legislative, executive, and judicial powers. However, the same norm was also found in the Cambodian legal system in the past, and was continuously practised until the arrival of the French in 1863. Legislative power was invested in the *privy councillors*[42] of the King. The King himself was invested with executive and judicial powers. Thus, the Cambodian norm of separation of powers is divided into these two personalities.

iii. *The Main Points of Conflict and Resolution*

There have not been any notable conflicts from adopting these norms in the Constitution of Cambodia. Khmer culture and Buddhism closely parallel the general principles and norms of constitutional law from the western world. The concepts of basic rights, the rule of law, separation of powers, and democracy can also be found in Khmer culture and the *Theravada* Buddhist tradition. However, some challenges remain, such as in the patron-client relationships prevalent in Cambodia, and in political and cultural values.

Cambodia is a country with a strong patronage system, with a notable divide between the powerful groups and the less-powerful groups. Article 31 was inserted into the Constitution in an attempt to solve this problem. This article is a key tool in guaranteeing equality before the law among all citizens regardless of race, sex, language, belief, religion, political tendency, origin, social status, wealth or other situations.

On the other hand, Cambodia is also a notable nation due to its political and cultural values. The last decade of this nation's history demonstrates political conflict and suffering. Citizens may label each other with different political stripes, hence embittering the political environment. Thus, the Constitution is meant to be a core instrument to keep Cambodia in peace and prosperity, but this is dependent on the Constitution being respected. For instance, in order to guarantee respect for the right to life, the Constitution was made with no death penalty, as stated in article 32.

C. Constitutional Structure

i. *The Overall Arrangement*

After several rounds of revisions and amendments, the 1993 Constitution now consists of 160 articles in 12 Chapters, which are: Chapter I on sovereignty; Chapter II on the King; Chapter III on the rights and duties of Khmer citizens; Chapter IV on the political regime; Chapter V on the economy; Chapter VI on education, culture, and social affairs; Chapter VII on the National Assembly;

---

[42] *Raja Guru* of the King or other members of *Purohita* from Hinduism or *Sangha* are among very influenced group, who advised the King in legislative law making process.

Chapter VIII (New) on the Senate; Chapter IX (New) on the congress of the National Assembly and the Senate; Chapter X (New) on the Royal Government, Chapter XI (New) on the Judiciary; Chapter XII (New) on the Constitutional Council; Chapter XIII (New) on the organisation of the administration; Chapter XIV (New) on the National Congress; Chapter XV (New-two) on the Electoral Organisation; Chapter XVI (New-two) on the effect, the revision, and the amendment of the Constitution; and Chapter XVII (New) on transitional provisions. Besides these chapters, there is also a preamble, seven Annexes, and one Additional Constitutional Law consisting of seven articles.

a. Preamble of the Constitution

The preamble of the Constitution of 1993 starts with 'We, Khmer citizens …', followed by four paragraphs. The first paragraph is a reminder of the prosperous history of the Kingdom of Cambodia; the second paragraph is a reminder of the mass destruction of the past few decades; the third paragraph shows the awareness of Khmer citizens in creating this Constitution; while the fourth paragraph expresses the people's unshakable will in enshrining this Constitution.

b. Annexes of the Constitution

The Constitution of Cambodia of 1993 consists of seven Annexes, which are (i) Annex 1 on the national flag; (ii) Annex 2 on the national anthem; (iii) Annex 3 on the national coat of arms; (iv) Annex 4 on the oath of the King; (v) Annex 5 on the oath of the President, Vice Presidents, and members of the national assembly; (vi) Annex 6 on the oath of the Prime Minister and members of the royal government; and (vii) Annex 7 on the oath of the President, Vice Presidents, and members of the senate.

c. Additional Constitutional Law

The additional constitutional law was created in 2004 to resolve the political deadlock of 2003. This law is considered part of the Constitution, and its constitutionality cannot be examined by the Constitutional Council. Thus, its publication is attached to the Constitution.

d. Arrangement of the Chapters and Articles

Interestingly, the Cambodian Constitution consists of 'Chapters', with each chapter followed by 'Articles'. There are no 'Parts' or 'Sections'. Some Articles contain 'New', 'New (One)' or 'New (Two)' in their titles, which indicate that these articles have been amended. An article containing 'New' in the title means that it has been amended once. 'New (One)' indicates that the article has been amended twice, while 'New (Two)' means that the article has been amended three times.

Another point to note is that some articles contain the terms 'New' as well as 'Former Article …'. This indicates that the location of these articles within the Constitution have shifted, but it does not mean that the wording of these articles has been amended. The use of this technique started after the Senate was created in 1999. Chapter VIII (New) on the Senate and Chapter IX (New) on the Congress of the National Assembly and the Senate were designed to come after Chapter VII on the National Assembly and to replace Chapter VIII on the Royal government, which begins at article 99. Hence, all articles of the aforesaid two new chapters contain the word 'New' to indicate that they were newly created; namely, article 99 (New) to article 117 (New). Once these two new chapters were inserted into the Constitution, the original Chapter VIII on the Royal government was moved back to Chapter X (New). This relocated Chapter on the Royal government also contains the word 'New' and starts with article 118, the title of which contains the words 'New' and 'Former Article 99' to indicate that the current article 118 was previously article 99. The re-titling of Chapters and articles can be confusing if a reader is not aware of how the Cambodian Constitution is revised.

ii. The Relationship Between Constitutional Ideas/Values and Constitutional Structure

The constitutional ideas/values are translated into provisions in each article of the Constitution. An article may consist of one or more paragraphs, depending on the respective constitutional idea/value that is engaged. The relationship between constitutional ideas/values and the constitutional provisions is crucial in shaping the entire Constitution. For instance, in accordance with a constitutional norm, the Constitution of Cambodia does not contain punishment provisions; instead, it refers to the relevant laws to be created at a later stage in conformity with the constitutional provisions. In this way, constitutional ideas/values play the role of key ideas that guide subsequent law creation.

iii. Designation of the Legislative Election System to Respond to Plurality

Following the key tenets of a Liberal Multi-Party Democracy, article 76 of the Constitution sets out the principles for holding legislative elections in Cambodia. Accordingly, elections must be (i) universal: elections shall be held homogenously and at the same time nationwide; (ii) free: elections shall be carried out without oppression or threats; (iii) equal: every voter, regardless of class, shall equally have one vote; (iv) carried out through direct suffrage: every voter shall vote directly at the polling station; and (v) administered via secret ballot: every voter shall fill in his ballot paper in a secret room. Elections are administered by the National Election Committee (NEC), which is stipulated to be an independent and neutral body in Article 12 of the Law on Elections of Members of the National Assembly (LEMNA). All members of the National Election Committee are thus supposed to be impartial and neutral in carrying out their electoral duties.

iv. *The Effect of Plurality on the Choice of System of Government*

In the Cambodian context, plurality in the form of a parliamentary system is a crucial means of promoting representative democracy. Thus, plurality has positively affected the formation of government and legislative organs in this country. Every five years, different political parties can register to participate in universal elections. Khmer people of both sexes have the right to elect their representatives. Thus, since 1993, there have been representatives from different political parties present in the National Assembly. This system promotes contestation between the winning party and the opposition, which is beneficial to the democratic system in the National Assembly and in the government. The Members of the National Assembly represent their people by electing the Royal government through a vote of confidence.[43] This means that both the National Assembly and the government are formed on the conceptual basis of plurality, which includes different groups of Khmer people.

Even though plurality positively affects the government system, some negative aspects have emerged in practice in terms of the different values espoused by the majority group and the minority group in the legislative organ. In this context, the minority group's voice is respected by allowing their representatives to negotiate with the majority, thus upholding the '*culture of dialogue*'.

Dialogue among political parties is a crucial means of promoting constitutional pluralism in Cambodia. It is a floor for parties to share different points of view and encourage one another to adjust their policies for governing the state. Respecting each party's values, which can be defined as the ideas of a particular group on the concepts of '*good and bad*', can help to reduce political tension and political extremism. A positive political atmosphere can be formed through the friendly acceptance of plurality. In short, the benefits of pluralism depend on whether parties are able to smartly navigate plurality.

v. *The Distinctive Points of the Organisation, Operation, and Relations of the Three Branches of the State (Legislature, Executive, and Judiciary) in Cambodia*

According to article 51 (New) of the Constitution, the Legislative, Executive, and Judicial powers shall be separated. As Cambodia adopts a bicameral system, legislative power is invested in both the National Assembly and the Senate.

---

[43] Art 90 New (Two) of the Constitution of 1993 states that the National Assembly grants a vote of confidence to the Royal Government through an absolute majority of all its Members.

The National Assembly plays the role of (i) debating and (ii) adopting draft laws[44] or proposed laws,[45] while the Senate plays the role of (i) examining and (ii) giving recommendations on text laws[46] which have already been adopted by the National Assembly. The National Assembly is formed through universal elections every five years and consists of at least 120 members; while the Senate is formed through restricted suffrage elections every six years, where the number of Senate members cannot exceed half of the National Assembly's members. According to article 112 (New) of the Constitution, the Senate is the legislative organ that regulates the work of the National Assembly and the government. The role of the Senate in regulating the work of the National Assembly and the government was defined in the Constitutional Council's interpretation of article 112 (New) of the Constitution.[47]

According to article 1 of the Law on the Organisation and Functioning of the Council of Ministers, the Royal government of Cambodia[48] has the duty of determining and implementing state policies in accordance with the principles enshrined in the Constitution. The Royal government oversees the application of laws and directs the general affairs of the state, except those that come within the competencies of the legislative organ and the judicial organ.[49] The Royal government owes responsibilities to the National Assembly for its general policies and its activities. The Royal government governs and commands the administration in all of these bodies' activities.[50] The Royal government also manages the general affairs of the state in compliance with the political program and plans approved by the National Assembly.[51]

In addition, according to article 128 (New) (former article 109) of the Constitution, the judiciary has independent power. The judicial power is the guarantor of impartiality and the protector of the citizens' rights and liberties. The judicial power has jurisdiction over all forms of litigation, including administrative litigation. This power is entrusted to the Supreme Court and to the jurisdictions of various categories and degrees. The three layers of the court system in Cambodia are (i) Provincial/municipality courts; (ii) Appellate court; and (iii) Supreme Court. Article 130 (New) (former article 111) of the Constitution prohibits any organ of the Legislative Power or the Executive Power from exercising

---

[44] Laws initiated by the Royal government.
[45] Law initiated by the National Assembly or by the Senate.
[46] Draft laws or proposed laws that have been adopted by the National Assembly are called Text Laws.
[47] For more details, please refer to Taing Ratana, 'The Influence of Constitutional Law on Administrative Law: The Influence of the Constitutional Council's Decisions on the Administration in Cambodia' in Kai Hauerstein and Jörg Menzel (eds), *The Historical Development of Cambodian Administrative Law* (Cambodia, Konrad Adenauer Stiftung 2014) 133.
[48] The Council of Ministers is the Royal Government of the Kingdom of Cambodia and is headed by the Prime Minister. He is assisted by Deputy Prime Ministers as well as by Senior Ministers, Ministers and Secretaries of State as members.
[49] Art 2 of The Law on the Organization and Functioning of the Council of Ministers.
[50] ibid Art 3.
[51] ibid.

judicial powers. According to article 132 (New) (former article 113), the King of Cambodia plays the symbolic role of Guarantor of the independence of the Judiciary. However, the same article states that the Supreme Council of Magistracy assists the King in this task.

vi. The Election of the Selected Head of State and the Effect of Plurality to this Selection

The King of Cambodia is the Head of State. According to article 14 of the Constitution, a member of the royal family who is at least 30 years old and a descendant of King *Ang Duong*, King *Norodom*, or King *Sisowath*[52] qualifies for election as King of Cambodia. Before ascending the throne, the King must take his oath in accordance with the stipulations in Annex 4.[53]

Cambodia's monarch is elected by the crown council. This council comprises nine notable personalities, namely (i) the President of the Senate; (ii) President of the National Assembly; (iii) Prime Minister; (iv) First Vice President of the Senate; (v) First Vice President of the National Assembly; (vi) Second Vice President of the Senate; (vii) Second Vice President of the National Assembly; (viii) Supreme Patriarch of the *Maha Nikaya* Buddhist order of the Kingdom of Cambodia; and (ix) the Supreme Patriarch of the *Dhammayutika Nikaya* Buddhist order of the Kingdom of Cambodia.[54]

The council membership reflects the plurality of three institutions: (i) the Legislative; (ii) the Executive; and (iii) Buddhism. This plurality has a positive effect on the workings of democracy in Cambodia because it lends credence to the idea that the King is elected by the people. However, according to the provisions of the Constitution, the power of the King is very limited. This has been criticised by some scholars and members of the public, who wish to see more power invested in the King. Some have complained that the limitations on the King's power was deliberately introduced by political parties during the constitutional drafting process. However, the reality of the matter can be found in the minutes of the second plenary session of the Constitutional Assembly, which is kept in the library of the National Assembly.

In the second plenary session of the Constitutional Assembly held on 15 September 1993, H.E. *Chem Snguon*[55] reported that the crown council had

---

[52] King Norodom (1834–1904) and King Sisowath (1840–1927) were the sons of King Ang Doung (1796–1860). King Ang Doung was a popular king because he freed slaves in the entire country using his own royal property. The slavery regime thus ended during his reign.

[53] See Annex 4 of the Constitution of 1993, the oath of the King: "I swear to perform my duty in conformity with the constitution and laws of the Kingdom, and to be beneficial to the State and Citizen."

[54] Art 13 (New) of the Constitution of 1993.

[55] He is a Constitutional Assembly member from the Cambodian People's Party (CPP) and was the former personal secretary to King Norodom Sihanouk during the first Kingdom.

initially been proposed by the former King *Norodom Sihanouk*, who was at that time the Head of the Supreme National Council (SNC). The former King also suggested that the crown council, in order to be truly democratic, must not contain any member of the royal family. This is the historical reality of article 13 (New). H.E. *Chem Snguon* also said in this session that when he visited Pyongyang in North Korea on 30 August 1993 to report on the progress of the constitution-making process to former King *Norodom Sihanouk*, he was advised by the former King to limit, as far as possible, the important rights of the King. The powers to be limited are:

(i) The right to assign the dignity of leading the council of ministers (but upon the proposal of the President of the National Assembly);
(ii) The right to veto draft and proposed laws;
(iii) The right to directly lead the armed forces;
(iv) The right to grant pardons; and
(v) The right to preside over sessions of the council of ministers.

The most notable point about this constitution-making process is that the former King accepted the constitutional monarchy at 9.30pm on 31 August 1993 as proposed by representatives from three winning parties, who submitted their request to him at *Changsuwon* palace,[56] the royal residence in Pyongyang. However, the former King again suggested to the delegation from the three winning parties that the following points should be enshrined in the Constitution[57]:

(i) The King reigns, but does not govern;
(ii) The provisions stating that the King reigns but does not govern absolutely cannot be amended;
(iii) The King has no right to appoint his heir to the throne (instead, he proposed forming the Crown Council to carry out this duty); and
(iv) The consort of the King shall not engage in politics.

As a result, the Head of State of Cambodia is now elected in accordance with the principles of pluralism and democracy. Cambodia can be said to be a true democratic constitutional monarchy based on historical and legal fact. Furthermore, as the above explanation shows, the limitations on the King's power were suggested by the King himself and approved by the constituent assembly.

vii. *The Claims of the Branches of Government for their Legitimacy*

Article 51 (New) of the Constitution provides that '*All powers shall belong to the citizens. The citizens shall exercise their powers through the National Assembly, the*

---

[56] This palace was built in 1974 by Kim Il Sung of North Korea for the exiled King Norodom Sihanouk of Cambodia and it was where the King would entertain foreign diplomats. Kim Il Sung of North Korea and King Norodom Sihanouk had a very good relationship, which King Sihanouk called a 'Brother Bond'.

[57] Minutes of the second plenary session of the Constituent Assembly.

Senate, the Royal Government and the Jurisdictions'. This article explains that the Royal government of Cambodia is the representative of Khmer citizens. Thus, citizens elect the government through universal elections, in line with the principles of a liberal multi-party democracy, which is enshrined in paragraph 1 of article 51 (New) of the Constitution. The legitimacy of the Royal government of Cambodia is therefore based on (i) universal elections; (ii) the vote of confidence by the National Assembly; (iii) a Royal Decree appointing the Council of Ministers; and (iv) oath-taking.

(i) *Universal Elections*: Since 1993, Cambodia has organised universal elections every five years to allow Khmer citizens to exercise their right to elect their representatives, in accordance with the principles of a parliamentary system and a liberal multi-party democracy. All political parties registered with the Ministry of the Interior (MoI) and the National Election Committee (NEC) will appoint one of their members to stand as a candidate for Prime Minister and present their policies before taking part in the election to form the National Assembly, which comprises at least 120 members.[58] The candidate for Prime Minister from the winning party in the election will then be elected through a vote of confidence by the National Assembly.

(ii) *Vote of Confidence by the National Assembly*: According to article 119 (New) (Former article 100), upon the proposal of the President of the National Assembly and with the agreement of the two Vice-Presidents, the King will assign a high-ranking Member of the National Assembly from the winning party with the task of forming the Royal government. This assigned Member, along with fellow Members of the National Assembly or members of the parties represented in the National Assembly who are in charge of ministerial functions within the Royal Government, will then solicit the vote of confidence from the National Assembly.

(iii) *Royal Decree appointing the Council of Minister*: Once the National Assembly has carried out the vote of confidence, the King will sign a Royal Decree appointing the full Council of Ministers.

(iv) *Oath-taking*: Before assuming office, the Council of Ministers, comprising the Prime Minister, Deputy Prime Ministers, Senior Ministers, and Ministers and Secretaries of State will take their oaths according to the text in Annex 6 of the Constitution. The oath-taking usually takes place in the throne hall of the Royal Palace, with the exception of the second mandate of 1998 where the oaths were taken at the Temple of *Angkor Wat* in *Siem Reap* province.

According to Annex 6, the Council of Ministers shall take their oaths before:

(i) *His Majesty the King*: This means that the King of Cambodia must preside over this religious ceremony in the Royal Palace. However, one question that has not been addressed is: can the King assign a representative to replace him if he is abroad or seriously ill?

---

[58] Art 76 provides that the National Assembly shall comprise at least 120 members.

(ii) *The Supreme Patriarch of Theravada Buddhism*: There are two main sects of Theravada Buddhism in Cambodia – the *Dhammayutikanikaya* and the *Mahanikaya*. Each sect is headed by a Supreme Patriarch (*Samdach Preah Sangha Raja*). The two *Sangha Raja* must be present at the oath-taking ceremonies in the throne hall of the Royal Palace.

(iii) *Devata Raksa Svetachhatra*: The Khmers believe that a well-known *Devata* (Deity) is the guardian of the nine-tiered white umbrella (*Svetachhatra*), which symbolises the 10 rules of the King (*Dasapit Raja Dhamma*). This *Devata* is the only deity to be recognised by the Constitution of this Kingdom. The nine-tiered white umbrella, which also symbolises the King's power, is installed over the golden throne in the royal palace of Phnom Penh.

Hence, the Royal government of Cambodia gains its legitimacy by following the steps and rituals set out in the Constitution; otherwise, the government can be declared to be unconstitutional. Significantly, this legitimacy is binding in both law and religion. It is an example of how constitutional pluralism is conceptualised in this Kingdom, where people practise both state law (*Anacakra*) and customary law (*Buddhacakra*).

viii. Other Distinctive Constitutional Institutions Beyond the Usual Branches of Legislature, Executive, and Judiciary

Beyond the three branches of power, there are other distinctive constitutional institutions with functions spelled out in the Constitution of Cambodia:

(i) *The National Congress*: This institution is described in Chapter XIV (New) of the Constitution. The National Congress allows citizens to be directly informed about various affairs of national interest, to raise issues, and to submit suggestions to the State authorities. Khmer citizens of both sexes have the right to participate in the National Congress.[59] The National Congress meets once a year, usually in early December, upon the convening of the Prime Minister. It conducts its proceedings under the High Presidency of the King.[60] The National Congress can submit suggestions to the Senate, the National Assembly, and State authorities for consideration. The organisation and functions of the National Congress are stipulated by law.[61]

However, it can be argued that such an institution is contrary to the principle of representative democracy in Cambodia. A National Congress is more applicable to a society with direct democracy but not one with representative

---

[59] Art 147 new (former art 128) of the Constitution of 1993.
[60] ibid Art 148 new (former art 129).
[61] ibid Art 149 new.

democracy. Hence, some questions that remain to be answered are: Is it necessary to keep Chapter XIV (new) relating to the National Congress in the 1993 Cambodian Constitution? Why was this chapter created when Cambodia practises representative democracy? No one can provide the answers except the Constitution makers of 1993.[62]

(ii) *The Congress of National Assembly and the Senate*: This organ, which is essentially a congress of the National Assembly and the Senate, can be convened if necessitated and required. This Congress can call for meetings involving both bodies to resolve important national issues. The plurality inherent in the Congress's structure promotes democracy in Cambodia's bicameral system because both legislative organs can exchange points of view in finding resolution for national issues.

(iii) *The Constitutional Council*: The nine members of the Constitutional Council come from three different institutions. Three members are appointed by the King, three members are elected by the National Assembly, while the remaining three are elected by the Supreme Council of Magistracy. The plurality in the composition of the Council plays a crucial role in promoting the independence and impartiality of the institution, which is then empowered to promote the rule of law in Cambodia.

(iv) *The National Election Committee*: The current structure of the National Election Committee (NEC) is the result of a political agreement on 22 July 2014 between the Cambodian People's Party (CPP) (the ruling party) and the Cambodia National Rescue Party (CNRP) (dissolved). This agreement was made in order to resolve the political deadlock after the fifth universal election of 28 July 2013, to respect the common will of the Khmer citizens, and to work towards the national benefit. Thus, the reformed NEC has nine members comprising four members from the ruling party, four members from parties with seats in the National Assembly and which did not form the government, and the last member from civil society who is selected and approved by all parties with seats in the National Assembly. As a result, the plurality in the composition of the NEC has had a positive effect on free and fair elections in Cambodia and has increased the trust of all concerned parties and Khmer citizens in the functions of the NEC.

ix. *The Judicial Review Mechanisms to Adjudicate upon the Constitutionality of State Action*

The Constitutional Council is the sole organ for judicial review in Cambodia. The Constitutional Council is a supreme, neutral, and independent institution that came into effect with the promulgation of the 1993 Cambodian Constitution.

---

[62] Taing (n 46).

This institution has functioned effectively since 15 June 1998. There has not been a clear reason explaining this five-years delay of creation, but it might be caused by the fact that, rather than establishing the Constitutional Council, there had been a lot of other priorities to be attended to after the first election of 1993.

The Constitutional Council consists of one President and eight Members. The President is elected by the nine Members of the Council and an absolute majority is required. The election of the President is conducted every three years, when three new members come into office. The President's rank and prerogatives are equal to those of the President of the National Assembly, while the Constitutional Council Members' rank and prerogatives are equal to those of the Vice-Presidents of the National Assembly. The usual term of office of the Constitutional Council Members is nine years. Every three years, three members of this Council are replaced. There were exceptions to these rules in the first Constitutional Council, when some members were appointed and elected for terms of three, six, and nine years.

Three members are appointed by His Majesty the King, while the National Assembly and the Supreme Council of Magistracy are each entitled to elect three members. The Members of the Constitutional Council must be high-ranking personalities who are Khmer nationals by birth; are at least 45 years old; have higher education qualifications in the fields of law, administration, diplomacy, or economy; and who have at least 15 years of professional experience in the above-mentioned fields of work.

According to the Constitution and the Law on the Organisation and the Functioning of the Constitutional Council, the Council has three main duties:

(i) *To guarantee respect for the Constitution*: The Constitutional Council interprets the Constitution as well as the laws adopted by the National Assembly and reviewed by the Senate, and examines the constitutionality of these laws.[63]
(ii) *To examine and rule on electoral litigation*: The Council examines and rules on litigation involving the election of the Members of the National Assembly and the election of the Senators.[64]
(iii) *To notify His Majesty the King*: The King consults the Constitutional Council on all proposals to amend the Constitution.[65] The initiative of the revision or the amendment of the Constitution belongs to the King, Prime Minister, and President of the National Assembly, on the proposal from one-fourth of all the National Assembly's Members.[66]

As a rule of thumb, the Constitutional Council cannot examine any matter on its own initiative. The Constitutional Council can examine the constitutionality of a

---

[63] Art 136 (New) of the Constitution of 1993.
[64] ibid.
[65] ibid Art 143 (New) (former art 124).
[66] ibid Art 151 (New) (former art 132).

law before (*A priori*) or after (*A posteriori*) its promulgation. Article 140 (New) of the Constitution states that the King, the Prime Minister, the President of the National Assembly or one-tenth of the National Assembly's Members, or the President of the Senate or one-fourth of the Senators, may send a law adopted by the National Assembly to the Constitutional Council for examination before promulgation.

In addition, the rules of procedure of the National Assembly, the rules of procedure of the Senate, and organic laws – laws on the organisation and the functioning of institutions – must be submitted to the Constitutional Council for examination before their promulgation. The Constitutional Council must pronounce within 30 days whether the laws or the rules of procedure conform to the Constitution.

According to article 141 (New) of the Constitution, the King, the President of the Senate, the President of the National Assembly, the Prime Minister, one-fourth of the Senators, one-tenth of the National Assembly's Members, or the courts can request for the Council to examine the constitutionality of a law after its promulgation. Citizens thus have the right to raise the unconstitutionality of a law through the avenues of the National Assembly's Members, the President of the National Assembly, the Senators, or the President of the Senate.

x. *The Vertical Separation of Power (Federalism and Decentralisation) Responding to Plurality*

Cambodia has implemented a policy of decentralisation since 2002. It is considered a key tool to promote local democracy and ownership as the central government can delegate power and responsibility to local governments. It has been a notable democratic development in Cambodia.

According to article 145 (New-One) of the Constitution, the territorial administrative organisation of Cambodia is divided into *Reach Theany* (the Royal Capital City), *Khet* (provinces), *Krong* (municipalities), *Srok* (districts), *Khan* (arrondissements), *Khum* (communes), and *Sangkat* (quarters).

Reach Theany, Khet, Krong, Srok, and *Khan* are administered by councils, which are elected via indirect elections every five years. In contrast, *Khum*[67] and *Sangkat* are administered by councils elected through universal elections. All councils must consult citizens within their jurisdictions on the formulation and implementation of development plans. They must also consult the other types of councils within their jurisdiction, the relevant ministries, and other stakeholders.

Decentralisation in Cambodia is thus applied at the communal/Sangkat levels. In promoting decentralisation at this level, the Royal government of Cambodia has also established two main laws to govern decentralisation: (i) the Law on Administrative Management of Commune/Sangkat; and (ii) the Law on the Election of the Communal/Sangkat Council.

---

[67] *Khum* and *Sangkat* are at the same level. *Khum* is used for communes in districts while *Sangkat* is used for communes in *Krong* or *Khan*.

The Communal/Sangkat Councils are vested with the autonomy to run their own administration and budget. They have the power to develop their own communities. Chapter 2 of the Law on Administrative Management of the Commune/Sangkat defines the Communal/Sangkat Council as an organisation that represents the citizens in its commune/Sangkat and carries out its functions in order to benefit citizens. The Communal/Sangkat Council is elected by the citizens of each commune/Sangkat in accordance with the Law on the Election of the Communal/Sangkat Council. The Communal/Sangkat Council has a mandate of five years and this mandate is determined when the new council takes office. The Communal/Sangkat Council can have five to eleven members, depending on the demographics of the Commune/Sangkat.

The Commune/Sangkat is envisioned to fulfil the following objectives: promote good governance, manage the resources required by the local communities, serve the common good of the citizens, and respect the national benefit in compliance with the general policies of the State. In order to achieve these goals, the Commune/Sangkat has two main roles:

(i) The role of implementing the affairs of the local communities in order to promote the benefit of the Commune/Sangkat and of its citizens: Here, the Communal/Sangkat Council is in charge of (i) guaranteeing public security and order; (ii) organising public services, and examining these services to ensure that they function properly; (iii) promoting the health of citizens; (iv) promoting the development of the economy and the living standards of citizens; (v) protecting and preserving the environment, natural resources, as well as the national culture and heritage; (vi) taking in the ideas of citizens; and (vi) meeting the needs of the citizens.

(ii) The role of agents representing the state through the delegation of power by the state: Here, the Communal/Sangkat Council has the duty of implementing laws, royal decrees, sub-decrees, proclamations, and other related regulations made under the law.

As result, decentralisation is an important method of creating local government. It also contributes to democratic development by promoting effective participation by local residents even though they hold different political beliefs.

D. Constitutional Rights

i. *The Principles of Constitutional Rights*

According to article 31 of the Constitution of 1993, the Kingdom of Cambodia recognises and respects human rights as enshrined in the United Nations Charter, the Universal Declaration of Human Rights, and all the international treaties and conventions relating to human rights, women's rights, and children's rights. According to paragraph 2 of article 31, Khmer citizens are equal before the law and enjoy the same rights, liberties, and duties regardless of race, colour, sex, language, belief, religion, political tendency, birth origin, social status, wealth or other circumstances. Furthermore, according to the same article, the exercise of personal rights and liberties by any individual shall not adversely affect the rights and freedom of others; while the exercise of such rights and liberties shall be in accordance with the law.

ii. Specific Rights Included in the Constitution to Address Plurality

The rights and obligations of Khmer citizens are stated in Chapter III of the Constitution. The specific rights to address plurality are likewise found in this chapter. Besides paragraph 2 of article 31, which has already been discussed above, article 35 provides that 'Khmer citizens of both sexes have the right to participate actively in the political, economic, social and cultural life of the nation'. Based on those provisions, one can elucidate specific rights to do with plurality:

(i) *Political rights to address plurality*:
- Khmer citizens of both sexes shall enjoy the right to vote and to stand as candidates for the election.[68]
- Khmer citizens of both sexes shall enjoy the right to strike and to organize peaceful demonstrations within the framework of the law.[69]
- Khmer citizens shall have the freedom to express their personal opinions, and shall have the right to freedom of the press, freedom of publication, and freedom of assembly. No one can take advantage of these rights to impinge on the dignity of others, to affect the good mores and customs of society, and to affect public order and national security.[70]
- Khmer citizens shall have the right to create associations and political parties. This right is to be determined by law. Khmer citizens may participate in mass organisations meant for mutual assistance, the protection of national realisations, and social order.[71]

(ii) *Economic Rights to address plurality*:
- Khmer citizens of both sexes have the right to choose any form of employment according to their ability and according to the needs of society. Khmer citizens of both sexes shall receive equal pay for equal work. The work of housewives at home shall have equal value as remunerated work done outside the home. Khmer citizens of both sexes shall also have the right to enjoy social security and other social benefits as determined by law. Khmer citizens of both sexes shall have the right to create trade unions and to participate as their members.[72]

---

[68] The Constitution of 1993, Para 1 of Art 43 (New).
[69] ibid Art 37.
[70] ibid Para 1 of Art 41.
[71] ibid Art 42.
[72] ibid Art 36.

(iii) *Social Rights to address plurality*:
- All Khmer citizens of different origins, individually or collectively, shall have the right to ownership. However, only natural persons or legal entities of Khmer nationality shall have the right to land ownership. Legal private ownership shall be protected by law. Expropriation is possible only if public utility demands it in specific circumstances stipulated by the law, and if prior appropriate and fair compensation is granted.[73]

(iv) *Civil Rights to address plurality*:
- Citizens' freedom to travel, far or near, and to legally settle down shall be respected. Khmer citizens have the right to settle abroad or to return home. The protection of the right to the inviolability of residence and to the confidentiality of correspondence by mail, telegram, telex, facsimile, and telephone shall be guaranteed. Searches of residences and properties and body searches shall be done only in accordance with legal stipulations.[74]

(v) *Cultural and Religious Rights to address plurality*:
- Khmer citizens of both sexes shall have the right to freedom of belief. Freedom of belief and freedom of religious practice shall be guaranteed by the State, provided such freedoms do not impinge upon other beliefs or religions or on public order and security.[75]

IV. Key Observations on How the Pluralistic Sources Shape/Affect the Constitutional Law and Politics

The pluralistic sources of the Constitution affect constitutional law and politics in both positive and negative ways. It is important to note that these pluralistic sources are a result of adopting democracy and pluralism in the Cambodian Constitution and adapting these concepts to the Cambodian context. These two concepts have had great political, economic, social, and cultural impact on this Kingdom.

The adoption of pluralism and democracy has shaped the Cambodian Constitution along the lines of modern constitutionalism. Some important points to be noted in the Cambodian Constitution:

(i) *Fundamental rights* as enshrined in the United Nation Charter, UDHR, and other international instruments are accepted and expressed in the Cambodian Constitution, which is beneficial to the Khmer people as a whole.
(ii) *The separation of powers* is very clearly defined in the Cambodian Constitution, thereby setting Cambodia on the path to becoming a state with real checks and balances.

---
[73] ibid Art 44.
[74] ibid Art 40.
[75] ibid Art 43.

(iii) *The rule of law* is a common demand of Khmer citizens. Pluralism has played a crucial role in allowing all key actors to perform their rights and duties in a way that achieves rule of law.
(iv) *Democracy* is re-implanted in Cambodia after its absence for decades during the period of war and conflict. This principle is very beneficial to both institutional and human resource development in Cambodia. Even though democracy is quite young for this country and is a subject to be discussed, in reality Cambodian people have benefited from it in present times.

On the other hand, the adoption of pluralism and democracy can cause some challenges to the constitutional law and politics of Cambodia:

(i) *The problem of achieving quorums:* The political deadlock of 2003 was caused by the need for a two-third-majority vote in the National Assembly. The winning party could not form the National Assembly and the government because it lacked the necessary majority and quorum. Thus, political pluralism can cause political deadlock or conflict after the elections. In some cases, the majority may be kidnapped by the minority voice if it cannot form the requisite quorum.
(ii) *Constitutional fragmentation:* Given the existence of pluralistic sources, the Cambodian Constitution of 1993 has been placed in danger several times since its promulgation. The 2003 political deadlock could have led to the extinguishing of the Constitution if the additional constitutional law had not been created. Pluralistic sources could thus, in some cases, affect the sustainability of constitutional practices in Cambodia.
(iii) *Political deadlock:* Pluralism may thus have a negative effect on political sustainability if it is not used and governed properly and carefully. Cambodia has experienced this negative impact on its constitutional law and politics many times throughout its history.
(iv) *Development delay:* Political deadlock and conflicts, for instance in 1997 and 2003, caused delays in Cambodia's development process. However, political parties tried to find a resolution by adopting a win-win policy for building national reconciliation in the pluralistic state.

V. Conclusion

As has been observed, '*difference shall produce harmony*'. A melodic song is always produced by many musical instruments. A beautiful garden cannot be formed with just one type of flower. However, different musical instruments could spoil a nice song if the instruments are not in tune with one another, and a garden could become messy if the different kinds of flowers are not planted with some form of order. Thus, the art of reaping the benefits of pluralism must be based on the specific nation's distinctive needs. All citizens are the masters of their own nation's destiny; hence, the responsibility of shaping pluralism to the nation's needs is that of all citizens representing the full diversity of the nation.

Cambodia is walking on the path towards this idea of pluralism. In the meantime, smiling and shedding tears are inevitably part of the road towards constitutional pluralism, which is a new experience for this young democratic state. However, Cambodia has demonstrated commitment and patience in reaching the goal of re-creating the nation and achieving the *'Oasis of Peace'* set out in the Constitution's preamble. Even in the face of challenges, its pluralist constitution has provided avenues for Cambodia to choose the best way of reconciling constitutionalism within the Cambodian context and values.

The important concept of a pluralist constitution is crucial in ensuring that democracy survives in Cambodia by encouraging the acceptance of different opinions in all activities of the state. Thus, what all concerned actors in Cambodia must continue doing, in the present and in the future, is to guarantee the respect of the Constitution and to effectively carry out the functions enshrined in the Constitution with *unshakeable virtue and confidence*. If citizens in Cambodia can do so, Cambodia will realize the ideals of its pluralist constitution in the developmental process of the nation and all Khmer citizens will become real masters of their country's destiny.

Bibiliography

—— Agreement on a Comprehensive Political Settlement of the Cambodia Conflict (Paris Conference, 23 October 1991).
—— Decision N° 092 /003/2007 CC.D (10 July 2007).
—— Decision N° 107/003/2009 CC.D (23 December 2009).
—— Law on Elections of Members of the National Assembly (LEMNA).
—— Law on the Organization and Functioning of the Council of Ministers.
—— Minutes of the second plenary session of the Constituent Assembly (Secretariat General of the National Assembly's Archives, August 1993).
—— Paris Peace Accords of 1991.
—— United Nations Charter.
—— Universal Declaration of Human Rights.
Bowen G T, 'Khmer Republic' in Blaustein A P and Flanz G H (eds), *Constitutions of the Countries of the World* (New York, Oceana Publication 1972).
—— and Sheldon S, 'Cambodia' in Blaustein A P and Flanz G H (eds), *Constitutions of the Countries of the World* (New York, Oceana Publication 1982).
Constitutional Council of Cambodia, Law on the Organization and the Functioning of the Constitutional Council (published 1998).
—— 'The Internal Rules on the Procedure implemented in front of the Constitutional Council' (1998).
—— 'The Rules of Procedure of the Constitutional Council' (1998).

—— Law on the Amendment of the Law on the Organization and the Functioning of the Constitutional Council (published 2007).
—— The Constitution of the Kingdom of Cambodia (published March 2010).
—— Constitution of Cambodia (published 2016).
Chuon Nath, *Khmer Dictionary* (Buddhist Institution Press 1967).
Chandler D, 'The Constitution of Democratic Kampuchea: The Semantics of Revolutionary Changes' (1976) 49(3) Pacific Affairs 506.
—— *Cambodia's Historical Legacy* (1998) 5 Conciliation Press 19.
Cedès G, *Pour Mieux Comprendre Angkor* (Jouve 1947); (Minh Nakry trs, unpublished).
HE Ieng Moly, 'The Making of the Cambodian Constitution' (Presentation at the 10th Konrad Adenauer Stiftung Law Talk, Sihanoukville, 11 October 2013).
Jennar R M, *The Cambodian Constitutions (1953–1993)* (Phnom Penh 1995) 36.
HE Ouch Borith, 'Cambodia's Peace-building Experience' (Presentation at 'Tokyo Peace-builder Symposium 2008', Tokyo, 24–25 March 2008).
Taing Ratana, 'The Influence of Constitutional Law on Administrative Law: The Influence of the Constitutional Council's Decisions on the Administration in Cambodia' in Hauerstein K and Menzel J (eds), *The Historical Development of Cambodian Administrative Law* (Cambodia, Konrad Adenauer Stiftung 2014) 133.
Thong Thel, *Language Planning and Language Policy of Cambodia* (Pacific Linguistics, A-67, 1985).
Troeung Ngea, *Khmer History: From the Beginning to Abandon of Angkor* (1st ed, Phnom Penh 1973).

8
Constitutions in Ethnically Plural Societies: Laos and Vietnam

BUI NGOC SON

I. Introduction: Beyond Constitutional Design in Divided Societies

A body of recent scholarship focuses on constitutions in divided societies. Little attention, however, has been paid to the constitutions in plural, but not divided, societies. Two reasons account for this phenomenon. First, the pragmatic concern is that divided societies are more or less associated with constitutional arrangements, which require grave positive explanation and normative construction. Second, there may be an implicit assumption that if a society is plural but not deeply divided, its Constitution may be silent about plurality because there is no serious social and political problems that require constitutional treatments. Drawing on constitutional expressivism in comparative constitutional epistemology, this chapter makes the case that constitutions may respond to plurality in plural but not divided societies, and the function of this constitutional response is expressive rather than regulative.

Laos and Vietnam are used as case-studies. This chapter focuses on the current socialist constitutions of the two countries: the Lao 2015 Constitution and the Vietnamese 2013 Constitution. The two societies are ethnically plural but not divided: there are no severe ethnic conflicts which have been translated in severe political conflicts. However, their constitutions are not silent about ethnic plurality. At the same time, there is no deliberate constitutional design to regulate ethnic plurality. Rather, from the preamble to constitutional provisions on the fundamental principles of the regime, the bill of rights and the structural institutions, both constitutions seek to express the reality of ethnic plurality, the aspiration towards continuing ethnic unity, the sovereignty of a unified people, and the state's commitments to the promotion of socio-economic development of the different ethnic groups and the protection of their rights.

An important implication arises from this experience. Expressive functions are not unique to democratic constitutions: they can be performed by authoritarian constitutions as well. The exploration of this experience is important to expand our comparative knowledge about the Constitution in plural societies.

In this Chapter, Part II lays down the conceptual framework of constitutional expressivism. Part III briefly introduces the background of constitutional history and the context of ethnic plurality. Part IV considers the constitutional expression of ethnic plurality. Part V concludes.

II. Constitutional Expressivism

Most contemporary societies are more or less plural, but not all are divided where 'ethnocultural diversity translates into political fragmentation.'[1] As a constitution, *qua* the fundamental document of a polity, occupies the paramount role in the legal system, political order, and society, it is often practically summoned as the framework to mollify social and political conflicts engendered by ethnocultural plurality. Understandably, pundits of comparative constitutional law have focused on normative and empirical questions regarding constitutional design in divided societies.[2] However, constitutions also engage with plural but not divided societies. In this case, the function of the constitution vis-à-vis plurality is not to regulate social and political conflicts rooted in plurality but as an expression of the plurality.

This is connected to the concept of constitutional expressivism in comparative constitutional epistemology. Although expressivist thought is not constitutionally distinctive,[3] gurus of comparative constitutional law, such as Garry Jacobsohn, Mark Tushnet, Vicki Jackson, and Cheryl Saunders, have consolidated the expressivist constitutional epistemology, indicating that the Constitution is not merely about rules and institutions but is also expressive of values and commitments of a community.[4] This mode of thinking is traceable to G. W. F. Hegel's 'immanent' theory of constitutional law, which conceives of the Constitution as the expression of the spirit of the people.[5] The German philosopher contends that 'the constitution of any given people depend in general on the character and development of its

---

[1] Sujit Choudhry, 'Bridging Comparative Politics and Comparative Constitutional Law: Constitutional Design in Divided Societies' in Sujit Choudhry (ed), *Constitutional Design for Divided Societies: Integration or Accommodation?* (OUP 2008) 5.

[2] See eg, Aslı Ü. Bâli and Hanna Lerner (eds), *Constitution Writing, Religion and Democracy* (CUP 2017).

[3] See Cass R Sunstein, 'On the Expressive Function of Law' (1996) 144 *University of Pennsylvania Law Review* 2021.

[4] Mark Tushnet, 'The Possibilities of Comparative Constitutional Law' (1999) 108 *Yale Law Journal* 1269; Cheryl Saunders, 'Towards a Global Constitutional Gene Pool' (2009) 4(3) *National Taiwan University Law Review* 12; Gary Jacobsohn, *Constitutional Identity* (Harvard University Press 2010); Vicki Jackson, 'Comparative Constitutional Law: Methodologies' in Michel Rosenfeld and András Sajó (eds), *The Oxford Handbook Of Comparative Constitutional Law* (OUP 2012) 66–67.

[5] For detailed analysis, see Michael Salter and Julia J A Shaw, 'Towards a Critical Theory of Constitutional Law: Hegel's Contribution' (1994) 21(4) *Journal of Law and Society* 464.

self-consciousness. In its self-consciousness, its subjective freedom is rooted and so, therefore, is the actuality of its constitution.'[6]

Constitutional expressivism has to do with the conceptions of the nature, forms, and effects or consequences of constitutional expression. By *nature*, scholars argue that constitutions are expressive of national values, constitutive political commitments, and sovereignty.[7] Existing accounts, however, tend to focus on the expressive substance of democratic constitutions. In fact, the expressive function is not distinctive to democratic constitutions but can be performed by authoritarian constitutions as well. While the instrumental functions of authoritarian constitutions are more prominent, this does not mean that they are purely instrumental to those in power.[8] When authoritarian constitutions are enacted under plural conditions, they may express the ethno-cultural plurality of the polity beyond the material political calculus. Moreover, authoritarian leaders cannot simply ignore the historical and identitarian values of their nation, and this enables an authoritarian Constitution to perform expressive functions.

In addition, the nature of constitutional expression is not necessarily analogous to that of constitutional aspiration. Constitutional expressivism can be both positivist and aspirationalist. The Constitution can be expressive of existing and historical values and normative aspirational commitments that guide the direction of the whole polity. Furthermore, constitutional expressivism is essentially different from constitutional instrumentalism: the former is axiological and underlying while the latter is materialist and hegemonic. Constitutional expressivism is about underlying values and principles of a polity, independent from the instrumental concerns of constitution-makers and politicians. In this regard, the incorporation of transnational norms into domestic constitutions for material interests of political elite (e.g. attracting foreign investments)[9] is better conceptualised from an instrumentalist, rather than an expressive, perspective.

The *forms* of constitutional expression are varied, ranging from constitutional preambles to constitutional principles and constitutional rights.[10] Two types of constitutional principles may perform the expressive function: the constituent and directive principles. The former defines the nature of polity, while the latter guides policy.[11] In addition, the bill of rights is not merely the regulatory ambit which

---

[6] G W F Hegel, *Outlines of the Philosophy of Right* (T. M. Knox tr, Stephen Hougate ed, OUP 2008) 263.
[7] Denis Galligan and Mila Versteeg, 'Theoretical Perspectives On The Social And Political Foundations of Constitutions' in Denis J Galligan and Mila Versteeg (eds), *Social And Political Foundations Of Constitutions* (CUP 2015) 8–13, 16–18.
[8] Mark Tushnet, 'Authoritarian Constitutionalism' (2015) 100(2) *Cornell Law Review* 391 (rebutting instrumental accounts of authoritarian constitutions).
[9] Galligan and Versteeg (n 7) 14.
[10] Jeff King, 'Constitutions as Mission Statements' in Denis J Galligan and Mila Versteeg (eds), *Social And Political Foundations of Constitutions* (CUP 2015) 82–85; Maarten Stremler and Wim Voermans, *Constitutional Preambles: A Comparative Analysis* (Edward Elgar Publishing 2017), see particularly ch 5: The function of preambles).
[11] On the latter, see Lael K Weis, 'Constitutional Directive Principles' (2017) 37(4) Oxford Journal of Legal Studies 916.

limits the state actions; it also expresses certain values and principles guiding state actions. Apart from these, the underexplored form of constitutional expression is structural constitutional provisions. These provisions do not merely regulate (disable or enable) state functions and lay down institutional architecture; more than that, they can also express values and commitments underlying the institutional structure.

Finally, the *social consequences or effects* of expressive constitutional provisions vary across different countries, and require empirical verification.[12] The effects of expressive constitutional provisions can be judicial, political, administrative, and social. These provisions may inform constitutional interpretation by courts in some ways, but are not limited to the judicial constitutional interpretation. They may also inform legislations, administrative regulations, and public discussion of the society.

III. Background

A. Constitutional History

The history of the Laotian State can be traced back to the Kingdom of Lan Xang (literally Million Elephants), a united kingdom which existed from 1354 to 1707 and was one of the largest kingdoms in Southeast Asia.[13] The political structure of this kingdom is marked by two important features: *meuang* and Buddhism. *Meuang* are tributary principalities, which all together constituted the kingdom.[14] Each *meuang* was headed by a *chao meuang*, or 'ruling prince, who was always drawn from the leading aristocratic family',[15] not officially appointed by the central imperial government. Therefore, Stuart-Fox remarks that 'Lao *meuang* were thus far more autonomous than were Chinese or Vietnamese provinces. They might independently enter into relations with other powers. Moreover, what happened within their jurisdictions depended on local laws and customs, whose application might be known to the centre only through the reports of spies and itinerant merchants.'[16] This suggests that Lan Xang was a heterarchical kingdom in which a plurality of local laws and customs coexisted.

The second feature, Buddhism, makes Lan Xang a polity of constitutional relevance. Buddhism was spread to Laos in the seventh to eighth centuries CE, via the Kingdom of Dvaravati.[17] Buddhism was reinforced in the Kingdom of Lan Xang,

---

[12] Galligan and Versteeg (n 7) 11.

[13] For an extensive study of this kingdom, see Martin Stuart-Fox, *The Lao Kingdom of Lan Xang: Rise and Decline* (Bangkok, Thailand, White Lotus Press 1998).

[14] Martin Stuart-Fox, *Laos: Politics, Economics, and Society* (Lynne Rienner Publishers 1986), 7.

[15] Martin Stuart-Fox, 'Politics and Reforms in the Lao People's Democratic Republic' Murdoch University's Asia Research Centre, Working Paper No. 126 (November 2005) 3.

[16] ibid 5.

[17] Stuart-Fox, *Laos: Politics, Economics, and Society* (n 14) 3.

for which Stuart-Fox identifies the kingdom as a 'Buddhist kingdom.'[18] Together with heredity, Buddhism constituted one of primary sources of the legitimacy of the ruler.[19] Particularly, the Buddhist concept of *karma* suggests that 'a king must have accumulated considerable religious merit in previous existences' and therefore 'he owned his exalted position primarily to the workings of the immutable law of *karma*.'[20] Stuart-Fox observes:

> Theoretically the king wielded absolute power, of life and death over his subjects and of ownership over the territories subject to him. In fact he was constrained both by the expectation that as a Buddhist monarch he would abide by the ten Buddhist precepts of just rule, and by his need for the support of the powerful members of the aristocracy and regional *chao meuang* who sat on the King's Council. In cases where the code of royal conduct was flagrantly violated, a king might be deposed. In fact, extreme autocratic behavior was quite rare in Lao history.[21]

This observation suggests that the Kingdom of Lan Xang may be an example of what can be called 'Buddhist constitutionalism.' The imperial government was limited ideationally by Buddhist principles of just rule and institutionally by local autonomous actors. This is comparable to Confucian constitutionalism in China and Vietnam in which imperial power was constrained by the Confucian principles of just rule and by scholars siting in different imperial institutions.[22]

The unity of the Kingdom of Lan Xang was undermined by dynastic disputes, which led to the division of the kingdom into three kingdoms in the eighteenth century: Luang Prabang in the North, Champasak in the South, and Vientiane in the Central.[23] During the second half of the twentieth century, Laos was colonised by France.[24] In 1893, the French Indochina was added with Laos together with Cambodia, and three Vietnamese regions of Tonkin (north), Annam (centre), and Cochinchina (south).[25] Since then, Laos has experienced four constitutions: the 1945 provisional Constitution of the Lao Issara government; the 1947 Constitution of the royal government; the 1991 socialist Constitution of the communist government – Lao People's Democratic Republic (LPDR), amended in 2003; and the 2015 Constitution of the current government.[26]

---

[18] Martin Stuart-Fox, *Buddhist Kingdom, Marxist State: The Making of Modern Laos* (Bangkok, Cheney: White Lotus 1996).
[19] Stuart-Fox, 'Politics and Reforms' (n 15) 5.
[20] Stuart-Fox, *Laos: Politics, Economics, and Society* (n 14) 5.
[21] Stuart-Fox, 'Politics and Reforms' (n 15) 5.
[22] See Bui Ngoc Son, *Confucian Constitutionalism in East Asia* (Routledge 2016) ch 2.
[23] Stuart-Fox, *Laos: Politics, Economics, and Society* (n 14) 8.
[24] For this period, see Martin Stuart-Fox, *A History of Laos* (CUP 1997) ch 2.
[25] For the making of Indochina, see Pierre Brocheux and Daniel Hémery, *Indochina: An Ambiguous Colonization, 1858–1954* (Ly Lan Dill-Klein, Eric Jennings, Nora Taylor, and Noémi Tousignant trs, University of California Press 2009).
[26] For more details on Lao constitutional history, see Gerald Leather, 'Laos: A Constitution in Search of Constitutionalism' in Clauspeter Hill and Jörg Menzel (eds), *Constitutionalism in Southeast Asia, Vol. 2 – Reports on National Constitutions* (Konrad-Adenauer-Stiftung 2008).

Vietnam is geologically located in Southeast Asia but culturally belongs to the East Asian world, dominated by Vietnam's great neighbour of China.[27] The nation has a long history. The Văn Lang Kingdom of Hùng Kings is considered the first Vietnamese state, existing in the legendary Hồng Bàng age (2879–258 BC). In 111 BC, Chinese military commander Zhao Tuo (known in Vietnam as Triệu Đà), who gained autonomy upon the collapse of the Qin Dynasty and established the Nanyue (Vietnamese: Nam Việt) dynasty, conquered Vietnam (known as Âu Lạc at that time) and divided the colony into two districts, namely Chiao-chih (Giao Chỉ) and Chiu-chen (Cửu Chân), initiating the millennial period of Chinese dependency ('*Bắc thuộc*') in Vietnam. During that period, there were brief independent times after some revolts, such as the times of the Trưng Sisters (40–43) and the Kingdom of Vạn Xuân (541–602). The dependency was terminated in 905 when a military governor named Khúc Thừa Dụ regained the national sovereignty from the Tang dynasty (618–907).[28] After that, Vietnam entered a new era of national independence with successive dynasties of Ngô (938–967), Đinh (968–980), Former Lê (980–1009), Lý (1009–1225), and Trần (1225–1400), Hồ (1400–1407), Latter Lê (1428–1527, 1533–1789), and Nguyễn (1802–1886), independence; 1887–1945, French colonialism). Basically, the government of pre-modern Vietnam followed monarchical polity.

Like Laos, constitutional history of modern Vietnam began in the early years of the twentieth century when France colonised the country. Under the communist rule, Vietnam has enacted five constitutions: the 1946 Constitution of the Democratic Republic of Vietnam (DRV); the DRV's 1959 Constitution; 1980 Constitution of the Socialist Republic of Vietnam (SRV); SRV's 1992 Constitution, amended in 2001; and the SRV's 2013 Constitution.[29]

B. Ethnic Plurality

Both Laos and Vietnam possess the condition of ethnic plurality. Laos is perhaps the 'most ethnically diverse'[30] in the region. The country is the home of some 6.5 million people[31] divided into four main linguistic groups and 49 ethnic groups:

1. The Lao-Tai Family having eight ethnic groups: Lao, Phouthai, Tai, Lue, Gnouane, Young, Saek and Thai Neua.

---

[27] William J Duiker, *Vietnam: Revolution in Transition* (WestView Press 1995) 165.
[28] For more details, see Keith Weller Taylor, *The Birth of Vietnam* (University of California Press 1976).
[29] For more details on Vietnamese constitutional history, see Mark Sidel, *The Constitution of Vietnam* (Hart Publishing 2009).
[30] Elizabeth M King and Dominique van de Walle, 'Laos' in Gillette H Hall and Harry Anthony Patrinos (eds), *Indigenous Peoples, Poverty, And Development* (CUP 2012) 249.
[31] Lao Statistics Bureau, 'Results of Population and Housing Census 2015' (21 October 2016) 21 http://lao.unfpa.org/en/publications/results-population-and-housing-census-2015-english-version accessed 21 September 2018.

2. The Mon-Khmer Family having 32 ethnic groups: Khmu, Pray, Singmou, Khom, Thene, Idou, Bid, Lamed, Samtao, Katang, Makong, Try, Trieng, Ta-oi, Yeh, Brao, Harak, Katou, Oi, Krieng, Yrou, Souai, Gnaheune, Lavy, Kabkae, Khmer, Toum, Ngouane, Meuang and Kri.
3. The Tibeto-Burmese Family having 7 ethnic groups: Akha, Singsali, Lahou, Sila, Hayi, Lolo and Hor.
4. The Hmong-Loumien category having 2 main tribes: Hmong and Loumien (Yao).[32]

It is indicated that 'these multi-ethnic people are scattered across the country each with their own unique traditions, culture and language.'[33] The Lao ethnic group is the largest group, occupying 50% the country's population.[34] The second and third largest groups are Khmou and Hmong respectively.[35]

Like Laos, Vietnam is an ethnically plural society. The country has 54 ethnic groups, classified into eight groups according the languages they use:

1. Việt-Mường Group: Chứt, Kinh, Mường, Thổ.
2. Tày-Thái Group: Bố Y, Giáy, Lào, Lự, Nùng, Sán Chay, Tày, Thái.
3. Mon-Khmer Group: Ba na, Brâu, Bru-Vân kiều, Chơ-ro, Co, Cơ-ho, Cơ-tu, Cơ-tu, Gié-triêng, Hrê, Kháng, Khmer, Khơ mú, Mạ, Mảng, M'Nông, Ơ-đu, Rơ-măm, Tà-ôi, Xinh-mun, Xơ-đăng, Xtiêng.
4. Mông-Dao Group: Dao, Mông, Pà Thẻn.
5. Kađai Group: Cờ Lao, La Chí, La ha, Pu Péo.
6. Austro-Polynenisian Group: Chăm, Chu-ru, Ê đê, Gia-rai, Ra-glai.
7. Chinese Group: Hoa, Ngái, Sán Dìu.
8. Tibeto Group: Cống, Hà Nhì, La Hủ, Lô Lô, Phù Lá, Si La.[36]

According to the Vietnamese government, 'the Viet (Kinh) people account for 87% of the country's population and mainly inhabit the Red River delta, the central coastal delta, the Mekong delta and major cities. The other 53 ethnic minority groups, totalling over 8 million people, are scattered over mountain areas (covering two-thirds of the country's territory) spreading from the North to the South.'[37]

The above narratives reveal three common features. First, both Laos and Vietnam are ethnically plural societies, and the two have some similar ethnic groups. Second, they are not divided societies in the sense that ethnic plurality is

---

[32] 'Minorities in Laos' (Facts and Details) http://factsanddetails.com/southeast-asia/Laos/sub5_3c/entry-2962.html accessed 21 September 2018.
[33] ibid.
[34] Lao Statistics Bureau (n 31) 36.
[35] ibid.
[36] 'List of Vietnamese ethnic groups' (Viet Nam Government Portal) www.chinhphu.vn/portal/page/portal/English/TheSocialistRepublicOfVietnam/AboutVietnam/AboutVietnamDetail?categoryId=10000103&articleId=10002652 accessed 21 September 2018.
[37] ibid.

not translated into serious political cleavages. Third, consequently, the constitutions do not regulate but express this plurality.

Notwithstanding the similarities, the difference is that the Lao ethnic group does not predominantly occupy the nation's population as the Viet-ethnic group does in Vietnam. Unlike societies in Laos and many other Southeast Asian countries, Vietnamese society is relatively homogeneous. A commentator observed that 'the Vietnamese people [the Kinh people] constitute a single, relatively homogeneous group, regardless of geographic location.'[38] However, this creates light differences in constitutional expression of plurality in the two societies. For example, the idea and phrase called 'multi-ethnic Lao people' runs throughout the Lao Constitution.

IV. Constitutional Expression

A. Nature

The constitutions of Laos and Vietnam have multiple functions. They have instrumental functions of authoritarian charters in the sense that they serve those in power.[39] They, however, also express the values and principles rooted in ethnic plurality in the two societies, which is not necessarily associated with the material calculation of those in power.

Multi-functionalism may be an apt approach to understand the functions of the constitutions in Laos and Vietnam specifically and authoritarian constitutions in general. These constitutions have different provisions and statements, each of which perform different functions. Constitutional rules and institutions (especially the structural ones) may be more instrumental, while constitutional preambles and principles may be more expressive. In this regard, while the provisions on the state structure in the constitutions in Laos and Vietnam are employed for instrumental purposes, their preambles and constitutional principles may express values shared by the communities, including the one associated with ethnic plurality. However, the distinction should not be very strict: constitutional preambles and principles can be used for instrumental purposes, while constitutional structure may be expressive of underlying values.

In engaging with ethnic plurality, the constitutions in Laos and Vietnam are expressive of the reality of ethnic plurality, the principles and aspirations to ethnic unity, equality of ethnic groups, and the state's commitments to promotion of socio-economic development of ethnic groups and protection of their rights.

---

[38] A Terry Rambo, 'Vietnam: Searching for Integration' in Carlo Caldarola (ed), *Religions and Societies, Asia and the Middle East* (Mouton 1982) 407.

[39] For more details about the four instrumental functions (namely operating manuals, billboards, blueprints, and window dressing) of authoritarian constitutions, see Tom Ginsburg and Alberto Simpser, 'Introduction: Constitutions in Authoritarian Regimes' in Tom Ginsburg and Alberto Simpser (eds), *Constitutions in Authoritarian Regimes* (CUP 2015) 2

The expressive function stems from the following factors. First, as these documents were drafted in plural societies, they cannot simply ignore the plurality of values, ideas, and interests. In addition, the constitutions are subjected to different influences by different actors of the society: political elite, civil society and ethnic groups. Consequently, constitutions are expressive of different ideas and values, including the ones associated with ethnic plurality.

The expression of ethnic plurality consolidates the sociological foundation of the constitutions. This expression enables the Constitution to be regarded as socially acceptable, and fortifies especially the recognition of ethnic groups. This sociological constitutional legitimacy is not necessarily associated with the material interests of political elites.

B. Form

The forms for constitutional expression of ethnic plurality in Laos and Vietnam include: (1) the constitutional preamble; (2) constituent constitutional principles; (3) directive constitutional principles; (4) constitutional rights; and (5) the constitutional structure.

i. Constituent Preamble

Both constitutions of Laos and Vietnam have a preamble. Like many constitutions around the world, preambles are the ideal place to express national history, and identity, and aspirational goals. They are also the platform to express values, principles, and aspirations associated with ethnic plurality.

The first sentence of the Lao Constitution's preamble reads: 'The multi-ethnic Lao people have existed and developed on this beloved land for thousands of years.'[40] The 'multi-ethnic Lao people' denotes the idea of 'unity in diversity.'[41] The idea is that the Lao people are a united community of diverse ethnic groups. The tradition of 'multi-ethnic Lao people' is said to have emerged with the reign of Chao Fa Ngum, who was founder of the united Lane Xang Kingdom.[42] Therefore, the constitutional preamble further underlines this idea: 'Starting from the middle of the 14th century, during the time of Chao Fa Ngum, our ancestors founded the unified Lane Xang country and built it into a prosperous land.'[43] This expresses the regime's central constitutional aspiration towards 'unity'. Indeed, the preamble explicitly establishes 'unity' as one of 'the long-standing aspirations and strong determination of the national community.'[44]

---

[40] Constitution of The Lao People's Democratic Republic (2015) Preamble.
[41] Vatthana Pholsena, *Post-war Laos: The Politics of Culture, History, and Identity* (Institute of Southeast Asian Studies; NIAS Press; Silkworm Books 2006) 59.
[42] ibid.
[43] Constitution of The Lao People's Democratic Republic (2015) Preamble.
[44] ibid.

212 *Bui Ngoc Son*

Vietnam has a similar aspiration to achieve the constitutional unity of one people: 'Throughout their millennia-old history, the Vietnamese People, working diligently and creatively and fighting courageously to build and defend their country, have forged a tradition of patriotism, solidarity, humanity, justice, resilience and indomitableness, and have created the civilisation and culture of Vietnam.'[45] The statement defines the Vietnamese people as one people sharing a history, fundamental values, and characters.

ii. Constituent Constitutional Principles

The second form for constitutional expression refers to constituent constitutional principles. The first chapter of both constitutions is titled 'political regime'. These chapters include foundational principles defining the nature of constitutional system, which are also expressive of ethnic plurality.

To begin with, these chapters include provisions expressive of the principle of unity. Article 1 of the Lao Constitution defines that the Lao People's Democratic Republic is 'a unified country belonging to all multi-ethnic people and is indivisible.'[46] Article 1 of the Vietnamese Constitution also defines the Socialist Republic of Vietnam as 'an independent, sovereign and united country'.[47] The idea of a 'united country' also implies the unity of ethnic groups. In other words, ethnic unity is a constituent feature of the regime.

The first two chapters also include provisions expressive of sovereignty of a single people. Article 2 of the Lao Constitution provides that all powers belong to the people and are exercised for 'the interests of the multi-ethnic people.'[48] Article 3 ensures 'the rights of the multi-ethnic people to be the masters of the country.'[49] In the same vein, article 2 of the Vietnamese Constitution defines the people as 'the masters of the Socialist Republic of Vietnam State.'[50] That means, despite ethnic plurality, power is not divided among ethnic groups but is practised by a single unified people.

Apart from expressing unity and sovereignty, the two chapters are also expressive of the state's commitments to the promotion of ethnic unity and fundamental principles guiding the state policy regarding ethnic groups. To illustrate, article 8 of the Lao Constitution details the state's commitment to promotion of unity among ethnic groups, protection of their rights, and prohibition of ethnical discrimination, and support of the socio-economic development of all ethnic groups:

> The State pursues the policy of promoting unity and equality among all ethnic groups. All ethnic groups have the right to protect, preserve and promote the fine customs and

---

[45] Constitution of the Socialist Republic of Vietnam (2013) Preamble.
[46] Constitution of The Lao People's Democratic Republic (2015) art 1.
[47] Constitution of the Socialist Republic of Vietnam (2013) art 1.
[48] Constitution of The Lao People's Democratic Republic (2015) art 2.
[49] ibid art 3.
[50] Constitution of the Socialist Republic of Vietnam (2013) art 2.

cultures of their own tribes and of the nation. All acts creating division and discrimination among ethnic groups are prohibited. The State implements every measure to gradually develop and upgrade the socio-economic levels of all ethnic groups.[51]

Similarly, article 5 of the Vietnamese Constitution comprehensively expresses the regime's commitment to ethnic unity and fundamental principles guiding the state policy regarding ethnic groups:

1. The Socialist Republic of Vietnam is a unified nation of all ethnicities living together in the country of Vietnam.
2. All the ethnicities are equal and unite with, respect and assist one another for mutual development; all acts of discrimination against and division of the ethnicities are prohibited.
3. The national language is Vietnamese. Every ethnic group has the right to use its own spoken and written language to preserve its own identity and to promote its fine customs, practices, traditions and culture.
4. The State shall implement a policy of comprehensive development and create the conditions for the minority ethnicities to draw upon/further their internal strengths and develop together with the country.[52]

The fact that the above two provisions are incorporated into the first chapters under the title of 'political regime' indicates that these provisions express constitutional principles constituent to the nature of the polity. The promotion of ethnic unity, protection of the rights of ethnic groups, prohibition of ethnic discrimination, and support for the socio-economic development of ethnic groups are fundamental, aspirational goals that both define and direct the regime's developmental path and state's specific policy.

One distinctive feature of the constitutional system in Laos and Vietnam is the existence of mass organisations integral to this system, whose roles are defined in the constitutions. These mass bodies are also the socio-political platforms for the promotion of the unity of ethnic groups. In Laos, they include: The Lao Front for National Construction, the Lao Federation of Trade Unions, the Lao People's Revolutionary Youth Union, the Lao Women's Union and other social organisations, constitutionally defined as 'the organs to unite and mobilize all strata of the multi-ethnic people to take part in the tasks of protection and construction of the country; to develop the right of self-determination of the people and to protect the legitimate rights and interests of members of their respective organizations.'[53]

Vietnam has similar bodies. They include the Vietnam Fatherland Front and its major members, namely the Trade Union of Vietnam, the Vietnam Peasants' Association, the Ho Chi Minh Communist Youth Union, the Vietnam Women's Union and the Vietnam War Veterans' Association. The Front is constitutionally defined as 'a political alliance and a voluntary union of the political organisation,

---

[51] ibid art 8.
[52] Constitution of the Socialist Republic of Vietnam (2013) art 5.
[53] Constitution of The Lao People's Democratic Republic (2015) art 7.

socio-political organisations and social organisations, and prominent individuals representing their class, social strata, ethnicity or religion and overseas Vietnamese.'[54] The Constitution defines the latter bodies as the 'socio-political organisations established on a voluntary basis to represent and protect the rights and lawful and legitimate interests of their members; and together with other member organisations of the Vietnam Fatherland Front coordinate and unify action within the Front.'[55] These mass organisations are not ethnic-based bodies but are instrumental to ethnic unity particularly and national unity in general.

iii. Directive Constitutional Principles

The third form of constitutional expression are the directive constitutional principles. The constitutions of Laos and Vietnam have separate chapters which stipulate principles guiding the state's socio-economic policy. These principles also express fundamental commitments that guide the state's policy pertaining ethnic plurality. Like constituent principles, these principles guide the state's policy. However, the directive principles focus on guiding the state's specific actions rather defining the state nature.

Article 22 of the Lao Constitution provides that: 'The State and society attend to developing high quality national education, to create opportunities and [favourable] conditions in education for all people throughout the country, especially people in remote areas, ethnic groups, women, disadvantaged children and disable people.'[56] Article 23 expresses the state's commitment to the promotion of both 'fine tradition of the country and its ethnic people' and 'selected progressive cultures from around the world.'[57] The Constitution of Vietnam also expresses the state's commitments and directive of the state's policy, to address ethnic plurality. To illustrate, article 58 indicates the state's commitment to 'exercise a priority policy of health care for highlanders, national minorities, islanders, and people living in extremely difficult economic and social conditions.'[58] Article 26 is committed to prioritising 'the educational development in mountainous and island areas, regions inhabited by ethnic minority people and regions encountering exceptional difficulties.'[59]

iv. The Bill of Rights

The fourth form of constitutional expression is the bill of rights. The Constitutions of Laos and Vietnam have separate chapters on fundamental rights. The bills

---

[54] Constitution of the Socialist Republic of Vietnam (2013) art 9.
[55] ibid.
[56] Constitution of The Lao People's Democratic Republic (2015) art 22.
[57] ibid art 23.
[58] Constitution of the Socialist Republic of Vietnam (2013) art 58.
[59] ibid art 26.

of rights do not stipulate specific rights of ethnic groups, but are applied nationwide and exclusively to individuals. Both Constitutions underline the principle of citizen equality under the law. To illustrate, the Lao Constitution provides that: 'Lao citizens are all equal before the law irrespective of their gender, social status, education, beliefs and ethnic groups.'[60] In the same vein, the Vietnamese charter states: '1. All people are equal before law. 2. No one is subject to discriminatory treatment in political, civil, economic, cultural or social life.'[61] The Vietnamese bill of rights has a provision, which is specifically expressive of ethnic plurality: 'A citizen has the right to determine his or her ethnicity, use his or her mother tongue and choose his or her language of communication.'[62]

Although these provisions are presented in the form of rights provisions, they are not significantly different from provisions on directive principles. The rights provisions are not meant to establish legal restraints on state power, but they are expressive of principles positively guiding the state's actions. To illustrate, the statement on equality of ethnic groups empowers the state to make policy to promote this equality. In this sense, these provisions are directive to the state's policy.

v. Constitutional Structure

Several provisions in the Constitutions of Laos and Vietnam on the state structure are not merely designed to regulate and structure state power. They are also expressive of fundamental values and principles that the regime is committed to, including those pertaining ethnic plurality.

To illustrate, the Constitution of Laos defines the unicameral National Assembly as 'the representative of the rights, powers and interests of the multi-ethnic people.'[63] The Vietnamese Constitution also defines the National Assembly as 'the highest representative body of the People.'[64] These provisions are expressive of the commitment to a single people represented by a popularly elected legislature.

The legislatures in both Laos and Vietnam include a specific body responsible for ethnic affairs. The Lao Constitution is silent about this body; instead, the body known as the Ethnic Affairs Committee is created according to the Law on the National Assembly.[65] In Vietnam, a body called the Ethnic Council possesses constitutional status. The Constitution provides for fundamental principles about the structure and authority of this body and its relationship with other state institutions, stating that:

1. The Ethnic Council is composed of the Chairperson, Vice Chairpersons and members. The Chairperson of the Ethnic Council shall be elected by the National

---

[60] Constitution of The Lao People's Democratic Republic (2015) art 35.
[61] Constitution of the Socialist Republic of Vietnam (2013) art 16.
[62] ibid art 42.
[63] ibid art 52.
[64] ibid art 69.
[65] Law on the National Assembly (Laos) (2006) art 31.

216   *Bui Ngoc Son*

> Assembly; Vice Chairpersons and members of the Ethnic Council shall be approved by the Standing Committee of the National Assembly.
> 2. The Ethnic Council shall study and make proposals on ethnic issues to the National Assembly; exercise the power of overseeing the implementation of policies on ethnic groups, programs and plans for socio-economic development in mountainous and ethnic minority areas.
> 3. The Chairperson of the Ethnic Council may be invited to attend Government meetings to discuss the implementation of policies on ethnic groups. The Government shall consult the Ethnic Council before promulgating regulations on the implementation of policies on ethnic groups.[66]

The Ethnic Council is not designed to regulate ethnic divisions but is an institutional embodiment of the constitutional commitments to ethnic unity and promotion of the socio-economic development of the minority ethnic groups.

C. Effects

In Laos, several policies introduced to implement the provisions regarding ethnic plurality in the previous constitution of 1991 still remains in force after the enactment of the new 2015 Constitution. For example, the *1992 Resolution of the Party Central Organization Concerning Ethnic Minority Affairs in the New Era*, introduces these general policies concerning ethnic minorities which require the government to take positive actions to:

> build national sentiment (national identity); realize equality between ethnic minorities; increasing the level of solidarity among ethnic minorities as members of the greater Lao family; resolve problems of inflexible and vengeful thinking, as well as economic and cultural inequality; improve the living conditions of the ethnic minorities step by step; expand, to the greatest extent possible, the good and beautiful heritage and ethnic identity of each group as well as their capacity to participate in the affairs of the nation.[67]

In addition to the Party policy, the eighth Five-year National Socio-economic Development Plan (2016–2020) adopted by eighth National Assembly's Inaugural Session on 20–23 April 2016 provides for general policies of socio-economic development,[68] including the ones pertaining ethnic groups, which reflects the constitutional provisions expressive of ethnic plurality. To illustrate, one of the main outcomes that the Development Plan aims to achieve is that 'poverty in all ethnic groups is reduced, all ethnic groups and both genders have access to quality

---

[66] Constitution of the Socialist Republic of Vietnam (2013) art 75.
[67] Ministry of Health of the Lao People's Democratic Republic, 'Ethnic Group Development Plan for Health Governance and Nutrition Development Project Based on Health Services Improvement Project Ethnic Group Development Plan' (Ministry of Health 2015) 8.
[68] '8th Five-year National Socio-economic Development Plan (2016–2020)' (Officially approved at the 8th National Assembly's Inaugural Session, Vientiane, Laos, 20–23 April 2016).

education and health services.'[69] To achieve this outcome, the Plan provides for this direction:

> To solve the poverty of the population and ethnic minorities across the country by enhancing robust and firm political roots and carry out comprehensive rural development linked to the building of developed villages according to the 4 statements and 4 targets: economic development is regarded as the central task, along with sociocultural development and environmental protection, to safeguard the national defence and security and to maintain political stability; agglomerate big villages into small towns in rural areas linked to production facilities in the local regions and territories; resettle the displaced people by allocating new places to stay and permanent professions in a priority manner; create rural employment and income-generating activities for poor and vulnerable rural households through an integrated approach; continue putting e orts into clearing the UXOs from development territories, tourist sites, and agricultural production, livestock raising and residential areas. In parallel, pay attention to carrying out treatment, health rehabilitation and assistance for UXO victims.[70]

In accordance with this direction, the Plan proposes implementing these policies and legal instruments, which require the government to:

1. Improve and set investment policies serving the areas of production, tourist service, education and health in the remote rural areas to clarify them in order to attract more private investments, aiming to create employment and further income generation for the people by focusing on the investments that employ rural labour, as in the activities of the agriculture and forestry sector, mining, power and processing industries, etc. In parallel, develop professional training in various special ties to upgrade the labour skills and expertise of the rural people to reduce the ow of labour into cities and spread more development out to rural areas.
2. Issue appropriate policies for customs and tax collection, credit issuance, site resources utilisation and asset capitalisation; objectively promote the entrepreneurs and others in the dangerous, rural, remote and poor areas.
3. Improve and issue regulations at the lowest administrative level of local areas to render them consistent with actual conditions, deriving them from general regulation and principle.
4. Strengthen the sectors' responsibility and ownership in the detailed implementation of sector policies and concentrate on objectively directing and supervising the staff and funds used in the actual operation in the local areas.
5. Issue policies that promote the staff at central, provincial and district levels who carry out their old mission in remote and dangerous areas, consistent with the actual situation and fitting their capacities.
6. Formulate a national strategy on rural employment that defines strategies, methodology and projects for promoting rural employment and income generation.

[69] ibid 89.
[70] ibid 124–25.

218 Bui Ngoc Son

7. Increase coordination within the government organisations and involve civil society in implementing the UXO clearance, as civil society plays a very critical role in supporting the government.[71]

In Vietnam, ethnic diversity is reflected in the components of the National Assembly. For example, in the fourteenth term of the National Assembly following the election in June 2016, 85 deputies among 496 National Assembly came from minority groups.[72] The ministerial body inside the government is called Committee for Ethnic Minority Affairs.[73] The departments of ethnic minority affairs are also created in the local government where the presence of the minority groups is significant. This institutional arrangement is the embodiment of the constitutional commitments to the promotion of socio-economic development of ethnic groups. These institutions regulating ethnic affairs should be distinguished from constitutional design to regulate ethnic plurality. The former is the managing function of the administrative system, while the latter is the political function of the constitution. Administrative regulation of ethnic affairs is the quotidian function of administrative bodies, while constitutional regulation of ethnic affairs arises when ethnic plurality translates into serious political conflicts.

In addition to institutional embodiment, after the adoption of Vietnam's 2013 Constitution, the provisions expressive of ethnic plurality are subjected to political and scholarly discussions.[74] The discussions focus on explaining the meaning of the provisions and related laws and policies which have been previously enacted and remain in force. The legislations related to the protection of the rights of the ethnic groups include: Law on Vietnamese Nationality, Law on Education, Law on Administrative Procedure, Civil Code, Criminal Code, Criminal Procedure Code, Law on Elections.[75] The government also issued many policies regulations

[71] ibid 127.
[72] Hoàng Duân '86/496 đại biểu Quốc hội khóa 14 là người dân tộc thiểu số,' (Công Thương, 15 June 2016) http://congthuong.vn/86496-dai-bieu-quoc-hoi-khoa-14-la-nguoi-dan-toc-thieu-so.html accessed 21 September 2018.
[73] 'Committee for Ethnic Minority Affairs' <www.cema.gov.vn/home.htm> accessed 21 September 2018.
[74] Tòng Thị Phóng, 'Hiến pháp và thực hiện chính sách dân tộc của Đảng và Nhà nước' ['The Constitution and the Implementation of the Party and State's Policy in Ethnic Groups] (Nhân Dân, 21 January 2014) www.nhandan.com.vn/chinhtri/tuyentruyenhienphap/item/22196802-hien-phap-va-thuc-hien-chinh-sach-dan-toc-cua-dang-va-nha-nuoc.html accessed 21 September 2018; Phạm Hồng Thuý, 'Những điểm mới của Hiến pháp nước Cộng hòa XHCN Việt Nam về lĩnh vực dân tộc, công tác dân tộc' [New Points in the Constitution of The Socialist Republic of Vietnam Related in Ethnic Affairs'] (Uỷ ban Dân tộc [CEMA], 24 April 2014) http://cema.gov.vn/2014/04/24/2aa1978043c02299b3b0bb79efc62112-cema.htm accessed 21 September 2018; Đặng Văn Hường, 'Vấn đề dân tộc trong Hiến pháp năm 2013' ['Ethnic Issues in the 2013 Constitution'] (Tạp chí Quốc Phòng Toàn dân, 16 June 2014) http://tapchiqptd.vn/vi/tuyen-truyen-ve-thuc-hien-hien-phap/van-de-dan-toc-trong-hien-phap-nam-2013/5763.html accessed 21 September 2018; Thiên Phương, 'Quyền của các dân tộc thiểu số ở Việt Nam thể hiện trong Hiến pháp sửa đổi' ['The Rights of Minority Ethnic Groups in Vietnam in the Amended Constitution'] (Nhân dân, 01 August 2014) www.nhandan.com.vn/chinhtri/tuyentruyenhienphap/item/22084802-quyen-cua-cac-dan-toc-thieu-so-o-viet-nam-the-hien-trong-hien-phap-sua-doi.html accessed 21 September 2018.
[75] Lừ Văn Tuyên, 'Quyền của các dân tộc thiểu số trong pháp luật quốc tế và pháp luật Việt Nam,' ['The Rights of Minority Ethnic Groups in International Law and Vietnamese Law'] (Lý Luận Chính

aimed to promote the socio-economic developments of the minority ethnic groups. These include, among many others, Decision to Approve The Program On Socio- Economic Development In Mountainous, Deep-Lying And Remote Communes With Special Difficulties (1998); Decree on Commercial Development in Mountainous and Island Areas and Areas of Minority Ethnic Groups (1998); Decree on Ethnic Affairs aiming to Ensure and Promote Equality, Unity, Mutual Helps in Development, Respects and Preservation of Cultural Identity of Ethnic Groups (2011).[76]

A related aspect is that ethnic plurality is the source of legal pluralism. Vietnam is replete with indigenous laws of minority groups in the Western Highlands and Northwest of Vietnam, called Hịt khỏng (Thái), Phat kđi (Êđê), Phat Ktuôi (M'nông), and N'ri (Mạ).[77] The Constitution does not mention the possible practice of indigenous law. However, the Civil Code recognises the applications of customary law, which is defined as 'rules of conduct obvious to define rights and obligations of persons in specific civil relations, forming and repeating in a long time, recognized and applying generally in a region, race, or a community or a field of civil.'[78] That allows the practice of legal pluralism.[79]

One may argue that expressive constitutional provisions do not have any binding legal effect since they are not judicially enforceable. However, judicial constitutionalism is not the only way to conceptualise constitutionalism. Expressive constitutional provisions may inform political actions and discourse. In Laos and Vietnam, courts do not have power to conduct judicial review such that constitutional provisions expressive of ethnic plurality are not enforced in judicial platform. This, however, does not mean that these provisions are meaningless. They inform legislations, party policies, and government policies which are introduced to implement constitutional commitments to ethnic unity and promotion of socio-economic developments of minority ethnic groups. This practice is connected to the political form of constitutionalism. More generally, it can be said that expressive constitutional provisions are more likely to be implemented by political constitutionalism than judicial constitutionalism.

The discussion of the effects of constitutional provisions expressive of ethnic plurality here is limited to the laws and policies introduced to implement the constitutional provisions. The actual effect of these laws and these policies requires further empirical investigation.

---

trị, 22 July 2016) http://lyluanchinhtri.vn/home/index.php/anh-chinh/item/1560-quyen-cua-cac-dan-toc-thieu-so-trong-phap-luat-quoc-te-va-phap-luat-viet-nam.html accessed 21 September 2018.

[76] ibid.

[77] See generally, Ngô Đức Thịnh, *Luật Tục Trong Đời Sống Các Tộc Người Ở Việt Nam [Customary Law in The Lives of Ethnic Groups in Vietnam]* (Judicial Publishing House 2010).

[78] Civil Code (2015) (Vietnam) art 5.

[79] For more details, see David Lempert, 'Ethnic Communities and Legal Pluralism: The Politics of Legal Argument in Market-Oriented Communist Vietnam' (2001) 25 Legal Studies Forum 539.

V. Conclusion: The Pluralist Constitutions

I conclude this chapter with a reflection on whether we can think about the constitutions in Laos and Vietnam as pluralist constitutions. A pluralist Constitution is one that is committed to different values, principles, and goals. In this sense, the constitutions of the two countries can be understood as pluralist constitutions.

On one hand, they are instrumental to realising the Communist party's socialist aspirations, principles, and goals. On the other hand, the constitutions are expressive of the reality, values, aspirations, and principles associated with ethnic plurality, such as unity, the commitments to socio-economic developments of ethnic groups and the protection of their rights. This constitutional expression is determined by the reality of ethnic plurality and reflects the concerns of ethnic groups, and is not necessarily associated with the instrumental concerns of political elite. This suggests that constitutions are committed to different values, principles, and goals, which renders them pluralist documents.

That said, there is a balance between the instrumental concerns and the expressive values in the constitutions. Instrumental concerns remain hegemonic while expressive values still have room in a plural constitutional platform. Constitutional expressivism captures the partial expressive function of the constitutions in Laos and Vietnam.

Bibliography

—— '8th Five-year National Socio-economic Development Plan (2016–2020)' (Officially approved at the 8th National Assembly's Inaugural Session, Vientiane, Laos, 20–23 April 2016).
—— 'Committee for Ethnic Minority Affairs' <www.cema.gov.vn/home.htm> accessed 21 September 2018.
—— Constitution of The Lao People's Democratic Republic (2015).
—— Constitution of the Socialist Republic of Vietnam (2013).
—— Law on the National Assembly (Laos) (2006).
—— 'List of Vietnamese ethnic groups' (Viet Nam Government Portal) www.chinhphu.vn/portal/page/portal/English/TheSocialistRepublicOfVietnam/AboutVietnam/AboutVietnamDetail?categoryId=10000103&articleId=10002652 accessed 21 September 2018.
—— 'Minorities in Laos' (Facts and Details) http://factsanddetails.com/southeast-asia/Laos/sub5_3c/entry-2962.html accessed 21 September 2018.
Bâli A Ü and Lerner H (eds), *Constitution Writing, Religion and Democracy* (CUP 2017).
Brocheux P and Hémery D, *Indochina: An Ambiguous Colonization, 1858–1954* (Dill-Klein LL, Jennings E, Taylor N and Tousignant N trs, University of California Press 2009).

Bui N S, *Confucian Constitutionalism in East Asia* (Routledge 2016), ch 2.

Sunstein C R, 'On the Expressive Function of Law' (1996) 144 University of Pennsylvania Law Review 2021.

Sujit Choudhry, 'Bridging Comparative Politics and Comparative Constitutional Law: Constitutional Design in Divided Societies' in Choudhry S (ed), *Constitutional Design for Divided Societies: Integration or Accommodation?* (OUP 2008) 5.

Đặng Văn Hường, 'Vấn đề dân tộc trong Hiến pháp năm 2013' ['Ethnic Issues in the 2013 Constitution'] (Tạp chí Quốc Phòng Toàn dân, 16 June 2014) <http://tapchiqptd.vn/vi/tuyen-truyen-ve-thuc-hien-hien-phap/van-de-dan-toc-trong-hien-phap-nam-2013/5763.html> accessed 21 September 2018.

Duiker W J, *Vietnam: Revolution in Transition* (WestView Press 1995).

Galligan D and Versteeg M, 'Theoretical Perspectives On The Social And Political Foundations of Constitutions' in Galligan D J and Versteeg M (eds), *Social And Political Foundations Of Constitutions* (CUP 2015),

Ginsburg T and Simpser A, 'Introduction: Constitutions in Authoritarian Regimes' in Ginsburg T and Simpser A (eds), *Constitutions in Authoritarian Regimes* (CUP 2015).

Hoàng Duân '86/496 đại biểu Quốc hội khóa 14 là người dân tộc thiểu số,' (Công Thương, 15 June 2016) http://congthuong.vn/86496-dai-bieu-quoc-hoi-khoa-14-la-nguoi-dan-toc-thieu-so.html accessed 21 September 2018.

Hegel G W F, *Outlines of the Philosophy of Right* (Knox T M tr, Hougate H ed, OUP 2008).

Jackson V, 'Comparative Constitutional Law: Methodologies' in Rosenfeld M and Sajó A (eds), *The Oxford Handbook Of Comparative Constitutional Law* (OUP 2012).

Jacobsohn G, *Constitutional Identity* (Harvard University Press 2010).

King E M and van de Walle D, 'Laos' in Hall G H and Patrinos H A (eds)., *Indigenous Peoples, Poverty, And Development* (CUP 2012).

King J, 'Constitutions as Mission Statements' in Galligan D J and Versteeg M (eds), *Social And Political Foundations of Constitutions* (CUP 2015).

Lao Statistics Bureau, 'Results of Population and Housing Census 2015' (21 October 2016) 21 http://lao.unfpa.org/en/publications/results-population-and-housing-census-2015-english-version accessed 21 September 2018.

Leather G, 'Laos: A Constitution in Search of Constitutionalism', in Hill C and Menzel J (eds), *Constitutionalism in Southeast Asia, Vol. 2 – Reports on National Constitutions* (Konrad-Adenauer-Stiftung 2008).

Lempert D, 'Ethnic Communities and Legal Pluralism: The Politics of Legal Argument in Market-Oriented Communist Vietnam,' (2001) 25 Legal Studies Forum 539.

Lừ Văn Tuyên, 'Quyền của các dân tộc thiểu số trong pháp luật quốc tế và pháp luật Việt Nam,' ['The Rights of Minority Ethnic Groups in International Law and Vietnamese Law'] (Lý Luận Chính trị, 22 July 2016) http://lyluanchinhtri.

vn/home/index.php/anh-chinh/item/1560-quyen-cua-cac-dan-toc-thieu-so-trong-phap-luat-quoc-te-va-phap-luat-viet-nam.html accessed 21 September 2018.

Ministry of Health of the Lao People's Democratic Republic, 'Ethnic Group Development Plan for Health Governance and Nutrition Development Project Based on Health Services Improvement Project Ethnic Group Development Plan' (Ministry of Health 2015) 8.

Ngô Đức Thịnh, *Luật Tục Trong Đời Sống Các Tộc Người Ở Việt Nam [Customary Law in The Lives of Ethnic Groups in Vietnam]* (Judicial Publishing House 2010).

Phạm Hồng Thuý, 'Những điểm mới của Hiến pháp nước Cộng hòa XHCN Việt Nam về lĩnh vực dân tộc, công tác dân tộc' [New Points in the Constitution of The Socialist Republic of Vietnam Related in Ethnic Affairs'] (Uỷ ban Dân tộc [CEMA], 24 April 2014) http://cema.gov.vn/2014/04/24/2aa1978043c02299b3b0bb79efc62112-cema.htm accessed 21 September 2018.

Pholsen V, *Post-war Laos: The Politics of Culture, History, and Identity* (Institute of Southeast Asian Studies; NIAS Press; Silkworm Books 2006).

Rambo A T, 'Vietnam: Searching for Integration' in Caldarola C (ed), *Religions and Societies, Asia and the Middle East* (Mouton 1982).

Saunders C, 'Towards a Global Constitutional Gene Pool' (2009) 4(3) National Taiwan University Law Review 12.

Salter M and Shaw J J A, 'Towards a Critical Theory of Constitutional Law: Hegel's Contribution' (1994) 21 (4) Journal of Law and Society 464.

Sidel M, *The Constitution of Vietnam* (Hart Publishing 2009).

Stremler M and Voermans W, *Constitutional Preambles: A Comparative Analysis* (Edward Elgar Publishing 2017).

Stuart-Fox M, *Laos: Politics, Economics, and Society* (Lynne Rienner Publishers 1986).

—— *Buddhist Kingdom, Marxist State: The Making of Modern Laos* (Bangkok, Cheney: White Lotus 1996).

—— *A History of Laos* (CUP 1997) ch 2.

—— 'Politics and Reforms in the Lao People's Democratic Republic,' *Murdoch University's Asia Research Centre, Working Paper No. 126* (November 2005) 3.

—— *The Lao Kingdom of Lan Xang: Rise and Decline* (Bangkok, Thailand, White Lotus Press 1998).

Taylor K W, *The Birth of Vietnam* (University of California Press 1976).

Thiên Phương, 'Quyền của các dân tộc thiểu số ở Việt Nam thể hiện trong Hiến pháp sửa đổi' ['The Rights of Minority Ethnic Groups in Vietnam in the Amended Constitution'] (Nhân dân, 01 August 2014) <www.nhandan.com.vn/chinhtri/tuyentruyenhienphap/item/22084802-quyen-cua-cac-dan-toc-thieu-so-o-viet-nam-the-hien-trong-hien-phap-sua-doi.html> accessed 21 September 2018.

Tòng Thị Phóng, "Hiến pháp và thực hiện chính sách dân tộc của Đảng và Nhà nước" ['The Constitution and the Implementation of the Party and State's

Policy in Ethnic Groups] (Nhân Dân 21 January 2014) www.nhandan.com.vn/chinhtri/tuyentruyenhienphap/item/22196802-hien-phap-va-thuc-hien-chinh-sach-dan-toc-cua-dang-va-nha-nuoc.html accessed 21 September 2018

Tushnet M, 'The Possibilities of Comparative Constitutional Law' (1999) 108 Yale Law Journal 1269.

—— 'Authoritarian Constitutionalism' (2015) 100(2) Cornell Law Review 391.

Weis L K, 'Constitutional Directive Principles' (2017) 37(4) Oxford Journal of Legal Studies 916.

9

Volcanic Constitution: How is Plurality Turning Against Constitutionalism in Thailand?

APINOP ATIPIBOONSIN

I. Introduction

Late 2013 was the middle of the political crisis that had been looming since Yingluck Shinnawatra had risen through a 50-day election campaign from a sister of the ex-Prime Minister Thanksin Shinnawatra to the Prime Minister of Thailand. It was also when the Constitutional Court considered a draft amendment of the Thai Constitution,[1] which would allow relatives of the Representatives to become Senators and revert the Senate into a fully elected chamber.[2] The Court ultimately held that the proposed amendment was unconstitutional on both procedural and substantive grounds.[3] This was especially because a fully-elected senate would destroy the bicameral system, and become a prohibited exercise of rights or liberties to overthrow the democratic regime under the Constitution.[4]

How could an elected Senate be considered as backward as well as undemocratic and unconstitutional? The answer belies the Court's rationale based on the distrust of Thai politicians and the dilution of bicameralism,[5] and can instead be found within the complicated and conflicting versions of constitutional democracy in Thailand.

Thai constitutional law, coinciding with those in emerging constitutional regimes worldwide, does not simply fall into a category of normative constitutions. Its text and practice do not constantly align, and constitutionalism as a

---

[1] Constitution of the Kingdom of Thailand 2007 ch VI, Pt III.
[2] As was the case in the previous Constitution of the Kingdom of Thailand BE 2540 (1997), 11 October 1997.
[3] Constitutional Court Decision No. 15–18/2556 (20 November 2013).
[4] Constitution of the Kingdom of Thailand BE 2550 (2007) Art 68.
[5] As noted in the decision in *supra* note 3, '[t]he modification of the senatorial sources and qualifications which bring the Senators into close relations with the political sectors would considerably impair the principles of check and balance under the bicameral system, as it would allow the political sectors to absolutely overshadow the NA without any check and balance.'

value is not evenly upheld among the people.[6] As discussed by a prominent Thai constitutional scholars, Thailand has struggled to close the gap between constitutional principles, its aims to make its Constitution respectable for the people, and political reality.[7] Now, after the period of 20 years and rigorous state-sponsored research by public law scholars on the constitutional problems and solutions of Thai politics,[8] the formal and doctrinal approach applied by the original constitutional drafters should be challenged with a different take on Thai constitutions.

The term *'volcanic constitution'* is employed here to reflect the co-existence of – and thus the contest among – different layers of constitutional authorities of equal weight. Much like a volcanic eruption where the pressure accumulated through various molten rocks erupts through a vent, such a Constitution is tested each day from various pluralities in the system. If this tension continues unabated, it would lead to the constitutional system reaching its breaking point or falling apart. This is precisely the case in Thailand: resistance against having constitutionalism as its core value and ideology lets non-constitutional and non-democratic norms co-exist under and over conventional constitutional law. Ultimately, when conflicts cannot be contained in the constitution, society resorts to the extra-constitutional measures such as coup d'état and abrogation of the Constitution. As long as there is a strong challenge from other sets of antagonistic ideas and values, the Constitution cannot grow into a stable system.

It is poignant to consider a quote from the latest coup leader as he defends his authoritarian regime. Prime Minister Prayuth Chan-O-Cha sheds light on the uniqueness of the Thai constitution against the monistic understanding of constitutionalism:

> Please tell the United States that in tailoring you cannot just cut one dress and expect it to fit all. There must be many sizes for each to fit. That is why a tailor is needed. You cannot tailor one dress and expect the whole world to wear it. Each nation has its own problems that differ …[9]

The turbulent history of the Thai Constitution, especially since the polarisation following the 1997 Constitution, showcases the clash between multiple fundamental ideas about how Thailand should govern itself. The Thai experience cannot be relegated as a freak accident particular to one country; this analysis resonates with

---

[6] Karl Loewenstein, *Political Power and the Governmental Process* (University of Chicago 1957) 147ff.

[7] 'Professor Likhit Theerawin on the Thai Constitution: Constitution Must be Respected and Implemented' (*Thai PBS News*, 21 November 2016) https://news.thaipbs.or.th/content/257946> accessed 21 September 2018.

[8] Somchai Preechasinlapakun, '20 Years of the 1997 Constitution: Reform of Thai Politics in the enforcement of Public Law Enforcement' (*The 101*, 16 March 2017) www.the101.world/20-year-constitution-2540/ accessed 21 September 2018.

[9] 'US must not impose its idea of democracy: PM' (*The Nation*, 14 March 2015) www.nationmultimedia.com/politics/US-must-not-impose-its-idea-of-democracy-PM-30256005.html accessed 21 September 2018.

the growing polarisation and hostility against constitutional democracy worldwide. Thailand is special only insofar as it has a history and tendency to allow constitutional breakdown with relative ease compared to many new democracies.

This chapter thus serves as an attempt to investigate the presence of plurality which affects the reality of Thai constitutional law. Part II introduces the facts of plurality in Thailand and its connection with the law. Part III then provides a brief history of Thai constitutional law, which furnishes the political and legal background necessary for readers to understand the long and complicated story leading to the current 2017 Constitution. Part IV further examines pluralism in various areas of Thai constitutional law – from the structure of constitutional government, to the regime of a constitutional bill of rights. Thereafter, the cases, events, and their constitutional contexts will be cumulatively analysed in Part V. Here, a new perspective on how the current 2017 Constitution responds to Thailand's plurality is proposed.

II. Law and Plurality in Thailand

Thailand is arguably among the countries with spectacular diversity in ethnicities, cultures and languages. Within the Association of Southeast Asian Nations (ASEAN), it is the third largest with a total area of 513,000 km^2, and the fourth most populous with 69 million people. Understandably, Thailand's sheer size contributes to a robust and diverse background. Its position and connectivity with Southeast Asia add significantly to this as the region is also the epicentre of many pluralities.[10]

The population of Thailand may seem ostensibly homogeneous with up to 98.5% in their census registry being of '*Thai ethnicity*'.[11] However, off these official records the Thai consist of a plethora of various ethnicities and origins. At least 13% of them are identified as Thai-Chinese, without considering many more who had previously severed their Chinese roots.[12] Most of them come from a mixture of ethnic groups that can be classified into 62 ethnic groups such as Thai-Malay or Thai-Lao.[13] No official classification of population number by racial or ethnic group exists because these ethnic groups have mixed together through history.[14]

---

[10] RobertoRegala, 'The Stakes of the Free World in Southeast Asia.' (1953) 28(6) Phil LJ 889.
[11] National Statistical Office, 'Thailand: Multiple Indicator Cluster Survey 2012' (UNICEF 2012) 16.
[12] Leo Surayadinata, *The Ethnic Chinese in the ASEAN States: Bibliographical Essays* (Institute of Southeast Asian Studies 1989) 6.
[13] Office of the National Culture Commission, 'Ethnolinguistic Maps of Thailand' www.newmandala.org/wp-content/uploads/2015/05/Thailand-Ethnolinguistic-Maps.pdf accessed 21 September 2018.
[14] UN Committee on the Elimination of Racial Discrimination, 'Reports submitted by States parties under article 9 of the Convention: International Convention on the Elimination of All Forms of Racial Discrimination: 1st to 3rd periodic reports of States parties due in 2008' (Thailand, 5 October 2011) CERD/C/THA/1-3 www.refworld.org/docid/506406442.html accessed 21 September 2018.

It is eminent that Thailand and Thai people have successfully built a pluralistic society – merged in a melting pot 'fuelled by the norms and value' in a way echoing American ideals.[15] Identification as a Thai pivots on one's overall worldview as a Thai national over mere physical appearance.

Likewise, Thailand may boast an impressive percentage of up to 93.5% of its population listed as being Buddhist,[16] but the minimum threshold to identify as a Buddhist varies between individuals. A Thai Buddhist might be in one of the two distinct sects of Theravada Buddhism – namely, *'Dhammayuttika Nikaya'* and *'Maha Nikaya'*. Both are officially recognised and organised by the state. Individuals may even be part of more radical Buddhist groups beyond state recognition.[17]

These distinctions do not pose a serious problem to the harmony of the people like those with a declared national religion.[18] In fact, as long as one does not compete directly with the official monastic vision,[19] he or she will be recognised as a Buddhist just like any another who professes to be part of an official sect.

Interestingly, Islamism is also prominent in Thailand with approximately 5% of the population being a Muslim. Most of them reside in the Southern Thailand.[20] Despite the overwhelming number of Buddhists, the Constitution does not openly declare Buddhism as a national religion and legal scholarship generally promote the doctrine of separation of state and religion.[21] Moreover, according to the constitutional text, 'any person shall enjoy full liberty to profess a religion'.[22] These positive accounts of religious plurality will be discussed how it performs rather different in practice later in Part III.

In effect, Thailand has long been pluralistic under its seemingly monistic façade. Such pluralism is further concealed under the legal and constitutional order. Notwithstanding the impressive account of plurality discussed earlier, there is little evidence of legal recognition. It is one thing to appreciate plurality as an observer like a tourist in a foreign country, but it is an entirely different challenge to make rules and principles in support of these factual phenomenon. The government's promoting of a *'Thai'* identity effectively belittles these pluralities

---

[15] Michel Rosenfeld, 'Constitutional Identity' in Michel Rosenfeld and András Sajó (eds), *The Oxford Handbook of Comparative Constitutional Law* (OUP 2012) 763–64.

[16] See National Statistical Office, 'Table4: Population by religion, sex and area'; 'Census tables – table of statistics from pre-release report and complete report' http://popcensus.nso.go.th/table_stat.php?yr=2553 accessed 21 September 2018.

[17] Frank Reynolds, 'Dhamma in Dispute: The Interactions of Religion and Law in Thailand' (1994) 28(3) Law & Society Review 433, 444–449.

[18] Eg, consider countries with a majority professing Sunni or Shia Islamism like Iran or Iraq.

[19] Reynolds (n 17).

[20] National Statistical Office (n 16).

[21] Arnon Mamout, 'The Separation of State and Church: a Concept in Legal Philosophy and Public Law'; Khemthong Tonsakulrungruang, 'The Relationship between State and Religion' (*Public Law Net*, 23 September 2012) http://public-law.net/publaw/view.aspx?id=1770 accessed 21 September 2018.

[22] See art 37 of the 2007 Constitution, which provides that '[a] person shall enjoy full liberty to profess a religion, a religious denomination or creed, and observe religious precepts or commandments or exercise a form of worship in accordance with his belief; provided that it is not contrary to his civic duties, public order or good morals.'

into nothing but a backdrop to the unity achieved through assimilation and government policy. It is reflective of nationalistic inclinations.[23] Those who are unable to become one with the Thai, such as people from indigenous hill tribes, are deprived of citizenship along with the rights and privileges protected under the Constitution.[24] Those who are not practicing Buddhism find little to no support from the state, contrary to how it allocates resources to support Buddhist organisations.[25]

The mystery here is truly what happened to the pluralities seen in Thailand, and why they are disregarded under the legal system. One approach is to look at how scholarship on historical facts or origins of these pluralities is often neglected or abandoned. Most claims of plurality are but superficial narratives involving only the praising of diversity, but omitting aspects that could be interpreted as inciting conflicts among the people. The abandonment of pluralist scholarship can also be attributed to the administration's effectiveness in fabricating a shared nationhood through various policies and propagandas. Another factor is the versatility of *Thainess* with its indefinite origins and embracing nature. Thai language, Thai-Kadai ethnicity and Thai culture are equally indefinite and unreliable that it is difficult to find a point of departure for a meaningful social or political movement.[26]

Alternatively, it is possible to focus on how the Thai legal system is in favour of the monistic idea of Thainess over pluralism from what the law provides. While there are laws and institutions watching over Thai nationalistic values (such as *lese majeste* law, laws imposing duty to stand before the national anthem and national flag,[27] or the National Office of Buddhism under the command of Prime Minister) there is no such luxury for the engagement with plurality. In a rare event where the state indeed recognises that many other identities exist, it does so minimally and adopts precautions against encouraging unconformity. For instance, while the preservation of Islamic law as personal law for Muslims in the deep south of Thailand is often praised today as an ingenious policy to harmonise the majority Malay Muslims with the Thai Buddhist in the area,[28] this move was actually inspired by the techniques of the colonial British against its native subjects.[29]

---

[23] See the discussion in Pt IV below.
[24] See the details in Network of Indigenous Peoples in Thailand, *The Rights of Indigenous Peoples in Thailand* (Advocacy Factsheet for Thailand's 2nd Cycle Universal Periodic Review, 2016) http://tbinternet.ohchr.org/Treaties/CCPR/Shared%20Documents/THA/INT_CCPR_ICO_THA_23570_E.pdf accessed 21 September 2018.
[25] Mamout (n 21).
[26] See generally in Sujit Wongthes, *A Social and Cultural History of Language and Literature in Thailand* (Matichon 2003).
[27] Surasak Boonruang, 'Legal Aspect of a Duty to Respect the National Anthem' (2017) 46(2) Thammasat University Journal of Law 614.
[28] Just Pornvinsin, *Islamic Law and Heritage Management: A Case Study of Satun Provincial Court* (Bangkok: Institute for Judicial Training 2012) 9–10.
[29] Tamara Loos, 'Competitive Colonialisms: Siam and the Malay Muslim South' in Rachel V Harrison and Peter A Jackson (eds), *The Ambiguous Allure of the West: Traces of the Colonial in Thailand* (Hong Kong University Press 2010) 75, 77–79.

The Islamic law in the Thai court today, although showing a sign of the plural legal system, is limited to only four southernmost provinces and is applicable only within the court; not to mention several practical problems that prevent its effectiveness.[30]

For Thai people, the law has been – and will always be – a tool in melding together differences, not in promoting plurality. Field Marshal Phibun's chauvinistic government had even forced the people to call themselves '*Thai*' without the identification of regional or ethnic plurality since 1939. This practice is still effective, especially with the North-eastern Thai whose shared ethnic and cultural roots with the Laos were once a threat to the secession from Thailand.[31]

III. Constitutional Context

Several accounts have been made on the history of Thai constitutional law and also on possible causes for its tragic track record. Historical recounts of a nation normally lead to partisan or biased accounts especially from those who are part of that society themselves.[32] The following analysis minimises this by navigating contradictory versions of history, and presenting facts relevant to pluralistic features in Thailand.

At the heart of any consideration of Thai politics – especially the many Constitutions of Thailand – is the fact that Thailand has never been through a dramatic change in structure. The institutions and ideologies from the distant past continue to influence the country.[33] The monarchy, for instance, maintains its high regard among other institutions notwithstanding the revolution, various political crises, and both World Wars. Likewise, the Westminster parliamentary system which was fully formed with a bicameral legislature since 1946 is still alive and well in the 2017 Constitution. These foundations which shape and strengthen the values, ideologies and constitutional institutions will be discussed with regard to how they interact or affect plurality in the many constitutions they have witnessed.

Beginning with the first Constitution, Pridi Banomyong is credited as the author of the short-lived 1932 Temporary Charter[34] which took effect just three days after the democratic revolution. The document is often described as a tool

---

[30] See Ustaz Abd Shakur Bin Shafi-e (Abdulsuko Din-a), 'The Future of Islamic Law in Thailand' (*OK Nation Blog*, 26 December 2010) http://oknation.nationtv.tv/blog/shukur/2010/12/26/entry-3 accessed 21 September 2018.

[31] Thongchai Winichakul, *Siam Mapped: A History of the Geo-Body of a Nation* (Silkworm Books 1994) 164–165.

[32] Charnvit Kasetsiri, *A Political History of Thailand 1932–1957* (4th edn, Bangkok: The Foundation for the Promotion of Social Sciences and Humanities Textbooks Project 2001) 1–9.

[33] Likit Teerawakin, *Evolution of Politics in Thailand*, (9th edn, Thammasat Press 2003) 2–3.

[34] Temporary Charter for the Administration of Siam Act BE 2475 (1932), 27 June 1932. This was also formally known as the Provisional Constitution for the Administration of Siam.

for the unavoidable transitional period following the revolution. The Temporary Charter was, in fact, intended to be rather permanent;[35] but because of disagreements between the parties on the text of the document, the King added the word 'temporary' in the title of the signed document. He then initiated fresh discussions for compromises before the arrival of the 1932 Constitution[36] later that year. From the very first constitutional text, there were already competing authorities on the substance and form of the constitution.

The causes of initial disagreement between the monarchy and the People's party are mostly attributed to the reduced status of the monarchy in the 1932 Temporary Charter; for instance, by providing that the King can be prosecuted in criminal cases, and allowing the Assembly to preside over the case.[37] The subsequent 1932 Constitution was thus drafted to better suit the needs of the monarchy with provisions that placed the monarchy at the centre of constitutional governance. Under the 1932 Constitution, the status of the King was enthroned in a position of revered worship and was not to be violated.[38] As Head of State the King could exercise sovereign power through constitutional organs.[39] These clauses have remained in every permanent constitution since.

While free from colonial history, the drafters of Thailand's constitutions chose to adhere to the dogma of constitutional monarchy from legal scholars and political thinkers in Thailand. Archetypal models were referenced from Germany, France and the UK. Even today, most critics of Thai constitutional law and politics in general often recite institutions, legal doctrines or precedents from these jurisdictions as a minimum standard. Jurisprudence from these countries remains determinative of Thailand's success and failure in becoming a democratic nation. As can be seen in the drafting of recent constitutions, the committees heavily consulted on comparative materials to come up with the draft.[40] Nonetheless, while many provisions derive their form from foreign sources, they are still open for original and peculiar adaptations in content.

Before any drafts of modern Thai constitutions were made, the earliest account of constitutionalism and democracy can be traced back to as early as in the reign of King Chulalongkorn. In his response to an appeal from group of young Thai royals and high-ranking officers to change Siam into a constitutional monarchy, King Chulalongkorn stated that:

> I am strongly determined to accomplish the task. Do not suspect that I will object to the loss of absolute powers, for I have experienced it since I was merely a puppet

---

[35] Eg, ibid Art 10 envisions the progression of the parliament into 3 stages from wholly appointed members to wholly elected members.
[36] Constitution of the Kingdom of Thailand BE 2475 (1932), 10 December 1932.
[37] Temporary Charter (n 34) Art 6.
[38] 1932 Constitution (n 36) Art 3.
[39] ibid.
[40] Eg, in 2015 the government invited French and German constitutional scholars, ie, Prof. Dominique Rousseau, Prof. Michel Troper and Prof. Ulrich Karpen to give a lecture to the drafting committee and those involved in constitutional making on resolving political crisis to achieve democratic reform.

monarch ... Thus, please understand that I am not the King who should be forced to the moderate way as were Kings in the European history. ...[41]

In the same fashion, the King commented that the Western parliamentary system and political party are not appropriate for the people.[42] The two succeeding monarchs, King Vajiravudh and King Prajadhipok, followed suit in adopting democratic projects for the future while mindful that the people were not ready for immediate change.[43] The monarchy knew all along about the need for a Constitution, but the exact timing was never settled. Eventually, the people acted to promulgate a Constitution after King Prajadhipok failed to give a Constitution on the 6 April 1932. When he resiled from previous promises due to both economic condition and the opposition from other princes, the People's Party led a bloodless revolution on the 24 of June.[44] This was followed by a few days of negotiation and anticipation, with the King ultimately signing the 1932 Temporary Charter. The Charter is thus the first ever constitution of Thailand and created Parliament with both elected and appointed members.

Yet the ongoing conflict between the two sides spiralled into a crisis after a proposal on socialist economic reform was presented at the Parliament and a struggle for a constitutional amendment to again empower the monarchy became futile.[45] This left King Prajadhipok no choice but to abdicate as the last measure to counteract the People's Party. He did so then with a final remark that resonates well into today's Thai politics.

> I feel that the government and its party employ methods of administration incompatible with individual freedoms and the principles of justice. I am unable to agree to any person or any party carrying on such government in my name.
>
> I am willing to surrender the powers I formerly exercised to the people as a whole, but I am not willing to turn them over to any individual or any group to use in an autocratic manner without heeding the voice of the people.[46]

In the official version of Thai history, King Prajadhipok is regarded as a democratic King who crafted a long-term plan for his country to progress gradually into a true democracy.[47] The People's Party and later politicians are seen as mere

---

[41] Chai-anand Smudhvanich and Khattiya Kannasut, *Documents on Thai Politics and Government (1874–1934)*, (Social Sciences and Humanities Handbook Project 1975) 76.

[42] Winichakul (n 31) 3–4.

[43] King Vajiravudh initiated a pilot project launching a model democratic city with a constitution and a parliament called 'Dusit Thani', while King Prajadhipok commissioned the two different versions of drafted constitutions with limited monarchy as a core principle.

[44] For more details on the 1932 revolution, see Andrew Harding and Peter Leyland, *The Constitutional System of Thailand: A Contextual Analysis* (Hart Publishing 2011) 10–14.

[45] Kasian Tejapira, 'The Democratic Regime with the King as Head of State: Causes and Effects' (2011) Fah Diew Kan 89, 90–93.

[46] Kobkua Suwannathat-Pian, *Kings, Country and Constitutions: Thailand's Political Development 1932–2000* (Routledge 2013) 96.

[47] King Prajadhipok's Institute, an academic arm of the Parliament with its main mission to develop democracy in Thailand is named after the King coinciding with the 100th anniversary of his birthdate.

opportunists wrestling power using the name of the people.[48] In furtherance of this narrative, the history following King Prajadhipok's abdication has mostly been about the fight for power and not much else. This began in 1947 when a group of military leaders led the coup that would be a model (known as the 'vicious circle') for all later coups to follow. The military publicised corruption and election fraud by politicians and reset the Constitution with a provisional charter following with the drafting a new permanent constitution.

A glorious process to break the vicious loop with a new Constitution began after the massacres of protestors by Thai army in 1992. By that time, public sentiment shifted in pursuit of a change to known methods of governance as those had led them nowhere close to a stable and legitimate government. It is the first time a Constitution was drafted under the Constitutional Assembly with elected members in Thai history, and the drafters also ensured direct deliberation with an unprecedented number and variety of people.[49] Against all odds, the Constitutional assembly created the 1997 Constitution with faith in the proficiency of the public lawyers involved.[50] This Constitution aimed on one hand to strengthen the stability of the government through mechanisms such as majoritarian voting system and strong political parties. On the other, it sought to regulate democratic power and limit the role of partisanship with a well-designed framework overseeing the corrupted politics – such as independent institutions, a constitutional court, and a non-partisan senate.[51]

However, the attempt to fix past mistakes created yet another challenging crisis leading to the coup d'état of 2006. After the rise of Thaksin Shinawatra (arguably the most popular politician in recent Thai politics) the institutions and constitutional checks and balances carefully planned to curb government power and maintain stability failed to deliver because the Senate and most watchdog agencies were politically captured. The 2006 coup then came as a surprise since it was believed at the time that the military would no longer be able to legitimise its intervention. Then, in a timely fashion, a civilian government replaced the military government and held an election according to the newly drafted 2007 Constitution within the next year.

With the new 2007 Constitution, the drafters tried to fix all the weaknesses that led to inefficient checks and balances in the previous document. However, the country faced another political crisis and even more polarisation stemmed from the past crises. The cycle repeated with another coup in 2014.

Looking back, the controversial introduction of a proposed amnesty bill that could bring back former Prime Minister Thaksin Shinawatra from his self-imposed exile sparked a rising of protestors and a new round of confrontation

---

[48] For an example of an archetypical account of Thai politics, see Pinai Nanakorn, 'Re-making of the Constitution in Thailand' (2002) 6(1) Sing Journal of International and Comparative Law 90.

[49] Tom Ginsburg, 'Constitutional afterlife: The Continuing Impact of Thailand's Postpolitical Constitution' (2009) 7 International Journal of Constitutional Law 83, 89–90.

[50] Preechasinlapkun (n 8).

[51] Nantawat Bannanun, *The Constitution of 1997* (Bangkok: Institute of Policy Studies 1998) 1.

between the supporters of the two sides. This polarisation then gained a momentum that led to a prolonged protest against the government and Thanksin's influence on Thai politics as a whole. The battle on the street escalated to a legal battle in the Constitutional Court, with the Prime Minister Yingluck Shinawatra ousted from the position by the Court in the end due to the transfer of a high-ranking officer appointed from the earlier government. But it was too late to stop the political movement which seeks a complete reform and impartial caretaker government. Many extra-constitutional measures were deployed to end the crisis such as a call for a royally-appointed Prime Minister to oversee the reform and the Military's imposition of martial law. After these measures and negotiations between stakeholders failed to solve the problem the military finally made another coup d'état in the name of peace and order as well as a great reform for the country.

Having learned from the mistakes of the latest coup and constitution, drafters of the new 2017 Constitution devised a scheme that would let the power of the coup live on to oversee politics. This is done by providing special channels for the appointment of the Prime Minister during the first five years of the operation of the 2017 Constitution.[52] By looking beyond safeguards against another crisis and the return of past political deadlock, this Constitution also improves by emphasising informal and traditional values. Unlike its predecessors, the 2017 Constitution departs from the standard format since the political reform in the 1997 Constitution in trying to solve the conflict between liberal constitutionalism and the traditional and conservative force emerging from nationalistic claim of Thainess.

IV. Volcanic Constitution

The tumultuous history in Part III does present one clear pattern amongst the chaos: there is a constant tug-of-war between the two extremes of authoritarian military rule and malfunctioning constitutional democracy. The tension is most noticeable from 1997 which saw the draft of a long and sophisticated Constitution and the coup d'état which ended its short lifespan. However, it is along these two extremes that we can see the clash of norms which caused the swing between these two opposites. Thus, this part will try to explain the nature and the cause of this volcanic constitution by introducing the main players and institutions as well as the overall structure and design that have been influenced by this plurality.

In general, the Thai people have a unique belief in an ultimate goal of the country. This is connected to the Thainess which is identified both by reference to the national identity, and in juxtaposition with foreigners. Although a precise definition of Thainess is impossible, the tricolor national flag of Thailand captures the three fundamental institutions held dear by the people, namely: nation, religion, and monarchy. A Thai should think in accordance with what these institutions

---

[52] Art 272 of the Constitution of the Kingdom of Thailand BE 2560 (2017), 6 April 2017.

lead and while those thinking differently from the norm may exist, the improbability of expressing dissidence is a reality. Thus, these things come closest to the notion of shared common goods for Thai people. It is indeed a state religion that is treated as unquestionable for mainstream media. The uniqueness and capability of Thainess in identifying the right thing for the county ultimately clouds the meaning and aspiration for democratic constitutionalism thought as inappropriate for Thailand.

Despite the seemingly narrow conception of Thainess, there seems to be a high degree of tolerance for difference. This may stem from a cultural trait: Thai people avoid conflicts at all costs and opt to tolerate differences rather than risk conflict. Thus, sensitive issues in other jurisdictions such as discrimination against Lesbians, Gays, Bisexuals, Transgenders or Queers ('*LGBTQ*') or racism can be discussed generally without much hatred and resistance.

As a result, the plurality in cultural ethnic, racial, linguistic, territorial or even religious factors is accepted as long as the core identity of Thainess is intact. *Otherness*, its corollary, is then something that is in conflict with Thainess. As long as these pluralistic features abstain from interfering with the core of the nation or, even better, try assimilating and embracing *Thainess*, there is always a place for plurality. But this category of plurality does not have its effect on the legal sphere as discussed in Part III. The fact that the legal system does not ban or discourage the plurality is the farthest extent that Thai law will go to accommodate plurality with regard to constitutional pluralism. Tolerance just does not equate to acceptance and accommodation.

Consequently, as concrete and tangible pluralities such as those in ethnicity, religion or language in Thailand are not recognised or could be considered as non-existent in constitutional practice; the plurality, if any, can only surface through a more abstract form. The earliest attempt to look into plurality through this lens was the cultural and regional plurality between the rural Thai and the more educated urban Thai.[53] The study concludes that the rural Thai who are greater in number would determine the winner of the election, while the urban Thai's opinions would affect the policy and longevity of the government. In other words, the problem of Thai politics is simply an initial shortage of an urban middle class in the population. Once most people fill the urban middle class, the tension that plagues Thai politics will subside.[54]

Recent research has pointed out that the unexpected tension between the urban middle class and the newly established ones from outside of Bangkok is responsible for the last political crisis which led to the coup d'état in 2014.[55] A simplistic

---

[53] Anek Laothammathat, *A Tale of Two Cities of Democracy: Directions for Reform in Politics and Economy for Democracy* (Matichon 1995).

[54] Funatsu Tsuruyo and Kagoya Kazuhiro, 'The Middle Classes in Thailand: The Rise of the Urban Intellectual Elite and their Social Consciousness' (*The Developing Economies* XLI-2 2003) 243–263.

[55] Apichart Satitlamai and Anusorn Unno, '"Good man's politics": Political Thoughts, Practices and identities of the "Change Thailand Movement" supporters' (2017) The Thailand Research Fund

idea of plurality that merely associates the urban Thai with proper judgment, and the rural Thai with money politics, cannot truly capture the complicated conflicts in ideology which lie deeply in another layer beyond the regional or locational plurality. This is why attempts to use the constitutional organs and mechanics to eradicate money politics and corruption – weaknesses of Thai democracy on the part of the rural Thai majority – are not sufficient to cure constitutional defects.

This chapter hence focuses on ideational plurality instead. Solely reading the text of the past constitutions would not reveal many pluralistic features mentioned earlier since the Constitution was never intended as a tool to promote or engage with plurality. After all, the ultimate goal of the Constitution is to unite the people around the vision of Thainess with the monarchy at the centre through the legitimacy of constitutionalism.[56] The government and governing laws are determined to suppress or ignore the pluralistic features of Thai people. As a result, the account of a positive constitutional pluralism, if any, can only be found in the dialogue existing in constitutional practice and conventions along with those unwritten or extraconstitutional powers.

The main thrust of the volcanic constitution's occurrence in Thailand is therefore the struggle for plurality of constitutional ideas. Two monist aspirations are drawn from different sets of constitutional thinking. While constitutional democracy focuses on the will of the people and give rise to opportunities for plurality to express in the regime through empowering its citizen, Thainess and traditional ideas act to limit the range of plurality allowed under the regime. It is precisely because of this aforementioned connection between plurality and constitutional democracy that makes the government and its monistic idea of Thainess against the adherence of western constitutional law. Ultimately, the vicious circle of Thai constitutions may lie in the inflexibility of the system to let the two different ideas of constitution coexist.

A. The Monarchy and Buddhism: The Force behind the Idea of 'Thai-ness' in the Constitution

From the context given in Part II, the monarchy has been shown to 'selectively [adopt] only good things from the West for the country while preserving the traditional values at their best'[57] when it comes to the adoption of constitutional democracy. This monarchy's claim of wisdom confers it the most authority to challenge the monistic model of Constitution based on ideas from the West. The institution has gone to greater lengths to continue leading the competition against constitutional democracy.

Complete Research Paper 135–136. https://elibrary.trf.or.th/downloadFull.asp?proid=RDG5810002 accessed 15 August 2018.
[56] See the discussion below in Pt V.
[57] Winichakul (n 42) 3.

At the time of the revolution, the popularity and significance of the monarchy shrank from both the transition from absolute to constitutional monarchy and the King's lack of presence. After the abdication in 1935, Parliament chose a young prince to become King Ananda. As he was a 9-year-old prince studying in Switzerland at the time, his regents appointed by the National Assembly dealt with royal affairs in his absence throughout his brief reign. Also contributing to the fading influence of the monarchy was the ascendancy of Field Marshal Plaek Phibunsongkhram, who tried to establish himself as the centre of Thai nationalism between World War II to 1957. In effect, he replaced the monarchy in society.

The tide has started to turn for the monarchy when the late King Bhumibol began his reign in 1946 and it was during his reign that the whole fabric of current Thai constitutional principles and practice was made. With a new government led by Field Marshal Sarit Thanarat, the monarch was once again the centre of the nation as part of a scheme to strengthen the legitimacy of the Field Marshal's autocratic government.[58] Apart from the return of ceremonial and symbolic features of the past era, academics and lawyers took part in rewriting the relationship between the monarchy and the constitution. The essential theory here is the conception of a 'Democratic Form of Government with the Monarch as the Head of the State', where:

(1) the King is above politics;
(2) he retains specific powers acquired through tradition and personal prestige;
(3) the 1932 Revolution is not a regime change but a seizure of power which result in vicious circles; and
(4) the king is always the one who gives the constitution.[59]

The effect of this is that the King performs his role in accordance with that of a Buddhist King. Although the constitutional text especially since the 1997 Constitution may present the monarchy as identical to those in European countries with only ceremonial roles and nominal powers,[60] the King is in practice more powerful and capable of more due to his status as a Buddhist King presiding over the whole nation by consent, subject to the 'Ten Principles of a Righteous King' (*Dasavidha-rājadhamma*).[61] As teachings in Buddhism suggest that the King should be elected,[62] the past Thai Kings also adopted this concept in their selection under the

---

[58] See Duncan McCargo, 'Network Monarchy and Legitimacy Crises in Thailand' (2005) 18(4) The Pacific Review 499, 503.

[59] Piyabutr Saengkanokkul, 'Constitution: Conceptual History, Constituent Power, and Transition' (2016) Fah Diew Kan 178–179.

[60] Harding and Leyland (n 44) 29–30.

[61] Thomas Voss, 'King Asoka as a Role Model of Buddhist Leadership' (MA thesis, University of Kelaniya 2015) 4.

[62] Tawee Surarithkul, 'Democracy with the King as the Head of the State (26)' (*Siamrath Online*, 29 May 2017) https://siamrath.co.th/n/16281 accessed 21 September 2018.

Palace Law of Succession.[63] This arrangement is comparable to a social contract that made the monarchy a functioning branch of the state and legitimises many powers outside the constitutional text. The Palace Law of Succession remained in force until during the reign of King Vajiravudh in 1924.

Buddhism here bridges the gap between the monarchy and democratic ideas and claims a special place for the monarchy in Thai democracy. A statement from Kukrit Pramoj, a former Prime Minister and prominent writer seems the most illustrative here: '…it is a joint governance of the monarch and the people, empowering the royal powers than in democracy and empowering the citizen than any previous system …'[64]

The role of the King is thus both a figure above politics and an actor in constitutional law at the same time. He is the source of national legitimacy and sets the national agenda through his royal speeches; but he has also proven to be the arbiter in political crises.[65] For example, the King had appointed the Prime Minister in time of crisis more than once starting with the appointment of Sanya Dharmasakti after the popular uprising of October 1973, a precedent which was sought for by political movements during the crises before both the 2006 and 2014 coup d'états. However, King Bhumibol kept stating that the royal appointment of the Prime Minister is constitutional due to the constitutional text being open to interpretation.[66]

That said, the King also has his source of powers embedded in the constitutions. The 1997 Constitution opened up a myriad of powers on the King by adding Article 7 which states that 'Whenever no provision under this Constitution is applicable to any case, an act shall be performed or a decision shall be made in accordance with the constitutional conventions of Thailand under the democratic regime of government with the King as Head of State.'[67] The provision was intended as a sweeping clause to make the constitution more flexible;[68] but the unspecified constitutional conventions here have since been a source of contention regarding the power of the King.

B. Sources of Constitutional Norms

For every Thai lawyer, there is a strong teaching of the hierarchy of law influenced by the Pure Theory of Law by Hans Kelsen. The written Constitution is at the apex

---

[63] Soontri Asawai, *Cakkravatti-Vatta of King Bhumibol Adulyadej* (Thammasat University 2004) 36–38.
[64] Kukrit Pramoj, 'Daily Discussion' *Siamrath* (Bangkok, 11 Dec 1971).
[65] McCargo (n 58) 501.
[66] See Charter for Administration of the Kingdom 1972, Constitution of the Kingdom of Thailand 2007 art 14 which broadly gives the King the power to appoint the Prime Minister without any specific requirements or procedures.
[67] Constitution of the Kingdom of Thailand 2007 ch I, art 7.
[68] Montri Rupsuwan et al, *Constitutional Intent* (Winyuchon 1999) 68–70.

of the hierarchy order; it informs the validity of law the way the 'rule of recognition' works in common law countries.

The written Constitution acquires its content and legitimacy from the participation of the people. This is the Constitution in its classical sense of a document imbued with powers and functions given by the sovereign. But piercing the veil of its monism and absolute authority, the entire source and content of another constitutional order in Thailand will unfold.

According to Bawornsak Uwanno, a prominent Thai constitutional scholar, the power of the monarchy was intact from the time before the revolution till today. Hence whenever a coup d'état succeeds, the sovereign power returns in full to the King.[69] The principle is deeply rooted to the extent of being part of unwritten constitutional law strictly followed by previous coup makers who were royally appointed as the leader of the coup.[70] This will lead to a different constitutional order in Thailand as this assumption of the sovereign power indicates more involvement and constitutional power on the part of the monarchy. Moreover, there were already many instances where the written constitution is overwritten by virtue of this hidden constitutional order as will be discussed.[71]

The monarchy, the court and the military then go hand in hand in creating a different source of constitutional law; and it is in fact a different constitutional order within the same domestic territory. As evidently shown in the case regarding the voiding of elections in 2006, in the mode of crisis and after the influential royal speeches hinting at a more active role of the judiciary,[72] the court was prepared to decide based on a different constitutional order and against the written text of the Constitution. While some scholars may refer to this phenomenon under the name of 'network monarchy'[73] or 'deep state'[74] according to each approach towards the matter, this is constitutional pluralism in its truest form: a situation in which there is more than one constitutional order claiming ultimate authority over the other.[75]

But this hidden constitutional order is not visible to the public at all. When the constitutional organs decide to yield to this order, it is often portrayed as a temporary measure in time of crisis or under necessary circumstances. The result is that the written Constitution is preserved intact and there is no situation of pluralism apart from temporary and recurrent constitutional setbacks.

---

[69] Borwornsak Uwanno, *Public Law Volume 2: Separation between Public and Private Law and the Development of Public Law in Thailand* (1994).

[70] For example, Prayuth Chan-O-Cha was appointed by the King on 26 May 2014 (four days after the coup).

[71] See the discussion below in Pt V.

[72] See a detailed account in Björn Dressel, 'Judicialization of Politics or Politicization of the Judiciary? Considerations from Recent Events in Thailand' (2010) 23(5) The Pacific Review 679–680.

[73] McCargo (n 58).

[74] Eugénie Mérieau, 'Thailand's Deep State, Royal Power and the Constitutional Court (1997–2015)' (2016) 46(3) Journal of Contemporary Asia 445.

[75] Miguel Poiares Maduro, 'Three Claims of Constitutional Pluralism' in Matej Avbelj and Jan Komarek (eds), *Constitutional pluralism in the European Union and beyond* (Hart Publishing 2012) 67, 70–72.

C. Constitutional Rights

The constitutional bill of rights first came with the 1932 Permanent Constitution. Since this second Constitution was promulgated, successive permanent constitutions have always included a chapter on rights and liberties of the Thai people. Like many contemporary constitutions, Thai constitutions from the 1997 Constitution to the current 2017 Constitution have an admirable and pervasive range of constitutional rights that could boast as a masterpiece from each drafting committee.[76] The stipulated rights in Thailand are mostly derived from and already exist under international obligations. Exceptionally, Thai constitutions since the 1997 iteration have imported 'human dignity' and its principles from the German constitutional system as a central concept in rights protection.[77]

However, it took more than half a century before the Constitutional and Administrative Courts were established under the 1997 Constitution to practically enforce the rights and freedom of the people. By that time, people came to ignore constitutionally protected rights due to the ineffectiveness of the constitutional system as a whole and the underwhelming performance of the judiciary in implementing it.[78] Instead, in the wake of populist policy and public welfarism under the 1997 Constitution, the advancement of basic needs was driven in many ways outside the ambit of the constitution such as universal healthcare and free public transportation. This has strikingly led to constitutions being recently considered by scholars as mainly a tool in controlling the abuse of populist policy and maintain fiscal discipline.[79]

Interestingly, with regard to the problem of inequality and poverty, there is indeed no applicable social and economic right in the Constitution. The absence of these rights reflects the view that while inequality remain prevalent in Thai society due to the social and economic structure,[80] the influence of both Buddhism and the monarchy subdue the urge for such advancement. Buddhism favours status quo and relate misfortune to previous lives, and to act against Karma and seek justice through litigation simply runs against the vision of a proper Buddhist.[81]

---

[76] See Somkit Lertpaitoon, 'The Origins and Spirit of the 2007 Constitution' in Wootisan Thanchai, *Exploring the 2007 Constitution* (Nonthaburi: King Prajhadipok's Institute 2007) 11–12 and 17–18.

[77] Boonsri Meewongse-Ukos, *Texts on Comparative Constitutional Law: The German Constitution* (Bangkok: Textbook and Supplementary Teaching Materials Project, Faculty of Law, Thammasat University 1992) 110.

[78] See eg, Constitutional Court Decision No.25/2547 (15 January 2004). The Court decided there that since the phrase '*as prescribed by law*' was appended to most provisions granting constitutional rights in the 1997 Constitution, those rights could not be applied by the plaintiffs until legislation prescribing them was available. Moreover, the direct constitutional compliant which came about in the 2007 Constitution had just been updated to match with the original in Germany with s 213 in the Current Constitution.

[79] Somkiat Tangkitvanich, *Democratic Crisis, Populism and Democratic Solutions* (KPI Yearbook 2558, King Prajadhipok's Institute 2015) 110–124.

[80] National Human Rights Commission of Thailand, 'Human Rights Situation in Thailand' (Paper submitted to the United Nations Human Rights Council under the UPR Process, 2011).

[81] See in general David Engel and Jaruwan Engel, *Tort, Karma and Custom: Globalization and Legal Consciousness in Thailand* (Standford University Press 2010).

Now, the 2017 Constitution pushes another step towards a stronger set of constitutional rights by giving a new concept of 'universal rights' to the people. Article 26 describes clearly the ideas that all Thai people are imbued with rights from birth, and grants individuals the liberty to claim constitutional rights and freedoms in every action so long as it is not explicitly limited by the Constitution or other laws. Although this provision was influenced by the teaching of administrative law in Thailand with an emphasis on the constraint of government power, the principle of universal rights is beneficial for minorities and pluralities not mentioned in the Constitution. That said, the constitutional text on rights are unlikely to realize with the attitude of the people discussed earlier.

On a more worrying note, the present 2017 Constitution also departs from the two previous constitutions with regard to the rights and freedom of the people. No explanation is proffered, and instead of guaranteeing the human dignity for the people as a whole, the text of the 2017 Constitution clearly specifies that it will only protect those with Thai nationality. There is no question now that the constitution will only take care of those who are Thai, but not the others. This perhaps is another hint at the importance of Thainess in the Constitution.

D. Constitutional Structure

Initially envisioned as a country with a parliamentary system prior to the Revolution,[82] Thailand has maintained this ideal structure even in times when the country was under military control. From the first permanent Constitution of 1932, all constitutions have conformed to the idea of having Parliament among two other branches of the state – namely, the executive and the judiciary. The classical concept of checks and balances were in place to guarantee an appropriate government resembling that of its origins such as the UK.

Indeed, the system was heavily influenced by the form of government made popular also in many new democracies. Thailand also struggled to stabilise under the framework like many of them. Many causes had been attributed to the failure of democratic governance in Thailand including corruption and quality of education.

Nevertheless, the democratic side of these arrangements – the problem of the chain of delegation – were never seriously discussed among the people. To most constitutional scholars, the overwhelming power of the unelected military and the bureaucracy in general are threats to a healthy democracy, especially in one prone to coup d'étas like Thailand. One prominent instance would be the power of the military to declare unilaterally the state of emergency without consultation from the civilian government within certain areas.[83] Applying this at its zenith, Prayuth

---

[82] See Nanakorn (n 48) 92.
[83] Section 4 of the Martial Law BE 2457 (1914).

Chan-o-cha himself illegally declared a state of emergency before the 2014 coup d'état.[84] It is clear that the attitude of the military is far away from constraint from the text of the constitution.

More importantly, the interrelationship of the three branches of the state are not adapted for Thailand's plurality. The competition between political parties in the original UK parliamentary system which generally overcome the structural weakness of parliamentary dictatorship does not operate the same way in Thailand. Thai political parties hardly gained serious membership or operate with democratic processes. Likewise, there were no provisions directly addressing the power of the military or the monarchy under the constitution. In other words, the Constitution only governs some parts of the political reality with its basic institutions and structures. However, the constitutional framework does not go beyond the expectation to truly affect the players in politics.

E. The Judiciary

The supremacy of the Constitution is reserved in Thai constitutions since its first iteration.[85] The implementation and protection of this supremacy were, however, absent in practice until the 1997 Constitution instituted the Constitutional Court. Indeed, the introduction of the Thai Constitutional Court surprised observers with a sudden change towards judicialisation of politics (and thus the involvement of the judiciary.) In one account of pre-1997 Thailand it is stated that:

> A majority of the Southeast Asian countries are unlikely candidates for the judicialization of politics because they are ruled by regimes that, by any standard of judgment, are distinctively, if not ruthlessly, undemocratic and non-constitutional.[86]

The failure of the Constitutional Court to address the plurality of claims in Thailand may be the ultimate cause to the deadlock that inevitably leads to the coup d'état. The presence of competing constitutional claims requires the Court to function as a bridging agent if it is ever to overcome the old vicious circle of Thai politics and achieve stability. Unfortunately, the Court so far has failed in discharging this role.

During the peak of the 2006 crisis over the controversial election, King Bhumibol gave birth to a movement of judicial activism by encouraging judges to use the judicial power in solving the crisis. However, the movement failed to stop the crisis and the military intervened with another coup. The Court

---

[84] Art 188 of the Constitution of the Kingdom of Thailand BE 2550 (2007): "The King has the prerogative to declare and lift the martial law in accordance with the conditions and manner under the Martial Law."

[85] Art 31 of the Temporary Charter (n 34) provides: '... what is against the order or rules of the People's Committee of Siam or impermissible under the Charter shall be void.'

[86] Neal C Tate, 'The Judicialization of Politics in the Philippines and Southeast Asia' (1994) 15(2) International Political Science Review 187 188.

was seen as part of the hegemonic anti-democratic institution, rather than being an arbiter respected by both sides to the crisis.

V. Analysis

Despite the robust ideational plurality already discussed, plurality does not work in favour of the will of the people. In this chapter, we see how Thai people are pluralistic by virtue of its long history of interrelationship and an open border; but those pluralities are often neglected formally in law as part of state policy towards unity or harmony. While the Constitution occupies the apex of the legal system, concerns relating to pluralistic features of the people are left to deliberations at the level of ordinary legislation. The Constitution may naturally guarantee equality and protects the people against discrimination,[87] but does not entrench pluralistic features. Absent such entrenchment, it is unlikely that a highly nationalist state policy would account for pluralities instead through a politicised process of law-making. Examples of pluralities that have been blotted out are manifest in the cases of Shariah law and rights of the indigenous people mentioned above.

Ideational plurality is thus the primary contention. With concrete pluralities being accepted superficially, the struggle for pluralities and self-determination continues in pluralities of idea and politics which are subtler. This hidden constitutional order is not visible to the public, but when organs of state decide to yield to this order, it is often portrayed as a temporary measure in time of crisis or under necessary circumstances. The written Constitution remains intact but pluralism remains absent with a temporary constitutional setback suffered. Buried deep in the Thai legal practice and politics is the face of traditional Thai constitutional values and resilient norms planted in the mind of the people. This phenomenon is called 'Volcanic Constitution' – it is only in those times of crises (or when the constitution does matter) that the struggle begins to erupt with all its strength.

Of course, this awkward position of constant contest within the constitutional system is unpleasant and unpredictable. This is why the drafters of the 2017 Constitution went the extra mile to incorporate this other side of pluralist constitutional law into formal textual platforms. The elements of this formal incorporation are detailed as follows.

A. Constitutional Conventions

While upholding the Constitution as supreme, the Constitution still left open the vent of Constitutional Conventions[88] even though, time and again, the provision

---

[87] 2017 Constitution (n 52) Art 27.
[88] 2017 Constitution (n 52) Art 5.

had been the Pandora box with a potential for norms that do not conform to constitutionalism to emerge such as a request for a royally appointed Prime Minister during the political crisis in 2006.

At one time before the promulgation of the current Constitution, it is believed that the royal succession would see the end of a well-respected and charismatic leadership which had been a stable source of legitimacy.[89] The drafters thus considered that constitutional conventions were not viable as an emergency exit and decided to relocate the authority of defining these conventions to a meeting between constitutional institutions including the judiciary.[90] However, the current text does not depart from its predecessors. The only constitutional and formal portal for norms from Thainess hegemony remains in business.

B. Changes to the Draft Constitution before Promulgation

Even before the promulgation of the current Constitution, King Vajiralongkorn already tested the nature of this Constitution by making amendments to the constitutional text regarding his powers even after the referendum process. This goes to show how the discrepancies between constitutional principles and unwritten norms arising of Thainess tradition are now publicly announced, without the need to discreetly bypass the written constitution.[91] The idea that the King is always the one with constituent power as discussed in Part IV is thus highlighted here.

C. State Policies

Again, the informal and traditional Thai norms are written with reference to Buddhism under the Chapter VI 'Directive Principles of State Policies'. Instead of limiting itself to support and protect Buddhism and other religions as before, Article 67 now goes further by stating that Buddhism is a religion long professed by most Thai people, and that the state 'should promote and support education and dissemination of dharmic principles of Theravada Buddhism for the development

---

[89] Serhat Ünaldi, 'Thailand: A Coup, the Crown, and the Middle Classes' (*The Diplomat*, 23 May 2014) https://thediplomat.com/2014/05/thailand-a-coup-the-crown-and-two-middle-classes/ accessed 6 July 2018.

[90] Art 7 of the Council of State's draft in April 2015 for the Constitution of the Kingdom of Thailand. An unofficial translation is available at www.student-weekly.com/pdf/200415-constitution-en.pdf accessed 21 September 2018 while the original is accessible at www.student-weekly.com/pdf/200415-constitution-th.pdf accessed 21 September 2018.

[91] 'Thai parliament approves king's constitutional changes request, likely delaying elections' (*Reuters*, 13 January 2017) www.reuters.com/article/us-thailand-king-constitution/thai-parliament-approves-kings-constitutional-changes-request-likely-delaying-elections-idUSKBN14X0IF accessed 21 September 2018.

of mind and wisdom development, and shall have measures and mechanisms to prevent Buddhism from being undermined in any form.' This new addition may be a compromise given to movements demanding the recognition of Buddhism as a national religion.[92] Indeed, with its focus on a more purist Theravada Buddhism, some even considered the new constitution as 'Anti-heresy Constitution' due to its potential to curb the incorrect teachings that could undermine Buddhism.[93]

Surprisingly, within the same Chapter VI, 'Various Thai Ethnic Groups' is mentioned for the first time in Thai constitutional history. The entry which seems controversial from the hegemonic concept of Thainess has passed into the Constitution without public discussion or even academic debate.

Nonetheless the gravity of these two provisions above is limited by the fact that Chapter VI is not legally enforceable. They are in the Constitution with the sole purpose of keeping the government cognisant of its long-term plan, but do not impose constitutional duties. There may, however, be symbolic and social effects in the near future when the 2017 Constitution is fully implemented.

D. The Military

When extra-constitutional powers function under the written and formal Constitution, the invisible becomes visible and thus accountable to the people over its political actions. The military, as the law enforcement of the norms from Thainess, are now a subject under the Constitution. Nevertheless, it is written discreetly such as by retaining the National Council for Peace and Order (the military hunta responsible for the 2014 Coup d'état) in office even after the 2017 Constitution went into effect and the authoritative powers from the 2014 Interim Constitution remain in place.[94]

Although its powers are still largely unconstrained, the military will have the same fate as other institutions previously subject under the same treatment like the Privy Council or political parties; they have become part of the basic constitutional structure. The military may not be able to erase itself from constitutional system with ease and could end up losing the coup d'état from the shrinking arsenal of extraconstitutional movement. This is a strange move from the constitutional drafters but an albeit appropriate plan for the legitimisation and constitutionalisation of the military.

---

[92] 'Constitution Drafting: The Constitution Drafting Committee ("KRA") does not write "Buddhism is the national religion", but the state supports Theravada Buddhism' (*iLaw*, 25 April 2016) www.ilaw.or.th/node/4080 accessed 21 September 2018.

[93] Surapap Thaweesak, 'Hailed as "Constitutional Draft against Immoral Monks" the draft reveals a "Theravada Buddhism State"' (*Prachatai*, 31 May 2016) https://prachatai.com/journal/2016/05/66077 accessed 21 September 2018.

[94] See 2017 Constitution (n 52) Art 265.

VI. Conclusion

Thai constitutional law is a volcano. Looking through the lens of constitutionalism, this volcano is the result of intense struggles for dominance between the hegemony of Thainess and progressive liberal constitutionalism, with the Constitution as the arena. This chapter proposes an alternative view by applying the idea of constitutional pluralism and transcending the explanation that struggle for political power is the cause of constitutional failure. Following the framework proposed by Maduro, there are indeed 'competing claims of final authority between and within different institutions and legal orders'[95] in Thailand.

However, the competing claims are not simply between groups or sections in Thai society; they are actually between the anatomical understanding of constitutionalism and its connecting principles, such as rule of law and democracy vis-à-vis the Thainess hegemony's deviant adaptation of the same. The hope for these people suppressed by the omnipresent Thainess is to look into the constitution to advance their causes. If democracy and representative politics can truly operate in accordance with the will of the people as these ideas strive to be, there is a chance for pluralities buried below the law to emerge and flourish.

Ultimately, this chapter argues that the turbulent Thai constitutional history is the consequence of the aforementioned conflicts. It is the fight between recognition and self-determination, against uniformity and nationalistic interests. This plurality of ideas is the vent where all other suppressed pluralities try to emerge from. This explains the boom-and-bust of coups and new constitutions – the phenomenon of a volcanic constitution.

At the end of this chapter, the volcanic constitution as seen in Thailand is not an outlier which has no relevance to the international world. Comparatively, it sheds some light on the possibility of democracy and constitutionalism to adapt themselves to a designated polity at the time of democratic decline. Can constitutionalism, a sordid concept with identifiable institutions and principles, actually stand another test of localisation or legal transplant fuelled by pluralities in a particular regime? The new 2017 Constitution with its compromising features might soon be able to provide this challenging answer to the world.

Bibliography

—— Charter for Administration of the Kingdom 1972.
—— Constitutional Court Decision No.25/2547 (15 January 2004).
—— Constitutional Court Decision No. 15–18/2556 (20 November 2013).

---

[95] Maduro (n 75).

—— 'Constitution Drafting: The Constitution Drafting Committee ("KRA") does not write "Buddhism is the national religion", but the state supports Theravada Buddhism' (*iLaw*, 25 April 2016) www.ilaw.or.th/node/4080 accessed 21 September 2018.
—— Constitution of the Kingdom of Thailand BE 2475 (1932), 10 December 1932.
—— Constitution of the Kingdom of Thailand BE 2540 (1997), 11 October 1997.
—— Constitution of the Kingdom of Thailand 2007.
—— Constitution of the Kingdom of Thailand BE 2550 (2007).
—— Constitution of the Kingdom of Thailand BE 2560 (2017), 6 April 2017.
—— Martial Law BE 2457 (1914).
—— 'US must not impose its idea of democracy: PM' (*The Nation*, 14 March 2015) www.nationmultimedia.com/politics/US-must-not-impose-its-idea-of-democracy-PM-30256005.html accessed 21 September 2018.
—— 'Professor Likhit Theerawin on the Thai Constitution: Constitution Must be Respected and Implemented' (*Thai PBS News*, 21 November 2016) https://news.thaipbs.or.th/content/257946 accessed 21 September 2018.
—— 'Thai parliament approves king's constitutional changes request, likely delaying elections' (*Reuters*, 13 January 2017) www.reuters.com/article/us-thailand-king-constitution/thai-parliament-approves-kings-constitutional-changes-request-likely-delaying-elections-idUSKBN14X0IF accessed 21 September 2018.
—— Temporary Charter for the Administration of Siam Act BE 2475 (1932), 27 June 1932.
Asawai S, *Cakkravatti-Vatta of King Bhumibol Adulyadej* (Thammasat University 2004) 36–38.
Bannanun N, *The Constitution of 1997* (Bangkok: Institute of Policy Studies 1998) 1.
Boonruang S, 'Legal Aspect of a Duty to Respect the National Anthem' (2017) 46(2) Thammasat University Journal of Law 466.
Council of State, 'Draft Constitution of the Kingdom of Thailand' (2015) (trs) www.student-weekly.com/pdf/200415-constitution-en.pdf accessed 21 September 2018.
—— 'Draft Constitution of the Kingdom of Thailand' (2015) www.student-weekly.com/pdf/200415-constitution-th.pdf accessed 21 September 2018.
Dressel B, 'Judicialization of Politics or Politicization of the Judiciary? Considerations from Recent Events in Thailand' (2010) 23(5) The Pacific Review 679–680.
Engel D and Engel J, *Tort, Karma and Custom: Globalization and Legal Consciousness in Thailand* (Standford University Press 2010).
Ginsburg T, 'Constitutional afterlife: The Continuing Impact of Thailand's Postpolitical Constitution' (2009) 7 International Journal of Constitutional Law 83, 89–90.
Harding A and Leyland P, *The Constitutional System of Thailand: A Contextual Analysis* (Hart Publishing 2011) 10–14.

Kasetsiri C, *A Political History of Thailand 1932–1957*, (4th edn, Bangkok: The Foundation for the Promotion of Social Sciences and Humanities Textbooks Project 2001) 1, 1–9.

Laothammathat A, *A Tale of Two Cities of Democracy: Directions for Reform in Politics and Economy for Democracy* (Matichon 1995).

Lertpaitoon S, 'The Origins and Spirit of the 2007 Constitution' in Thanchai W, *Exploring the 2007 Constitution* (Nonthaburi: King Prajhadipok's Institute 2007) 11–12 and 17–18.

Loewenstein K, *Political Power and the Governmental Process* (University of Chicago 1957) 147ff.

Loos T, 'Competitive Colonialisms: Siam and the Malay Muslim South' in Harrison R V and Jackson P A (eds), *The Ambiguous Allure of the West: Traces of the Colonial in Thailand* (Hong Kong University Press 2010) 75, 77–79.

Maduro M P, 'Three Claims of Constitutional Pluralism' in Avbelj M and Komarek J (eds), *Constitutional pluralism in the European Union and beyond* (Hart Publishing 2012) 67, 70–72.

Mamout A, 'The Separation of State and Church: a Concept in Legal Philosophy and Public Law'; Tonsakulrungruang K, 'The Relationship between State and Religion' (*Public Law Net*, 23 September 2012) http://public-law.net/publaw/view.aspx?id=1770 accessed 21 September 2018.

McCargo D, 'Network Monarchy and Legitimacy Crises in Thailand', (2005) 18(4) The Pacific Review 499, 503.

Meewongse-Ukos B, *Texts on Comparative Constitutional Law: The German Constitution* (Bangkok: Textbook and Supplementary Teaching Materials Project, Faculty of Law, Thammasat University 1992) 110.

Mérieau E, 'Thailand's Deep State, Royal Power and the Constitutional Court (1997–2015)' (2016) 46(3) Journal of Contemporary Asia 445.

Nanakorn P, 'Re-making of the Constitution in Thailand' (2002) 6(1) Sing Journal of International and Comparative Law 90.

National Human Rights Commission of Thailand, 'Human Rights Situation in Thailand' (Paper submitted to the United Nations Human Rights Council under the UPR Process, 2011).

National Statistical Office, 'Table4: Population by religion, sex and area'; 'Census tables – table of statistics from pre-release report and complete report' http://popcensus.nso.go.th/table_stat.php?yr=2553 accessed 21 September 2018.

—— 'Thailand: Multiple Indicator Cluster Survey 2012' (UNICEF 2012) 16.

Network of Indigenous Peoples in Thailand, *The Rights of Indigenous Peoples in Thailand* (Advocacy Factsheet for Thailand's 2nd Cycle Universal Periodic Review, 2016) http://tbinternet.ohchr.org/Treaties/CCPR/Shared%20Documents/THA/INT_CCPR_ICO_THA_23570_E.pdf accessed 21 September 2018.

Office of the National Culture Commission, 'Ethnolinguistic Maps of Thailand' www.newmandala.org/wp-content/uploads/2015/05/Thailand-Ethnolinguistic-Maps.pdf accessed 21 September 2018.

Pornvinsin J, *Islamic Law and Heritage Management: A Case Study of Satun Provincial Court* (Bangkok: Institute for Judicial Training 2012) 9–10.

Pramoj K, 'Daily Discussion' *Siamrath* (Bangkok, 11 Dec 1971).

Preechasinlapakun S, '20 Years of the 1997 Constitution: Reform of Thai Politics in the enforcement of Public Law Enforcement' (*The 101*, 16 March 2017) www.the101.world/20-year-constitution-2540/ accessed 21 September 2018.

Regala R, 'The Stakes of the Free World in Southeast Asia' (1953) 28(6) Phil LJ 889.

Reynolds F, 'Dhamma in Dispute: The Interactions of Religion and Law in Thailand' (1994) 28(3) Law & Society Review 433, 444–449.

Rosenfeld M, 'Constitutional Identity' in Rosenfeld M and Sajó A (eds), *The Oxford Handbook of Comparative Constitutional Law* (OUP 2012) 763–764.

Rupsuwan M, et. al, *Constitutional Intent* (Winyuchon 1999) 68–70.

Saengkanokkul P, 'Constitution: Conceptual History, Constituent Power, and Transition' (2016) Fah Diew Kan 178–179.

Satitlamai A and Unno A, '"Good man's politics": Political Thoughts, Practices and identities of the "Change Thailand Movement" supporters' (2017) The Thailand Research Fund Complete Research Paper 135–136. https://elibrary.trf.or.th/downloadFull.asp?proid=RDG5810002 accessed 15 August 2018.

Smudhvanich C and others, *Documents on Thai Politics and Government (1874–1934)*, (Social Sciences and Humanities Handbook Project 1975) 124.

Sujit W, *A Social and Cultural History of Language and Literature in Thailand* (Matichon 2003).

Surarithkul T, 'Democracy with the King as the Head of the State (26)' (*Siamrath Online*, 29 May 2017) https://siamrath.co.th/n/16281 accessed 21 September 2018.

Surayadinata L, *The Ethnic Chinese in the ASEAN States: Bibliographical Essays* (Institute of Southeast Asian Studies 1989) 6.

Suwannathat-Pian K, *Kings, Country and Constitutions: Thailand's Political Development 1932–2000* (Routledge 2013) 96.

Tangkitvanich S, *Democratic Crisis, Populism and Democratic Solutions* (KPI Yearbook 2558, King Prajadhipok's Institute 2015) 110–124.

Tate N C, 'The Judicialization of Politics in the Philippines and Southeast Asia' (1994) 15(2) International Political Science Review 187 188.

Teerawakin L, *Evolution of Politics in Thailand*, (9th edn, Thammasat Press 2003) 2–3.

Tejapira K, 'The Democratic Regime with the King as Head of State: Causes and Effects' (2011) Fah Diew Kan 89, 90–93.

Thaweesak S, 'Hailed as "Constitutional Draft against Immoral Monks" the draft reveals a "Theravada Buddhism State"' (*Prachatai*, 31 May 2016) https://prachatai.com/journal/2016/05/66077 accessed 21 September 2018.

Tsuruyo F and Kazuhiro K, 'The Middle Classes in Thailand: The Rise of the Urban Intellectual Elite and their Social Consciousness' (*The Developing Economies* XLI-2 2003) 243–263.

UN Committee on the Elimination of Racial Discrimination, 'Reports submitted by States parties under article 9 of the Convention: International Convention on the Elimination of All Forms of Racial Discrimination: 1st to 3rd periodic reports of States parties due in 2008' (Thailand, 5 October 2011) CERD/C/THA/1-3 www.refworld.org/docid/506406442.html accessed 21 September 2018.

Ustaz Abd Shakur Bin Shafi-e (Abdulsuko Din-a), 'The Future of Islamic Law in Thailand' (*OK Nation Blog*, 26 December 2010) http://oknation.nationtv.tv/blog/shukur/2010/12/26/entry-3 accessed 21 September 2018.

Voss T, 'King Asoka as a Role Model of Buddhist Leadership' (MA thesis, University of Kelaniya 2015) 4.

Winichakul T, *Siam Mapped: A History of the Geo-Body of a Nation* (Silkworm Books 1994).

Ünaldi S, 'Thailand: A Coup, the Crown, and the Middle Classes' (*The Diplomat*, 23 May 2014) https://thediplomat.com/2014/05/thailand-a-coup-the-crown-and-two-middle-classes/ accessed 6 July 2018.

Uwanno B, *Public Law Volume 2: Separation between Public and Private Law and the Development of Public Law in Thailand* (1994).

10
The Philippine People Power Constitution: Social Cohesion through Integrated Diversity

BRYAN DENNIS GABITO TIOJANCO*

I. The Pluralist Promise of Integrated Diversity

Like most countries of the modern world,[1] the Philippines is a diverse society.[2] The 103 million native Filipinos scattered among the archipelago's more than 7,000 islands and across the globe belong to different ethnic categories[3] and speak more than a hundred languages (although nine in ten speak one of the nine major languages and a large chunk speak English).[4] The country is predominantly Roman Catholic (eight in ten Filipinos (80.9%)), but it is also home to many non-Catholic Christian sects, and at least one in twenty (5%) of the citizenry are Muslims.[5] There are also around 12 million tribal indigenous peoples (nearly 14% of the population) living on the outskirts of Philippine society.[6] In addition, the country's

---

* I would like to acknowledge Raul Pangalangan, Dante Gatmaytan, and Oscar Tan, whose course syllabi in their respective constitutional law and local government courses were helpful guides in the writing of this chapter.

[1] Samuel P Huntington, *Political Order in Changing Societies* (YUP 1968) 8; Robert Dahl, 'Introduction' in Robert Dahl (ed), *Regimes and Oppositions* (YUP 1973) 1 & 5; Robert A. Dahl, *Dilemmas of Pluralist Democracy: Autonomy vs. Control* (1st edn, YUP 1983).

[2] David Joel Steinberg, *The Philippines: A Singular and a Plural Place xiii* (4th edn, Westview Press 2000).

[3] 28.1% Tagalog, 13.1% Cebuano, 9% Ilocano, 7.6% Bisaya/Binisaya, 7.5% Hiligaynon Ilonggo, 6% Bikol, 3.4% Waray, 25.3% other.

[4] Tagalog, Cebuano, Ilocano, Hiligaynon or Ilonggo, Bicol, Waray, Pampango, Pangasinan, and Maranao, David Joel Steinberg, n 2 at 39; US Central Intelligence Agency, 'The World Factbook – Philippines' <https://www.cia.gov/library/publications/resources/the-world-factbook/geos/rp.html> accessed 18 September 2018.

[5] The non-Catholic Christian sects are the Aglipayans (2%), Evangelicals (2.8%), Iglesia ni Kristo (2.3%), and other Christians (4.5%). Only 1.8% of the population are listed for other religions, 0.1% list no religion, and the remaining 0.6% are unaccounted for; see CIA (n 4) citing a 2000 census.

[6] David De Vera, 'Indigenous Peoples in the Philippines: A Country Case Study' (RNIP Regional Assembly, Hanoi, 2007).

discrete and insular Chinese minority have historically held a sizable share of its wealth.[7] Like in other countries, occupational, professional, and class groupings supplement these various identities.[8]

Despite this diversity, the Philippines was, in 1896, the first in colonial Asia to exude a sense of common nationality that was mature enough to transcend regional, religious, ethnic, and linguistic identities.[9] By the 1980s, this sense of common nationality had spread from elite circles to the country's peripheries.[10] Citizen loyalty to such a historical collectivity as the Filipino nation is a minimum condition of an enduring democracy.[11] Beyond this minimum, however, democratic integration in the Philippines remains incomplete.[12] In an ideal democracy, civic virtue – ie, a political attitude which constantly prioritises the public good over private interests – would be widespread among the citizenry.[13] Since this lofty ideal is hardly realistic,[14] a democratic citizenry is regarded as *completely integrated* if in their political wheeling-and-dealings they routinely consider common interests and prefer cooperation over one-upmanship.[15]

Even this more realistic goal, however, has proved hard to attain in the Philippines – where citizens seldom sufficiently trust those outside their informal network of family and friends.[16] Centuries of unreliable governments have taught Filipinos to depend upon informal, hierarchical webs instead of public institutions for their needs.[17] Their political 'We', therefore, do not usually refer to 'the People', but to the hierarchy of blood and ritual and pragmatic ties to which one belongs.[18] Everyone else are considered rivals – ie, 'They'.[19] Individuals are most loyal to

---

[7] David Wurfel, *Filipino Politics: Development and Decay* (Cornell Univesity Press 1988) 31–33; Steinberg (n 2) 42–44; Alfred W. McCoy, 'Preface: The Philippine Oligarchy at the Turn of the Twenty-First Century' in Alfred W. McCoy (ed), *An Anarchy of Families: State and Family in the Philippines* (1st edn, University of Wisconsin Press 2009), xxi–xxiii.

[8] Jean Grossholtz, *Politics in the Philippines: A Country Study* (Little, Brown 1964) 6, 13; Huntington (n 1) 8.

[9] Raul Manglapus, 'The State of Philippine Democracy' (1960) 38 Foreign Aff. 613, 616; Wurfel (n 7) 50–51.

[10] Wurfel (n 7) 24–27.

[11] Dahl, *Dilemmas of Pluralist Democracy* (n 1) 96; Juan J. Linz & Alfred C. Stepan, *Problems of Democratic Transition and Consolidation: Southern Europe, South America, and Post-Communist Europe* (The John Hopkins University Press 1996) 16–37.

[12] Steinberg, (n 2) 38.

[13] Dahl, *Dilemmas of Pluralist Democracy* (n 1) 142 & 145.

[14] Bruce Ackerman, *We the People, Vol. 1: Foundations* (HUP 1991) 230–265.

[15] Dahl, *Dilemmas of Pluralist Democracy* (n 1) 79.

[16] Wurfel (n 7) 35.

[17] O.D. Corpuz, 'Cultural Foundations', in Jose Abueva & Raul de Guzman (eds), *Foundations and Dynamics of Filipino Government and politics* (Manila, Bookmark 1969), 13–14; Luis Francia, *A History of the Philippines: From Indios Bravos to Filipinos* (Overlook Press 2014) 14.

[18] I elaborate this point in Bryan Dennis Gabito Tiojanco, 'We the Dutertards, You the Dilawan' (*Inquirer.Net*, 9 October 2017) http://opinion.inquirer.net/10M7742/we-the-dutertards-you-the-dilawan accessed 18 September 2018.

[19] Richard L. Stone, 'Philippine Urbanization: The Politics of Public and Private Property in Greater Manila' (Special Report No 6, Center for Southeast Asian Studies, Northern Illinois University 1975) 112–113; Steinberg (n 2) 3.

informal networks and private interests, not official rules and the public good.[20] Nepotism and corruption are thus accepted as routine realpolitik, and bending rules to favour bosses, patrons, clients, blood or ritual kin, friends, classmates, etc is considered normal.[21]

Moreover, many Filipinos are linked to the national government only indirectly, ie, as clients of one of a few wealthy patrons to whom they feel dutybound – out of a socially enforced debt of gratitude[22] – to lifelong loyalty.[23] These ties have been historically lopsided in favour of patrons,[24] and are sometimes wounded around threats, bribes, and the like. During elections, these hierarchical ties often translate into an exchange of vote banks for particularistic rewards (eg, exemption from laws, preferential government contracts, jobs on public works projects, school houses, roads, etc).[25] Political parties are structured along these lines: personal followings link village leaders, mayors, and governors to congressmen, senators, and the President in a system of shifting coalitions where votes flow upward and patronage downward.[26]

This sort of patronage is 'the bread and butter' (or, if you prefer, 'the oil') of Philippine politics.[27] The extended kinship networks which are their basic units, however, are woefully neglected in juristic talks and writings about democratic pluralism. Instead, these networks are usually pigeonholed into more studied identity groupings such as religion, language, race, ethnic group, region, socioeconomic class or status, occupation, educational level, etc.[28]

Patterns of pluralism vary very much from country to country, and imputing on one the pluralist traits of another can fog up comparative analysis.[29] It would be helpful, therefore, to begin with a definition of pluralism and then assess whether a grouping being considered as a source of plurality is consistent with

---

[20] Stone (n 19) 21.

[21] US Central Intelligence Agency, 'The Philippine Political System (1965)', in Daniel Schirmer and Stephen Shalom (eds), *The Philippines Reader: A History of Colonialism, Neocolonialism, Dictatorship, and Resistance* (South End Press 1987), 126; Steinberg (n 2) 6.

[22] 'Utang na loöb,' in the vernacular. Those who don't pay back this debt are considered shameless ('walang hiya'): Grossholtz (n 8) 95–97; Onofre D. Corpuz, *The Philippines* (Pretince-Hall 1965) 90; Wurfel (n 7) 34; Remigio E. Agpalo, *Adventures in Political Science* (University of the Philippines Press 1992) 114–115; Diana Mendoza, 'Understanding The Philippine Political Culture', in *Politics and Governance: Theory and Practice in the Philippine Context* (Ateneo de Manila University Press 1999) 32; Steinberg (n 2) 4; Benedict J Tria Kerkvliet, *Everyday Politics in the Philippines: Class and Status Relations in a Central Luzon Village* (Ateneo De Manila University Press 2013) 244.

[23] Kerkvliet (n 22) 214–220.

[24] ibid 220–227.

[25] Cristina Montiel & Victoria Marie Chiongbian, 'Political Psychology in the Philippines' (1991) 12 Political Psychology 759, 763.

[26] Grossholtz (n 8) 136–154; Carl H. Lande, *Leaders, Factions, and Parties* (Southeast Asian Studies, Yale University 1965) 1–2; Corpuz (n 22) 99; Francia (n 17) 14–15.

[27] Grossholtz (n 8) 113; Mark R. Thompson, *The Anti-Marcos Struggle: Personalistic Rule and Democratic Transition in the Philippines* (YUP 1995) 32.

[28] See eg, Robert Alan Dahl, *Polyarchy; participation and opposition* (YUP 1971) 106–108.

[29] Dahl, *Dilemmas of Pluralist Democracy* (n 1) 54 & 75.

this definition. In this chapter, I borrow Robert Dahl's definition of pluralism as 'the existence of a plurality of relatively autonomous (independent) organizations (subsystems) within the domain of a state'.[30] Relative autonomy here means that it would be highly costly – though not impossible – to unduly restrict an organisation's independence. If we accept this definition, then all modern democracies are pluralist, ie, there are always some relatively independent organisations in largescale democracies.[31] These can be governmental organisations like legislatures, courts, or local governments; political organisations like parties and interest groups; or economic organisations like business firms. Theories of constitutional democracy usually take the relative autonomy of these groups for granted, especially since the extent of independence guaranteed to them is what distinguishes modern democracies from other (eg, authoritarian, totalitarian) regimes.[32] When a Constitution is qualified as pluralist, therefore, I take it to mean that it gives relative autonomy not only to these sorts of organisations which democracies across centuries and continents have left independent. A Constitution is pluralist, therefore, when relative autonomy is also granted to groupings of what Dahl calls 'subcultural pluralism', ie, groups which adopt 'ways of life, outlooks, identifications, loyalties, organizations, social structures' that are different from mainstream, publicly held comprehensive viewpoints, but which nevertheless accept the legitimacy of the political system.[33] Dahl lists 'differences in religion, language, race, or ethnic group, and region' as the defining identity markers of these subcultural groups.[34]

Kinship networks, much like these other subcultural groups, are also often deeply rooted not only individually in their members' personal identities, but also historically in the country's demographic makeup.[35] In fact, in the Philippines – as in most developing countries – kinship networks, particularly of elite families, have long been among the most influential social forces driving national politics.[36] Also like these other subcultural groups, kinship networks are autonomous (independent) organisations (subsystems) within the domain of a state. Moreover, they, too, adopt ways of life, outlooks, identifications, loyalties, organisations, social structures that are different from mainstream, publicly held comprehensive

---

[30] ibid 5.

[31] Of course, pluralism is not unique to democracies: ibid 29–30, 36, The last century's Christian authoritarian regimes, eg gave relative autonomy to the Catholic Church, Jan-Werner Müller, *Contesting democracy: political ideas in twentieth-century Europe* (YUP 2011) 108–112; This includes the Marcos dictatorship, Robert Youngblood, *Marcos Against The Church: Economic Development and Political Repression in the Philippines* (Cornell University Press 1993).

[32] Dahl, *Dilemmas of Pluralist Democracy* (n 1) 5, 26–30.

[33] Dahl, *Polyarchy* (n 28) 106–108; John Rawls, *Political Liberalism: Expanded Edition* (Columbia University Press 2011) 133–172.

[34] Dahl, *Polyarchy* (n 28) 106.

[35] ibid 106–108. See eg, the essays collected in Alfred W. McCoy (ed), *An Anarchy of Families: State and Family in the Philippines* (1st edn, University of Wisconsin Press 2009).

[36] Alfred W. McCoy, '"An Anarchy of Families": The Historiography of State and Family in the Philippines' in Alfred W. McCoy (ed), *An Anarchy of Families: State and Family in the Philippines* (1st edn, University of Wisconsin Press 2009).

viewpoints, but nevertheless accept the legitimacy of the political system.[37] Why, then, are they not considered a standard grouping of subcultural pluralism? Why are they neglected in juristic theories of democratic pluralism?

I think that the gap between this political reality of kinship networks and its scholarly absence in juristic theories can be explained by what I presume is the inherent goal of pluralist constitutions, which we may call *integrated diversity*. The right to form and join relatively autonomous associations, particularly for the purpose of political participation, is necessary if a democracy is to live up to its promise of government of, by, and for the people.[38] Beyond this baseline, pluralist constitutions also promote and protect the relative autonomy of subcultural groups for various reasons. One is because diversity in itself is worth valuing – not only on utilitarian grounds, but also out of respect for everybody's 'right to one's own identity, personhood, personality, culture'.[39] Another is to integrate these diverse groups into national politics, ie, to encourage them to routinely consider common interests and prefer cooperation over one-upmanship in their political wheeling-and-dealings. By giving these groups an influential voice in the country's governance, pluralist constitutions foster their loyalty to the regime's fundamental principles and discourage them from placing their political faith elsewhere, eg, would-be dictators or local bosses.[40] Their loyalty to the regime helps steady the charter ship amid siren calls of populists, demagogues, etc to abandon enduring principles in favour of expedient policies, and their voice serves as a corrective compass whenever policies veer too far away from their expectations.[41] Ideally, fostering constitutional faith would encourage civic virtue. More realistically, constitutional faith would channel political energies through democratic processes where the cooperation, compromise, and coalition-building needed to succeed would encourage citizens to champion collective norms, consider complementary interests, and pursue win-win solutions.[42]

The problem is that, much like monopolies abuse property rights to defeat the economic goal of free competition, some groups can also abuse their relative autonomy to defeat the pluralist goal of integrated diversity.[43] Kinship networks, particularly of 'the wealthy and well-born', have historically been one such culpable grouping.[44] The Philippines, for example, is lorded by wealthy oligarchs knitted together by blood and marriage.[45] For more than a century, a few powerful families

---

[37] See Benedict Anderson, 'Cacique Democracy in the Philippines: Origins and Dreams' (*New Left Review* I/169 May-June 1988), https://newleftreview.org/I/169/benedict-anderson-cacique-democracy-and-the-philippines-origins-and-dreams accessed 18 September 2018.

[38] Dahl, *Polyarchy* (n 28) 2-3; Dahl, *Dilemmas of Pluralist Democracy* (n 1) 36-40.

[39] Dahl, *Dilemmas of Pluralist Democracy* (n 1) 101.

[40] Heather Gerken, 'The Loyal Opposition' (2014) 123 Yale Law Journal 1958, 1978; 'maintaining an opposition that is loyal' is 'one of the basic aims of democracy,' ibid at 1959.

[41] Albert O. Hirschman, *Exit, Voice, and Loyalty: Responses to Decline in Firms, Organizations, and States* (HUP 1970) 76-105.

[42] Dahl, *Dilemmas of Pluralist Democracy* (n 1) 161 & 188.

[43] Dahl, *Dilemmas of Pluralist Democracy* (n 1) 166.

[44] Sheila S Coronel, *The Rulemakers: How the Wealthy and the Well-Born Dominate Congress* (2004).

[45] Anderson (n 37); McCoy (n 35).

have dominated Philippine society through 'the active pursuit of political influence to gain market advantage'.[46] From its founding until the present, Philippine government 'has remained weak and incapable of controlling the powerful families that plunder its assets, rule its provinces, and contend for control of national politics'.[47] Thus, while the 1987 Constitution 'recognizes the Filipino family as the foundation of the nation' and promises to 'strengthen its solidarity and actively promote its total development'[48] as 'a basic autonomous social institution',[49] it also seeks to limit the family's political clout: 'The State shall guarantee equal access to opportunities for public service, and prohibit political dynasties as may be defined by law'.[50] These two policies indicate the Constitution's recognition that the oligarchical political strength of elite kinship networks have historically been a stumbling block to the pluralist goal of integrated diversity. Kinship networks are often neglected in the pluralism literature, I suppose, largely because they have not historically been a peripheral subcultural grouping to integrate, but a disintegrative political force to tame.

One of the main reasons why elite families have dominated the country as much as it has is 'the relative weakness of countervailing social forces'.[51] Structural innovations introduced in the 1987 Constitution were designed precisely to address this by empowering these latent social forces and giving them effective channels to assert their rights. These innovations aim to close the gap between the potential influence which universal suffrage gives these subcultural groups, and the actual influence they have given their relatively limited wealth and weak organization.[52] Particularly, the Constitution follows 'the principle of unity in diversity'.[53] Although this principle is mentioned under the subheading 'Arts and Culture', I argue that it is also a structural principle that frames the whole document. The Philippine Constitution promotes civic virtue and constitutional loyalty through a pluralist framework of integrated diversity. Its strategy is to promote the organization and introduction of more and more diverse groups into democracy's pluralist bazaar. By addressing their systemic bargaining disadvantage, the Constitution aims to enable these groups to more effectively compete democratically against the historically dominant kinship networks of elite families.[54]

---

[46] McCoy (n 7) xii.
[47] Id. at xiii.
[48] The 1987 Constitution of the Republic of the Philippines, art XV sec. 1; See also The Family Code of the Philippines, Exec Order No 209 Art 149 (1987) ("The family, being the foundation of the nation, is a basic social institution which public policy cherishes and protects.").
[49] ibid art II, sec 12.
[50] ibid art II, sec 26. The country has not yet enacted such an anti-political dynasty law.
[51] McCoy (n 7) at xxv.
[52] Dahl calls this gap "slack" political resources, and observes that "The existence of a great deal of political slack seems to be a characteristic of pluralistic political systems and the liberal societies in which these systems operate," Robert A Dahl, *Who Governs? Democracy and Power in an American City* 305 (1961).
[53] The 1987 Constitution of the Republic of the Philippines, art. XIV sec 14.
[54] For a similar line of thought, see Bruce Ackerman, 'Beyond Carolene Products' (1985) 98 Harv L Rev 713.

Like the other chapters in this book, this chapter will examine the relationship between plurality, whether in the form of culture, ethnicity, race, nationality, language, ideology, and territory, and constitutional attempts to address them. Furthermore, this chapter will also examine extended kinship networks as a source of plurality in the Philippines' constitutional system, and argue that it is this extended kinship network that critically shapes much of the country's pluralist constitution.

II. Constitutional Context

A. Drafting History

The 1987 Philippine Constitution is a product of the People Power Revolution.[55] Many are familiar with its most reported, remembered, and replayed episodes: then President Ferdinand Marcos ending Philippine democracy by proclaiming martial law on black-and-white television in 1972; the violence and corruption of the ensuing Marcos dictatorship; the bloodied corpse of the dictator's archrival, former Senator Benigno 'Ninoy' Aquino, Jr., shot dead at the airport tarmac upon his return from exile in 1983; the million mourners who attended Ninoy's wake and marched at his funeral; the big crowds that Ninoy's widow, Corazon 'Cory' Aquino, regularly drew while running for President against Marcos during the 1986 'Snap' elections which public clamour for the ballot had forced upon the dictator; the widespread election violence, cheating, and fraud documented by a nationwide citizen election watchdog campaign; the broadcasted defection of about 300 soldiers who pleaded for the people to protect them; and finally, in February 1986, People Power itself: the four days of courage along the country's main highway (Epifanio de los Santos Avenue, or 'EDSA') where the citizenry – chanting 'Co-ry! Co-ry! Co-ry!' – formed a human shield around the rebel soldiers and peaceably stood their ground against the dictator's tanks and soldiers, and which ended with Cory taking the Presidential Oath and the People flooding the Presidential Palace after Marcos and his family had hurriedly fled the country.[56]

Notably, the term 'people power' had already been around for at least a decade before those four courageous days of Filipino patriotism in 1986 at EDSA.[57] Community organisers had often used the term since the early 1970s as a catch-all

---

[55] Whether People Power was a revolution, a coup, an uprising, a revolt, etc is today still hotly contested. See the collection of essays by J Paul Manzanilla and Caroline Hau (eds), *Remembering/Rethinking EDSA* (Kyoto University Press 2016). I think that if we accept Bruce Ackerman's definition of revolution as 'a successful effort to transform the governing principles and practices of a basic aspect of life through an act of collective and self-conscious mobilization,' Bruce Ackerman, *The Future of Liberal Revolution* (YUP 1992) 5–6, then People Power is a textbook example of it.

[56] For an excellent introduction to these events, see Thompson (n 27).

[57] Mary Racelis Hollnsteiner, 'People Power: Community Participation in the Planning and Implementation of Human Settlements' (1976) 24 Philippine Studies 5–36.

label for various related concepts including 'popular participation', 'empowerment of people' and 'community organising and mobilisation' – ie, whenever plenty enough individuals organise and act to better their lot (eg, their individual incomes, community safety, etc). The organised efforts of around 26,000 urban poor families to make their interests and demands a part of a 1974 government urban renewal project, for example, was then referred to as people power.[58] People power gave a name to the 'collective power through mass action' generated by the 'militant approach' of a group of citizens 'banding together' and acting in a way which 'forces negotiation on an equal bargaining basis and promotes immediate, specific gains for the poor and powerless'.[59]

It is this democratic entry of grassroots groups into a political stage historically dominated by elite patrons that is the essence of People Power.[60] It undermined the usual logic of patronage politics as usual in the Philippines. While traditional politicians parceled out government pork in piecemeal to clients, these new groups mobilised members to push for the changing and implementation – wholesale, local, or sectoral – of public policies. Their entry is helped by the People Power Principle which pervades the 1987 Constitution. As this principle is embedded in so many new constitutional rules, tests, and standards, as well as in landmark laws and precedents of the Cory era, the charter may be properly called a People Power Constitution, and the Philippines a People Power Republic.[61]

B. Constitutional Rights

The People Power Principle institutionalises the revolutionary spirit of people power[62] by promoting 'the right of citizens to [political] participation'.[63] Individuals and groups now have greater democratic space to directly participate

---

[58] Patricia Licuanan, 'People Power: A Social Psychological Analysis' in *Understanding People Power: A Collection Of Papers Presented at A DAP Symposium on People Power* (Development Academy of the Philippines 1987) 18–19.

[59] Hollnsteiner (n 57) 6.

[60] This is the main thesis of my Yale Law J.S.D. Dissertation, Bryan Dennis Tiojanco, *People Power Republic: Rebirth by Revolution of Philippine Constitutional Democracy*. This thesis diverges from standard narratives, analyses, and accounts of People Power, and will understandably raise some eyebrows. Unfortunately, fully recounting my argument here would be beyond the scope of this chapter.

[61] People Power, therefore, can be said to have made the Philippines a modern state: Huntington (n 1) 36 ('More than by anything else, the modern state is distinguished from the traditional state by the broadened extent to which people participate in politics and are affected by politics in large-scale political units … The most fundamental aspect of political modernization, consequently, is the participation in politics beyond the village or town level by social groups throughout the society and the development of new political institutions, such as political parties, to organize that participation.').

[62] Closing remarks of the President of the Constitutional Commission at the final session (GOVPH, 15 October 1986).

[63] Dante Gatmaytan, 'Tradition, Contestation and Democratization: Law and the Challenge of Philippine 'Folk Democracy'' (2001) 76 Philippine Law Journal 77, 99. Gatmaytan calls it 'the principle of democratization.' Although I agree with Gatmaytan in essence, I propose a wider conception of the principle.

in policymaking through initiative (ie, the power of the people to propose laws, including constitutional amendments, and to enact or reject them through an election), referendum (ie, the right reserved to the people to adopt or reject, through an election, a legislative act that is submitted for their consideration), or recall (ie, the power of the people to remove a public official through an election).[64] It is also now easier for them to affect policymaking indirectly through the decentralisation of national governmental powers[65] in favour of local governments,[66] autonomous regions,[67] indigenous cultural communities,[68] etc. Moreover, the Constitution now politically empowers the different kinds of citizens and their groups which embodied People Power: workers,[69] farmers,[70] the urban and rural poor,[71] people's organisations,[72] non-governmental, community-based, or sectoral organisations,[73] etc.[74] These innovations establish a framework for integrated diversity, which aim to break the historical dominance of the oligarchy by bringing in more of the citizenry into the formal channels of law and democracy.

Both civil and political as well as socioeconomic rights enshrined in the Constitution promote integrated diversity by establishing a robust infrastructure of democratic pluralism.[75]

---

[64] The 1987 Constitution of the Republic of the Philippines art VI, 32; art X, 3; art XVII, 2, art VI, s 32; art X, s 3; art XVII, s 2; The Initiative and Referendum Act, Republic Act No. 6735 3 (a) & (c) (1989); Local Government Code of 1991, Republic Act No. 7160 69–75 (1991); *Garcia v. Commission on Elections* (1993) G.R. No. 111511; *Subic Bay Metropolitan Authority v. Commission on Elections* (1996) 330 Phil. 1082.

[65] Florin T. Hilbay, 'The Revolution after EDSA: Issues of Reconstruction and People Empowerment' in *Law and Newly Restored Democracies: The Philippine Experience in Restoring Political Participation and Accountability* (Institute of Developing Economics (IDE-JETRO 2002) 4.

[66] The 1987 Constitution of the Republic of the Philippines at art X, ss 1–14, art. X, ss 1–14; Local Government Code of 1991 (n 64).

[67] The 1987 Constitution of the Republic of the Philippines art X, ss 15–21, art X, ss 15–21; An Act Providing for an Organic Act for the Cordillera Autonomous Region, Republic Act No. 6766 (1989); An Act Providing for an Organic Act for the Autonomous Region in Muslim Mindanao, Republic Act No. 6734 (1989); An Act to Establish the Cordillera Autonomous Region, Republic Act No. 8438 (1997); An Act to Strengthen and Expand the Organic Act for the Autonomous Region in Muslim Mindanao, Amending for the Purpose Republic Act No. 6734, entitled 'An Act Providing for the Autonomous Region in Muslim Mindanao' as amended, Republic Act No. 9054 (2001); Constituting the Transition Commission and for Other Purposes, Executive Order 120 (s 2012) (2012); Amending Further Executive Order No. 120 (s.2012), as Amended by Executive Order No. 187 (s 2015), on the Bangsamoro Transition Commission and for Other Purposes, Executive Order No. 08 (s 2016) (2016); Organic Law for the Bangsamoro Autonomous Region in Muslim Mindanao, Republic Act No. 11054 (2018).

[68] The 1987 Constitution of the Republic of the Philippines art XII, s 5; The Indigenous Peoples' Rights Act of 1997, Republic Act No. 8371 (1997); *Cruz v National Commission on Indigenous Peoples* (2000) G.R. No. 135385.

[69] The 1987 Constitution of the Republic of the Philippines art 2, s 18; art XIII, s 3.

[70] ibid art XIII, ss 4–7.

[71] ibid art XIII, ss 9–10.

[72] ibid art XIII. ss 15–16.

[73] ibid art II, s 23.

[74] See eg, ibid art VI, 5(1)–(2).

[75] For a similar claim on how the First Amendment to the U.S. Constitution creates 'an *infrastructure of free expression*', see Jack Balkin, 'The First Amendment is an Information Policy' (2013) 41 Hofstra Law Review 101, 104.

First, the right of suffrage allows all adult citizens – whatever their ethnicity, class, ideology, etc – to have a voice in choosing the country's highest officials.[76] The new party-list system also gives national, regional, and sectoral parties 20% of the seats in the House of Representatives.[77]

The right of suffrage can help make government responsive and accountable to the citizenry only if the electorate is both well-informed of and can freely debate about all issues which concern government.[78] Thus, secondly, the Bill of Rights guarantees the freedom of speech, of expression, and of the press, as well as the right of the people to peaceably assemble and petition the government for redress of grievances.[79] Further, no person may be detained solely by reason of their political beliefs and aspirations.[80] These freedoms encourage the citizenry to settle disputes discursively through ballots instead of repressively through bullets. They provide 'a framework in which the conflict necessary to the progress of a society can take place without destroying society'.[81]

Thirdly, since public debate needs accurate information, the Constitution guarantees '[t]he right of the people to information on matters of public concern', and affords the citizenry reasonable '[a]ccess to official records, and to documents, and papers pertaining to official acts, transactions, or decisions, as well as to government research data used as basis for policy development'.[82] The State also 'adopts and implements a policy of full public disclosure of all its transactions involving public interest'.[83] Pursuant to this, the Commission on Audit submits to the President and Congress an annual report covering the financial condition and operation of the government.[84] The Office of the Ombudsman also publicises matters covered by their investigations of public officials.[85]

Fourthly, the Constitution guarantees the right of the people to form unions, associations, and societies for lawful purposes.[86] This encourages non-governmental, community-based, and sectoral organisations that promote the welfare of the nation.[87] The Constitution also mandates Congress not only to provide for sectoral representation in local legislative bodies,[88] but also to 'create an agency to promote the viability and growth of cooperatives as instruments for social justice and economic development'.[89]

---

[76] The 1987 Constitution of the Republic of the Philippines art V.
[77] ibid art VI, s 5(1)-(2).
[78] Charles Lund Black, *Structure and Relationship in Constitutional Law* (Ox Bow Press 1985) 41–43; Balkin (n 75) 102.
[79] The 1987 Constitution of the Republic of the Philippines art III, s 4.
[80] ibid art III, s 18(1).
[81] *Estrada v Desierto* (2001) G.R. Nos. 146710-15.
[82] The 1987 Constitution of the Republic of the Philippines art III, s 7.
[83] ibid art II, s 28.
[84] ibid art IX-D, s 4.
[85] ibid art. XI, s 13(6).
[86] ibid art III, s 8.
[87] ibid art II, s 23.
[88] ibid art X, s 9.
[89] ibid art XII, s 15.

Fifthly, the following provisions empower non-kin groupings in various ways:

First, the Constitution promises to 'afford full protection to labour', guaranteeing 'the rights of all workers to self-organisation, collective bargaining and negotiations, and peaceful concerted activities, including the right to strike in accordance with law'.[90] Workers are also 'entitled to security of tenure, humane conditions of work, and a living wage', and have the right to 'participate in policy and decision-making processes affecting their rights and benefits' as well as a 'just share in the fruits of production'.[91]

Second, it recognises 'the right of farmers, farmworkers, and landowners, as well as cooperatives, and other independent farmers' organizations to participate in the planning, organization, and management' of the Constitution's mandated 'agrarian reform program founded on the right of farmers and regular farmworkers, who are landless, to own directly or collectively the lands they till or, in the case of other farmworkers, to receive a just share of the fruits thereof'.[92]

Third, it respects 'the role of independent people's organisations [ie, grassroots organisations[93]] to enable the people to pursue and protect, within the democratic framework, their legitimate and collective interests and aspirations through peaceful and lawful means'.[94] In an often overlooked clause, the Constitution guarantees the 'right of the people and their organizations to effective and reasonable participation at all levels of social, political, and economic decision making' and promises 'the establishment of adequate consultation mechanisms'.[95]

Fourth, the Constitution 'recognizes and promotes the rights of indigenous cultural communities within the framework of national unity and development'.[96] It promises to consider and respect 'the rights of indigenous communities to preserve and develop their cultures, traditions, and institutions ... in the formulation of national plans and policies,'[97] and 'protect the right of indigenous cultural communities to their ancestral lands to ensure their economic, social, and cultural well-being.'[98] The Indigenous Peoples' Rights Act of 1997 was enacted for this purpose.[99] Despite this, however, indigenous peoples are still 'among the poorest and most disadvantaged social group in the country' and live in settlements which are 'remote, without access to basic services, and are characterized by a high incidence of morbidity, mortality and malnutrition'.[100]

---

[90] ibid art XIII, s 3.
[91] ibid art XIII, s 3.
[92] ibid art XIII, ss 4–5.
[93] Sidney Silliman & Lela Garner Noble, *Introduction*, in Sidney Silliman & Lela Garner Noble (eds), *Organizing for Democracy: NGOs, Civil Society, and the Philippine State* (Ateneo de Manila University Press 1998) 6.
[94] The 1987 Constitution of the Republic of the Philippines art. XIII, s 15 ('People's organizations are bona fide associations of citizens with demonstrated capacity to promote the public interest and with identifiable leadership, membership, and structure.').
[95] ibid art XIII, s 16.
[96] ibid art II, s 22.
[97] ibid art XIV, s 17.
[98] ibid art XII, s 5.
[99] The Indigenous Peoples' Rights Act of 1997 (n 86); *Cruz v. National Commission on Indigenous Peoples* (n 68).
[100] De Vera (n 6).

Any discussion of the Philippines' pluralist constitution would not be complete without mentioning the Constitution's handling of religion. The Preamble to the Constitution 'implor[es] the aid of Almighty God.' 'So help me God' is also a part of the oath which both the President, the Vice-President, or the Acting President must take before they enter office (although they can omit this sentence if they choose to take an affirmation instead of an oath).[101] And yet, the Constitution declares that '[t]he separation of Church and State shall be inviolable.'[102]

The Record of the Constitutional Commission of 1986 throws some light into this apparent contradiction. There was a long debate during one of their sessions about how to refer to God. 'Divine Providence,' 'God Almighty,' 'God of History,' and 'Lord of History' were also suggested. 'Almighty God' was finally accepted right after Muslim Commissioner Lugum Uka noted that 'if we use the word "Almighty God" instead of other appellations, there will be no objections from the other sects,' including your 'brother Muslims'.[103] This suggests that what the Constitution refers to as '[t]he separation of Church and State' does not mean the *exclusion* of religion from politics. Indeed, Philippine law features many 'explicit concessions to certain religions'.[104] The Philippine Supreme Court has also adopted 'the benevolent neutrality approach in interpreting the [Constitution's] religion clauses,' which 'recognizes the religious nature of the Filipino people and the elevating influence of religion in society,' and thus 'gives room for accommodation' in order 'to uphold religious liberty' whenever government 'laws or actions of general applicability ... inadvertently burden religious exercise'.[105] Thus, consistent with the overarching goal of integrated diversity, the formal separation of Church and State more accurately refers to the equal *inclusion* of all religious denominations within the political system. 'The ideal,' says the Supreme Court, 'is the protection of religious liberty not only for a minority, however small – not only for a majority, however large – but for each of us to the greatest extent possible within flexible constitutional limits.'[106] In short, the constitutional separation of Church and State refers to the nondomination of any one or more religious denominations in political decisionmaking.

---

[101] The 1987 Constitution of the Republic of the Philippines art VII, s 5.
[102] The 1987 Constitution of the Republic of the Philippines art II, s 6.
[103] Record of the Constitutional Commission of 1986, Vol. I, No. 8 (11 June 1986) ('MR. TINGSON: ... our Committee [The Committee on Preamble, National Territory, and Declaration of Principles] was wondering whether our Muslim brothers from the South would accept the phrase ALMIGHTY GOD when we discussed this even this morning. We are very happy that our Muslim brother, Commissioner Lugum Uka, has now placed upon the record that they are also accepting the phrase ALMIGHTY GOD.').
[104] Raul C. Pangalangan, 'Religion and the Secular State: National Report for the Philippines' in Javier Martínez-Torrón and W. Cole Durham, Jr (eds), *Religion and the Secular State: National Reports* (International Center for Law and Religion Studies 2014) 559, 564 www.iclrs.org/content/blurb/files/Philippines%20wide.pdf accessed 18 September 2018.
[105] *Estrada v. Escritor*, A.M. No. P-02-1651 (4 August 2003) http://sc.judiciary.gov.ph/jurisprudence/2003/aug2003/am_p_02_1651.htm accessed 18 September 2018, affirmed in *Estrada v. Escritor*, A.M. No. P-02-1651 (22 June 2006) http://sc.judiciary.gov.ph/jurisprudence/2006/june2006/A.M.%20No.%20P-02-1651.htm accessed 18 September 2018.
[106] *Estrada v Escritor* (4 August 2003) (n 105).

This formal separation has 'a special place in Philippine history', since the nation's formative revolution against Spain was 'an "anti-Monastic" revolution, a rebellion against the abuses by the friar orders under a "unity of Church and State"'.[107] The Bill of Rights thus guarantees the free exercise of all religions and the non-establishment of any religion:

> No law shall be made respecting an establishment of religion, or prohibiting the free exercise thereof. The free exercise and enjoyment of religious profession and worship, without discrimination or preference, shall forever be allowed. No religious test shall be required for the exercise of civil or political rights.[108]

Government may also not tax '[c]haritable institutions, churches and parsonages or convents appurtenant thereto, mosques, no-profit cemeteries, and all lands, buildings, and improvements, actually, directly, and exclusively used for religious, charitable, or educational purposes'.[109] It is also prohibited from funding any religion or religious exercise, except only when a 'priest, preacher, minister, or dignitary is assigned to the armed forces, or to any penal institution, or government orphanage or leprosarium'.[110]

III. The Pluralist Constitution: Commonalities, Inclusion, and Exclusion

As mentioned above, the Philippines is a highly diverse society. However, as with most peoples,[111] there is a sense of a common Filipino nationality founded on a history of common struggle.[112] It is a story of uprisings, rebellions, and revolutions – first against foreign colonisers (Spain, America, Japan) and then against a home-grown dictator (Ferdinand Marcos). This explains why the executions of Gomburza and Rizal by the Spaniards, Bonifacio's Katipunan revolt against Spain, Aguinaldo's war against the Americans, the defence of Bataan against the Japanese, and the People Power Revolution against Marcos are what most Filipinos remember about Philippine history.[113]

---

[107] Raul C. Pangalangan, 'Transplanted Constitutionalism: The Philippine Debate on the Secular State and the Rule of Law' (2008) 82 Philippine Law Journal 1, 2.
[108] The 1987 Constitution of the Republic of the Philippines art III, s 5.
[109] ibid art. VI, s 28 (3).
[110] ibid art VI, s 29 (2).
[111] Ernest Renan, *Qu'est-ce qu'une nation?* [What is a nation?] (Wanda Romer Taylor trs, Tapir Press 1996) 47.
[112] Uldarico S. Baclagon, *Philippine Campaigns* (Graphic House 1952) 130; Reynaldo Clemeña Ileto, *Filipinos and their Revolution: Event, Discourse, and Historiography* (Ateneo de Manila University Press 1998) 178. See also Renato Constantino & Letizia R. Constantino, *The Philippines: A Past Revisited* (Tala Pub. Services 1975) 85 ('The most fundamental aspect of Philippine history is the history of the struggles of its people for freedom and a better life.').
[113] Constantino and Constantino (n 112) 1–9; Steinberg (n 2) 38.

This history of common struggle emphasises two founding events. The first is the country's national founding; the second, its constitutional one. The nation's founding at the turn of the nineteenth century drew together the heretofore warring groups of mestizos, native aristocrats, intellectuals, native clergymen, and peasants into a common struggle for independence against Spain and then the US.[114] The unity achieved there spread gradually towards the other islands until an archipelago of diverse ethnic groups and languages came to imagine themselves as one nation. The constitutional founding, in turn, culminated in those four courageous days of 1986, which paved the way for the present 1987 Constitution. The People Power Revolution reaffirmed the national founding's commitment to popular sovereignty, democracy, and the rule of law.[115]

In addition, faith in Christ was a common social glue in the country's two founding events. Introduced by Spain partly as a tool of colonisation, Catholic ideas and images were then converted into shared referents of thought and action by the popular movements for independence against that empire and then the US.[116] The Anti-Marcos struggle – led by devout Catholic Cory Aquino and Manila Archbishop Jaime Cardinal Sin – also tapped these religious referents in their moral crusade against dictatorship.[117] Today, a towering, bronze statue of the Virgin Mary stands as the largest monument commemorating the 1986 Revolution: a symbol of the Catholic Church's claim that People Power was also Prayer Power – *ie*, a miracle from God.[118]

The country's predominant Roman Catholicism makes Christian symbolism a powerful adhesive in the Philippines. This shared faith in the Christian God shapes not only the country's politics, but also its laws.[119] Roman Catholicism's influence comes not only from the sheer number of its faithful, but also by its Church hierarchy's 'close ties to a feudal-minded elite'.[120] Moreover, although Church and State in the Philippines are formally separate,[121] Filipino politicians often avoid clashing with the Church on major policy issues, for fear of being 'chastised from the pulpit of every church in their district'.[122]

Roman Catholicism, as a predominant, crosscutting identity, has been a crucial commonality for integrating the country's diverse groups.[123] But it has also worked to exclude some discrete and insular minorities within the country. First, the prevalence of Catholicism in Philippine politics, law, and culture partly explains nearly

---

[114] Nick Joaquin, *A Question of Heroes* (Anvil Publishing Inc. 1981) 152–153.

[115] The 1987 Constitution of the Republic of the Philippines (n 82) Preamble; For the ideological commitments (and contradictions) of the national founding, see Joaquin (n 114).

[116] Reynaldo C Ileto, *Pasyon and Revolution: Popular Movements in the Philippines* (Ateneo de Manila University Press 1979) 1840–1910.

[117] Thompson (n 27) 138–161.

[118] Lisandro E Claudio, *Taming People's Power: The EDSA Revolutions and their Contradictions* (Ateneo de Manila University Press 2013) 27–57.

[119] See Pangalangan, 'Religion and the Secular State' (n 104).

[120] Pangalangan, 'Transplanted Constitutionalism' (n 107) 1 & 5.

[121] The 1987 Constitution of the Republic of the Philippines art II, s 6.

[122] Pangalangan, 'Transplanted Constitutionalism' (n 107) 7.

[123] See Dahl, *Polyarchy* (n 28) 108–110.

five decades of Islamic secessionist rebellion in the southern island of Mindanao, which has claimed more than 120,000 lives.[124] It also explains why many of the roughly three million Muslims in that island consider Philippine government as a *gobyerno a-sarwang a tao*: an alien government.[125] Most of them neither call themselves Filipinos, which for them refers to the country's ninety million Christians, nor follow generally applicable Philippine laws.[126] Instead, they identify themselves as Moros, a term comprising all of the region's Islamic groups, and govern themselves in accordance with Islamic Law, which was enacted in a separate code in 1977 to govern them.[127]

Second, the millions of Indigenous Peoples living on the outskirts of Philippine society had been once upon a time officially classified as 'non-Christians' who – because they were considered 'citizens of a low degree of intelligence' and consequently 'not the equals' of Christian Filipinos – could be forcefully segregated into reservations for their own 'protection'.[128] Although most of them share the majority's Malayo-Polynesian roots, these indigenous tribes have maintained the distinct languages, religions, artworks, dress, and customary laws of their precolonial ancestors (who resisted assimilation into the Spanish and American colonial empires).[129]

Aiming to accommodate the Muslim community's hopes for a Bangsamoro, which literally means a nation (*bangsa*) of Muslims (*moro*), the Constitution endorses the creation of an autonomous region in Muslim Mindanao.[130] The Organic Law for the Bangsamoro Autonomous Region in Muslim Mindanao was recently enacted for this purpose.[131] The Bangsamoro Autonomous Region would be established if the Organic Law is approved in the ratification plebiscite that would be held in the region on January 21, 2019.[132] The rights, well-being, and national integration of Muslim Filipinos outside this autonomous region are ensured primarily by the National Commission on Muslim Filipinos, which is in charge of preserving and developing their culture, tradition, institutions, and well-being.[133]

Just like in Muslim Mindanao, the Constitution also endorses the creation of an autonomous region in the neighbouring mountainous northern provinces of

---

[124] Francisco J Lara Jr, *Insurgents, Clans, and States: Political Legitimacy and Resurgent Conflict in Muslim Mindanao, Philippines* (Ateneo de Manila University Press 2014) 61–62.

[125] Bryan Dennis G Tiojanco, 'Thoughts on the Bangsamoro Peace Agreement' *The Manila Times* (Manila, 9 February 2014) www.manilatimes.net/thoughts-on-the-bangsamoro-peace-agreement/74435/ accessed 18 September 2018.

[126] Lara Jr (n 124) 71–118.

[127] Ferdinand E Marcos, Code of Muslim Personal Laws of the Philippines Presidential Decree No. 1083 (1977).

[128] *Rubi v The Provincial Board of Mindoro* (1919) G.R. No. L-14078.

[129] Owen J Lynch, Jr, 'Native Title, Private Right and Tribal Land Law: An Introductory Survey' (1982) 57 Philippine Law Journal 268; William Henry Scott, *Cracks in the Parchment Curtain and Other Essays in Philippine History* (New Day Publishers 1982) 28–41.

[130] The 1987 Constitution of the Republic of the Philippines art X, s 15.

[131] Republic Act No. 11054 (2018).

[132] ibid art. V; Paterno Esmaquel II, 'Plebiscite on Bangsamoro Organic Law set for January 2019' (*Rappler*, 5 September 2018) www.rappler.com/nation/211191-plebiscite-bangsamoro-organic-law-january-21-2019 accessed 18 September 2018.

[133] National Commission on Muslim Filipinos Act of 2009, Rep. Act No. 9997 (2009).

the island of Luzon called the Cordilleras.[134] The two organic acts that have been passed to bring this about,[135] however, were both rejected by voters in separate plebiscites.[136]

The plebiscite requirement for the creation of autonomous regions for these historically marginalised groups are part of the 1987 Constitution's general infrastructure of democratic pluralism. Similarly, no local government unit 'may be created, divided, merged, abolished, or its boundary substantially altered' without the 'approval by a majority of the votes cast in a plebiscite in the political units directly affected'.[137] As discussed above, this framework is crystallised in the Constitution's People Power Principle, which allows the citizenry 'greater opportunities for the substantive exercise of the sovereign powers' than previous constitutions.[138] The Initiative and Referendum Clause, for example, commands Congress to create a process for people to directly propose and enact laws, or wholly or partly approve or reject national statutes and local ordinances.[139] This Congress did in both The Local Government Code of 1991 and The Initiative and Referendum Act.[140] Considering that these laws 'institutionalized people power in law-making' and implemented the People's 'residual and sovereign authority to ordain legislation directly', the Supreme Court has interpreted the provisions for initiative and referendum 'liberally ... to facilitate and not to hamper the exercise by the voters'.[141] However, the Court has also held that the People cannot at present exercise their power to directly amend the Constitution because (1) the system of initiative on constitutional amendments requires an implementing law, and (2) The Initiative and Referendum Act is inadequate for this purpose.[142] No such implementing law has yet being enacted.

IV. Constitutional Institutions and Structure

A. Separation of Powers featuring a Dominant Executive

The Philippine government is presidential, and separation of powers is its keystone principle. The legislative power (except to the extent reserved to the people) is

---

[134] The 1987 Constitution of the Republic of the Philippines art X, ss 15–21.
[135] An Act Providing for an Organic Act for the Cordillera Autonomous Region 1989 (n 67); An Act to Establish the Cordillera Autonomous Region (n 67).
[136] Miriam Coronel Ferrer, 'Cordillera autonomy – Miriam Coronel Ferrer' (*ABS CBN News*, 9 April 2010) http://news.abs-cbn.com/insights/04/08/10/cordillera-autonomy-miriam-coronel-ferrer accessed 18 September 2018.
[137] The 1987 Constitution of the Republic of the Philippines art X, s 10.
[138] Florin T. Hilbay (n 65) 4.
[139] The 1987 Constitution of the Republic of the Philippines art VI, s 32.
[140] Local Government Code of 1991 (n 64) 120–127; The Initiative and Referendum Act (n 64).
[141] *Subic Bay Metropolitan Authority v. Commission on Elections* (n 64).
[142] *Defensor Santiago v. Commission on Elections* (1997) 336 Phil. 848.

vested in Congress,[143] the executive power in the President,[144] and the judicial power in the judiciary.[145] In theory, the legislative, executive, and judicial departments are coordinate and coequal.[146] In practice, however, the President has historically dominated Philippine government.[147] This reflects the country's 'historic background and experience as well as our political culture'.[148]

The judiciary comprises one Supreme Court and lower courts which are established by law (ie, an anti-graft court known as the Sandiganbayan, the Court of Appeals, the Court of Tax Appeals, regional trial courts, metropolitan trial courts, municipal trial courts, and municipal circuit trial courts).[149] The Supreme Court is composed of a Chief Justice and 14 Associate Justices. It sits *en banc* in some important cases (eg, those involving the constitutionality of a treaty, international or executive agreement, or law; when modifying or reversing its own precedents), but in three divisions of five Justices each in most cases.[150] Although Congress has the power to define, prescribe, and apportion the jurisdictions of the various lower courts, it may neither deprive the Supreme Court of its jurisdiction over cases enumerated by the Constitution,[151] nor increase the appellate jurisdiction of the Supreme Court without its advice and concurrence.[152] The Members of the Supreme Court and judges of lower courts are appointed by the President from a list of at least three nominees prepared for every vacancy by a Judicial and Bar Council.[153] They hold office during good behaviour until they reach the age of 70 years or become incapacitated to discharge the duties of their office.[154]

Congress consists of a Senate and a House of Representatives.[155] The Senate is composed of 24 Senators elected nationwide, 12 at a time, every three years.[156] The term of office of the Senators is six years, and no Senator may serve for

---

[143] The 1987 Constitution of the Republic of the Philippines art VI, s 1.
[144] ibid art VII, s 1.
[145] ibid art VIII, s 1.
[146] *Neri v Senate Committee on Accountability of Public Officers and Investigations*, G.R. No. 180643 (Sep. 4, 2008).
[147] Vicente V Mendoza, *From McKinley's instructions to the new Constitution: documents on the Philippine constitutional system* (Central Lawbook Pub. Co. 1978) 53; Remigio E. Agpalo (n 22) 187.
[148] Mendoza (n 147) 53; See Leia Castañeda Anastacio, *The Foundations of the Modern Philippine State: Imperial Rule and the American Constitutional Tradition in the Philippine Islands* (CUP 2016) 1898–1935.
[149] The 1987 Constitution of the Republic of the Philippine 1987 art VIII, s 1; art XI, s 4; An Act Reorganizing the Judiciary, Appropriating Funds therefor, and for other Purposes, Batas Pambansa Blg. 129 (1981); An Act Expanding the Jurisdiction of the Court of Tax Appeals (CTA), Elevating its Rank to the Level of a Collegiate Court with Special Jurisdiction and enlarging its Membership, amending for the purpose certain sections of Republic Act No. 1125, as amended, otherwise known as the Law Creating the Court of Tax Appeals, and for other purposes, Republic Act No. 9282 (2004).
[150] The 1987 Constitution of the Republic of the Philippines art VIII, s 4.
[151] ibid art VIII, s 2.
[152] ibid art VI, s 30.
[153] ibid at art VIII, secs. 8–9.
[154] ibid at art VIII, s 11.
[155] ibid at art VI, s 1.
[156] ibid at art VI, s 2.

more than two consecutive terms.[157] The House of Representatives is presently composed of 292 house members.[158] 235 of them are elected from 238 districts (note: two are now deceased and one was appointed cabinet Secretary)[159] that are apportioned every three years among the provinces, cities, and the Metropolitan Manila area in accordance with the number of their respective inhabitants and on the basis of a uniform and progressive ratio.[160] Each city with a population of at least 250,000 and each province is entitled to at least one district representative.[161] The remaining 57 of the members of the House[162] (20% of the total membership of the House) are elected though a party list system of registered national, regional, and sectoral parties or organisations.[163] The Members of the House of Representatives are elected for a term of three years, and none of them may serve more than three consecutive terms.[164]

The President and the Vice-President are elected by direct, nationwide vote of the people for a term of six years. The President is not eligible for any re-election, and the Vice-President may not serve more than two successive terms.[165] The President 'has the authority to directly assume the functions of the executive department',[166] eg, by promulgating executive orders, administrative orders, proclamations, etc.[167] But of course the President cannot execute the laws alone, and needs the assistance of subordinates.[168] One check on presidential power is that the President always needs Congress to either create public offices, or delegate to him or her the power to do so.[169]

In practice, however, Congress has consistently delegated to the President almost unlimited authority to structure the bureaucracy at will.[170] The General

---

[157] ibid at art VI, s 4.
[158] Republic of Philippines, House of Representatives, House Members http://congress.gov.ph/members/ accessed 18 September 2018.
[159] Republic of Philippines, House of Representatives, District Representatives http://congress.gov.ph/members/?v=district accessed 18 September 2018.
[160] The 1987 Constitution of the Republic of the Philippines art VI, s 5(1) & (4).
[161] ibid art VI, s 5(3).
[162] Republic of Philippines, House of Representatives, Party List Representatives http://congress.gov.ph/members/?v=pl accessed 18 September 2018.
[163] The 1987 Constitution of the Republic of the Philippines art VI, s 5(1)-(2).
[164] ibid art VI, s 7.
[165] ibid art VII, s 4.
[166] *Biraogo v The Philippine Truth Commission of 2010* (2010) GR. Nos. 192935-36.
[167] Administrative Code of 1987, Executive Order No. 292 (1987) Book III, Title 1, ch 2.
[168] See *Myers v United States* (October 25, 1926) 272 U.S. 52.
[169] *Biraogo v The Philippine Truth Commission of 2010* (n 166).
[170] The Supreme Court has sanctioned this practice, *Larin v Executive Secretary* (1997) G.R. No. 112745 ('Presidential Decree No. 1772 which amended Presidential Decree No. 1416 ... expressly grant the President of the Philippines the continuing authority to reorganize the national government, which includes the power to group, consolidate bureaus and agencies, to abolish offices, to transfer functions, to create and classify functions, services and activities and to standardize salaries and materials. The validity of these two decrees are unquestionable.'); The Supreme Court has reaffirmed *Larin* in *Buklod ng Kawaning EIIB v Executive Secretary* (2001) G.R. No. 142801-802; and *Banda v Ermita* (2010) G.R. No. 166620 ('an inclusive and broad interpretation of the President's power to reorganize executive offices has been consistently supported by specific provisions in general appropriations laws.').

Appropriations Act for Fiscal Year 2017, for example, authorises the President 'to create new offices and modify the existing organizational structure of the agencies in the Executive branch, as well as create new positions or modify existing ones whenever public interest so requires'.[171] In particular, the President is authorised to pursue 'institutional strengthening measures to enhance productivity and improve service delivery' through 'the: (i) creation, abolition, renaming, consolidation or merger of bureaus, offices and units within their coverage; or (ii) creation, abolition, reclassification, conversion or transfer of existing positions, from one unit to another'.[172] Since money saved from 'unfilled, vacant or abolished positions' are considered savings[173] and money needed to fund newly created bureaus and offices are considered deficiencies,[174] the President may transfer funds from one to the other.[175] Moreover, the Supreme Court has read into the President's broad duty to 'ensure that the laws be faithfully executed'[176] a specific power to create ad hoc committees for ascertaining facts and determining the faithful execution of laws.[177]

Separation of powers is a crucial part of the Constitution's framework for integrated diversity. It 'expands the points of access to government,' increasing the ability of various groups to participate in the policymaking process.[178] This was in fact why Montesquieu – who was the first to articulate separation of powers in its modern form[179] – had trumpeted the separation of powers:

> The different powers are accessible to different social groups, so each group can check its rivals, while their entanglement means the executive can influence the conduct of Parliament and vice versa ... What Montesquieu praised was [the] multiple points of access to political institutions for different social groups, and the readiness of those who operate the various institutions to stand up for themselves.[180]

---

[171] An Act Appropriating Funds for the Operation of the Government of the Republic of the Philippines from January One to December Thirty-One, Two Thousand and Seventeen and for Other Purposes (2016) S 82; see also Administrative Code of 1987 (n 172) s 31, ch 10, Title III, Book III.

[172] General Appropriations Act, FY2017, s 83.

[173] ibid s 67.

[174] ibid s 68. ('A deficiency in a program, activity or project may result from: [a] Unforeseen modifications or adjustments in the program, activity or project; or [b] Re-assessment in the use, prioritization and/or distribution of resources ... In no case shall a non-existent program, activity or project be funded by augmentation from savings or by the use of an appropriations authorized in this Act.').

[175] ibid s 66; see also Administrative Code of 1987 (n 172) ss 39 & 42, ch 5, Book VI ('When ... a function or an activity is transferred or assigned from one agency to another, the balances of appropriations which are determined by the head of such department to be available and necessary to finance or discharge the function or activity so transferred or assigned may, with the approval of the President, be transferred to and be made available for use by the agency to which said function or activity is transferred or assigned for the purpose for which said funds were originally available.').

[176] The 1987 Constitution of the Republic of the Philippines art VII, s 17.

[177] *Biraogo v. The Philippine Truth Commission of 2010* (n 166).

[178] Jules Lobel, 'The Political Tilt of Separation of Powers' in David Kairys (ed.), *The Politics of Law: A Progressive Critique* (3rd edn, Basic Books 1998) 591, 608.

[179] Alan Ryan, *On Politics: A History of Political Thought from Herodotus to the Present* (Liveright 2012) 528.

[180] ibid 528–530.

Thus, for Montesquieu, 'separation of powers was not primarily institutional':[181] 'Social and economic pluralism preserved liberty,' and their multiple points of access to the different powers is what 'secures the "balance"'.[182] Unfortunately, Congress's longstanding practice of delegating bushels of decision making power to the President has caused political blockage in these multiple access points – thus undermining the democratic pluralism envisioned by the People Power Principle.

B. Local Autonomy under a Unitary State

Philippine government is also unitary.[183] The President has control of all the executive departments, bureaus, and offices,[184] and exercises general supervision over local governments and autonomous regions.[185] He is also the Commander-in-Chief of all of the armed forces of the Philippines.[186]

Nevertheless, the country's territorial and political subdivisions (viz., the provinces, cities, municipalities, and barangays) enjoy local autonomy, can create their own sources of revenues, and can levy taxes, fees, and charges (subject to congressional guidelines and limitations) which accrue exclusively to them.[187] Moreover, pursuant to Congress's constitutional mandate to 'enact a local government code which shall provide for a more responsive and accountable local government structure instituted through a system of decentralization',[188] the Local Government Code of 1991 implements the state's policy to give local governments 'genuine and meaningful local autonomy to enable them to attain their fullest development as self-reliant communities and make them more effective partners in the attainment of national goals'.[189] The policy 'recognizes the wholeness of the Philippine society in its ethnolinguistic, cultural, and even religious diversities'.[190] It aims to imbue locals 'with a deepened sense of involvement in public affairs as members of the body politic'.[191] Years after the statute's enactment, it was observed that 'the Philippines enjoys the most supportive statutory environment for local political participation in all of Southeast Asia'.[192]

---

[181] ibid 529.
[182] Ryan (n 179) 528; Charles Louis de Secondat, Baron de Montesquieu, *The Complete Works of M. de Montesquieu* (W. Watson, 1777) 1, 200.
[183] *Funa v Chairman of the Civil Service Commission* (25 November 2014) G.R. No. 191672.
[184] The 1987 Constitution of the Republic of the Philippines art VII, s 17.
[185] ibid art X, ss 4 & 16.
[186] ibid art VII, s 18.
[187] ibid art X, ss 1–2, 5 & art II, s 25.
[188] ibid art X, s 3.
[189] Local Government Code of 1991 (n 64) s 2(a).
[190] *Disomangcop v Secretary of the Department of Public Works and Highways* (2004) G.R. No. 149848.
[191] *Belgica v Executive Secretary* [2013] 721 Phil 416 quoting *Philippine Gamefowl Commission v Intermediate Appellate Court* (1986) G.R. No. 72969-70.
[192] Terrence George, 'Local Governance: People Power in the Provinces?' in Sidney Silliman and Lela Garner Noble (eds), *Organizing for Democracy: NGOs, Civil Society, and the Philippine State* (Ateneo de Manila University Press 1998) 225.

The principle of local autonomy intends to sever congressional control of some local affairs, eg, local legislation.[193] The principle 'is not instantly self-executing, but subject to, among other things, the passage of a local government code, a local tax law, income distribution legislation, and a national representation law, and measures designed to realize autonomy at the local level'.[194] It also 'involves a mere decentralization of administration, not of power, in which local officials remain accountable to the central government'.[195] Decentralisation of administration means delegation of 'administrative powers to political subdivisions in order to broaden the base of government power'.[196] It is different from 'decentralization of power,' where 'the autonomous government becomes accountable not to the central authorities but to its constituency'.[197]

Local autonomy is thus different from federalism in that it 'does not ... contemplate making mini-states out of local government units'.[198] Although the Constitution intends 'to deny legislative control over local governments', it did not exempt local governments from legislative regulations that are 'consistent with the fundamental premise of autonomy'.[199] In fact, Congress, through a local government code, is mandated to provide for all 'matters relating to the organization and operation of the local units', including 'the qualifications, election, appointment and removal, term, salaries, powers and functions and duties of local officials'.[200] Congress may delegate the exercise of some of these powers, eg, the disciplinary power, to the President – who may then remove erring local officials.[201] Congress may also provide guidelines and limitations on the power of local governments to create their own sources of revenues and to levy taxes, fees, and charges.[202]

Two regions – Muslim Mindanao and the Cordilleras – are entitled to greater autonomy once organic acts for each of them are approved by the local electorate in a plebiscite.[203] These organic acts would give the autonomous regions legislative powers over administrative organisation; creation of sources of revenues; ancestral domain and natural resources; personal, family, and property relations; regional urban and rural planning development; economic, social, and tourism development; educational policies; preservation and development of the cultural heritage; and such other matters as may be authorised by law for the promotion of the general welfare of the people of the region.[204] The idea is 'to allow the separate

---

[193] *Ganzon v. Court of Appeals* (1991) G.R. No. 93252.
[194] ibid.
[195] ibid.
[196] ibid.
[197] ibid.
[198] ibid.
[199] ibid.
[200] The 1987 Constitution of the Republic of the Philippines art X, s 3.
[201] *Ganzon v Court of Appeals* (n 193).
[202] The 1987 Constitution of the Republic of the Philippines art X, s 5.
[203] ibid art X, ss 1, 15, 18.
[204] ibid art X, s 20.

development of peoples with distinctive cultures and traditions. These cultures, as a matter of right, must be allowed to flourish'.[205]

The autonomous regions are entitled to 'political autonomy', which is 'greater than the administrative autonomy granted to local government units'.[206] This greater autonomy would extend to the people there 'the right to self-determination', ie, 'a right to choose their own path of development; the right to determine the political, cultural and economic content of their development path within the framework of the sovereignty and territorial integrity of the Philippine Republic'. It addresses the 'need for a political structure that will respect the autonomous peoples' uniqueness and grant them sufficient room for self-expression and self-construction'.[207] Greater autonomy is intended to be 'the appropriate vessel of deliverance for Muslim Filipinos and the ultimate unity of Muslims and Christians in this country'.[208] But any grant of autonomy must respect the unity of the Philippine State. It should neither treat any part of the Philippine territory as an independent state, nor 'provide for a transitory status that aims to prepare any part of Philippine territory for independence'.[209] For example, it may not grant the autonomous regions with treaty-making power, which only the President may exercise.[210]

Congress in 1989 passed a statute providing for an organic act for Muslim Mindanao.[211] Four provinces voted for the creation of an autonomous region and became the Autonomous Region in Muslim Mindanao (ARMM).[212] The intent of this act was 'to cede some, if not most, of the powers of the national government to the autonomous government in order to effectuate a veritable autonomy'.[213] Congress later passed a statute strengthening and expanding the organic act for the ARMM.[214] It was ratified in a plebiscite held in 2001, and two more provinces voted to join the ARMM.[215] Because these organic acts 'enjoy affirmation by a plebiscite', they 'cannot be amended by an ordinary statute': 'The amendatory law has to be submitted to a plebiscite'.[216] Consistent with this, the recently enacted Organic Law for the Bangsamoro Autonomous Region in Muslim Mindanao

---

[205] *Disomangcop v Secretary of the Department of Public Works and Highways* (n 190).
[206] ibid.
[207] ibid.
[208] ibid.
[209] *Province of North Cotabato v. Government of the Republic of the Philippines Peace Panel on Ancestral Domain* (2008) G.R. No. 183591.
[210] ibid.
[211] An Act Providing for an Organic Act for the Autonomous Region in Muslim Mindanao (n 67).
[212] *Disomangcop v Secretary of the Department of Public Works and Highways* (n 190).
[213] ibid.
[214] An Act to Strengthen and Expand the Organic Act for the Autonomous Region in Muslim Mindanao, Amending for the Purpose Republic Act No. 6734, entitled 'An Act Providing for the Autonomous Region in Muslim Mindanao' as amended (n 67).
[215] *Disomangcop v Secretary of the Department of Public Works and Highways* (n 190).
[216] ibid.

requires it to be approved in a ratification plebiscite within the region if its envisioned Bangsamoro Autonomous Region is to be established.[217]

V. Kinship Networks as a Source of Plurality in the Philippines

Filipinos are largely suspicious of their government, and for their everyday needs depend mostly on kin, clan, patrons, etc instead of formal state institutions. Local leaders thus act as go-betweens between their constituents and national leaders in the recurring exchange of votes for patronage. Loyalties, values, identity, and interests thus often attach more to personal ties than to notions of the public good.[218] Despite the Constitution's promise to 'guarantee equal access to opportunities for public service, and prohibit political dynasties',[219] 'political power remains concentrated in the hands of a relatively few families', and 'political parties serve primarily as a means of building national coalitions'[220] among this handful of families.

Moreover, despite the Constitution's prohibition of private armies and paramilitary forces outside the citizen armed force,[221] Philippine government has yet to fully disarm the country's oligarchs.[222] Many of them still employ private militias or hire bands of soldiers or motley goon squads as part of their means to defend their wealth against redistribution.[223] They use 'guns, goons, and gold' to win elections,[224] and whatever minimum standards of fair play and decency they maintain during elections have given 'the appearance for decades that the rule of law existed'.[225] Benedict Anderson had long ago observed that 'Congressional control of the purse, and of senior judicial appointments, taught the oligarchy that the "rule of law", provided it made and managed this law, was the firmest general guarantee of its property and political hegemony'.[226] Elections, for these oligarchs, have become a means to periodically determine who among them gets to feed at the public trough.[227] The extreme wealth they accumulate, in turn, makes an oligarch 'a quasi-patriarchal landlord who dispense[s] justice and favors in return

---

[217] Rep. Act No. 11054 (2018) art. V.
[218] Luis Francia (n 17) 14–15.
[219] The 1987 Constitution of the Republic of the Philippines art 2, s 26.
[220] Sidney Silliman and Lela Garner Noble, 'Citizen Movements and Philippine Democracy' in Sidney Silliman and Lela Garner Noble (eds), *Organizing for Democracy: NGOs, Civil Society, and the Philippine State* (Ateneo de Manila University Press 1998) 282.
[221] The 1987 Constitution of the Republic of the Philippines art XVIII, s 24.
[222] Jeffrey A Winters, *Oligarchy* (CUP 2011) 197.
[223] ibid 193.
[224] P N Abinales & Donna J Amoroso, *State and Society in the Philippines* (Rowman and Littlefield Publishers 2005) 15.
[225] Winters (n 222) 199.
[226] Anderson (n 37) 12.
[227] Winters (n 222) 193, 198.

for the complete subservience and total loyalty of his labor force'.[228] This loyalty earns them votes, which local oligarchs can then use to barter with national politicians in exchange for more favourable laws, monopolistic licences, etc.[229] In short, bullets beget ballots that bring patronage and bias rules.

Philippine government has thus been unable to govern independently – let alone effectively – amid a handful of oligarchic families that largely succeed in bending public policies towards their private interests. Fortunately, the country also features a robust civil society, ie, intersecting, politically active groups that work alongside government to promote the public good and help marginalised sectors of society.[230] It is civil society that 'encompasses pluralism and diversity' in the country.[231] In particular, the community nongovernmental organisations (NGOs) in the Philippines 'shares the core values of autonomy, pluralism, diversity, closeness to the grassroots, a bottom-up perspective, and volunteerism'.[232] NGOs are voluntary organizations which are 'independent of both the government and the private business sectors'.[233] The core of the NGO community are grassroots organisations which pursue collective goals of their sectoral groups.[234] The Philippine NGO community is 'large, highly organized, and politically prominent'.[235] They have been effective in expanding political participation and redressing socio-economic inequalities 'to an extent greater than anywhere else in Southeast Asia'.[236]

The People Power Revolution envisioned NGOs as 'the vehicle by which political power would be democratized'.[237] Cory's administration encouraged their growth by allocating funds for many NGOs.[238] She even gave some prominent NGO activists leadership roles in her government 'to an extent that is "historically unprecedented"'.[239] Regarding the Local Government Code of 1991 (discussed above), it has been observed that '[n]owhere in Asia does a law so explicitly accord NGOs a role in local governance'.[240] This proliferation and empowerment of NGOs has significantly improved Philippine democracy. NGOs have profoundly reshaped the public agenda by putting a spotlight (and loudspeaker) on issues which the country's oligarchical elite have either hid or ignored, and have enjoyed 'modest success' in influencing government policy. Participation of NGOs in government

---

[228] ibid 196.
[229] ibid 197.
[230] Silliman and Noble (n 93) 13, 20–21.
[231] Larry Diamond, 'Toward Democratic Consolidation' (1994) 5 Journal of Democracy 4, 6.
[232] Silliman and Noble (n 93) 18.
[233] ibid 6.
[234] ibid 10–11.
[235] ibid 13.
[236] ibid 3.
[237] Silliman and Noble (n 220) 288.
[238] ibid 289. ('The President's Social Fund provided an estimated one billion pesos in financing for potable water systems, school buildings, livelihood projects, and rehabilitation of disaster areas to an estimated four hundred NGOs.')
[239] ibid 297.
[240] George (n 192) 227.

programs also increases the likelihood that they will be implemented even against members of the elite.[241]

The reluctance and inability of NGOs to participate more directly in politics, however, limits their impact. NGOs rarely field candidates during elections. They prefer to remain outsiders, influencing politics through mass demonstrations, letter-writing campaigns, publications, etc. As a result, NGOs have not been able to consolidate power, and government policy remains the domain of the traditional elite.[242] It takes great effort and extraordinary linkages for bureaucrats to do their job of enforcing social justice rights against recalcitrant elites.[243] For example, in two important case studies, Jennifer Franco found that:

> rights-based demands for land reform took flight only after the respective communities of tenants and farm workers gained effective access to a rights-advocacy organization that was willing and capable of (1) reaching into areas under the influence of cacique hacienda law; (2) working to expand an alternative "rights consciousness" inside "captive lands"; (3) facilitating the birth of alternative rural collective identities geared toward resisting the hegemonic power of cacique law and initiating political-legal engagement with the state; (4) assisting in mobilizing the material support needed to sustain a long political-legal struggle for land reform; and (5) facilitating connections with potential allies within the state and in society beyond the local level.[244]

Without this kind of multitiered aid, landlords tend to dominate the countryside, and the pluralism of sectoral and local values encouraged by the Constitution is displaced by an anarchy of oligarchical interests and corrupt practices.[245]

Fortunately, the country's diverse groups have time and again proven the potency of the People Power Principle. With some help from rights advocates and a lot of persistence, for example, around 45,000 farmer households successfully asserted their constitutional right to land redistribution against a powerful landlord.[246] In the same way, indigenous communities preserved their rights over ancestral lands in a lawsuit involving big mining corporations.[247]

Further, such civil society mobilisation has also challenged the dominance of the Roman Catholic Church over moral-political issues. In 2012, The Responsible Parenthood Reproductive Health Act of 2012 was passed by Congress despite staunch resistance from the historically politically dominant Roman Catholic Church.[248] The statute requires hospitals to provide a full range of modern family

---

[241] Silliman and Noble (n 220) 283, 291 & 302.
[242] ibid 295, 300 & 305.
[243] Jennifer Franco, *Bound by Law: Filipino Rural Poor and the Search for Justice in a Plural-Legal Landscape* (Ateneo de Manila University Press 2011) 104–108.
[244] ibid 102.
[245] ibid 157.
[246] ibid 62–72.
[247] *Cruz v National Commission on Indigenous Peoples* (n 68); Allan Chester Nadate, 'Constitutional Redemption and the Road to Recognizing Indigenous Filipinos in a Transplanted Charter' (2014) 88 Philippine Law Journal 640.
[248] The Responsible Parenthood and Reproductive Act of 2012 (2012), www.officialgazette.gov.ph/2012/12/21/republic-act-no-10354/ accessed 18 September 2018.

planning methods, and prohibits the withholding of information about and access to family planning services.[249] It also requires government to distribute family planning supplies (eg, contraceptives) nationwide.[250] The proposal for this law languished for over a decade, meeting resistance from the Church, principally the conservative Catholic Bishops' Conference of the Philippines.[251] It was passed with the dedicated support of 'a loose alliance of women's groups, medical professionals, academics, business leaders, celebrities and a few progressive Catholic organizations', as well as a President 'who ignored threats of excommunication to actively campaign for its approval'.[252]

Finally, mass public protest expressing popular will has also been a robust source of constitutional norms. The Supreme Court had earlier placed such protests in 'the realm of politics where only the people of the Philippines are judge'.[253] Thus, the 1986 People Power Revolution was a judgement of the Filipino People to accept the government of President Corazon Aquino as 'not merely a de facto government but [also] a de jure government'.[254] In 2001, however, the Court distinguished between 'EDSA I' (ie, the 1986 Revolution) and 'EDSA II' (ie, similar popular protests along the same highway in 2001 that led to mass defections of both military and civilian officials and which forced President Joseph Estrada out of office):

> EDSA I involves the exercise of the people power of revolution which overthrew the whole government. EDSA II is an exercise of people power of freedom of speech and freedom of assembly to petition the government for redress of grievances which only affected the office of the President. EDSA I is extra constitutional ... EDSA II is intra constitutional and the resignation of the sitting President that it caused and the succession of the Vice President as President are subject to judicial review.[255]

The Court, in ruling that Estrada had 'resigned as President', considered 'the totality of prior, contemporaneous and posterior facts' – including the fact that 'the resignation is the result of his repudiation by the people'.[256]

Mass protests also reshaped constitutional norms in the 2013 Pork Barrel Decision. The Supreme Court had long sanctioned the allotment of 'pork barrels' (ie, lumpsum discretionary funds) to individual members of Congress from which they could propose and identify government projects.[257] Following exposés of

---

[249] ibid s 7.
[250] ibid s 10.
[251] Francia (n 17) 330.
[252] Tom Hundley, 'Philippines reproductive-health law tests power of Catholic Church as it lobbies Supreme Court' *The Washington Post* (Manila, 17 June 2013) www.washingtonpost.com/world/asia_pacific/philippines-health-law-tests-power-of-catholic-church/2013/06/16/36bc3bdc-d36a-11e2-8cbe-1bcbee06f8f8_story.html?utm_term=.572094b63cb2 accessed 18 September 2018.
[253] *Lawyers League for a Better Philippines v. Corazon C. Aquino* (1986) G.R. No. 76180.
[254] ibid.
[255] *Estrada v. Desierto* (n 81) (emphases omitted).
[256] ibid (emphases omitted).
[257] *Philippine Constitution Association v Enriquez* (1994) G.R. No. 113105; *Lawyers against Monopoly and Poverty v Secretary of Budget and Management* (2012) G.R. No. 164987.

massive corruption enabled by this practice, however, numerous 'gatherings in ... public places throughout the Philippines' where 'tens of thousands ... converged ... to express their demand for the abolition of the Pork Barrel' took place.[258] The Supreme Court promptly abandoned its previous decisions which sanctioned the Pork Barrel System, and ruled that such lumpsum discretionary funds violated the principle of separation of powers.[259]

VI. Conclusion

The People Power Principle enables various types of citizens, particularly the poor, to form or join an array of civil society groupings to effectively help them voice their grievances, pursue their interests, and participate in politics. These kinds of groupings (eg, labour unions, NGOs, etc) promote stability in democracies.[260] The idea is that citizens would each become members of overlapping associations, and this pluralism would encourage a 'peaceful, even if highly contentious, coexistence' that would 'tie all the groups (or, perhaps better, all their individual members) together, creating something larger and more encompassing than any of them.'[261] In addition, 'the sense of being a citizen' is 'strengthened by empowerment', ie, a 'sense of efficacy' which 'leads them to think, not wrongly, that they have more power than they had before, not only to shape their own lives within their groups but also to influence the life of the larger community.'[262] In short, people empowerment leads to citizen mobilization and constitutional faith; these, in turn, foster social cohesion.

Because 'it is a general rule of civil society that its strongest members get stronger,' weaker members and groups continually need the help of the state; otherwise a creeping domination of the weak by the strong will unavoidably ensue.[263] This, in sum, is the idea motivating the People Power Principle. Without the integrated diversity which this principle aims to foster, government would drift towards becoming, 'as Marx argued, the ruling committee of the strongest.'[264] In this case, when they lack a realistic chance of success via their own groupings, the unorganised masses have, at least in the Philippines, historically tended to place their faith in populists who rely on personalistic appeal to obtain power. Such populism was early on entrenched in post-Marcos Philippines in the person of Erap Estrada, who won as Vice President in 1992 and President in 1998.

---

[258] *Petition for Prohibition with the Supreme Court of the Philippines, Social Justice Society v. Hon. Franklin Drilon* (28 August 2013) G.R. No. 208493.
[259] *Belgica v Executive Secretary* (n 191).
[260] Silliman and Noble, (n 220) 307.
[261] Michael Walzer, *Politics and Passion: Toward a More Egalitarian Liberalism* (YUP 2005) 68.
[262] ibid 42.
[263] ibid 73–74 & 78.
[264] ibid 74.

Erap was mostly an embodiment of the poor's resentments against elite domination.[265] He was 'a demobilising populist': instead of empowering citizen groupings of the poor so that they could better help themselves, Erap discouraged 'the self-organisation of the poor, and the establishment of regularized, organized access to the government'.[266] Instead he rewarded bloc voting in his favour with political patronage to their communities which were 'not aimed at changing the political culture, but at fulfilling basic, material needs'.[267] This kind of patronage is episodic and does not politically empower the poor.[268] Today, the country's President, Rodrigo Duterte, is again such a demobilising populist.

Populism is 'the antithesis of democratic reform' because it 'feeds on the anguish of the poor without providing anything other than temporary access to symbolic goods' and 'does not facilitate the organisation of the poor'.[269] If democracy is to improve in the Philippines, our robust civil society must transform itself into an effective political society. It must learn how to better tap the People Power Principle of the Constitution so that more and more citizens are mobilised into pursuing their local, sectoral, class, etc concerns through modern political parties.[270] In this way, the People themselves will be able to more effectively realise their pluralist constitution's goal of integrated diversity.

Bibliography

—— Closing remarks of the President of the Constitutional Commission at the final session (GOVPH, 15 October 1986).

—— Record of the Constitutional Commission of 1986, Vol. I, No. 8 (11 June 1986).

—— Republic of Philippines, House of Representatives, District Representatives http://congress.gov.ph/members/?v=district accessed 18 September 2018.

—— Republic of Philippines, House of Representatives, House Members http://congress.gov.ph/members/ accessed 18 September 2018.

—— Republic of Philippines, House of Representatives, Party List Representatives http://congress.gov.ph/members/?v=pl accessed 18 September 2018.

---

[265] Joel Rocamora, 'Estrada and the Populist Temptation in the Philippines' in Kosuke Mizuno and Pasuk Phongpaichit (eds), *Populism in Asia* (Kyoto University Press 2009) 41–43, 58.
[266] ibid 48 & 58.
[267] ibid 59–60.
[268] ibid 61.
[269] ibid 62.
[270] ibid 63; happily there is much reason for optimism: Nathan Quimpo, *Contested Democracy and the Left in the Philippines after Marcos* (Ateneo de Manila University Press 2012) 53 ('Since ... 1995, PO/NGO-based forces have built new political parties representing marginalized sectors [which] have managed to win congressional seats and/or a number of local government posts.').

Abinales P N & Amoroso D J, *State and Society in the Philippines* (Rowman and Littlefield Publishers 2005) 15.
Ackerman B, 'Beyond Carolene Products' (1985) 98 Harv L Rev 713.
—— *The Future of Liberal Revolution* (YUP 1992) 5–6.
—— *We the People, Vol. 1: Foundations* (HUP 1991).
Agpalo R E, *Adventures in Political Science* (University of the Philippines Press 1996).
Anastacio L C, *The Foundations of the Modern Philippine State: Imperial Rule and the American Constitutional Tradition in the Philippine Islands* (CUP 2016) 1898-1935.
Anderson A, 'Cacique Democracy in the Philippines: Origins and Dreams' (*New Left Review* I/169 May-June 1988) https://newleftreview.org/I/169/benedict-anderson-cacique-democracy-and-the-philippines-origins-and-dreams accessed 18 September 2018.
Baclagon U S, *Philippine Campaigns* (Rev. Ed. Graphic House 1952) 130.
Balkin J, 'The First Amendment is an Information Policy' (2013) 41 Hofstra Law Review 101, 104.
Black C L, *Structure and Relationship in Constitutional Law* (Ox Bow Press 1985) 41–43.
Claudio L E, *Taming People's Power: The EDSA Revolutions and Their Contradictions* (Ateneo de Manila University Press 2013) 27–57.
Constantino R & Constantino L R, *The Philippines: A Past Revisited* (Tala Pub. Services 1975) 85.
Coronel S S, *The Rulemakers: How the Wealthy and the Well-Born Dominate Congress* (Philippine Center for Investigative Journalism, 2004).
Corpuz O D, *The Philippines* (Englewood Cliffs, N.J, Pretince-Hall 1965) 90.
—— 'Cultural Foundations' in Abueva J & de Guzman R (eds), *Foundations and Dynamics of Filipino Government and politics* (Manila, Bookmark 1969).
Dahl R A, *Who Governs? Democracy and Power in an American City* 305 (Yale University Press, 1961).
—— *Polyarchy; participation and opposition* (YUP 1971) 106–108.
—— 'Introduction' in Dahl R A (ed), *Regimes and Oppositions* (YUP 1973).
—— *Dilemmas of Pluralist Democracy: Autonomy vs Control* (1st edn, YUP 1983).
—— (ed), *Regimes and Oppositions* (YUP 1973) 1 & 5.
de Vera D, 'Indigenous Peoples in the Philippines: A Country Case Study' (RNIP Regional Assembly, Hanoi, 2007).
Diamond L, 'Toward Democratic Consolidation' 5 Journal of Democracy. 4, 6 (1994).
Esmaquel II P, 'Plebiscite on Bangsamoro Organic Law set for January 2019' (*Rappler*, 5 September 2018) <www.rappler.com/nation/211191-plebiscite-bangsamoro-organic-law-january-21-2019 accessed 18 September 2018.
Ferrer M C, 'Cordillera autonomy – Miriam Coronel Ferrer' *ABS CBN News* (9 April 2010) http://news.abs-cbn.com/insights/04/08/10/cordillera-autonomy-miriam-coronel-ferrer accessed 18 September 2018.

Francia L, *A History of the Philippines: From Indios Bravos to Filipinos* (Overlook Press 2014) 14–15.

Franco J, *Bound by Law: Filipino Rural Poor and the Search for Justice in a Plural-Legal Landscape* (Ateneo de Manila University Press 2011).

Gatmaytan D, *Tradition, Contestation and Democratization: Law and the Challenge of Philippine 'Folk Democracy,'* 76 Philippine Law Journal 77, 99 (2001).

George T, 'Local Governance: People Power in the Provinces?' in Silliman S and Noble L G (eds), *Organizing for Democracy: NGOs, Civil Society, and the Philippine State* (Ateneo de Manila University Press 1998) 225.

Gerken H, 'The Loyal Opposition' (2014) 123 Yale Law Journal, 1958, 1978.

Grossholtz J, *Politics in the Philippines: A Country Study* (Little, Brown 1964).

Hilbay F T, 'The Revolution after EDSA: Issues of Reconstruction and People Empowerment' in *Law and Newly Restored Democracies: The Philippine Experience in Restoring Political Participation and Accountability* (Institute of Developing Economics (IDE-JETRO 2002) 4.

Hirschman A O, *Exit, Voice, and Loyalty: Responses to Decline in Firms, Organizations, and States* (HUP 1970) 76–105.

Hollnsteiner M R, 'People Power: Community Participation in the Planning and Implementation of Human Settlements' (1976) 24 Philippine Studies 5–36.

Hundley T, 'Philippines reproductive-health law tests power of Catholic Church as it lobbies Supreme Court' *The Washington Post* (Manila, 17 June 2013) www.washingtonpost.com/world/asia_pacific/philippines-health-law-tests-power-of-catholic-church/2013/06/16/36bc3bdc-d36a-11e2-8cbe-1bcbee06f8f8_story.html?utm_term=.572094b63cb2 accessed 18 September 2018.

Huntington S P, *Political Order in Changing Societies* (YUP 1968).

Ileto R C, *Filipinos and their Revolution: Event, Discourse, and Historiography* (Ateneo de Manila University Press 1998) 178.

—— *Pasyon and Revolution: Popular Movements in the Philippines* (Ateneo de Manila University Press 1979) 1840–1910.

Joaquin N, *A Question of Heroes* (Anvil Publishing Inc. 1981) 152–153.

Kerkvliet B J T, *Everyday Politics in The Philippines: Class and Status Relations in a Central Luzon Village* (Ateneo de Manila University Press 2013) 244.

Lande C H, *Leaders, Factions, and Parties* (First Am ed. Southeast Asian Studies, Yale University 1965) 1–2.

Lara Jr F J, *Insurgents, Clans, and States: Political Legitimacy and Resurgent Conflict in Muslim Mindanao, Philippines* (Ateneo de Manila University Press 2014) 61–62.

Licuanan P, 'People Power: A Social Psychological Analysis' in *Understanding People Power: A collection Of Papers Presented at A DAP Symposium on People Power* (Development Academy of the Philippines 1987) 18–19.

Linz J J and Stepan A C, *Problems of Democratic Transition and Consolidation: Southern Europe, South America, and Post-Communist Europe* (The John Hopkins University Press 1996) 16–37.

Lobel J, 'The Political Tilt of Separation of Powers' in Kairys D (ed.), *The Politics of Law: A Progressive Critique* (3rd edn, Basic Books 1998) 591, 608.

Lynch Jr O J, 'Native Title, Private Right and Tribal Land Law: An Introductory Survey' (1982) 57 Philippine Law Journal 268.

Manglapus R, 'The State of Philippine Democracy' (1960) 38 Foreign Affairs 613, 616.

Manzanilla J P and Hau C (eds), *Remembering/Rethinking EDSA* (Kyoto University Press 2016).

Mccoy A W (ed), *An Anarchy of Families: State and Family in the Philippines* (1st edn, University of Wisconsin Press 2009).

—— 'Preface: The Philippine Oligarchy at the Turn of the Twenty-First Century' in Mccoy A W (ed), A*n Anarchy of Families: State and Family in the Philippines* (1st edn, University of Wisconsin Press 2009), xxi-xxiii.

—— '"An Anarchy of Families": The Historiography of State and Family in the Philippines' in Mccoy A W (ed), *An Anarchy of Families: State and Family in the Philippines* (1st edn, University of Wisconsin Press 2009).

Mendoza D, 'Understanding the Philippine Political Culture' in *Politics and Governance: Theory and Practice in the Philippine Context* (Ateneo de Manila University Press 1999) 32.

Mendoza V V, *From Mckinley's Instructions to The New Constitution: Documents on the Philippine Constitutional System* (Central Lawbook Pub. Co. 1978) 53.

Montiel C and Chiongbian V M, 'Political Psychology in the Philippines' (1991) 12 Political Psychology 759, 763.

Müller J-W, *Contesting Democracy: Political Ideas in Twentieth-Century Europe* (YUP 2011) 108–112.

Nadate A C, 'Constitutional Redemption and the Road to Recognizing Indigenous Filipinos in a Transplanted Charter' (2014) 88 Philippine Law Journal 640.

Pangalangan R C, 'Transplanted Constitutionalism: The Philippine Debate on the Secular State and the Rule of Law' (2008) 82 Philippine Law Journal 1.

—— 'Religion and the Secular State: National Report for the Philippines' in Martínez-Torrón J and Durham Jr W C (eds), *Religion and the Secular State: National Reports* (International Center for Law and Religion Studies 2014) 559, 564 www.iclrs.org/content/blurb/files/Philippines%20wide.pdf accessed 18 September 2018.

Quimpo N, *Contested Democracy and the Left in the Philippines after Marcos* (Ateneo de Manila University Press, 2012) 53.

Rawls J, *Political Liberalism: Expanded Edition* (Columbia University Press, 2011) 133–172.

Renan E, *Qu'est-ce qu'une nation? (What is a nation?)* (Taylor W R trs, Tapir Press 1996) 47.

Rocamora J, 'Estrada and the Populist Temptation in the Philippines' in Mizuno K and Phongpaichit P (eds), *Populism in Asia* (Kyoto University Press 2009).

Ryan A, *On Politics: A History of Political Thought from Herodotus to the Present* (Liveright 2012) 528.
Scott W H, *Cracks in the Parchment Curtain and Other Essays in Philippine History* (New Day Publishers 1982) 28–41.
Secondat C L d, Montesquieu B d, *The Complete Works of M. de Montesquieu* (W. Watson 1777) 1, 200.
Silliman S & Noble L G (eds), *Organizing for Democracy: NGOs, Civil Society, and the Philippine State* (Ateneo de Manila University Press 1998).
—— 'Introduction' in Silliman S & Noble L G (eds), *Organizing for Democracy: NGOs, Civil Society, and the Philippine State* (Ateneo de Manila University Press 1998) 6.
Steinberg D J, *The Philippines: A Singular and a Plural Place xiii* (4th edn, Westview Press 2000).
Stone R L, *Philippine Urbanization: The Politics of Public and Private Property in Greater Manila* (Special Report No 6, Center for Southeast Asian Studies, Northern Illinois University 1975) 112–113.
Thompson M R, *The Anti-Marcos Struggle: Personalistic Rule and Democratic Transition in the Philippines* (YUP 1995) 32.
Tiojanco B D G, 'Thoughts on the Bangsamoro Peace Agreement' *The Manila Times* (Manila, 9 February 2014) www.manilatimes.net/thoughts-on-the-bangsamoro-peace-agreement/74435/ accessed 18 September 2018.
—— 'We the Dutertards, You the Dilawan' (*Inquirer.Net*, 9 October 2017) http://opinion.inquirer.net/10M7742/we-the-dutertards-you-the-dilawan accessed 18 September 2018.
US Central Intelligence Agency, 'The Philippine Political System (1965)' in Schirmer D and Shalom S (eds), *The Philippines Reader: A History of Colonialism, Neocolonialism, Dictatorship, and Resistance* (South End Press 1987).
—— 'The World Factbook – Philippines' www.cia.gov/library/publications/resources/the-world-factbook/geos/rp.html accessed 18 September 2018.
Walzer M, *Politics and Passion: Toward a More Egalitarian Liberalism* (YUP 2005).
Winters J A, *Oligarchy* (CUP 2011).
Wurfel D, *Filipino Politics: Development and Decay* (Cornell Univesity Press 1988)
Youngblood R, *Marcos Against The Church: Economic Development and Political Repression in the Philippines* (Cornell University Press, 1993).

INDEX

absolute monarchy *see under* **Brunei**
ASEAN (Association of Southeast Asian Nations) 1–2
see also Southeast Asia

Brunei
  Abdul Latif Ibrahim 107
  Abell, A F 92, 96–100
  absolute monarchy 84, 85, 89
  authoritarian mechanisms of colonial rule 85
  Brunei Code 86
  Constitution of 1959
    absolute monarchy 88, 91
    Council of Ministers 89, 90
    elections 1961 88–9
    history of 91–102
      Advisory Committee 94–5
      British drafts/negotiations 96–100
      British High Commissioner 92, 93, 96–8
      coming into force 100–1
      constitutional politics/public debates, post-WWII 92–3
      district advisory councils 97, 99
      enactments/amendments 3, 101–2
      legal status of colonial rule 93–4
      military/defence forces 100
      oil, discovery/revenues 92
      public participation, avoidance 102
      State Council 94
    Interpretation Tribunal 90, 106
    Islam in the Constitution 104–6
      invocation of faith 104–5
      key agencies 105–6
      MIB reaffirmation 105
      Ministry of Religious Affairs 105
      MUIB (Religious Council) 90, 105–6
    judicial system, appointments/system 91
    Legislative Council 90
    Malay element in 104
    monarchy and the Constitution
      amendment power, exclusive 106
      personal/official immunity 107
    Personaleinheit 84, 106
    public finance accountability 106
    Privy Council 89, 90
    state of emergency (1962) 89
    Syriah law/courts 91, 108–9
  constitutional rights
    disrespect of Islam/religious authorities 108–9
    international human rights 108
    just ruler/loyal subjects relationship 109
    other religions, practice of 108
  Haji Mohd Yusuf 94
  Hickling, R H 96
  historical context
    birth as Islamic nation 85–6
    as British Protectorate 86–7
    law in pre-colonial state 86
    MIB (*Melayu Islam Beraja*) as official state ideology 87–8
    Sunni Islam, adoption 86
  Hooker, M B 86
  Hussainmiya, B A 96
  indigenous ethnic groups 83
  Islamic/non-secular state 84–5
  Kershaw, R 102
  Malay as ethnic classifier 83–4
  Malay teachers group 94, 97, 99, 101, 102
  MIB (*Melayu Islam Beraja*)
    Bruneian/non-Bruneian views of 103
    in Constitution 105
    interaction between elements 107–8
    as official state ideology 87–8, 102–3
  monoculturalism as goal 83
  NDP (National Development Party) 89
  oil, discovery/revenues 92
  PRB (People's Party of Brunei) 88–9, 98–9, 100–1
  Sultan Hassanal Bolkiah 101–2
  Sultan as Head of State/Head of government 84, 89–90
  Sultan Muhammad Shah 85
  Sultan Omar Ali Saifuddin III 92–101 *passim*
  summary 18–19, 110
Burma *see* **Myanmar**

284 Index

Cambodia
  Additional Constitutional Law 182
  adoption/promulgation 178
  Angkor Empire 172, 179
  basic issues/summary 169, 200–1
  branches of the state/government 188–90
    Communal/Sangkat Council 197
    Congress of National Assembly and Senate 194
    Constitutional Council 194, 195–6
    Council of Ministers 189
    Head of State/monarch, election 74, 190–1
    judicial review mechanisms 194–6
    judiciary/court system 189–90
    legitimacy claims 191–3
    National Assembly/Senate 188–9
    National Congress 193–4
    National Election Committee 194
    oath-taking provision 182, 192–3
  Cedès, G 169
  civil rights and plurality 199
  communism and Khmer Rouge 175, 179–80
  conflict resolution 185
  Constitution of 1947 172, 174
  Constitution of 1972 175
  Constitution of 1976 175
  Constitution of 1981 175–6
  Constitution of 1989 176
  Constitution of 1993 176–8
  Constitutional Assembly 178
  constitutional enactments 3
  constitutional fragmentation 200
  constitutional monarchy 174, 190–1
  constitutional rights
    and plurality 198–9
    principles 197–8
    respect for 184
  coup d'etat (1970) and political conflict 174, 179
  cultural/religious rights and plurality 199
  decentralisation and plurality 196–7
  democracy principle 200
  development delay 200
  election system and plurality 187–8
  fundamental rights 181
  government system and plurality 188
  historical background 169–70
    founding history 170–2
    French civil law tradition 171
    post-WWII change/globalisation 171–2
    Princess *Nagi* legend 170–1
  ideas/values
    constitutional monarchy 181, 182
    ideational plurality 17
    localist-Cambodian values 181, 182
    and structure 187
    universalist values 180–1
    western liberalist values 181
  Jayavarman VII the Great, King 173
  Khmer Empire 169
  Khmer Republic 175
  Khmer Rouge and communism 175, 179–80
  Kingdom of Cambodia 176–8
  Lon Nol, General 179
  multi-party democracy 181
  National Assembly/Senate 188–9
  Paris Peace Accords (1991) 177
  People's Republic of Kampuchea 175–6
  pluralistic sources 199–200
  plurality of country
    Christianity/Islam etc 173–4
    Hinduism/Buddhism 173
    languages/ethnicity 172
    notable groups of foreigners/ethnic groups 173
  political deadlock 200
  quorums, achieving of 200
  rule of law 200
  separation of powers 181, 184–5, 196–7
  shared common goals of nation 179–80
  social rights and plurality 199
  sources of 182–4
  State of Cambodia 176
  structure of constitution 185–7
  Troeung Ngea 172
  written/unwritten sources 182–4
Chen, A H Y 5
constitutional expressivism *see under* **Laos and Vietnam**
constitutional law *see under* **Southeast Asia**

Dahl, R 13, 254

expressivism, constitutional *see* **Laos and Vietnam, constitutional expressivism**

Hamid, Justice Abdul 28
Harding, A 29
Horowitz, D 8, 55–6
human rights, and UDHR/ICCPR provisions 127

Ikenberry, G John 54
Indochina *see* **Laos and Vietnam**
Indonesia
    Asshiddiqie, J 139
    background 115–17
    Bandung coup 120
    basic issues/summary 116–17, 138–9
    BPUPKI Committee 118–19
    Constitution of 1945 and
        independence 117–21
      constitution-making debates 118–19
      early days of independence 119–20
      federalism issue 119–20
      Konstituante Council (1956–1959) 120–1
      Provisional Constitution of 1950 120
    constitutional enactments 3, 117–18
    constitutional structure and institutional
        arrangements 130–2, 139
      decentralisation initiatives 131
      institutions derived from legislation 131
      institutions recognised in
        Constitution 131
      nine key institutions 130
      President/Vice-President
        directly elected 132
        highest state executive authority 132
        legal accountability 132
      separation of powers 130–1
    courts
      Aceh/Papua, special autonomy for 134
      customary rights protection 133
      legal orders, plurality recognised 132–3
      plurality of legal systems
        acknowledged 134–5
      religious courts/adat courts 133
      state role in unifying 133–4
    decentralisation concerns 137–8
    democracy, post-Soeharto elements 116
    Drooglever, P J 119
    East Timor secession 138
    Habibie, President B J 137
    historical issues 117
    human rights 127–30
      amendments (1999–2002) 127, 128
      Blasphemy Law's constitutionality 129
      constitution guarantees (1945) 127
      judicial creativity/activism 129–30
      legal/social/political context 129
      religious values exception 127–8
      violations, post-1945 128
    Jakarta Charter 16, 117, 119, 121
    Joko Widoko (Jokowi), President 135
    Lev, D S 133
    Mahfud, M D 139
    MPR (People's Consultative Assembly) 122
    national emblem 115
    Noken electoral system, Papua 135–7
      court ruling 136
      fraud allegations 135–6
      nature of voting 135
      traditional voting custom upheld 137
    Numberi, Elion 135
    Pancasila's five principles 16–17, 32, 115–16,
        118–19, 121, 138–9
      as source of all legal sources 124–6
        aims of state 124–5
        and Preamble 124–5
        varying of interpretation/
          implementation 125–6
    post-authoritarian reforms
        (1999–2002) 122–4
      amendment matters 122
      constitutional democracy
        foundations 124
      context, differences from 1945 123
      Islam's role, debate 123
      Preamble 123, 124–5
    PPKI Committee 118–19
    rule of law, state that upholds 115–16
    Soeharto, President
      centralisation obsession 137
      fall of 122, 126
      Guided Democracy era/New Order
        regime 115–16
      human rights violations 128–9
      press freedom speech 125
      and unitary state 120–1
integrated diversity *see under* **Philippines**

Jennings, Sir I 28

Laos and Vietnam
    authoritarian experience 203–4
    constitutional expressivism 204–6
      and comparative law theorists 204–5
      effects/social consequences 206
      forms of 205–6
      nature of 205
      in plural (but not divided) societies 203,
        204
    current socialist constitutions 3, 203
    Hegel, G W F 204–5
    ideational plurality 16
    Jackson, V 204

Jacobsohn, G   204
Lan Xang, Kingdom of   206–7
Laos
    Bill of Rights   214–15
    Buddhism/Buddhist
        constitutionalism   206–7
    colonisation   207
    constituent preamble   211
    constituent principles   212–13, 213–14
    constitutional history   207
    constitutional structure   215–16
    directive principles   214
    effects of policies   216–18
    ethnic plurality   16, 208–9, 209–10
    ethnic unity commitment   212–13
    Five-year National Socio-economic
        Development Plan   216–18
    mass organisation   213
    Party policy   216
pluralist constitutions   220
Stuart-Fox, M   206, 207
Tushnet, M   204
Vietnam
    Bill of Rights   214–15
    Chinese dependency   208
    constituent preamble   212
    constituent principles   213–14
    constitutional dependency   208
    constitutional history   208
    constitutional structure   215–16
    directive principles   214
    effects of policies   218–19
    Ethnic Council   215–16
    ethnic plurality   16, 209–10
    ethnic unity commitment   213
    indigenous/customary law   219
    judicial constitutionalism   219
    mass organisation   213–14
    National Assembly components   218
    provisions expressive of ethnic
        plurality   218–19
Lijphart, A   8, 55–6

Malaysia
    background   25–6
    basic issues/summary   26, 48
    constitution-making process   25–30
        bill of rights   29–30
        controversial issues   27
        federalism   28–9
        fundamental liberties/human rights   29
        Islam's position   27–8
        terms of reference   26–7, 33

    constitutional enactments   3
    ideas/values   32–6
        constitutional monarchy   34
        constitutional supremacy   33
        federal system/federalism   33–4
        inter-group compromise   35–6
        national values (*Rukun Negara*)   32–3
        non-Malays' citizenship rights   35–6
    institutions/structure   36–41
        controversial laws   37–8
        executive powers   36–7
        federal-bias   40–1
        House of Representatives/Senate   37
        judiciary   38–9
        legislature   37–8
        Syariah jurisdiction   39–40
    Islam's position   27–8
        Islamic law traditions   34–5
        public service/business employment
            quotas   31–2
        Syariah jurisdiction   39–40
        temporary/provisional nature of
            privileges   32
    Mahathir Mohamad   37, 38–9
    Malaysian Islamic Development Department
        (JAKIM)   35
    Perak crisis   45, 46
    pluralistic sources   41–7
        civil/Syariah jurisdiction contests   43–4
        custody/child conversion cases   41–3,
            46–7
        heads of state involvement   47
        identity-based/instititution-based
            conflicts   45–6
        monarchy's role   44–5, 47
    pre-colonial elements   25–6
    Reid Commission   25, 28
    rights
        equality right exemptions   31–2
        protection/restriction   30–1
        religious freedom   31
    Rulers, executive power   36
    social fabric, diversity data   25
    YDPA (*Yang di-Pertuan Agong*)   32, 34
        executive power   36, 38
        Senate membership appointments   37
Mill, J S   13
Myanmar
    Anglo-Burmese War, Third   148
    Anti-Fascist People's Freedom League
        (AFPFL)   149–50
    Aung San   148–50
    Aung San Suu Kyi   152–3, 155–6

Aung San/Attlee Agreement   149
authoritarian regimes (1962-2011)   143-4
background   143-7
Bamar predominance   143, 145, 154, 156-7
basic issues/summary   147, 164-5
Burmese Independence Army (BIA)   148-9
Burmese/Myanmar language   146
Cheeseman, N   158
constitutional cycles   144-5, 146-7
constitutionalised pluralities   145-6
drafting history   147-53
  colonial origins   147-8
  Constitution of 1947   147-50
  Constitution of 1974   151-3
  Constitution of 2008   153
  constitutional enactments   3, 144
  constitutional paths   147
  constitutional process   149-50
  insurgencies   150-1
  nationalist movements (1930s/40s)   148-9
  secession rights   154
ethnic demography   143, 149
ethnic pluralities   145
  categories of ethnic rights   157
  citizenship right   157-8
  constitutional rights   156-9
  Ethnic Rights Protection
    Law of 2015   158-9
  national races concept   157, 158
  social/economic/cultural rights   158
institutions and structure   161-4
  chief ministers of states, appointment by
    President   163
  ethnic-state/non-ethnic-region/division
    structure   162
  key constitutional arrangements   161-2
  office of ministers for national races
    affairs   162-3
  people's representation   164
  union government and states/regions/
    self-administered areas, distribution
    of powers between   163
  Upper House composition/representation,
    as issue   163-4
Konbaung Dynasty   147
military's role   150-1, 152, 154-5
  in Constitution of 2008   155
  constitutional rights   160-1
  executive branch nominees   160
  legislature guardian role   160
  National Defence and Security Council
    (NDSC) composition   160-1
  and people's representation   164

political role   155-6
Presidential College role   160
republicanism/democracy envisaged   155
Ne Win, General   151-2, 155
Panglong Agreement   149
political pluralities   145
  constitutional rights   159-61
  foundational ideas   153-5
  individual rights   159
  military rights *see* military role *above*
SLORC/SPDC (State Law and Order
  Restoration Council/State Peace
  and Development Council)   153, 154,
  155-6, 162
Thein Sein, President   155, 161-2, 165
U Nu   150-1

Neo, J L   5

Philippines
Anderson, B   273
Aquino, Benigno   257
Aquino, Corazon   257-8, 264
autonomous regions, organic acts/plebicites
  for   265-6, 271-3
Bill of Rights   260
Church and State separation   262-3
commonalities/inclusion/exclusion
  autonomous regions   265-6, 271-3
  Constitution forming events   264
  founding events as   252, 263-4
  Islamic secessionism   265
  plebiscite requirement   266
  Roman Catholicism   264-5
Constitution 1987   256
constitutional enactments   3
constitutional rights
  Bill of Rights   260, 263
  Church and State separation   262-3
  farmers' rights   261
  grassroots organisation rights   261
  indigenous cultural communities'
    rights   261
  individual and group participation   258-9
  information access right   260
  labour/workers' rights   261
  non-kin grouping empowerment   261
  plebiscite requirement   266
  suffrage right   260
  unions/associations/societies, right to
    form   260
Cordilleras region   271
Dahl, R   13, 254

288 *Index*

democratic pluralism   253, 255, 259, 266, 270
Estrada, President Erap   277–8
indigenous cultural communities' rights   261
integrated diversity
　common nationality, sense of   252
　constitutional innovations   256
　definition of pluralism   253–4
　diversity   251–2
　elite family domination   255–6
　informal networks   252–3
　kinship networks   254–5
　patronage links   253
　pluralist goal   255, 277–8
kinship networks
　civil society   274–7
　family planning issues   275–6
　integrated diversity   254–5
　mass protest's effectiveness   276–7
　NGO's effect   274–5
　oligarch militias   273–4
　personal ties/public good distinction   273
　pork barrel system, abandonment   276–7
local autonomy
　administration, decentralisation of   271
　federalism, distinction   271
　principle   271
　regional autonomy   18
　regions, organic acts/plebicites for   265–6, 271–3
　territorial/political subdivisions   270
Local Government Code of 1991   270, 271
Marcos, President Ferdinand   257, 263
Mindanao island/region   265, 271–3
Montesquieu, Charles, Baron de   269–70
　1987 Constitution   256
People Power revolution   257–8, 277–8
　democratic pluralism   253, 255, 259, 266, 270
separation of powers
　basic principle   266–7
　and integrated diversity   269–70
　President's dominance   267, 268–70
　Senate/House of Representatives   267–8
　Supreme Court/lower courts   267
Sin, Cardinal Jaime   264
pluralism-in-fact *see under* **pluralist constitutions**
pluralist constitutionalism *see under* **Singapore**
pluralist constitutions
　accommodationism/integrationism   9
　ameliorating pluralities focus   9–10

centripetalism   9
consociationalism   8
definition/meaning   4
design-oriented approach, limitations   9–10
divided societies   10
institutional design   8–10
pluralism-in-fact   10–14
　convergence/divergence dynamics   12–13
　normative pluralism distinction   11–12
　state constitutional pluralism   12
　unity/plurality dynamic   13–14
religion, values, ideas, systems, as pluralities   10
see also Southeast Asia, pluralist constitutions

Reilly, B   9
Rosenfeld, M   10–11

Singapore
Association of Muslim Professionals (AMP)   58
basic issues   55
bilingualism
　in education system   67–8
　English language   68
　formal/substantive equality   68
　Malay as national language   67, 68
CDAC (Chinese Development Assistance Council)   59
constitutional enactments   3
electoral integration   69–75
formal/substantive equality   59–62
　complementary role   61
　equality of access to opportunity   60–1
　in founding documents   59
　individual premise   59–60
　Malay-Muslim community   61–2
　meritocracy   61
　non-discrimination   60
　objective   62
Goh Chok Tong   69–70
Group Representation Constituency (GRC)   69–72
　aims/objectives   69–70
　criticisms of   70–1
　deeming provision   70
　dominance   71–2
　electoral integration   69
　multi-member team   70
integration/accommodation in constitutional design   55–7
　conflict regulation typology   56

pragmatic approaches   56–7
theoretical basis   55–6
interests' centrality   75–7
Lee Hsien Loong   73
Lee Kuan Yew   63, 69
limited legal pluralism   65
Malay community
  directory/non-justiciable nature of Art 152   64
  as indigenous people   62, 64
  racial equality argument   63–4
  substantive equality   61–2, 63
  see also religious equality and pluralism below
MENDAKI(Council on Education for Muslim Children)   58
MUIS (Islamic Religious Council of Singapore)   65
Muslim community see under religious equality and pluralism below
pluralist constitutionalism   15
  civic citizenship as overarching identity   54–5
  colonial/decolonial policies   52–3
  constitutionalism defined   54
  domestic/geopolitical necessity   53
  as goal   77–9
  harmonious diversity   51
  individual rights/group rights distinction   53–4
  multiracialism policy   52
  nudges/incentives   75
race as organising principle   57–9
  Chinese-Malay-Indian-Others (CMIO) classification   57
  civic citizenship path dependence   57–8
  ethnic self-help groups   58–9
  integration/accommodation mix   58
religious equality and pluralism   65–6
  Malay-Muslim community significance   65, 66
  and personal law   65–6
  Pew Research Centre ranking   65
  secularism   65
reserved presidential election   72–5
  accessibility to all racial communities   73–4
  Elected Presidency (EP) (1991)   72–3
  electoral integration approach   72
  eligibility criteria   74
  potential difficulties   75

rights-based approach, avoidance   53, 64, 75–6, 78
SINDA (Singapore Indian Development Association)   59
Singaporean Singapore identity   52

Southeast Asia
'Asianization'   1
colonialisation history   2
comparative constitutional law   6–7
constitutional diversity   3–4
constitutional law   4–6
  contextualist accounts   5–6
  macro-historical contextualism   5
  methodological pluralism   6
  political/social contextualism   6
  textualist approaches   4–5
constitutional theory   7–8
ethnical diversity   2
legal diversity   2
pluralist constitutions
  constitutional pluralism   19
  ethnic plurality   15–16
  ideational plurality   16–17, 236
  ideological ideal   17
  monist de jure practice   18–19
  mutually reinforcing plurality   17–18
  pluralist constitutionalism   19
    global context   19–21
  plurality of pluralities   15
  range of questions   14–15
  regional autonomy   18
  religious plurality   16
  see also pluralist constitutions above
religious diversity   1–2
see also ASEAN (Association of Southeast Asian Nations)

Thailand
Ananda, King   237
basic issues/summary   227, 246
Bawornsak Uwanno   239
Bhumibol, King   237–8, 242
Buddhism
  Constitution of 2017   244–5
  and law   228
  see also monarchy and Buddhism below
Chan-O-Cha, Prayeuth   226, 242
Chulalongkorn, King   231–2
Constitution of 1997   233, 240–2
Constitution of 2007   233–4
Constitution of 2017   234

Buddhism reference   244–5
changes to draft constitution   244
constitutional conventions   243–4
ideational plurality   236, 243
military role   245
Thai ethnic groups   245
constitutional conventions   243–4
Constitutional Court   242–3
constitutional history   3, 230–4
  conflict and coups   233–4
  constitutional monarchy   231–3
  historical continuity   230
  revolution   232
constitutional rights
  Constitution of 1997   240–1
  inequality/poverty   240
  stipulated rights   240
  Thai nationality application   241
  universal rights concept   241
constitutional structure
  branches of state, interrelationship   242
  chain of delegation   241–2
  parliamentary system   241
Dharmasakti, Sanya   238
elected Senate proposal   225
judicial power   242–3
Kelsen, H   238
Kukrit Pramoj   238
monarchy and Buddhism   236–8
  Democratic Form of Government with Monarch as Head of State   237–8
  during revolution   237

power in Constitution   238
selective adoption from West   236
Plaek Phibunsongkhram, Field Marshal   237
plurality of constitutional ideas   236
plurality and law   227–30
  Buddhism   228
  Islamism/Islamic law   228, 229–30
  Thai ethnicity/identity   227–30
political reality and constitutional principles   225–6
Prajadhipok, King   232–3
Prayuth Chan-O-Cha   226
Sarit Thanarat, Field Marshal   237
Shinnawatra, Thanksin/Yingluck   225
sources of norms
  hierarchy of norms   238–9
  sovereign power returns to King   239
  written Constitution   239
Temporary Charter 1932   230–1, 232
Thai identity/Thainess
  ideational plurality   236, 243
  and law *see* plurality and law *above*
  nation/religion/monarchy as fundamental institutions   234–5
  plurality of constitutional ideas   236
  rural v urban cultures   235–6
  tolerance for difference   235
volcanic constitution   226–7, 234–8, 246

Vietnam *see* **Laos and Vietnam**
volcanic constitution *see under* **Thailand**